Equality of Arms in Criminal Procedure

Renato Stanziola Vieira

Equality of Arms in Criminal Procedure

An Analysis from a Brazilian Perspective

Springer

Renato Stanziola Vieira
São Paulo, São Paulo, Brazil

ISBN 978-3-032-03662-9 ISBN 978-3-032-03663-6 (eBook)
https://doi.org/10.1007/978-3-032-03663-6

The original submitted manuscript has been translated into English. The translation was done using artificial intelligence. A subsequent revision was performed by the author(s) to further refine the work and to ensure that the translation is appropriate concerning content and scientific correctness. It may, however, read stylistically different from a conventional translation.

Translation from the Portuguese language edition: "Paridade de Armas no Processo Penal" by Renato Stanziola Vieira, © Gazeta Jurídica 2014. Published by Gazeta Jurídica. All Rights Reserved.

This Springer imprint is published by the registered company Springer Nature Switzerland AG
The registered company address is: Gewerbestrasse 11, 6330 Cham, Switzerland

Foreword

Receiving the honorable invitation to write the preface for the present book, "Equality of Arms in Criminal Procedure," by Renato Stanziola Vieira, was for me a reason for great joy.

The book that I have been given to present to the reader is the result, with some changes and additions, of the master's dissertation presented by the student and friend Renato Stanziola Vieira. Even before entering the Master's course, the author always showed great academic interest, which was expressed in deep dedication to the activity of research and elaboration of the dissertation, which was defended with great elegance, confidence, and culture at the Faculty of Law of Largo São Francisco, resulting in unanimous approval with a vote of praise by the Examination Board.

The study embodied in this book fills a gap in the national doctrine, which had not yet dealt, in depth, with the theme of equality of arms in criminal procedure. The work is of great quality.

The work begins, in its Chap. 1, with a constitutional reading of equality, drawing from American constitutionalism, passing through the historical evolution in the various Brazilian constitutions, until reaching the current moment. Finally, equality is analyzed in the light of the theory of principles, taking as a premise the distinction between principle and rule, as formulated by Alexy, which has found deep acceptance in the national doctrine.

After a detailed analysis of the constitutional matrices related to the theme, Chap. 2 is dedicated to exposing the application of the principle of equality in Brazilian criminal procedure. To do so, it makes use of an important and deep historical study of the evolution of Brazilian criminal procedural legislation, in which little importance was given to equality of arms, from the Code of Criminal Procedure of the Empire, of 1832, passing through the codes and state legislations in criminal procedural matters, until reaching the Code of Criminal Procedure of 1941, both in its original wording, when in its subsequent reforms. It also analyses the theme in various Drafts of the Code of Criminal Procedure, reaching the current Bill No. 8.045/2012, which intends to establish the new Code of Criminal Procedure in Brazil, where greater concerns with equality of arms were shown.

After having analyzed the concept of equality, Chap. 3 is dedicated to the concept of "party" in criminal procedure. It begins by analyzing the nature of the criminal procedure itself, with special emphasis on the procedure as a legal situation. It then uses the concept of party in civil procedure to, afterwards, arrive at the detailed analysis of the parties in criminal procedure, where it analyzes the statute of the Public Prosecutor's Office, of the private accuser, of the accused, and, finally, of the third party in the criminal procedure, notably the assistant to the prosecution. Fundamental to the development of the theme was the position, which we have defended for a long time, that "the Public Prosecutor's Office acts as a party and not as a guardian of the law."

In Chap. 4, we move on to comparative analysis, with emphasis on *common law* models and, more specifically, the adversarial system, which is the most conducive model, although not essential, for the best development of equality of arms. Indeed, the text brings important and accurate criticisms of the American procedural model.

Then, in Chap. 5, we arrive at the formulation of a specific concept of equality of arms in criminal proceedings, making use of the judgments of international criminal courts, where the theme of equality of arms found strong development. This chapter is the heart of the work, in which an attempt is made to distinguish between equality of arms, on one hand, and *par condicio*, on the other, in a formulation unprecedented in national doctrine. The differences between equality of arms, presumption of innocence, and adversarial principle are also analyzed.

In summary, the author presents equality of arms as a principle of Brazilian criminal procedure, consisting of "an equal distribution, during the criminal process—from its pre-judicial phase to the executive—to those involved who defend opposing interests, of opportunities to present oral or written arguments and evidence with a view to prevailing their respective theses before a judicial authority." In addition to situating the reader on the state of the art of equality of arms, in comparative law and Brazilian law, in its various aspects, the book brings a critical analysis, in which the author confidently and convinced of his premises, expresses his point of view on controversial and disputed topics.

Finally, in Chap. 6, extracting the practical potential of the study developed and the concept of equality of arms proposed, it is subjected to a "test bank" throughout the various moments of the procedural dynamics, starting with the investigation phase, going through the procedural development in the first instance and reaching its application with very relevant practical repercussions in the appeal phase. The practical operability of the proposed concept is also tested in *habeas corpus*, in criminal review, and in criminal execution.

For all these reasons, I am sure that this book, which I now present to the public and which continues the Ada Pelegrini Grinover Collection, published by Gazeta Jurídica Publishing House, will be excellently received in the legal community, whether for its deep scientific content or for its practical importance.

Full Professor at Criminal Procedural Law at University of Sao Paulo
Lisbon, Portugal
May 2014

Gustavo Badaró

The principle of equality of arms between the prosecutor and accused in a criminal trial goes to the heart of the fair trial guarantee. (ICTY, *Prosecutor v. Tadic*. Appeals Chamber. 15 Jully 1999, § 44)

Acknowledgments

The following work is my master's dissertation entitled *Equality of Arms in Criminal Proceedings: From Concept to Application in Brazilian Criminal Procedural Law* defended at the Law School of the University of São Paulo on June 5, 2013, in a panel composed of my advisor, Associate Professor Gustavo Henrique Righi Ivahy Badaró, and the examiners Associate Professor Maurício Zanoide de Moraes and Doctor Professor Diogo Rudge Malan.

Publicly, I reiterate the admiration I have for each of them, in the greatest sense that this can mean. If Professors Gustavo Badaró and Maurício Zanoide were, for particular reasons of each one, closer to me throughout the research, Professor Diogo Malan, with his known elegance, gifted me, whenever he could—and there were not a few times—with reading recommendations that became central in the development of the work, as I highlighted in my argument. To all, I am immensely grateful for the criticisms and contributions, here incorporated to the extent that I deemed possible, which is due to my own limitations.

After defending the work before the panel, I was able to attend, alongside other Latin American students of criminal law and criminal procedure, the *Second Summer School in Criminal Sciences and German Dogmatic Criminal Law*, organized by the Department of Foreign Criminal Law and International Criminal Sciences of the Georg-August Universität Göttingen. On the occasion, in addition to the excellence of the course itself, I had access to other materials that, for the most part, are used here. To Professor Maria Laura Böhm, course coordinator, I am grateful for the welcome I received there, particularly for her availability in assisting me in research at the Criminal Law and Public Law Library.

Personally, I thank Professor Doctor Kai Ambos, creator of the course and largely responsible for the excellence of the International and Foreign Criminal and Procedural Law Library at the University of Göttingen, not only for the welcome and availability in assisting all those who were there, but also for the trust he bestowed upon me during and even after the course.

When I was in Germany, João Carlos Jorge Martini, my *Jota*, passed away. I also dedicate this work to him, for the friendship and the love with which he gifted me these years. You, *Jota*, have the admirable gift of knowing how to listen. He did not die young, but he left early. His physical presence is greatly missed.

I thank my parents and my brother. In absolutely all moments, the three—Gilberto, Leomar, Ricardo—were close to me. They never stopped supporting me, encouraging me, and giving directions for me to become a better person. It has always been like this. And it is like this.

I thank my supervisor, Associate Professor Gustavo Henrique Righi Ivahy Badaró. In this, which is no longer my first master's degree, I was able to enjoy a relationship of trust that was born years before my enrollment as a regular student in the Postgraduate Programme at the Faculty of Law of the University of São Paulo. Without foreseeing that I would be his supervisee, Gustavo, you already treated me with extreme respect and a cordiality that, as I have insisted on telling you, caught my attention from the beginning. And you, also from that time, trusted in my ability. Thank you very much. Thank you also for the enduring proof of patience with my anxieties, with my insistence on so many points about which you, with your discreet firmness, patiently showed me the best way to go. From the contact I had with you over the last four and a half years, I learned to admire you even more and to understand, after each of your teachings in the many meetings we had, why you are one of the greatest criminal proceduralists in the country.

Associate Professor Maurício Zanoide de Moraes, I must also express my sincere thanks for the always unimpeded tone with which you have received me. You, Professor, perhaps even for not having been formally my co-supervisor, ended up becoming something different and more important than that. Without any formal link, you were always by my side with an intellectual honesty and a remarkable detachment. With known and admirable seriousness, you always dedicated yourself to discussing the topic of equality of arms with me. Your attention, your kindness, and your deference in all our conversations gave more energy for this work to proceed to the end. On my part, with the expectations of seeing you again and exchanging frank ideas, I always tried to improve the text. Your help, Professor Maurício, also preceded by many of your arguments in the qualification board and followed them in other conversations we had, conversations that were as frank as pleasant and—for me—fruitful.

Both Professors Gustavo and Maurício need to know this: I really feel flattered to have had the supervisor I had and, besides him, the always present figure not of a formal co-supervisor, but of another master with whom I could share, not a few times, the anxieties of criminal procedure and particularly of equality of arms.

Regarding the qualification, I also thank Professor Titular Antonio Scarance Fernandes, who made important considerations for the direction that the work came to take.

During the postgraduate course, I could count on the brilliant and pleasant company of several friends. Among many, Décio "Turanza" Gomes and Danyele Galvão were always (fortunately for me and I hope for them too) closer and helped me a lot. Many other colleagues were important, but you made a big difference. Thank you very much.

I thank my colleagues and friends from the office. Not only did they have to live with my daily grumpiness, my bad moods, and my—let us face it—anxieties, but I always counted on the privileged intelligence of Fernando Gardinali Caetano Dias and José Roberto Coelho Akutsu. From both, I also enjoyed, in the afternoons when I had to be absent from the office to write the dissertation, all the perspicacity, dedication, and companionship in the practice of law that only someone more than a partner, but a friend, can give. More than the excellent lawyers that you two are, I have you in my heart as dear friends. From the hardships of advocacy to laughter, thank you very much for the moments that we spent together and those we spent apart, because you really were and are an important rearguard.

Speaking of friends, again, Andre... You, who every day show me how clear reasoning should be, who has an almost infinite good sense, were the one who helped me the most. Thanks, partner! Thanks for the tips, thanks for the tranquility that only you could provide me. One day, you told me that it is very good to have me as a partner and that it is even better to have me as a friend. True, mate. Very good to have you as a partner, but much better is to have you as a friend. Thank you.

Elisa, my dear proofreader: thank you very much for your care and, particularly, for the patience that only you, being who you are, could have with me.

Tucherman, Carina, Andre (with his always so precise comments), and Fernando (with his traditional and indispensable "telhadian" glosses), read in their own time, in the way and to the extent that was possible, the work. I thank them for their availability to help me make fewer mistakes than I would have made.

Cris, I owe you, besides the thanks, a huge apology. These hours, all of them, that we spent apart do not come back. I deeply felt every second of the early mornings when I was away from you, *hidden* here in my little corner. But, my love, more than saying that "I suffer in silence, not to tell you every second what a second without you is," I want you to know of my gratitude. No one would have understood me so well, no one would have ever imagined my needs, and no one would have noticed and respected any of this. Only you, with your infinite love, can perceive everything in me. Absolutely everything. I love you, also, for that.

Antonio, my son, my *little reason*. You still do not understand why Daddy *thanks* you. But as you were born with this work, son, I can already tell you: because you were born my companion and my friend. You already share time with me, in a way, and make my time also pleasantly yours (including in the early mornings). After you were born, Tom, I began to understand what Milton (that one...) meant with "I want happiness in a father's eyes." I love you, son, for a long time and a lot.

Cris, Tom and Isa, this work is for you.

For you, my love, who continue to take my life in your sweet and beautiful hands. With all my love.

For you, Tom, who gave a new meaning to the word *happiness*, with your way of smiling, with your curiosities all, with your look, for your existence. For you, Isa, when you arrived you made the challenges of my journey the best moments, and showed the most beautiful smile of the world. You teache me, always, to understand that life is worth living

You three are the center of my life.

Contents

Chapter 1
Of Equality: From Constitutional Contours to Application in the Brazilian Criminal Process

1.1 The Equality of Arms Against the Backdrop of Constitutional Law

Equality is a fundamental operative concept of democratic legal systems[1] and therefore, to reach its treatment in criminal proceedings, it should be considered from the philosophical-constitutional background.

The journey to try to grasp its main characteristics in the abstract plane and then to check how it has been treated in the field chosen as the theme of this work is inevitable. After all, if in the most abstract and ancient sense it was necessary to consider the principle as a consequence of equality among all citizens—and this is not the proper occasion to revisit Aristotle's distinction between slaves and citizens, or even the reasons then seen to distinguish one category from another[2]—in the choice that will be made here, there is a bias for specific action in criminal proceedings.

[1] "Equality is the fundamental sign of democracy," says José Afonso da Silva (2005a), p. 70. The umbilical connection between democracy and equality is dealt with by Augusto Cerri (2005), pp. 49–50. See also: Cerri (2007), p. 1; Ferreira (1977), p. 157. Cintra also discussed it, defining it as "one of the pillars of the so-called democratic regime" (1981/1982), p. 39.

[2] An elegant critique of the Stagirite was made by del Vecchio (1966), p. 26. Del Vecchio indicates that Aristotle would have surpassed the lesson of Pythagoras (according to whom justice would correspond to the notion of equality in the exchange of goods, i.e., equality in a commutative sense) to deal with equality also in the distributive aspect, which must consider the dignity, that is, the merit of each person. Del Vecchio's criticism regarding the aspect of distributive equality lies in the following observation: "it should be noted that Aristotle left undetermined the criterion for assessing 'dignity' and personal merit. He lacked the concept of the essential value of the human person, whose recognition must constitute the first postulate of justice; and this lack is evident in the justification of slavery."

R. S. Vieira, *Equality of Arms in Criminal Procedure*,
https://doi.org/10.1007/978-3-032-03663-6_1

From equality based on the nature of all (observed in antiquity, the distinction between Plato and Aristotle and with the passage through Christian history[3] culminating in lessons from authors like Ronald Dworkin[4]), we arrive at equality *in process*, not without first passing through the declarations of rights of the eighteenth century and the constitutions and current declarations of rights across the Western world. Considering that in the process it is not about *goods*, but about treatment before an impartial subject, it is transposed to this context an ideal not necessarily distributive, but of equality, on the part of the judge, in the treatment of those involved. Particularly in the *criminal* process, its configuration is the equality of arms.

Thus, as in any approach that has in view the system of positive law, it is assumed here that it is from the constitutional plane that the analysis begins,[5] descending in hierarchy—but increasing in concreteness—to the specific object of study. In addition, since talking about equality of arms refers to the cogitation between equalities and inequalities and their reasonable justifications for discrimination,[6] it is intended to question the widespread understanding that, even if the criminal process is legitimized based on the equality of all before the law, it "does not offer the parties equality of positions."[7]

The present proposal consists of, from the constitutional premises, investigating whether, in Brazilian positive law, the equality of arms echoes in the criminal process and whether, depending on the first answer that is reached, at least its cogitation is pertinent. With this, the idea is to stimulate the discussion about the treatment of the subjects of the criminal process from the perspective of procedural equality. Both a criticism (constitutionality) and the other (infraconstitutional provision) are equivalent, largely, to questioning the *mainstream* Brazilian doctrinal and

[3] Faria (1973), p. 7. There is a biblical passage reproduced in the booklet by Cerri (2005), p. 10, that shows the focus of Christianity when talking about equality: "it is often remembered, a passage from the epistle of Paul of Tarsus to the Galatians: 'there is neither Jew nor Greek, there is neither slave nor free, there is neither male and female: for you are all one in Christ Jesus'" (Gal 3, 26–28)

[4] Dworkin (2005), p. 199. Dworkin teaches that the "most abstract egalitarian principle" is that "the community treats all members with equal consideration."

[5] Jacques (1957), p. 89.

[6] Oppenheim mentions: "We can say that human beings are only equal or unequal in relation to certain characteristics that must be specified. It makes no sense to affirm that 'all men are equal'. Some may be as to a particular characteristic; others, not. [...] *A* and *B* are treated equally, not because both are targets of the same concession, but because the rule is applied to them impartially. [...] Equality and justice have, in reality, an important common characteristic: both can only be sustained by rules that determine how certain benefits or burdens are to be distributed among people" Bobbio et al. (2004), p. 598.

[7] Costa (2001), p. 10.

jurisprudential tradition that denies, either aprioristically,[8] or in its greater potentiality,[9] the suitability of the concept of equality of arms in our criminal procedural system.

What underpins the analysis of the equality of arms, therefore, before a judgment of procedural technique that will be dealt with in the text, is a perspective of purely constitutional equality. After all, if in the limit equality in the process could acquire the simple reading according to which "the principle of equality means that litigants should receive identical treatment from the judge"[10] or, in a well-known conception of the general theory of process, "the parties and attorneys should deserve equal treatment, so that they have the same opportunities to assert their reasons in court,"[11] the reflection is proposed first on the constitutional aspect and then on the technical-procedural.

The equality of arms in the Brazilian criminal process is, above all, a problem of constitutional law, because the very inequality in the process must meet, first and foremost, constitutional imperatives and justifications.[12]

---

[8] Costa considers "it better to admit, therefore, that the equality of arms is absent in the criminal process" (2001), p. 97.

[9] In the precedents of the Federal Supreme Court on equality of arms, it can be noted that the topic is not addressed from the evidentiary perspective but, mainly, about deadlines for manifestations. In this regard, see: Ag. Reg. in RE no. 1.310.109, Rel. Justice Edson Fachin, published on 10.05.2024; ADI no. 5567, Rel. Justice Alexandre de Moraes, *DJ* 24.01.2024; ADI no. 6298, Rel. Justice Luiz Fux, *DJ* 19.12.2023; Inq. no. 4325, Rel. Justice Edson Fachin, *DJ* 02.08.2023; *HC* no. 166.373, Rel. Justice Edson Fachin, *DJ* 18.05.2023; ADI no. 4768, Rel. Justice Carmen Lúcia, *DJ* 28.04.2023; Ag. Reg. in *HC* no. 158.538, Rel. Justice Edson Fachin, *DJ* 02.07.2021; HC no. 164.493, Rel. Justice Edson Fachin, *DJ* 04.06.2021; Ag. Reg. in *HC* no. 193.378, Rel. Justice Alexandre de Moraes, *DJ* 25.03.2021; HC no. 176.933, Rel. Min, Celso de Mello, *DJ* 18.11.2020; *HC* no. 178.856, Rel. Justice Celso de Mello, *DJ* 22.10.2020; Ag. in RHC no. 144.615, Rel. Justice Edson Fachin, *DJ* 27.10.2020; Ag. Reg. in Pet 7.494, Rel. Justice Edson Fachin, *DJ* 03.09.2020; MC *HC* no. 167.727, Rel. Justice Gilmar Mendes, *DJ* 18.02.2019; Ag. Reg. in RE 213.121, Rel. Justice Marco Aurélio, *DJ* 06.03.2009; *HC* n ° 86.816, Rel. Justice Gilmar Mendes, *DJ* 14.09.2007; *HC* n ° 87.567, Rel. Justice Marco Aurélio, *DJ* 17.08.2007; *HC* n ° 84.159, Rel. Justice Marco Aurélio; *DJ* 06.08.2004; *HC* n ° 83.917, Rel. Justice Marco Aurélio, *DJ* 25.06.2004; *HC* n ° 83.255, Rel. Justice Marco Aurélio, *DJ* 12.03.2004. Also noteworthy are monocratic decisions made in Rcl no. 36.378, Rel. Justice Gilmar Mendes, *DJ* 07.05.2021; Rcl 32.862, Rel. Justice Gilmar Mendes, *DJ* 28.08.2019; Ag. Reg. in *HC* no. 162.626, Rel. Justice Gilmar Mendes, 27.06.2019; *HC* no. 164.999, Rel. Justice Gilmar Mendes, *DJ* 30.04.2019; MC *HC* no. 166.694, Rel. Justice Gilmar Mendes, *DJ* 05.02.2019; and the judgment given in *HC* no. 166.694, Rel. Justice Gilmar Mendes, *DJ* 22.03.2019; which dealt with the theme and cited this work. Already in the scope of the Superior Court of Justice, the work was referred to in *HC* no. 903.753, Rel. Justice Sebastião Reis Júnior, *DJ* 06.09.2024.

[10] Nery Júnior (2016), p. 128.

[11] Dinamarco et al. (2020), p. 85.

[12] In the words of Bandeira de Mello in a reference text on the theme: "the advantages based on some distinctive peculiarity must be conferred by promoting positively connoted situations or, at least, compatible with the interests embraced in the constitutional system" Bandeira de Mello (1995), p. 42. This was, by the way, one of the reasons why the plenary of the Supreme Federal Court denied the order of *habeas corpus* of *HC* no. 106.212, under the rapporteurship of Justice

It is undeniable, in this regard, the reason of Antonio Carlos de Araújo Cintra when he exposes, from the constitutional extract, the so-called *procedural method.* The professor says:

> the procedural method requires the equality of the parties, regardless of the adoption of a political or ideological position similar to the one that inspired the constitutional precept of isonomy. It is because the procedural method is characterized by the collaboration of the parties[13] in the formation of the judicial provision of which they will be recipients, and this collaboration is made on the rational and ethical plane of the formulation of requests and the presentation of allegations and evidence. Now, the element of rationality inherent in the process and manifested in a special way in the motivation of judicial decisions, requires the dialogical (or dialectical) form of that collaboration of the parties, placing the 'dialoguers' on an equal footing, so that, rationally, their arguments and their evidence are evaluated for their own value and not in view of who presents them. The procedural method, therefore, equals the parties or presupposes their equality.[14]

It is after going through the constitutional plane that parity becomes a problem of specific technique of the process and particularly of the criminal process, in which it is important to deal with the parties, the procedural systems, and the possibility of application—in specific measures and phases—of the criminal prosecution.

1.1.1 Equality Linked to Ideas of Justice and Political Participation

It has never been a simple task to separate the equal from the unequal. It has also never been and is not easy to justify the distribution of a share of a good to each one, according to their respective inequalities. Equality and inequality, like twin sisters, only live together: with such difficulty and perennial impulse. After all, only by seeing what is unequal can equality be achieved in objects. As Fábio Konder Comparato said, "equality is a measure of comparison. There is no way to conceive the equality of one alone."[15]

Only when one compares, values and matches, in short, what is equal and what is unequal, is that, on the scale, the unequal is separated. And it is only through such valuation that one can consider the distribution of the equal portion to each one in

Marco Aurélio, in a judgment held on March 24, 2011, which discussed the constitutionality of Article 41 of the Maria da Penha Law (Law No. 10.340/2006).

[13] It will be seen in the text, however, that the cooperative aspect of the process—civil or criminal—is not immune to criticism.

[14] Cintra (1981/1982), p. 41.

[15] Comparato (1998), p. 18. Pizzorusso distinguishes equality (considered as synonymous with parity) from identity saying that the latter equates to a "total equality," which allows the conclusion that, according to that author, when talking about equality in politics or in jurisprudence, "it is almost always understood as a relative equality, referred to particular points of view" Pizzorusso (1983), pp. 12–13.

the measure of equality and, on the other hand, the unequal portion according to proportional inequality.[16]

This first logic—of distributive justice guided by a criterion of proportionality from the natural comparison between the equal and the unequal—goes back to a philosophical conception of absolute justice, typical of the Aristotelian model, which, according to the lesson of Maria da Glória Ferreira Pinto Garcia, lasted until the emergence of rationalism.[17] This way of treating equality, reminds the aforementioned author, is so emblematic that, in the ancient Greek context, the word *íson*, which means precisely the *equal*, was associated with the right. In the wake of what Michel Villey preached, the *equal* meant "the just place between an excess and a defect." It is no wonder that, both in Greek and Roman mythology, the right goes back to the idea of a balance in which the dishes are at the same level. It was a time, therefore, when equality was taken as synonymous with justice.

In that philosophical context, the notion of equality did not require positivation in legal texts and emanated from the natural concept of justice: all men, being equal, should be treated as such and, among them (as human genre, that is, as individuals), the goods should be distributed either according to numerical equality, or according to the proportion of goods and men who needed them more or less, or, still, according to the merit of each one.[18]

One can say that there is the broad and abstract notion of the principle of equality: one is not equal because the law says so, but, well before, because equality is the criterion of justice. Giorgio Del Vecchio reminds that for the first philosopher to delve into the theme, Pythagoras, justice was defined exactly as equality.[19] It is from this assumption that one starts: from the absolute, natural equality among men. Because it starts from such broad and absolute criterion, Maria da Glória Ferreira Pinto Garcia states that equality was presented "as a structural element of justice itself and that it is important not to confuse with the strict or legal concept, of equal treatment of citizens by public power."[20]

As a synthesis of this conception, Martim de Albuquerque recalls the following aspects:

(a) all men are naturally equal;
(b) equality is the essence of Justice;
(c) equality presupposes comparison and makes no sense among non-comparable things;

---

[16] Pontes de Miranda said that, "because men are not arithmetically equal and, moreover, equality is something to *be achieved*, and not achieved, the concept of 'equality' is always relative" (1960), p. 282. The lesson is repeated by Pizzorusso: "in this sense indeed equality is a goal, a target always difficult to reach, it is not calculable with the meter or with any other unit of measure" Pontes de Miranda (1983), p. 9.

[17] Garcia (2005), p. 32.

[18] This is, in summary, what Oppenheim named "traditional criteria of egalitarianism" in his approach to the entry *equality*.

[19] Del Vecchio (1966), p. 26.

[20] Ferreira (2005), pp. 33–34. In this sense, see: Cerri (2005), p. 11.

(d) equality obliges to treat equally what is equal, but unequally what is unequal;
(e) equality is the basis of democracy;
(f) equality is not necessarily arithmetic, it can (and should), in certain cases, be geometric;
(g) equality contains a component of adaptation to situations and ends;
(h) equality implies the participation of opportunities.[21]

Then, with the rationalism and individualism of the seventeenth and eighteenth centuries, it is argued that equality among all is not because the notion signifies justice, but because individuals are considered as qualitatively unequal among themselves. Man is no longer seen as representative of a geometric or proportional equality between him and the available goods, but between him and the context in which he is situated. Hence, the rethinking of the ideal distribution of goods in the community.

Especially in regard to relations between citizens and public power, the notion of equality, once again according to Maria da Glória Ferreira Pinto Garcia, acquires "a new and claimant force."[22] The treatment of what is equal or unequal, now, is no longer guided by the idea of natural justice, but rather by the idea of a justice to be achieved, of an equality to be achieved in a factually and legally unequal society.[23]

Such a context of the treatment of equality is the end of privileges that are not justified, even though we know of the factual inequalities between one social class and another. It was no longer the time for the treatment of equality in the static sense seen in the Greco-Roman origin, but, already then, on the dynamic side, it was about *equalizing* men in society. In this scenario, equality was protected by law. Indeed, Jean-Jacques Rousseau said at that time that "it is precisely because the force of things always tends to destroy equality that the force of legislation must always tend to maintain it."[24]

It was necessary to say that *all are equal before the law*, as if, with this, those who were not yet, given the factual distinctions (read: socio-economic), became so. There was inaugurated there the *civil equality* supported by law, the so-called *formal equality*, which was the first step to achieve—as we see today in constitutional theories and in positive law systems—to start thinking about material equality.

It was the time of Rousseau's contractualism, which proclaimed, among other revolutionary ideas then, that the fundamental pact that gives reason to be to the social contract exchanges natural equality for a "moral and legitimate equality," which replaces "what nature could bring of physical inequality among men, and, being able to be unequal in strength or in talent, all become equal by convention and

---

[21] Albuquerque (1993), pp. 15–16.

[22] Garcia (2005), p. 34.

[23] Just remember the tormenting examples of the revolutions of the seventeenth century (especially in England) and mainly the eighteenth century (American Independence, in 1776; French Revolution, in 1789; Declaration of the Rights of Man, of the same year; Constitution of France, of 1791; and Declaration of the Rights of Man and Citizen, of 1793).

[24] Rousseau (2003), p. 63.

by law."[25] It is also from Rousseau the attempt to convince his peers of his time of the idea according to which

> the social pact establishes such equality among citizens that all they commit under the same conditions and must enjoy the same rights. Thus, by the nature of the pact, every act of sovereignty, that is, every authentic act of the general will, obliges or favours equally all the citizens, so that the sovereign only knows the body of the nation and does not distinguish any of those who compose it.[26]

In this new context, the scenario of both the social pact inaugurated from inequalities (but with the aim of preserving the moral equalities of each one), as well as the historical and social struggle for the end of privileges, civil equality equates to an equality "against the State."[27]

The notion of civil equality, therefore, in the movement of constitutionalism, is typically liberal. It points in this direction the doctrine of José Joaquim Gomes Canotilho, when he says that

> men are born and remain free and equal in rights. Therefore it is considered that this equality is a prerequisite for the standardisation of regime of individual freedoms in favour of all subjects of a legal order. Legal equality thus emerges, inseparable from the very *freedom* individual.[28]

In the liberal period, as has already been seen and as will be better understood later, the notion of equality is exhausted in its formal establishment in constitutions and declarations of rights. It is the time of so-called negative *equality*, when the law supports equality so that the state does not invade its scope. The state is distrusted because it is believed that the best measure of equality is guaranteed *without* its intervention, and that the laws aim exactly to protect such a sphere of intangibility.

1.1.2 Equality from the Virginia Declaration of 1776

The documents that best reflect the notion of civil (or formal) equality are, first, the Virginia Declaration of Independence, of 1776, and then, the French Declaration of the Rights of Man, of 1789.[29] These were followed by a plethora of normative texts from various Western countries, either in the form of declarations or constitutions.

Even if many times their proclamations are nothing more than solemn sheets of paper, because—and this may be a problem that accompanies the relevance and difficulty of the concept throughout history—*equality* has also been a word noted for

[25] Rousseau (2003), pp. 29–30.
[26] Rousseau (2003), p. 41.
[27] Grinover (1975), p. 26.
[28] Canotilho (2003), p. 426.
[29] Ruffía (1973), p. 1088.

its adaptation to the ideological bias of each community,[30] the concept is today a constitutional unanimity.

As for the declarations of right that proclaimed it, the Virginia Declaration, of June 12, 1776, determined, for the first time in the West, that "all men are, by nature, equally free and independent, and have certain inherent rights."[31] Then, the Constitution of the State of Massachusetts was drafted on March 2, 1780, according to which:

> all men are born free and equal, and have certain natural, essential and inalienable rights, among which must be considered those of enjoying and defending life and liberty, of acquiring, possessing and protecting property, and, finally, of pursuing and obtaining their security and happiness.[32]

Then, the news that we have is that of the Declaration of the Rights of Man, promulgated in France on August 26, 1789, which again brought to light the treatment of formal equality by mentioning that "all men are born and remain free and equal in rights." As for the formation of the general will, the text establishes, in its Article 6, the equality of treatment between men in their formation.[33]

Following such documents, and not without noting, in the wake of Georg Jellinek, that the French declarations may have drawn from their American counterparts,[34] the Constitution of France, of 1791, was the first to deal with the principle of equality, and it did so, in the reading of Martim de Albuquerque, so that it would cease to

> exist nobility, peerage, hereditary distinctions, distinctions of order, nor feudal regime, or patrimonial justices, nor titles, denominations and prerogatives derived from them, nor any order of chivalry, corporation or decorations for which proofs of nobility were previously

[30] The proof of such moulding or ductility of the concept to accommodate the unequal and try to equalise them is seen not only in examples of the limits of distinction between the sexes—why is military service preferentially addressed to men?—and of distinction of stages of enjoyment of civil rights due to age—why is the age of criminal liability not the same as the electoral age?—but, as Del Vecchio reminded, even in the United Nations, which is notable, among other characteristics, for granting "important privileges to five States (*original members*), placing the others in conditions of serious and permanent inferiority," and also for, according to him, housing, with equal voting rights in general assembly, states "lacking organisation that guarantees fundamental rights" Del Vecchio (1966), pp. 34–35.

[31] Silva understands, however, that "it is in the French revolution that the legal idea of equality is formalised, inserted in art. 1 of the declaration of rights and of the citizen, of 1789" Silva (2001), p. 33. Menezes recalls that, besides this provision, in the outline of the configuration of formal freedom of that declaration, its Articles 4 (which prohibited the granting of special benefits and privileges and the hereditary transmission of these and specified offices), 5, and 6 (which ensured political participation equality) (2007), p. 175.

[32] Albuquerque (1993), p. 91.

[33] "The law is the expression of the general will. All citizens have the right to contribute, personally or through their representatives, to its formation. It must be the same for all, whether it protects or it punishes. All citizens, being equal in its eyes, are equally admissible to all dignities, places and public offices, according to their capacity and without any other distinction than that of their virtues and their talents."

[34] A comparison between them is made by Martim de Albuquerque (Albuquerque (1993), pp. 47 and foll.). About the positioning of Jellinek, see: Garcia (2005), p. 31, footnote no. 6.

> required, or that presuppose distinctions of birth, nor any superiority except that of public officials in the exercise of their functions.[35]

From then on, the formal protection of equality spread worldwide to the point that today[36] it is difficult to cite a constitution that does not provide for the clause, especially since there was still no commitment whatsoever with respect to equality—and to inequalities—*in* the law.[37] It was content with the proclamation of the principle of equality *of* the law, regardless of whether the law itself sponsors inequalities (in cases of equal situations) or arbitrariness (in cases of unequal situations that deserve treatment in such a proportional measure). This is the case remembered by Carlos Maximiliano: absolute equality is, in fact, the *paradox of equality*.[38]

The liberal notion was received in Brazil by the Imperial Constitution of 1824.

---

[35] Albuquerque (1993), p. 49.

[36] Regarding the ductility of the concept, it is emblematic that, in the United States, the equality clause—*equal protection clause*—only had constitutional shelter with the 14th Amendment, of 1868. Even after its adoption, the doctrine of *separate but equal* persisted from the famous Dred Scott case, considered one of the most infamous in the history of all constitutional jurisdiction, until the precedent review in 1954, with Brown v. Board of Education. In the entry *equal protection* in *Black's Law Dictionary*, one can see the distinction in concept only formal of equality and, currently, a concept more attentive to the content of inequalities. From there, it can be seen: "The 14th Amendment guarantees that the government must treat a person or class of persons the same as it treats other persons or classes in like circumstances. In today's constitutional jurisprudence, equal protection means that legislation that discriminates must have a rational basis for doing so. And if the legislation affects a fundamental right (such as the right to vote) or involves a suspect classification (such as race), it is unconstitutional unless it can withstand strict scrutiny" Garner (2009), p. 616.

[37] To stick to the most well-known and a curious case: the curious one is the provision of formal equality in the Constitution of the Republic of South Africa, adopted on May 8, 1996, which, in the preamble, recognises the unity in diversity of Africans living in that country and states that all citizens are equally protected by law. In its text, while in Article 1, "a," the need to achieve equality is recognised, in Article 3, 2, it is provided that all citizens are equally holders of rights, privileges, and benefits of citizenship, and equally subject to the tasks and responsibilities concerning citizenship. The Constitution of Italy, of December 7, 1947, in Article 3, provides that citizens have equal social dignity and are equal before the law, without distinction of sex, race, language, religion, political opinions, or personal and social conditions. Its text also states that it is the duty of the Republic to remove the economic and social obstacles that, by effectively limiting the freedom and equality of citizens, prevent the full development of the human person and the effective participation of all workers in the political, economic, and social organisation of the country. In Germany, in Article 3 of the Basic Law of May 23, 1949, both formal equality of all before the law, and equality between men and women were provided—hence the promotion of equality between both to eliminate existing differences, as well as the prohibition of favouritism or prejudicial treatment on the basis of sex, kinship, race, language, domicile or origin, belief or religious or political opinions. Such an article also determined that no one can be disadvantaged because of incapacity. In the Spanish Constitution of October 31, 1978, in its Article 14, it reads that Spaniards are equal before the law, without any discrimination on the grounds of birth, race, sex, religion, opinion, or any other personal or social condition or circumstance prevailing.

[38] Maximiliano (1948), p. 36.

1.1.3 The Development of Equality in Brazilian Constitutional History (1824 to 1969)

It is somewhat contradictory that in the midst of a monarchical regime, it was said that the Charter of 1824 had a *liberal* spirit, as it was supported by the winds that arrived here from the North (Virginia Declaration), or from the Atlantic (French declaration).[39] The liberal *tone* of the treatment of equality resonates from the provision of Article 179 of that Constitution, according to which, in its clause XIII, "the law will be the same for all, whether it protects, whether it punishes, and will reward in proportion to the merits of each one."

As Pandiá Calógeras said, attentive to the ideal that was being propagated at the time, at this point, the Constitution of 1824 was a "monument of liberalism."[40] And Paulino Jacques, considering the wording of the clause here transcribed to be almost a translation of what was contained in Article 3 of the French declaration adopted by the National Convention on May 29 of 1793, understood that "a more liberal source could not the precept of the monarchical Charter have found."[41]

The essence of this statement and its correctness are also noticeable because, in other four clauses (XIV to XVII), the constitutional provisions were nothing more than mere discipline for admission to public offices supported by "talents and virtues" (Art. 179, XIV), or of adequacy between the "proportion of assets" and the "contribution to the expenses of the State" (Art. 179, XV), or of reminiscence of privileges as long as they are linked to positions and have supposed public utility (Art. 179, XVI), or, still, of non-existence of privileged forum (Art. 179, XVII).

It did not escape from Anacleto de Faria's lesson the prohibition of "state intervention in the sense of reducing possible factual inequalities" (which already reinforced the liberal tone of the concept of equality),[42] it was the same author who brought to light other contradictions: the permanence of the strict income criterion for political participation in the life of the country (Articles 94 and 95 of the Constitution) and the maintenance of the *royal privileges* (distribution of honors that remained in the hands of the emperor).

We began the nineteenth century, therefore, with a chimera of equality, even because the state was not even secular and—as will be seen particularly with the

---

[39] Barroso recalls a passage from Raymundo Faoro, according to whom "liberalism was not, in its origin, democratic, but bourgeois, and, in many residues, aristocratic" Barroso (1986), p. 67. The contradiction in wanting to imitate the French and American bourgeois ideals lies exactly in the fact that the maturity that guided the egalitarian proclamation in those countries came along with the fight against the monarchical regime (France with its revolution and the United States with its independence from the English metropolis), and that, in both countries, equality served to diminish the differences between the classes with political representation due to the strengthening of the bourgeoisie. In Brazil, nothing like this was thought of.

[40] apud Faria (1973), p. 64. The passage from Pandiá Calógeras is in his work entitled *Historical formation of Brazil* (1935), p. 112.

[41] Jacques (1957), p. 97.

[42] Faria (1973), p. 65.

criminal process—the prevailing slavery regime prevented the labelling of such constitutional provisions as *liberal*.

With the republic, we advanced a little, because it began to admit "privilege of birth, forums of nobility and existing honorary orders and all their prerogatives and privileges, as well as the noble titles and council" (Art. 72, § 2°, 2nd part), and universal suffrage was accepted—although women's vote was only constitutionalized in 1934.

In dealing with the core of equality, however, the liberal handbook maintained that, purely and simply, "all are equal before the law" (Art. 72, § 2°). In this respect, Anacleto de Oliveira Faria is right when he says that "the equality advocated by the said Charter continued to be of a formal, negative and abstract character, provided for by the Constitution of 1824 and originating from the individualistic ideas then in force."[43] The synthesis of the affirmation of formal equality can be taken from the comment of João Barbalho, who summarizes Article 72, § 2°, of that Constitution in these terms:

> there are, before the republican law, neither great nor small, lords nor vassals, patricians nor plebeians, rich nor poor, strong nor weak, because it unites and levels everyone by right. There are no privileges of race, caste or class, nor distinctions as to the advantages and burdens established by the constitutional regime. And the inequality resulting from conditions of fortune and social position have not to influence in the relations between the individual and the public authority in any of its branches. The law, the administration, justice will be equal for all.[44]

With the Constitution of 1934, equality begins to be treated in the first of the clauses provided for individual rights and guarantees. Thus, in Article 113, I, it reads: "all are equal before the law. There will be no privileges or distinctions, due to birth, sex, race, own or parents' professions, social class, wealth, religious beliefs or political ideas."

Although one can notice the continuity of adhering to the liberal-individualist guide in the treatment of the theme, Anacleto de Oliveira Faria recalls, according to the interpretation made of Article 115 of that Charter (conditioning of economic freedom to offer "all" a "dignified existence"), that there was an attempt to move from mere formal equality to a "attempt at social and economic equality."[45] One could, in sequence, deal with the individualistic and liberal continuity of the prediction of equality in the Charter granted in 1937[46] (Art. 122, 1: "all are equal before the law"), but it is preferred to remember that the Constitution of 1937 did not even legally exist.

---

[43] Faria (1973), p. 68.

[44] Cavalcanti (2002), p. 303.

[45] Faria (1973), p. 71.

[46] Araújo Castro deserves important highlight, who, in his comments, followed the trail of João Mangabeira and postulated for a "protection that the State owes to the weak," affirming with this that "equality consists, above all, in considering unequal conditions unequally, in order to soften, as much as possible, by law, the social differences and promote social harmony, by the balance of interests and the fate of the classes" (2003), p. 267.

The passage from an interview with Francisco Campos, its architect, to the *Morning Mail*, on March 3, 1945, is enlightening:

> However, what is more serious is that the Constitution of 1937 is no longer in force. It is a document of purely historical value. It has entered the immense material that, having been or could have been legal, ceased to be or did not become legal, because it did not acquire or lost its validity.[47]

The principle of formal equality would be rescued in the Charter of 1946, simply and simply in § 1 of Article 141—"all are equal before the law"—were it not for the temperaments of the imperative of "social justice" as a criterion for organizing the economic order (Art. 145), the conditioning of "social welfare" in the use of property (Art. 147) and, finally, the distribution of property itself "with equal opportunity for all" (Art. 141, § 16).

For such temperaments, although the general rule in dealing with equality continued to be simply and simply equality *before* the law, authors like Themístocles Brandão Cavalcanti[48] and Carlos Maximiliano[49] already focused on the principle in light of its overcoming of individualistic treatment. And that is why Anacleto de Oliveira Faria remembered that such a constitution, "alongside the principle of isonomy, establishes rules related to the transposition to the substantial level of this principle and the establishment of greater possibilities of access to a minimum of material goods, on the part of all citizens."[50]

With the Constitution of 1967, later repackaged only in the form of agreement with the models of Constitutional Amendment No. 1 of 1969, it is maintained in Articles 150 (of the Charter of 1967) and 153 (in the terms of the aforementioned constitutional amendment) formal equality, in the sense that "all are equal before the law, without distinction of sex, race, work, religious creed and political convictions. Racial prejudice will be punished by law." In this particular, if on the one hand there was some optimism in the comment of Anacleto de Oliveira Faria from Article 168 of the Charter of 1967 (equality of opportunities by having established education as a right of all), there was no similar optimism in the comments of Francisco Cavalcanti Pontes de Miranda, who emphatically treated the principle as if it were mere formal equality.[51]

---

[47] The full interview is transcribed in Porto (2001), pp. 39–52. On the subject, Afonso Arinos de Melo Franco said: "there is no need to pay much attention to a text that was not applied, and that had been consciously written not to apply" Melo Franco (1976), p. 170.

[48] Cavalcanti (1952), p. 77.

[49] Maximiliano (1948), p. 36. The author also repeated a lesson according to which "the right of equality can only be admitted in the sense of an equality of rights in a corresponding equality of conditions" (p. 37).

[50] Faria (1973), p. 76.

[51] Pontes de Miranda (1974), p. 699.

1.1.4 The Constitution of 1988: From Formal Equality to Material Equality

If on the one hand José Afonso da Silva criticizes the observation that, in the dístico equality-freedom, more studies touch the latter to the detriment of those directed to the first,[52] on the other hand, in the light of the Charter of 1988, it is important to deal with the justification for adding to equality *before* the law that other, the *of* the law or, as Luiza Cristina Fonseca Frischeisen wants, built *by* the law.[53]

The current constitution, having provided right in the caput of its Article 5 that all "are equal before the law, without distinction of any nature," remained faithful to the liberal guide that equality is built in the dictates of the law. From this, it is repeated that any consideration of inequality cannot be *in the very* law, but in the treatment that the law operators give to the facts.

As the reason for the discrimination may be *in the very* law, the current constitution gives clues to overcoming the mere formal consecration of the principle of equality, that is, it gives clues that the interpretation that must prevail regarding equality goes beyond the *negative* and formal notion, adding to it the *positive* and substantial notion. It is because the objectives of the Brazilian Republic are the construction of "a free, fair and solidary society," and "the eradication of poverty and marginalisation, in addition to the reduction of social and regional inequalities" (Art. 3, I and III).

Such distinction between negative or *formal* equality and positive or *material* was outlined, in the Supreme Court Federal, in the Injunction Mandate No. 58, reported by Min. Celso de Mello, in these terms:

> This principle - whose observance binds, unconditionally, all manifestations of Public Power - must be considered, in its primary function of preventing discrimination and extinguishing privileges (RDA 55/114), under two aspects: (a) equality in law and (b) equality before the law. Equality in law - which operates in a phase of purely abstract generality - constitutes a requirement for the legislator who, at the time of its formation, cannot include in it factors of discrimination, responsible for the rupture of the isonomic order. Equality before the law, however, presupposing an already elaborated law, translates imposition destined to the other state powers, which, in the application of the legal norm, cannot subordinate it to criteria that lead to selective or discriminatory treatment.[54]

From the distinction made and in the wake of the lesson of Fernanda Duarte Lopes Lucas da Silva, the existence of a

> vacuum regarding the issue of material or real equality, as if the coincidence of the legal sense of the principle with the concept of formal equality was sufficient to satisfy the doctrinal positions and aspirations, relegating to other fields and areas of knowledge the problem of social inequality.[55]

---

[52] Silva (2013), p. 213.

[53] Frischeisen (2007), p. 34.

[54] STF, MI 58, Plenary, under the rapporteurship of Justice Celso de Mello, DJ 19.04.1991.

[55] Silva (2001), p. 52.

This is not a chorus here to the silence of the doctrinal sector that the Constitution of 1988 would have been merely content with its formal aspect.[56] In the words of José Afonso da Silva, here endorsed, "the understanding of the current provision, in the terms of Art. 5, *caput*, should not be so narrow."[57] The law itself is seen as a vehicle for overcoming existing inequalities, and not just as a means of formally declaring who is equal and to what extent this is given.

There was no Pontius Pilate's posture in the ideology of the current constitution, even because (and this matters to the theme of the equality of arms in criminal procedure) there is no way to achieve such a free, fair and solidary society, nor will it be possible to eradicate poverty and marginalization if, (in the constitution and) in the criminal procedure, the forces in play are not rebalanced, giving to the subjects who use their respective *arms* the necessary tools so that, in the process, equality is achieved. It is clear that the temperaments of such distribution of *arms* or the (re) balancing of forces is a matter to be dealt with later (from the glimpse of equality as a fundamental right and from the acceptances of its manifestation in criminal procedure). Still, the premise must be affirmed with vigor: the law not only declares who is equal and who is not; it is a channel of overcoming, to the extent that is factually and legally possible, inequalities.

The constitution also gives other quite evident indications that the desired equality is not formal, but substantial, material, when providing, for example, the social function of property (Art. 5, XXIII), the conditioning of the exercise of free initiative (Art. 170, *caput* and items) and the valorization of work (Art. 7). Particularly relevant is the establishment of public defenders of the states and the union, attributing to them the characteristic of an institution "essential to the jurisdictional function of the State" and imposing on them the "legal guidance and defence, at all levels, of the needy, in the form of art. 5, LXXIV" (Art. 134, CF).

The reminder of the public defenders was noted by José Afonso da Silva, once again on the point regarding material equality:

> the achievement of equality before justice, thus, requires the search for equalisation of conditions of the unequal, which implies leading the judge to two imperatives, as observed by Ingber: on one hand, it is incumbent upon him to recognise the existence of increasingly numerous and diversified categories, which replace the idea of man, an abstract entity, by the more precise notion of individual characterised by the group in which it is actually inserted; on the other hand, he must appreciate the relevance criteria that were adopted by the legislator.[58]

The 1988 Brazilian Constitution did not ignore the *differences* to try to eradicate the *inequalities*. It is impossible not to see that, if not in this way, even the constitutional promise of the two sections of Article 3 of the Republican Charter is not fulfilled. Therefore, there is no legal space in Brazil to turn a blind eye to inequalities, especially economic ones, which significantly spread to the legal plane. Once

---

[56] Moraes (2010), p. 36; Araújo e Nunes Júnior (2003), p. 96.

[57] Silva (2013), p. 217.

[58] Silva (2013), p. 222.

inequalities are perceived, they must be overcome to build a less unjust society. To imagine that today the constitution is fulfilled with the reasoning that formal equality, *formal*—before the law—therefore means disregarding the evolution already occurred in constitutional law and criminal procedure, not to mention the legal evolution provided for in successive international human rights treaties.[59]

Also noteworthy are the scope of constitutional jurisdiction, its legitimacy in controlling the *internal reasonableness* of laws, and the finding that absolute formal equality allows absolute inequality.[60] In this sense, equality in treatment outside the process is a point of arrival, not a starting point. Hence, it is sometimes necessary to discriminate in order to equalize. In the words of Luis Roberto Barroso, "it is by the very existence of inequalities—natural or not—that equality is aspired to."[61]

In the field of criminal procedure, it provokes reflection on the chronic dissonance between the Constitution and each of our Codes of Procedure, from the first to the current and, perhaps, the projected. This is what will be done next, from the specific focus of procedural equality. In the still expository development to be done next, the bipartite division of José Afonso da Silva will be adopted, according to whom

> the principle of jurisdictional equality or before the judge presents itself under two prisms: (1) as a prohibition to the judge to make a distinction between equal situations, when applying the law; (2) as a prohibition to the legislator to enact laws that allow unequal treatment to equal situations or equal treatment to unequal situations by Justice.[62]

1.2 Equality as a Fundamental Right: Aspects of Normative Incidence and Practical Consequences

The approach that allows achieving the concretization of equality in criminal procedure is not exhausted in the historical approach of its treatment from the point of view of constitutional law. After all, if what is being taken care of is the introjection in the criminal process of the constitutional provision, it is not possible to deal with

[59] Silva (2021), pp. 132–134.

[60] Among the vast doctrines that have already reached this conclusion, Maria da Glória Garcia recalls, without citing the reference work, that Pablo Lucas Verdú would have taken formal equality as an "evident hypocrisy" (2005), p. 12. For his part, Canotilho emphasizes that the mere abstract principle of formal equality "allows discrimination as to content (example: all individuals of Jewish race must have signage on the forehead; all individuals of 'black race' must be treated 'equally' in 'separate' schools from schools reserved for whites). The law treated equally all Jews and all blacks even if it created for them an intrinsically discriminatory discipline" (2003), p. 427. In procedural doctrine, it was Ada Pellegrini Grinover who said that the "absolute legal equality generated economic inequality: and from the primitive concept of equality, formal and negative, there was a call for the transition to real equality, in its positive aspect" Grinover (1975), p. 27.

[61] Barroso (1986), p. 70.

[62] Silva (2013), p. 220.

the equality of arms in criminal procedure without talking about equality as a fundamental constitutional right.

For this reason, the evolution of this study presupposes that one should discuss the approach of equality within the theory of principles, as treated by Ronald Dworkin and Robert Alexy, and followed in Brazil, within the scope of constitutional law, especially by Virgílio Afonso da Silva.[63]

After all, if up to now it has been seen that equality *in* the law is not enough to fulfil the promise of an egalitarian society (which in itself is already an important theoretical problem, but escapes the approach of this work[64]), it is necessary to consider, with Alexy, whether equality is a principle that, "*prima facie*, requires equal treatment and only allows unequal treatment if it can be justified with opposing reasons."[65]

The approach made from the so-called *theory of principles* seems opportune not only because the constitutional interpretation based on it allows constitutionally adequate solutions for difficult cases—hence it is an important practical application tool[66]—but also because it can be noted that the theory of criminal procedure has been attentive to this.[67]

For this work, assuming the approach that will be made from the referred theory, to define whether equality in criminal proceedings is a *rule* or *principle*, and, from there, to deal with its incidence in practical situations[68] proves to be relevant not only for the diagnosis to be made about the application of the *equality of arms in criminal proceedings*, but also for the formulation of criticisms of possible scenarios of legislative reforms.

If, like equality at the constitutional level, equality of arms is taken as having the normative aspect of a rule in criminal proceedings, the practical consequences will be different from those that will be reached if, as anticipated here, equality and equality of arms are taken as principles. Let us see why.

---

[63] In the article *Principles and Rules: Myths and Misconceptions About a Distinction*, the Brazilian author indicated the importance of foreigners and said that, for both, the distinction between principles and rules, within the scope of norms, is of "logical character" Silva (2003), p. 609. There are other authors who also showed attention to the incidence of principiological norms of constitutional law. Among them: (Stumm (1995), Barros (2006), Ávila (2003), Sarlet (2009), Sarmento (2003) and Pacheco (2007).

[64] For we are not going to deal here with the distinction, within the scope of legal norms, between *policies* (*policies*) and *rules* (*rules*), in the way Ronald Dworkin preaches. And neither is this the appropriate place to discuss—with the focus on the word *equality* that appears in the preamble of the Brazilian Constitution of 1988—the distinction between *rules, principles,* and *values*.

[65] Alexy (1997), p. 398.

[66] As understood by Queiroz (2002), p. 138.

[67] Zanoide de Moraes (2010), pp. 263–330; Badaró (2014), pp. 433–457.

[68] That is: to speak of the *scope of protection of the norm, its so-called factual support, and its hypotheses of restriction, limitation, and collision*.

1.2.1 *The Principles and Rules in the Theory of Fundamental Rights*

Legal principles have had a long dogmatic journey until they reached the conception of a legal norm, which happened, with nuances, from studies by two authors: Ronald Dworkin[69] and Robert Alexy.[70] If today it is certain that, among those who study fundamental rights from the bias of the theory of principles, they separate, within the scope of norms, the so-called *rules* from the *principles*, it is worth a brief digression, which is: what matters in the treatment that the theory of principles gives them does not result from their *fundamentality*, but rather from their structure of optimization command.[71]

Thus, it is not without purpose to remember that, before the approaches of Dworkin and, above all, those of Alexy, the *principles* were, with various semantic variations, likened to what is still known today as general principles of law. In a historical-legal sequence that goes beyond the limits of this work, it is worth saying, from the review made by Paulo Bonavides, that an important first approach in the treatment of principles was that which took them as "general principles of law" (and thus they were reproduced as such in Article 4 of the old Introduction to the Brazilian Civil Code – Decree-Law No. 4,657/42), to later, at the constitutional level, be raised to "fundamental principles."[72] From a subsidiary position, the principles reached, in theoretical evolution, the peak of positive law.

In such evolution, one could not approach the theme of the *principles* without mentioning the study of Josef Esser, who, in 1956, was pointed out as one of those responsible for the new theoretical treatment that was given to them.[73]

This overcoming of the private law approach that was given to principles, which occurred after the second post-war period and the provisions, particularly of the German, Portuguese, and Spanish Constitutions, still did not allow the bias that the theory of principles would later consecrate to them to be reached.

The authors who focused on principles from the point of view of their evolution from the so-called *general principles* of law to the *fundamental principles* of constitutional law cling, each with some variation in approach, to syntheses based on the *fundamentality* of the principle to the system (an example of which is, in Brazil, the doctrine of Bonavides and also, to some extent, that of Luis Roberto Barroso[74]), in

---

[69] Dworkin (1977).

[70] Alexy (1997).

[71] Silva (2005b), p. 36.

[72] Bonavides (1997), cap. 8. In a more summarized way, the panorama is outlined by Mendes e Branco (2024), pp. 37–39.

[73] Esser (1961). We were able to deal with this approach in an article written with Piovesan (2025), cap. 24.

[74] Barroso (1998), p. 141. He points out that constitutional principles "are the norms elected by the constituent as foundations or essential qualifications of the legal order it establishes." On the other hand, in Barroso (2024), pp. 162 and foll., the professor reviews the aspects that in constitutional

the *generality*[75] inherent in principles, or, finally, in the teaching of Celso Antonio Bandeira de Mello, according to which the principle is the

> nuclear command of a system, true foundation of it, fundamental provision that radiates over different norms composing their spirit and serving as a criterion for their exact understanding and intelligence, precisely by defining the logic and the rationality of the normative system, in what gives it the tone and gives it harmonious sense.[76]

Such an approach, which privileges principles from the side of their fundamentality—since the theoretical evolution of giving them to remove the privatization clothing and place it within the constitutional scope, and from there it is not possible to diminish the importance that the approach had, as summarized in Canotilho's own doctrine[77]—it is not the one followed by Alexy's theory of principles.

Nor is it, among the doctrines that began to worry about the way of incidence of the *norm* that the principle is, the one here accepted.[78] The choice made does not result from disparagement of the typology of principles or from an analysis that intends to sectorize them (special general principles, *more* or *less* fundamental than others). The reason is another: it matters, for the research, the form of the incidence of the norm. According to Virgílio Afonso da Silva and his reading of Alexy, the concept of principle is "axiologically neutral and its use does not express any option for this or that fundamental disposition, nor for this or that type of Constitution."[79]

It is not about the principle as a norm from its generality, or from its fundamentality, but rather from its form of incidence. As Virgílio Afonso da Silva says,

> a norm is a principle not because it is fundamental, but because it has the *structure* of an optimisation command. Therefore, a principle can be a 'nuclear command of the system',

---

law focus on the term *principle* and dwells more leisurely in the theory of principles. In Portugal: Canotilho; Moreira (1991), pp. 67–93. Professor Gomes Canotilho, incidentally, in *Constitutional Law and Theory of the Constitution* (pp. 1159 and foll.), exposes not only Alexy's theory, but also presents a review of the typology of principles already discussed here.

[75] On which Rothenburg (1999) and Tavares (2002), p. 87, have discussed, without prejudice to other aspects.

[76] Bandeira de Mello (1996), p. 545. When the theory of principles was not yet so thoroughly studied in Brazil, an important work was published, from the point of view of *cataloguing* doctrinal of the principles: Espíndola (1999). In more recent times, there are now repetitions of approaches that excel in the classification of principles according to their generality and abstraction, or others that excel in the acceptance of the theory of principles. About this, see: Leite (2003).

[77] "The law of the Rule of Law of the 19th century and the first half of the 20th century is the law of the rules of the codes; the Law of the Democratic Constitutional State and of Law takes the principles seriously, it is a law of principles" Canotilho (2000), p. 84.

[78] There are authors, like Silva (2005b), p. 31 and footnote 8, who say it is a *weak* conception that distinguishes principles from rules only by the criterion of degree or generality, and follow the so-called *strong* conception of the distinction, which is advocated by the theory of principles, which will be discussed here.

[79] Silva (2003), p. 615.

> *but it can also not be*, since a norm is a principle *only because of its normative structure* and not because of its fundamentality. The same applies to the rules.[80]

What the theory of principles preaches is that principles, unlike rules, are *optimization commands*. For this theory, and here we note an interweaving between Alexy and Dworkin that seems to be didactic, the norm (*norm*) brings as species the rules (*rules*) and the principles (*principles*). From this distinction, we can already say that the rule follows the system of *all-or-nothing* (*all or nothing fashion*), being that its incidence or non-occurrence in each concrete case is purely a matter of validity. With this, the incidence of a given rule in the concrete case, by itself, excludes that of others that do not perfectly fit that situation. With the principles, on the other hand, norms that they are, the dimension is already of value, of weight, hence the incidence of one of them does not necessarily exclude the incidence of another.[81]

Hence, the coexistence of rules is antinomic, and that of principles is conflictual. After all, while the rules exclude each other, the principles coexist; while in the strict model of the rules, there is a relation of total exclusion of one in the face of the incidence of another, with the principles, something different occurs, as it configures a balancing, a harmonization between both, a judgement of weighing.

In the words of Alexy, the solution between an antinomy of rules is always resolved by an "exception clause,"[82] while in the conflict of principles, one resorts to a criterion of "conditional precedence" dependent on weight, greater or lesser importance of each of the principles in comparison.[83] On this subject,

> the rule-norm is applied as it is provided, or it is not applied, it is the form 'all or nothing' ('*all or nothing*') of application. It cannot be partly set aside and partly applied. The rights-duties guaranteed by rules, unlike what happens with principles, are not susceptible to weighing with other norms in order to be, in certain cases, partly set aside and in another part produce legal effects. The rules are not restrictable, the principles are.[84]

---

[80] Silva (2005b), p. 36. From this cut, in the plane of the theory of principles, legality in criminal law is not a principle, but a rule. And it is also a rule, in matters of criminal law, the prohibition of double persecution for the same fact, and many others that, on the plane of *abstraction and fundamentality*, are traditionally seen as principles.

[81] Piovesan (2025), p. 359. About the criminal process, see: Badaró (2014), p. 437. See also: Zanoide de Moraes (2010), p. 271.

[82] And such exception clauses are the known rules of overcoming antinomies in positive law, such as specialty, anteriority, and superiority. Echo of this doctrine, in the procedural criminal field, can be seen in: Badaró (2014), p. 437; Zanoide de Moraes (2010), p. 271.

[83] Alexy (1997), p. 92. In Brazil, Barcellos (2002, p. 86) preaches that such a relationship of conditioned precedence is tied to the "social fundamentality" of the principles in question. In this regard, Silva (2005b), p. 32, states that, "according to Alexy, *principles* are norms that require that something be carried out to the greatest extent possible in the face of existing factual and legal possibilities. Defined in this way, the principles are clearly distinguished from the rules, because these, if valid, must always be fully realised. The degree of realisation of the principles, on the other hand, can always vary, especially in the face of the existence of other principles that impose the realisation of another right that collides with that required by the first."

[84] Zanoide de Moraes (2010), p. 271. In the lesson of Queiroz (2002), p. 134, "the main point of distinction between rules and principles points to a different quality, not a different nature between these two types of legal norms. The rules, unlike the principles, have the character of definitive

As Virgílio Afonso da Silva preaches,

> the main distinguishing feature between rules and principles is the structure of the rights that these norms guarantee. In the case of rules, definitive rights are guaranteed (or duties are imposed), while in the case of principles, rights (or duties) are guaranteed *prima facie*.[85]

Once again, the influence of the theory of principles in the field of criminal procedure is noted:

> In the case of collision between principles, the solution should be given by weighing or balancing. But, even after the solution of the conflict between principles, both will continue 'as valid as before', and it cannot be said that between them will consist exception to the other, since 'sometimes one prevails, sometimes the other', depending on the concrete conditions of each case in question.[86]

1.2.2 Equality as a Principle: The Contours of Broad Factual Support

Having exposed the complexity that surrounds the approach of the theory of principles about fundamental rights and established the methodological premise of this theory, regarding principles and rules, we can now go down a step.

It has already been seen, from the passages pertaining to the treatment of equality in the scenario of history (equality and inequality are the two sides of the same coin, even because both are *evaluative* and resulting from *characteristics* innate to the recipients of norms, and also because it is only by *differentiating* that the *equalities* are identified), that equality is not a legal notion tied to the rule of all-or-nothing. In the field of the theory of principles, Alexy points out that the principle of equality is the one that, "*prima facie*, requires an equal treatment and only allows an unequal treatment if it can be justified with opposing reasons."[87]

In agreement with Alexy and considering what has already been addressed so far, it is not possible to formulate an *a priori rule* (*all-or-nothing*) of equality, much less a universal rule. The examples of the German author are elucidative: it is the inconceivable inflexibility of equality to the point of imagining military service for children, penalties for all citizens regardless of age and imputation, or even that every voter is eligible to be elected and that the subordinates are also their own bosses. At the limit, and still in the field of Alexy's examples, not even the maxim of treating

mandates. Here there is no need for a weighting. The characteristic form of their application is not the weighting, but the subsumption."

[85] Silva (2009), p. 45.

[86] Badaró (2014), p. 438.

[87] Alexy (1997), p. 396.

everyone as equals and the unequal as unequal escapes this logic, since such reasoning would justify, including, the persecution of Jews.[88]

It cannot be denied, however, that the notion of *equality* as a right is linked to the *reasonable*, to the test of the *justifiable*, to the opposite of the *arbitrary*, all these semantic notions that indicate that it is a norm with the aspect of a principle. After all, it is indisputable that one of the ways to assess obedience or non-obedience to the principle of equality is to investigate whether the disparity results from arbitrariness, that is, from unjustifiable distinctions. Equality as a fundamental right has the logical aspect of a principle: it applies prima facie, as a norm guaranteeing a right, depending on the factual situation that allows it, observed the limitations of positive law.

It is necessary, then, to deal with the so-called factual support of the norm of fundamental right, since it is the "set of factual elements that the legal norm in abstract provides and to it imputes a certain consequence."[89] The theory of principles takes such a concept as determinant in the guarantee of the fundamental right, because, in the words of Virgílio Afonso da Silva,

> the form of application of fundamental rights - subsumption, weighing, concretisation or others - depends on the extension of the factual support; the requirements for justification in cases of restriction to rights fundamental depend on the configuration of the factual support; the very possibility of restriction to fundamental rights may depend on what is understood by factual support; the existence of collisions between fundamental rights also depends on a precise determination of the concept of factual support.[90]

As the mentioned author says in a doctrine that once again echoes in criminal procedure, here it is important to consider the answers to four questions: What is protected? Against what is the protection given? What is the legal consequence that can occur? What needs to happen for the consequence to occur?[91]

The example of the need to analyze the structure of the principled norm of the fundamental right from its factual support is pertinent to equality. In this regard, Virgílio Afonso da Silva says:

> therefore, when it is said that 'all are equal before the law', it is not the definition of what is protected - equality - enough to define the factual basis. What is protected is just a part - certainly, the most important part of the factual basis. This part is usually called the *scope of protection* of the fundamental right. But for the configuration of the factual basis a second element is necessary - and here comes the counter-intuitive part: the *state intervention*. Both

[88] "If the general principle of equality were limited to a universalist decision-making practice, the legislator could carry out any discrimination without violating it, as long as he presented it under the form of universal norms, something that is always possible. Under this interpretation, the National Socialist legislation against the Jews would not violate the formula 'Equal must be treated equally and unequal unequally'" Alexy (1997), p. 386.

[89] Silva (2009), p. 68.

[90] Silva (2009), p. 68. Zanoide de Moraes (2010), p. 274, in this regard, points out: "the factual support is formed by the fact, act or legal situation inserted in the scope of protection of the norm."

[91] Silva (2009), p. 70. Zanoide de Moraes (2010), p. 275.

> what is protected (scope of protection) and what against it which is protected (intervention, usually state) are part of the support factual of fundamental rights.[92]

Up to this point one could say that the factual basis of the right fundamental (of equality) is the sum of the *scope of protection* (What is protected, after all? What is the relevant good that motivates the existence of the norm?[93]) and the *state intervention* (What is the act that, occurred, triggers the legal protection, that is, the consequence and the recognition of its unconstitutionality?). Here is the so-called "dual composition of the factual basis."[94]

There is news, however, of a so-called *alternative model*, which is proposed by Virgílio Afonso da Silva[95] and followed, in the field of Brazilian criminal procedure, by Gustavo Henrique Righi Ivahy Badaró[96] and Maurício Zanoide de Moraes.[97] Such a model adds to the duality of *scope of protection* and *state intervention* a third element to make the fundamental right norm applicable: the absence of a constitutional justification for the intervention itself.

Thus, if a constitutional basis for the intervention is noted, the protection of the fundamental right does not apply, since there would not properly be a violation of such a right, but rather a restriction (constitutionally legitimate) of its exercise. The relevance to the criminal process of this alternative model is thus treated by Maurício Zanoide de Moraes:

> there are two forms of intervention: a legitimate one, called restriction, and which will be part of the factual basis in order to reduce the scope of protection of the constitutional norm; another illegitimate, called violation, and that if occurring will cause the legal consequence provided for in the norm.[98]

No less important problem is the amplitude of the factual basis, that is, the extent of the facts that, prima facie, can, if they occur, trigger the norm of fundamental right (of equality and, as will be seen, of equality of arms). It is that, if on the one hand, some argue that the factual basis is a notion *restricted*, others[99] advocate for a factual basis *wide*. And this is the position taken here.

---

[92] Silva (2009), p. 71.

[93] "The definition of the scope of protection of a fundamental right answers the question about what acts, facts, states or legal positions are protected by the norm that guarantees the said right" Silva (2009), p. 72. The distinction between the broad and narrow scope of protection is important in that, by the former, a greater range of goods protected by the norm is covered, and by the latter, not. Exemplifying, with the presumption of innocence, when it is provided that *no one* can be considered guilty before the final judgment of a conviction, Zanoide de Moraes (2010), pp. 282–283, defends the scope of protection of the norm in a broad sense.

[94] Silva (2009), p. 72. In the criminal process, it was addressed by Badaró (2014), p. 441 and Zanoide de Moraes (2010), p. 275.

[95] Silva (2009), p. 74.

[96] Badaró (2014), p. 442.

[97] Zanoide de Moraes (2010), p. 276.

[98] Zanoide de Moraes (2010), p. 277.

[99] Silva (2009), pp. 75 and foll.; Zanoide de Moraes (2010), pp. 278 and foll.

The option for a restricted concept of factual basis delimits, in advance, the incidence of the protective norm of fundamental rights. Thus, aprioristically factual situations are excluded from protection, which in the limit justifies, also in advance, state intervention. For the restrictive theory, says Maurício Zanoide de Moraes, "what is determined legislatively is already what is 'definitively protected by norm'."[100] Let us see an example taken from constitutional law with application in criminal procedure: the secrecy epistolary would not cover illicit practices,[101] that is, such practices would not be part of the factual basis of the protection of the fundamental right of freedom of communication.

It is important to realize that the restrictive theory, it seems, can even amount to going against the theory of principles, in measure that it does not sponsor an incidence prima facie of the protective norms, but their definitiveness, limiting it in function of choices already made legislatively, as the exclusions of the incidence of the norm are made in an abstract and definitive way. On the other hand, the broad theory of factual support, still in the conformation of the fundamental right norm, rejects the premise of "exclusions *a priori* of conducts or situations from the scope of protection of fundamental rights." With this, if by the restrictive theory of factual support what is protected is only what is *definitively* protected, in the expansive

> defining what is protected is just a first step, as conducts or situations covered by the scope of protection will still depend on a weighing in concrete situations before we can talk about definitive protection. Hence the distinction between what is protected *prima facie* and what is definitively protected.[102]

The theory of broad factual support, then, either by not excluding aprioristically from the incidence of the fundamental right norm its consequence, or by working with the idea of a prima facie judgement and not *definitive* of what it can protect, takes better care of fundamental rights. It does not restrict the normative protection, finally, to the mere existence of external factors to those that, from the point of view of the debated theme, would trigger the protection. This leads to another question, namely: the restrictions of fundamental rights.

---

[100] Zanoide de Moraes (2010), p. 280.

[101] Silva (2009), p. 79. In this regard, Zanoide de Moraes (2010), pp. 279–80, asserts (the example mentioned in this text, which is not his, is even relevant to what he exposes): "this exclusion *a priori* - and this point is what remains unanswerable by its supporters - is often done intuitively and in significant spaces of life goods." The author presents another example: the prohibition of provisional freedom to accused of the practice of heinous crimes and similar.

[102] Silva (2009), p. 125.

1.2.3 *Equality as a Principle: Hypotheses of Restriction of the Application of the Norm and the Problem of Limits and Essential Content*

The realization that the fundamental right is restrictable results in new difficulty, as the debate that is established is about the very essential conformation of the right and, in addition, about the limits of its restriction. If at stake are the restrictions on the exercise of fundamental rights, it is important to ask: what *defines* the right to, from this, qualify state intervention as legitimate (with which it is said to be a mere restriction) or illegitimate (with which we move to the field of violation)? In addition, *defined the content of the right*, how to reach the limit of the intervention itself, always taking into account the restriction or the violation?

Regarding the first question (restriction *vs.* violation), theoretically, two positions are known: the so-called theories *internal* and *external* of fundamental rights. By the first, the "process of defining the limits of each right is something internal to it,"[103] that is, internally, the fundamental right brings in itself its complete content, including its so-called immanent limits.[104] According to this line, then, because the conformation of the right is not *outside* of it, there is no consideration of defining its restriction from the criterion of weighing. Hence, in this case, according to the words of Badaró, "there is not even a question of applying the rule of proportionality, which requires weighing or balancing, in concrete, the fundamental right with another fundamental right."[105]

The main problem of this theoretical line of argument is in the realization that, by defining the content of the fundamental right aprioristically and internally, it is given the aspect of a *rule*, and not of a *principle*. Indeed, by treating the content and its limit together, the hypotheses of ponderation are excluded, and the fundamental right is no longer considered as a command of optimization.[106]

Opposite to the *internal* theory, the *external* theory shapes the fundamental right—that is, its core and therefore the division between restriction and violation—not from *inside*, but from *outside*. Restrictions or violations are defined exactly from the conflict between fundamental rights, with which we return to the idea of the

---

[103] Silva (2009), p. 128.

[104] In Brazilian doctrine, again, it is Silva (2009), p. 128, who most sharply discusses this, and he does so, as far as researched, without treating the theory of immanent limits as a consequence, or subdivision, of the external theory, in which he seems to be right. Although the author has not expressly stated in the text, from the between the lines of his work, one can even venture to say: immanent limits *imanentes* marry even to the internal theory *interna* insofar as, because of such theory to admit no criteria external to the fundamental right to give it its contours, such limits could only be *imanentes*.

[105] Badaró (2014), p. 443. According to Zanoide de Moraes (2010), p. 285, "for this theory, in the constitutional principle-norm the notion of restriction is replaced by the limit, which is already inherent to the 'definitive right': these are the so-called 'immanent limits'."

[106] That is why Silva points out: "the figure of immanent limits and the concept of weighing are mutually exclusive" (2009), p. 133.

theory of principles that they (the principles) are commands of optimization insofar as they do not define the content of rights definitively, but rather prima facie. There is a separation between the right and its restrictions.[107]

Following the external theory of the restriction of fundamental rights, therefore, is to privilege the conformation of the right not from itself but from outside, from collisions. In a word, it is about rescuing the notion of principle as a protection prima facie of constitutionally relevant good. Regarding, and with reflections in the criminal process:

> if the right is pre-formed definitively and without the possibility of restriction, in the face of the factual-legal conditions of the concrete case, it is a mistake to say that this right can undergo consideration or the scrutiny of proportionality when analysing the concrete case. Insofar as limits would be imposed on the right so as to conceive it, from the outset, in its definitive form (internal theory), there is no longer normative space for restriction, therefore, it is no longer possible to reduce it by force of consideration (proportionality *stricto sensu*) or the principle of proportionality *lato sensu* (necessity and adequacy).[108]

Once the external theory is adopted, the next step should take care of the limits of the restriction of the fundamental right, under penalty of annihilating its *essential core*. Again, what is imposed is the distinction between restriction and violation, but now no longer on the abstract plane (what is part and what is not part of the content of the fundamental right), but rather in the concrete (to what extent the right supports the collision).

Here, again, two theories are brandished: the so-called *relative* and the *absolute*. While the latter are concerned, in the language of Gilmar Ferreira Mendes, in establishing the "limits of the limits" for judicial intervention as acceptable, with which they work with the idea of pre-established barriers, the relative theories indicate that the essential content of the fundamental right is to be diagnosed only and solely from the conflict with another right, using a criterion of consideration to define it.[109]

The problem now, therefore, from the perspective of the essentiality of the fundamental right as a limit of intervention, continues to be either, on the one hand, the adoption of a pre-established and fixed measure (absolute theory), or, on the other, flexibility of the core, depending on the weighing. In Brazil, although Gilmar Ferreira Mendes and others have understood that the Federal Constitution adopted a model that tends towards the absolutization of the essential core due to the "guarantee model used by the constituent,"[110] there is a different position, by Virgílio Afonso da Silva, endorsed by the authors of criminal procedure who have most thoroughly studied the subject.

In the wake of the lessons of the aforementioned author, although counterintuitive, the relative theory better protects fundamental rights insofar as it does not fix in advance the essential content and, in doing so, demands exactly the best

[107] Alexy (1997), p. 138; Badaró (2014), pp. 443–444; Zanoide de Moraes (2010), p. 286.

[108] Zanoide de Moraes (2010), p. 287.

[109] Mendes e Branco (2024), pp. 182–183.

[110] Mendes e Branco (2024), p. 184.

argumentative density—read: constitutional reasoning—to justify the choice of one of them. In this sense, "the essential content of a fundamental right is not always the same, and may vary from situation to situation, depending on the rights involved in each case."[111]

In the context of criminal procedure, Maurício Zanoide de Moraes perceived the need for a relativistic approach to the essential content of fundamental rights, not without recognizing that the absolute theory is "doctrinally seductive" to assert that

> it appears to be safer for the fundamental right that a part of its content is considered unrestricted, however, by not defining what is this part by a clear and secure argumentation, nothing remains, in practical forensics, of the promise made. There is no theorist who has managed to delimit with secure and fixed criteria what is the portion of any fundamental right with a principle structure that is *a priori* and always unsusceptible to restriction.[112]

1.2.4 Equality as a Principle: Cases of Normative Conflicts

Among the complexities and subtleties outlined here, a fundamental aspect, although perhaps "the least explored of the theory of principles,"[113] is the normative collision. The particular difficulty of this approach lies in the distinction of the normative aspects between rules and principles. This is because, if on the plane of conflict between rules there are no imagined difficulties in solving practical problems and if, on the other hand, on the plane of collision between principles the weighing delimits the incidence of one of them for that case, without thereby denying the validity of the one that opposes it, the opposition between a principle and a rule is a point of heated doctrinal debates. After all, imagining weighing a rule when colliding with a principle is unthinkable, as the rule has definitiveness, and this characteristic does not integrate the structure of the principle.

The solution suggested by Alexy and criticized by his faithful follower in Brazil, Virgílio Afonso da Silva,[114] is that of an indirect weighing. Indirect because it does not occur between a principle and a rule (as this is prevented in light of the theory itself, as we have seen), but between that and the other principle from which the rule emanates. The criticism of this solution lies in the observation that it

---

[111] Silva (2009), p. 196.

[112] Zanoide de Moraes (2010), p. 333. Badaró (2014), p. 445, walks in the same direction: "The position adopted by the restrictive theory may seem to be less protective of fundamental rights, when compared to absolute theories. However, although in their appearance they entail a lower level of protection for fundamental rights, in truth, relative theories strengthen them, by requiring an argumentative justification of the restriction based on the circumstances of the case." Sarmento (2003), p. 113, also takes this position.

[113] Silva (2009), p. 51.

[114] Silva (2009), p. 51.

suggests that the law enforcer is always free, in any case and in any situation, to avoid the application of a rule because they understand that there is a more important principle that justifies this avoidance. This would result in a high degree of legal uncertainty.[115]

The solution proposed by Virgílio Afonso da Silva is distinct from that of Alexy because it does not conceive of the weighing, not even indirectly, between a rule and a principle. According to the lesson of the Brazilian author, the legal norm is applied by mere subsumption. The reasoning for this is the following: in the case of an antinomy between a principle and a rule, one resorts to the assumption that the legislator has already weighed, has weighed the interests at stake, so much so that they issued the rule. In this sense, the rule functions as a logical consequence of obedience to a principle, and, therefore, one does not go to the principle to find the solution to the problem affecting the antinomy of the principle that is opposed to it. The rule is applied. Virgílio Afonso da Silva says, in this regard: "the relationship between the rule and one of the principles is not, therefore, a relationship of collision, but a relationship of restriction. The rule is an expression of this restriction. This rule must, therefore, simply be applied by *subsumption*."[116]

Having made this brief digression on the theory of principles, in the course of the work, notably concerning the scope of the current and projected Brazilian criminal process, an attempt will be made to test its application with a view to the specific focus of the principle of *equality of arms*.

References

Albuquerque, M. (1993). *Da igualdade: introdução à jurisprudência*. Almedina.

Alexy, R. (1997). *Teoria de los derechos fundamentales*. Trad. Ernesto Garzón Valdés. Centro de Estudios Constitucionales

Araújo, L. A. D., & Nunes Júnior, V. S. (2003). *Curso de direito constitucional*. Saraiva.

Ávila, H. B. (2003). *Teoria dos princípios: da definição à aplicação dos princípios jurídicos*. Malheiros.

Badaró, G. H. R. I. (2014). *Juiz Natural no processo penal*. Revista dos Tribunais.

Bandeira de Mello, C. A. (1995). *Conteúdo jurídico do princípio da igualdade* (3rd ed.). Malheiros.

Bandeira de Mello, C. A. (1996). *Curso de direito administrativo* (8th ed.). Malheiros.

Barcellos, A. P. d. (2002). *A eficácia jurídica dos princípios constitucionais: o princípio da dignidade da pessoa humana*. Renovar.

Barros, S. d. T. (2006). *O princípio da proporcionalidade e o controle de constitucionalidade das leis restritivas de direitos* (3rd ed.). Brasília Jurídica.

Barroso, L. R. (1986). *Igualdade perante a lei*. Revista de Direito Público.

Barroso, L. R. (1998). *Interpretação e aplicação da Constituição* (2nd ed.). Saraiva.

Barroso, L. R. (2024). *Curso de direito constitucional contemporâneo* (12th ed.). SaraivaJur.

Bobbio, N., Matteucci, N., & Pasquino, G. (2004). *Dicionário de política* (C.C. Varialle, G. L. Mônaco, J. Ferreira, L. Guerreiro Pinto Caçais & R. Dini, Trans, Vol. 1, 5th ed.). Editora UNB.

---

[115] Silva (2009) cit., p. 52.

[116] Silva (2009), p. 52.

Bonavides, P. (1997). *Curso de direito constitucional* (7th ed.). Malheiros.
Canotilho, J. J. G. (2000). *A "principialização" da jurisprudência através da Constituição.* Revista de processo.
Canotilho, J. J. G. (2003). *Direito constitucional e teoria da Constituição* (7th ed.). Almedina.
Canotilho, J. J. G., & Moreira, V. (1991). *Fundamentos da Constituição.* Coimbra Editora.
Cavalcanti, J. B. U. (2002). *Constituição Federal Brasileira (1891): comentada.* Forense.
Cavalcanti, T. B. (1952). *A Constituição Federal Comentada. V. III.* Forense.
Cerri, A. (2005). *L'eguaglianza.* Editori Laterza.
Cerri, A. (2007). *Uguaglianza (principio costituzionale di).* Istituto della Enciclopedia Italiana Fondata da Giovanni Treccani.
Cintra, A. C. d. A. (1982). *O princípio da igualdade processual.* Revista da Procuradoria Geral do Estado de São Paulo.
Comparato, F. K. (1998). *Precisões sobre os conceitos de lei e de igualdade jurídica.* Revista dos Tribunais.
Costa, P. B., & Martins da, F. (2001). *Igualdade no direito processual penal brasileiro.* Revista Brasileira de Ciências Criminais.
Del Vecchio, G. (1966). *Igualdade e desigualdade perante a justiça.* Empresa Gráfica da "Revista dos Tribunais" S.A.
Dinamarco, C. R., Badaró, G. H. R. I., & Lopes, B. V. C. (2020). *Teoria geral do processo.* Malheiros.
Dworkin, R. (1977). *Taking rights seriously.* Cambridge University Press.
Dworkin, R. (2005). *A virtude soberana: a teoria e a prática da igualdade. Trad. Jussara Simões. Revisão técnica e da tradução: Cícero Araújo e Luiz Moreira.* Martins Fontes.
Espíndola, R. S. (1999). *Conceito de princípios constitucionais: elementos teóricos para uma formulação dogmática constitucionalmente adequada.* Revista dos Tribunais.
Esser, J. (1961). *Principio y norma en la elaboración judicial del derecho privado.* Bosch Editores.
Faria, A. d. O. (1973). *Do princípio da igualdade jurídica.* Revista dos Tribunais. Saraiva, São Paulo.
Ferreira, P. (1977). *Igualdade (direito constitucional).* Saraiva.
Franco, A. A. d. M. (1976). *Direito constitucional: teoria da Constituição; as Constituições do Brasil.* Forense.
Frischeisen, L. C. F. (2007). *Construção da igualdade e o sistema de justiça no Brasil: alguns caminhos e possibilidades.* Editora Lumen Juris.
Garcia, M. d. G. F. P. (2005). *Estudos sobre o princípio da igualdade.* Almedina.
Garner, B. A. (Ed.). (2009). *Black's Law Dictionary.* West Group.
Grinover, A. P. (1975). *Os princípios constitucionais e o Código de Processo Civil.* José Bushatsky Editor.
Jacques, P. (1957). *Da igualdade perante a lei: fundamento, conceito e conteúdo* (2nd ed.). Forense.
Leite, G. S. (Coord.) (2003). *Dos princípios constitucionais: considerações em torno das normas principiológicas da Constituição.* Malheiros
Maximiliano, C. (1948). *Comentários à Constituição Brasileira* (Vol. III). Freitas Bastos.
Mendes, G. F., & Branco, P. G. G. (2024). *Curso de Direito Constitucional* (19th ed.). SaraivaJur.
Moraes, A. d. (2010). *Direito constitucional* (26th ed.). Atlas.
Nery Júnior, N. (2016). *Princípios do processo na Constituição Federal: processo civil, penal e administrativo* (12th ed.). Editora Revista dos Tribunais.
Pacheco, D. F. (2007). *O princípio da proporcionalidade no direito processual penal brasileiro.* Lumen Juris.
Pizzorusso, A. (1983). *Che cos'è l'eguaglianza: il principio ético e la norma giuridica nella vita reale.* Editori.
Pontes de Miranda, F. C. (1960). *Comentários à Constituição de 1946.* Borsoi.
Pontes de Miranda, F. C. (1974). *Comentários à Constituição de 1967, com a emenda n. 1, de 1969.* Revista dos Tribunais.
Porto, W. C. (2001). *Constituições brasileiras: 1937.* Senado Federal.

Queiroz, C. (2002). *Direitos fundamentais (teoria geral)*. Coimbra.
Rothenburg, W. C. (1999). *Princípios constitucionais*. SAFE.
Rousseau, J.-J. (2003). *O contrato social*. Trans. Antonio de Pádua Danesi. Martins Fontes.
Ruffia, P. B. di (1973) Uguaglianza (principle of). In: Azara, Antonio; Eula, Ernesto (Dirs.). UTET
Sarlet, I. W. (2009). *Eficácia dos direitos fundamentais: uma teoria geral dos direitos fundamentais na perspectiva constitucional* (10th ed.). Livraria do Advogado.
Sarmento, D. (2003). *A ponderação de interesses na Constituição Federal*. Lumen Juris.
Silva, F. D. L. L. d. (2001). *Princípio constitucional da igualdade*. Lumen Juris.
Silva, J. A. d. (2005a). *Comentário contextual à Constituição*. Malheiros.
Silva, J. A. d. (2013). *Curso de direito constitucional positivo* (36th ed.). Malheiros.
Silva, V. A. d. (2003). *Princípios e regras: mitos e equívocos acerca de uma distinção*. Revista Latino-Americana de Estudos Constitucionais.
Silva, V. A. d. (2005b). *A constitucionalização do direito: os direitos fundamentais nas relações entre particulares*. Malheiros.
Silva, V. A. d. (2009). *Direitos fundamentais: conteúdo essencial, restrições e eficácia*. Malheiros.
Silva, V. A. d. (2021). *Direito Constitucional Brasileiro*. EDUSP.
Stumm, R. D. (1995). *Princípio da proporcionalidade no direito constitucional brasileiro*. Livraria do Advogado.
Tavares, A. R. (2002). *Curso de direito constitucional*. Saraiva.
Vieira, R. S., & Piovesan, F. (2025). *A força normativa dos princípios constitucionais fundamentais: a dignidade da pessoa humana*. Saraiva Jur.
Zanoide de Moraes, M. (2010). *Presunção de inocência no processo penal brasileiro: análise de sua estrutura normativa para a elaboração legislativa e para a decisão judicial*. Lumen Juris.

Chapter 2
Application of the Principle of Equality to Criminal Proceedings in Brazil

2.1 Equality in the Criminal Procedure Code of the Empire of 1832

There are two fundamental precautions in approaching the issue of procedural equality when one comes across the succession of Brazil's Criminal Procedure Codes.

The first is that one should always observe the historical reality of each period, with its complexities and its legal and sociological surroundings, so that, in judgments that are now intended to be made, one does not fall into a methodological error that undermines the credibility of the text. If one does not consider the details of the period in which the 1832 Code came to light, one overlooks all the repeated sayings of Brazilian authors[1] who, always comparing our first Criminal Procedure Code with the Philippine Ordinances (notably Book V), saw it as liberal and careful in dealing with the investigated and accused.

The second, no less important, lies in the answer to the following question: what kind of equality do we want to talk about? What concept, what type of equality: formal (procedural) equality, material (procedural) equality? If it is the latter, and this is the choice that is made,[2] one thinks of equality between the accused and accuser to establish a bias that aims to either justify or criticize the treatment given to them by the law and the judge.

---

[1] A summary of the opinions comparing the new Code to the Philippine Ordinances is presented by Frederico Marques (2000, p. 102): "With the foundation of the Empire, a period of reaction to the oppressive and monstrous laws of the Portuguese monarchy opens up for our criminal process, and from which the Criminal Procedure Code, of 1832, constitutes the culminating and most expressive legal diploma, synthesis of the humanitarian and liberal aspirations that throbbed in the heart of the people and nation."

[2] The constitutional premise of material equality cannot be forgotten in the formulations of the principle of equality in each infraconstitutional law that must be compatible with the 1988 Charter.

R. S. Vieira, *Equality of Arms in Criminal Procedure*,
https://doi.org/10.1007/978-3-032-03663-6_2

The distribution of opportunities for the presentation of the theses of those involved that bring cases to the judiciary is what drives the next lines. And it is here that the historical evolution of each Brazilian Criminal Procedure Code, including and particularly mentions of state codes in the period of the First Republic, helps in approaching the theme of equality of arms.

During the validity of the Brazilian Constitution of 1824, although liberal winds could be noticed in appearance, the realization of the beautiful promise could not happen. If then in Brazil it was said that "the laws of the process are the necessary complement of the constitutional laws"[3] and that "the steps of the criminal process are nothing less than the complement of the fundamental law of free States,"[4] in the state where the moderating power was the center of attention and the gravitational center of the distribution of power,[5] there was no development of the notion of procedural equality, even though the abstraction of the principle was provided for in Article 179, item XIII, of the Constitution.

As an example of the non-consecration of the constitutional principle of equality in the context of criminal proceedings, note that, in the Law of 29 November 1832, which became the first Brazilian Criminal Procedure Code, there was not even a systematic separation of the parties in the criminal process. This flaw contaminated our historical evolution of criminal procedure.

In the old Code, the attributions of the municipal judges (even because the notion of Federation was late here) were confused with those of the judges of law, and to the latter it was foreseen the accumulation even of police functions.[6] The first—and one of the few that exist—mention of the term parties in that order was seen in Article 46, § 5°, which provided as competence of the judge of law "to regulate the debate of the parties, the Lawyers and witnesses until the Jury is satisfied."

More than that, and faithful to the tone of the connection between Constitution and Criminal Procedure, Brazilian doctrine remembers, in unison, that the turbulent period that mediated the decline of the Empire and the proclamation of the Republic motivated changes in the Brazilian Code of Procedure.[7] Some of them, which matter for the theme of equality in criminal proceedings, have to do not only with the

---

[3] Almeida Júnior (1901), p. 5.

[4] Pimenta Bueno (1910), p. 8.

[5] It was not by chance that the formula of Benjamin Constant was brought to Article 98 of that Constitution, according to which: "The Moderating Power is the key to all Political organisation."

[6] Marta Saad (2004, p. 30) synthesizes: "The chief of police was also a judge of law." In the law, Article 35: "The Municipal Judge has the following attributions: 1st. Substitute in the Term to the Judge of Law in his impediments, or absences. 2nd. Execute within the Term the sentences and mandates of the Judges of Law, or Tribunals. 3rd. Exercise cumulatively the police jurisdiction." This provision lasted until 1871, when, with the advent of Law No. 2.033, of 20th September (Art. 1°, § 4°), complemented by Decree n° 4.824, of 22nd November of the same year (Art. 6°, § 1°, n. 3, and Art. 7°), the jurisdictional functions and those of the judicial police were separated.

[7] This "monarchist-conservative reaction, notably in the sphere of judicial and police organisation" was dealt with by Frederico Marques (2000), p. 104; Galdino Siqueira (1917), p. 13; and Joaquim Canuto Mendes de Almeida (1973), p. 64.

"growth of the Prosecutor's Office at the beginning of the Second Empire,"[8] but also with the institution of ex-officio criminal prosecution, which came to be implemented first with the Code itself (Arts. 138, 141, and 206) and then with Regulation No. 120, of 31 January 1842 (Arts. 256, 262, and ss.).

About this, José Antonio Pimenta Bueno anticipated a criticism that today is striking, especially in the light of the notion dear to the accusatory process: there is no conviction without accusation. At that time, the author said, "the good administration of criminal justice requires that there be a formal separation, not only between the criminal authority and the judicial police or Prosecutor's Office, but even between this and the judicial police itself." And he also affirmed, about the behavior of the judge in this delicate question:

> What does the judge do when he acts ex-officio? He constitutes himself simultaneously as judge and adversary of the offender; he gives the denunciation to himself, chooses the witnesses and questions them asking what he thinks is convenient, and finally evaluates the evidence that he created, and pronounces, or not, as he understands! Is there any guarantee in this? The judge should only be a judge, an impartial arbitrator, and not a party. Even disregarding the abuses that this accumulation facilitates, such confusion itself tends to unsettle the spirit of the judge. Indeed, when he is forced to create in his own mind the first suspicions of who is the author of the crime, instead of only appreciating those that are presented to him, these impressions will later influence in a dangerous way. The self-love of his foresight will invite him not to appreciate well the contradictions or opposing reasons, to make his penetration triumph: he will judge before it is time to.[9]

In the turbulent period that was that of the 1832 Code—whether because it started what was seen as promising for the time, or because it gave in to the police temptations[10] that led to the edition of Law No. 261, of December 3, 1841, and Regulation No. 120, of 1842,[11] or because the conservative turn ended up being overcome, decades later, by Law No. 2.033 and Decree No. 4.824, of 1871[12]—it should be remembered that it was not admitted a denunciation formulated by "slave against the master" (Art. 76, § 2° of the Criminal Procedure Code).

---

[8] Pierangeli (2004), p. 136. The author recalls that Decree n° 1.723, of 16th February 1856, was the first to foresee the need for manifestations of the Prosecutor's Office in the second degree and that from there, in the author's words, "in genuinely national legislation" a similarity between the body of the Prosecutor's Office and the Magistracy (pp. 141–142).

[9] Pimenta Bueno (1910), pp. 165–166.

[10] "Work of a monarchist-conservative nature, it presented authoritarian and centralising content," as Marta Saad warns (2004), p. 40.

[11] And it brought with it the numerical increase of prosecutors, in each instance, these prosecutors, moreover, were appointed directly by the emperor and dismissible *ad nutum*. Thus, Article 217 of Regulation No. 210 determines: "The prosecutors will be appointed by the Emperor in the Municipality of the Court, and by the Presidents in the Provinces, for an indefinite period; and they will serve as long as their conservation is convenient to the public service, being in the contrary case, indiscriminately dismissed by the Emperor, or by the Presidents of the Provinces in the same Provinces."

[12] Some say, like Paula Bajer Fernandes Martins da Costa (1997), p. 173, that in Regulation 4.824, in its Article 42, § 7°, "it is affirmed that the inquiries of the investigation will be done with the assistance of the indicted, if arrested, who could challenge the testimonies of the witnesses."

In the appeal scope, as provided in Article 80 of Law No. 261, of 1841,[13] none of the appeals provided for by law was applicable if the case passed in sentence was related to the provisions of the Law of June 10, 1835, which dealt exactly with the "slaves, who kill, wound or commit any other physical offense against their masters, etc."[14]

Emblematic: if on the one hand it was granted to the defendant, as far as possible, the right to confront the witnesses possibly heard in his absence (Art. 97 of the Criminal Procedure Code), on the other hand, and precisely because the act of interrogation is an act of instruction—or even "a simple formality and nothing more," as said by Councillor Vicente Alves de Paula Pessoa[15]—it was said that, "in the interrogation, the Lawyer does not intervene, it is necessary that the defendant answers the questions that are asked, without an artificial and anticipated defense disturbing the diligences employed, by the Judge, in the attempt to discover the truth."[16]

In the Imperial Code, the inequality alien to the norms of the process was reflected in it. That Criminal Procedure Code was a spirit of its time, and there was no space to deal with cogitations of equality between accuser and accused, let alone confer opportunities for the conviction of each thesis with a view to the pronouncement of sentences.

2.2 Equality in Criminal Procedure Codes of the Brazilian First Republic Until the Vicente Ráo Project

The advent of the Brazilian Republic (Provisional Decree No. 1, of November 15, 1889) and the Constitution that followed it (promulgated on February 24, 1891) meant, in the words of José Frederico Marques, a "blow given to procedural unity."[17]

The new Charter provided, in the Federation then inaugurated, that, in the field of legislative competences, to the Union it was up to (Art. 34) legislate "on the civil, commercial and criminal law of the Republic and federal justice procedural" (§ 23).

[13] Then replaced in Article 501 of Regulation No. 120, of 1842.

[14] They were punished with the death penalty "the slaves or slave women, who kill by any means, administer poison, seriously wound or commit any other serious physical offense to their master, to his wife, to descendants or ascendants, who live in his company, to the administrator, overseer and their wives, who live with them" (Art. 1°), and with lashes, if the offenses were of bodily harm.

[15] Paula Pessoa (1899), p. 159.

[16] Paula Pessoa (1899), p. 160, footnote no. 845. It is interesting how the same legal provision allows different readings. Pimenta Bueno (1910), p. 248, saw in the interrogation an act of defense of the defendant. And, it seems, he found it reasonable for the act to take place without the presence of the lawyer, because the defendant, "he is his own lawyer, it is nature that fights for the preservation of his freedom and life, who speaks before judges who observe his gestures and his emotions."

[17] Frederico Marques (2000), p. 108.

In the discussed perspective of the distribution of competences between what is residual and what is own,[18] said João Barbalho Cavalcanti:

> these words are a restriction to the competence that was left to the Union to legislate on the right: It has the power to regulate everything that concerns civil, commercial and criminal law, except as to procedural law (except for federal justice and local justice of the federal district, art. 34, ns. 23 and 30 and art. 67). The States were therefore reserved the competence (art. 65, n. 2°) for the laws of process and judicial organisation in civil, commercial and criminal matters that do not fall to the justices of the Union.[19]

In this context, state manifestations stood out, even though, on the one hand, not all have decided to implement their own Code, and, on the other hand, the Union has legislated on criminal procedural matters.[20] On a timeline and by the relevance of the treatment that was given to equality in the criminal process in state Criminal Procedure Codes, the matter can be seen under two main points: the production of evidence and the legal regime of the interrogation of the defendants.

Hence, it is important first to remember the Criminal Procedure Code of the State of Rio Grande do Sul, established by State Law No. 24, of August 15, 1898, and later reformed under the terms of State Law No. 141, of July 2, 1912. Although a systematic treatment of the parties in the criminal process could not yet be noticed, there was, as a novelty of that Code, in the so-called formation of guilt in the ordinary process, the provision of two types of procedures: the secret and the public. In addition, there was also the investigative diligence phase, with the typical attributions of judicial police, which had the following characteristics: "the process of police inquiry is secret and summary. During it no defence is admitted nor the

[18] In a simple perspective: is the legislative competence of the Union in a matter that concerns it *residual* or *exclusive*? According to the lesson of João Barbalho, it would be residual. From another point of view, the constitutional assignment of legislative competence for criminal procedure was seen, by José Henrique Pierangeli, only as implicit (2004), p. 150, and did not even exist, in the opinion of Galdino Siqueira (1917), p. 14.

[19] *Brazilian Federal Constitution* (1891), p. 128. In a passage of the text, a speech by the parliamentarian Gonçalves Chaves appears, according to whom "the laws of procedure are considered as part of what is called judicial organisation. Judicial institutions should belong to the political powers of the States."

[20] For Pierangeli (2004), p. 150, the States of Alagoas, Mato Grosso, and Goiás did not have their own criminal procedure codes. According to the same author, laws of a procedural nature enacted by the Union, such as Decree No. 4.780, of December 27, 1923, and Decree No. 167, of January 5, 1938, were applied at the state level. It is true that, in the last example cited, given the new Constitutional order, the competence of the Union to legislate on procedural matters was already imposed.

intervention of strangers" (Art. 85).[21] There, as Marta Saad recalls, the police inquiry was suppressed.[22]

About the phases of the ordinary process, in the first (secret) one, the defense of the investigated was prohibited.[23] It was already noticeable the inequality in the treatment of those involved in the process because, although the defense could not even witness the questioning of witnesses or attend any diligence, "the public prosecutor, however, can examine the process whenever he understands, and request the diligences that he considers appropriate" (Art. 344). The possibility of defense for the accused only began when the process was in its public phase, when the first act to be carried out would be the interrogation.[24] This act, contrary to the provision of the Brazilian Imperial Code, was taken in the presence of the defender and the Public Prosecutor (Art. 349), and could also be carried out on a new date, at the discretion of the party or by ex officio determination of the judge (Art. 287).

If in the secret phase of the ordinary process there were no proposed limits of witnesses by the parties (Art. 341[25]), in the public phase of the formation of guilt, the limit of five witnesses to be proposed by each party was established (Art. 351), although they could, under the terms of Article 160 of the Code, others be "ordered to be called by the judge ex officio."

[21] The exposition of the motives of the Code, signed by the President of the State, Júlio de Castilhos, dealt with such a police phase, called the *preparatory process*, in the following terms: "thus it is called the set of police diligences that must precede or serve as the basis for the repressive process. The police investigation is a merely administrative process, which is not subject to the formulas of the process in general; it has a separate existence, just as it is in charge of special officials. The police organisation law, abolishing the old inquiry in its written form, outlined broadly the course to be followed in the course of the police investigation. In practice, however, it has not received an exact and uniform interpretation, hence the need to specify rules for its good understanding and application" State of Rio Grande do Sul (1913), p. 232. Also: Mauro Fonseca Andrade (2021), p. 93.

[22] State of Rio Grande do Sul (1913), p. 59.

[23] Such a secret phase ended in the terms of Article 347 of the Code of Criminal Procedure and, in the ordinary phase of the formation of guilt (considered as the first phase of the accusatory process today similar to the criminal process of the jury—formation of guilt properly said), it was provided that "in the ordinary common process the defence is only allowed after the closing of the secret instruction."

[24] It is worth remembering that "the defendant who insists on not responding or does so in a disconnected way, is warned about the consequences of his act, which only results in prejudice to his own defence" (Art. 286).

[25] The judge could then "reduce the list to the number he considers sufficient, leaving to the parties the choice of those that should be excluded. If the parties omit or delay it, the choice is made by the judge himself. He can exclude altogether the witnesses who testify about superfluous circumstances or not pertinent to the cause." In this respect, Gonçalo Marinho (1917), pp. 179–180, stated: "This faculty to reduce the list of witnesses, offered by the Prosecutor's Office in the petition of denunciation, or by the complainant in the petition of complaint, should be used by the judge, in our view, with great discretion, and not simply because he is startled before the large number of witnesses listed, or because he has little willingness to inquire them all. There are cases in which the witnesses listed some testify in detail about the criminal fact, and others, not testifying in the same way, nevertheless provide important clarifications, with the reference made to facts or circumstances, which are linked to that, whose truth is sought to ascertain."

That Code innovated by providing, for the first time, legal assistance to the defendant who requested it (Arts. 304 to 315) and by intercalating, in the presentations of accusation and defense in the jury, the hearing of witnesses of each party after their respective manifestations.[26]

The Criminal Procedure Code of the State of Pará,[27] although it maintained the line of permission for criminal prosecution initiated ex officio (Art. 16), innovated in the treatment of interrogation, since the questions to the defendant in the formation of guilt began to be asked after the testimonies were collected,[28] and maintained the publicity as a rule of all the formation of guilt (Art. 116).

Moreover, besides not providing for the indication of witnesses by the judge himself, but only by the "complainant, representative of the public prosecutor and by the defendant" (Art. 436),[29] an important innovation was brought, in the wake of the embryo of the Brazilian Imperial Code, of what is now known as the right to confrontation. That is, according to Article 458 of that Code, "when the defendant, brought to the presence of the authority, requests that the witnesses questioned in his absence be re-questioned in his presence, it will be granted to him, if possible."[30]

On the other hand, in the Federal District, the Criminal Procedure Code of 1924 (Decree No. 16.751 would have been inspired by Decree No. 8.259, of 29 September 1910, which in that same year of 1910 had its execution suspended by order of Minister Rivadavia Correa.[31] From the idea germinated in 1910,[32] there were predic-

---

[26] After the sustenance of the accusatory libel, the witnesses listed by the prosecution were heard, and only after that the defence exposed its arguments to the jurors, followed by the defensive testimonies and, then, reply and rejoinder, as well as, if necessary, new hearings of the witnesses (Arts. 422 and ss.). It also dealt with the rights of the assistant in the criminal process in the same way that powers of action were granted to the Prosecutor's Office (Art. 7) and, in the provision of disaffection, being the motivation of the so-called "serious disturbance of public order," only the legitimacy for the request was attributed to the Prosecutor's Office, not to the investigated or accused (Art. 82).

[27] Decree No. 1,352, of January 21, 1905, gives criminal procedural regulation to Law No. 930, of October 25, 1905. Pierangeli (2004, p. 153) diminishes the importance of this Code, taking it as a mere subsequent modification implemented in the Code of the Empire.

[28] Article 108, paragraph only: "After the questioning of the witnesses and the above-mentioned diligences, the judge will interrogate the defendant, ordering the documents to be attached to the case file, justifications and defence that he produces. The defendant or his attorney may be granted a 3-day period to submit his defence in the registry." Such a sequence, with the court interrogation being carried out after the collection of testimonies, was also in the Code of Criminal Procedure of Maranhão (Law No. 507, of 22 March 1909, Art. 149).

[29] What was perceived differently in Minas Gerais, because, according to the *Consolidation of legislative and regulatory provisions relating to the organisation of justice and criminal procedure of the State of Minas Gerais*, approved by Decree No. 1,937, of 29 August 1906 (Belo Horizonte: Official Press of the State of Minas Gerais, 1906), admitted ex officio process *ex officio* (Art. 716), the witnesses could be "ordered to call ex-officio" (Art. 838).

[30] The model was followed by the Minas Gerais code, whose Article 846 provided that, "when the defendant, brought to the presence of the judge, requests that the witnesses questioned in his absence be re-questioned in his presence, it will be granted to him, if possible."

[31] Saad (2004), pp. 62–63, footnote no. 124.

[32] National Press (2010).

tions according to which, first, if in the interrogation the accused or complainant "refuses to answer, the judge must make him see that the fact of not answering about things that he should know could later be interpreted as an indication that he is guilty"(Art. 139, § 10), and, in the case of co-defendants, one was not allowed to hear the interrogation of the other (Art. 139, § 12). The breadth of the exploration of oral evidence distributed among the parties was an important characteristic insofar as the rule was not to refuse the questions asked by each party to the witnesses (Art. 152).[33]

Later, with the 1924 Code, a change in the investigation system was noted, with the suppression of the police inquiry and a more specific division between the so-called investigation acts and inquiry acts.

In the State of Bahia, the provisions of the criminal process were confined to the third book of its Process Code,[34] highlighting, in addition to the rules pertaining to the police inquiry (Arts. 1.725 and ss.),[35] the non-existence of prevention during the course of the inquiry that motivated a judicial request for any title (Art. 1.744).[36] In the production of evidence, in addition to the indication of witnesses by the parties, the judge was allowed to indicate of his own accord (Art. 1.822), it being certain that the parties were allowed to replace their indicated witnesses, "provided that this does not result prejudice to the progress of the process" (Art. 1.842).[37]

In the Bahian system, while in the formation of guilt the interrogation was the last act of the process, carried out after the collection of oral evidence (Art. 1.853),

[33] It was noted that the payment of a fine—if it was a misdemeanour or crime punished only with a fine—as an extinctive cause of punishability, if the fine was added to the costs of the process, even before the end of the instruction (Art. 180). It was foreseen that the hypothesis of the appeal called "protest for new trial," of exclusive handling of the defence, in cases where the applied penalty was imprisonment equal to or greater than 24 years and resulted from a non-unanimous trial regarding the proof of the crime and the responsibility of the accused (Art. 276).

[34] Law 1.121, August 21, 1915. Espínola (1916).

[35] In the inquiry system defined by that code, it was foreseen for the "defendant" to "challenge the testimonies of the witnesses" (Art. 1,735), while the Prosecutor's Office was allowed to "request to the police authority the diligences that seem convenient to him" (Art. 1,739), which is observed identically in the Code of Criminal Procedure of Maranhão (Law No. 1,318, of 11 April 1928, Art. 49). Still in the scope of the inquiry, it was foreseen that, "in crimes in which public action is not allowed, the inquiry, made at the request of the interested party, and reduced to an instrument, will be delivered to him for the use he understands, independent of transcript" (Art. 1,745).

[36] In addition to the Bahian system also allowing criminal action *ex officio* (Arts. 1,772, 1,779, 1,788 and following), it was opened to the "offended party or his legal representative" the possibility of intervening as an assistant to the Prosecutor's Office (Art. 1,792).

[37] As already seen in other state codes that preceded it, there was a specific provision for what is now conventionally called the right to confrontation in doctrine. In Article 1,843, it was foreseen that, "being the offender arrested or bailed, or residing in the district, in a way that he can be brought to the presence of the judge, he will attend the questioning of the witnesses, in which act he can contest them, and request that questions be directed to them." In Article 1,845, it was foreseen that, "if the defendant appears in court after the initiation of the formation of guilt, all the pieces of the process to which he is submitted will be read to him, and the witnesses will be re-questioned in his presence, if he so requests."

in the trial of the grand jury it was the first (Art. 1.920),[38] followed by the debates of accusation and defense (interspersed, also, by their respective witnesses – Arts. 1.921 and ss.).

In Sergipe, in the Criminal Process Code instituted by Law No. 753, of 7 September 1918, it was noted that in the inquiry, the proceedings were conducted with the assistance of the investigated person, if arrested, giving him even the possibility of challenging the testimonies of witnesses (Art. 21).

In Rio de Janeiro, book II of its Judicial Code (Law No. 1.580, of 20 January 1919)[39] also did not systematically provide the separation of the parties in the criminal process. In addition to the privilege of the existence of a police inquiry as a preliminary phase of the formation of guilt (Arts. 529 and ss.), the particular provision regarding the different forms of collecting testimonial evidence was noteworthy.[40] In the phase of the formation of guilt, at first, the system was presidential, with questions asked through the judge (Art. 634), with the re-questions being presented directly by the parties (Art. 638) and that, in the phase of instruction before the jury, the rule was the direct form of inquiry by the parties (Art. 635). The treatment of the accused had a curiosity: his interrogation was provided as an act subsequent to the collection of all the oral evidence, as re-recorded in Article 701, § 3: "once the inquiry of the witnesses is finished, the defendant will be interrogated, an act exclusively personal, dispensable in cases where the defendant can fail to appear, being represented by a lawyer."[41]

Conversely, the Criminal Process Code of the State of Paraná[42] admitted the ex-officio criminal action ex-officio (Art. 6°[43]) and placed the Prosecutor's Office in the position of "integral part of the criminal court," which is why it should be heard "in all terms of any action brought by the offended party, or by the judge or court,

[38] In Bahia, the separation between *grand jury* and *petit jury* had been instituted, affecting the nature of crimes, with the *petit jury*, provided for specific crimes and of lesser gravity, it provided a faster procedure, named "summarissimo" (Art. 1.960).

[39] State of Rio de Janeiro (1919).

[40] The judge would ensure that the witness did not know, not even the questions of the plaintiff and defendant, made to the other (Art. 632).

[41] The exception was due to the provisions of the instruction in a jury plenary, in which, in addition to the witnesses listed by the parties intercalating in the debates (after the accusation sustain the libel, its witnesses were heard, and, after the defence deduce the oral defence, it was time for theirs to be heard), the first, and not the last act, was the interrogation of the defendant (Arts. 800 to 804).

[42] State of Paraná (1924). In this regard, also check: Rodrigo Régnier Chemim Guimarães. (2021), pp. 56/7. The same was true with the Criminal Procedure Code of Amazonas, as can be seen from its Articles 2°, § 3°, and 6°. Fabrício Santos Almeida (2021), pp. 29/30. Also: Milton Gustavo Vasconcelos Barbosa and Mota (2021), pp. 25/6.

[43] Article 72: "The criminal action relating to an unaffordable crime, in the case of art. 6 of this Code will be initiated by written order of the judge or court, in which the facts will be exposed with their circumstances" (here, it is worth remembering that, in the system of the Rio Grande do Sul Code, in addition to prohibiting ex officio criminal action, the rule was provided that, from the knowledge of facts that demand criminal prosecution, communication was demanded to the Prosecutor's Office to act – Art. 110).

ex-officio" (Art. 12). As it also enshrined in the system, the provision of the police investigation phase (Arts. 41 and ss.), in that Code,

> the accused is allowed, at any term of the investigation, to accompany, re-question and contest the witnesses, present the evidence that he has of his innocence, and even request the diligences, or investigations, regarding plausible facts. Single paragraph. The accused may be accompanied by a lawyer or be represented by this one, not being a fugitive (Art. 48).

Regarding procedural equality, it was considered—at least in the part of the testimonial, literal, or documentary evidence—the application of rules of the Civil Procedure Code (Art. 294).

The confession also had specific treatment in the Code. First, it was an efficacy requirement ("proves the crime" – Art. 298) to be made in a competent court freely spontaneously and if it agrees with the other investigated circumstances; second, it was forbidden to judges or to the parties "to employ cunning means to obtain from the defendant the confession of the crime" (Art. 299).

The interrogation system was preceded by a warning that indicates the treatment of the party: "The interrogated will never be obliged to answer hastily, the authority should grant him the time that seems reasonable to recover the serenity that he has lost from the narration of the facts or particular circumstances or from more remote times" (Art. 328).[44] The provisions for the presentation of witnesses listed by prosecution and defense in the jury, with interruption of the flow of debates, followed the same idea of the State of Rio Grande do Sul Code (Arts. 501 and ss.).[45]

In the State of Minas Gerais, as João de Oliveira Filho accounts,[46] despite the persecution still prevailing ex officio (Arts. 1° and 5°), the confession was dealt with a greater requirement of fidelity to the investigated facts (Art. 230). Regarding the witnesses, it was allowed not only that they were listed by the parties, but also by the judge (Art. 240). And, as it was seen in the State of Rio de Janeiro, if during the formation of guilt, the rule was to follow the presidential system of collecting testimonies, in the jury plenary, the direct form of inquiry by the parties was privileged (Art. 248). As for the interrogation, its performance was reserved for the phase after

---

[44] Just like the novelty from Pará already discussed here, the Code provided for the right to confrontation. Article 347 stated: "the defendant arrested will always attend all acts of the process, under penalty of nullity; and, if he is arrested after the process has started and before the formation of guilt is finished, he will have the right to request the re-interrogation of witnesses questioned in his absence, not paying the respective costs in case of indigence."

[45] There was also the innovation—which also has clear relevance in the equality of treatment given to the parties in the process, of criminal review: Article 686: "The finished processes may be reviewed, at any time, in favour of the condemned, by the supreme federal court, to reform or confirm the sentence" (Art. 81 of the Federal Constitution).

[46] The consulted edition is the one referring to Decree n° 7.259, of June 15, 1926, which—in the sequence remembered by Pierangeli (2004), p. 153—after being issued by the then President of the State Fernando Mello Viana, came to be reissued on August 23, 1933. The version used of the Criminal Procedure Code of Minas Gerais was the following: Oliveira Filho (1927).

the collection of the testimonial evidence, considering it as "a means of defence, not of accusation."[47]

In none of these regional ordinances was systematic treatment of the parties in the process noted.[48]

If, in the multifaceted discipline of the state codes, there was no uniformity in the equality of the parties in the process, the picture would start to change with the Constitution of 1934, which provided in its Article 5, item XIX, letter "a," that the legislative competence in the field of procedural law was now exclusive to the Union. In Article 11 of the Transitional Constitutional Provisions, the need for a commission to "prepare a project for a Code of Criminal Procedure Penal" was established.

From this came the well-known Vicente Ráo Project,[49] given that the jurist was the Minister of Justice at the time and author of the statement of reasons, gateway of the project written by the commission composed by Bento de Faria, Plínio Casado, and Gama Cerqueira. According to the project, the modification that the system deserved, besides the resumption of procedural unity, was the institution of the instruction court. And this is because, at the time, it was said, with criticisms, that the judicial police,

> forms the content of the process and, anticipating the judicial authorities, practices unequivocally procedural acts, such as, for example, the statements of the accused and the testimony of the witnesses, which it takes in writing. This is what is called 'inquiry', or the piece from which the Prosecutor's Office, rarely collaborator of its making, extracts the elements for the indictment, handpicks the list of the witnesses of accusation and collects the indication of the others initially constituted, all of them, by the obliterated spirit, that the practice of the office determines of the respective police authority.[50]

The main idea of the diploma that did not come to be sanctioned was the institution of the instruction court that would, before the end of the first phase of criminal

---

[47] Oliveira Filho (1927), p. 243.

[48] As seen in the Codes to which access was possible, the points that linked one to another were few, and there were many differences between them. The State of São Paulo did not have its own Criminal Procedure Code. In this regard, it is worth seeing the effort made by Junio Soares Caiuby (1927), who sometimes collects scattered state laws on various subjects of criminal procedure; sometimes, in order to see uniformity in compliance with the laws of criminal procedure in São Paulo, he resorts to the still valid and general provisions of the Criminal Procedure Code of the Empire, from 1832.

[49] The 1935 Draft Code of Criminal Procedure became known as the "Projeto Vicente Ráo" because, at the time, that jurist was the Minister of Justice and Internal Affairs and presided over the commission established to draft the Code. One of the main ideas that emerged from that Commission was the elimination of the police inquiry (inquérito policial) and its replacement with the examining magistrate system (juizado de instrução). This draft was never enacted into law, and the ideal that underpins the current Brazilian Code of Criminal Procedure differs from that conception. On this topic, with some reservations regarding the author's interpretation, see: Mauro Fonseca Andrade. Juizado de Instrução. A Investigação Criminal Presidida pelo Poder Judiciário. Curitiba: Juruá Editora, 2005, pp. 63–65.

[50] Ráo (1935), p. 8.

prosecution, remove from the judicial police the instructive acts, leaving only the investigative ones, typically. In the terms of the statement of reasons for the project,

> the police is thus deprived of the function, which is not theirs, of interrogating the accused, taking the testimony of witnesses, in short, collecting evidence without legal value; however, the investigative function, which is inherent to it, is preserved, put in harmony and legalized by the co-participation of the judge, without which the results of the proceedings cannot and should not have probative value.[51]

Despite the interrogation being foreseen, once the procedural relationship was established, as the first act of the process (Arts. 112 and 113), followed by the requests for proceedings and evidence from the defense (Art. 127), in general, the idea that most motivated the studies that were made on the project was indeed the creation of the instruction court.

Finally, its progress was castrated with the coup of the New State on November 10, 1937.

2.3 Equality in the Brazilian Code of Criminal Procedure of 1941

The dictatorial tone of the diploma that inaugurated the period of standardization of Brazilian criminal procedural law is unmistakable. Right in the exposition of motives of Decree-Law No. 3,689, of October 3, 1941, criticism was introduced to what was then called "such an extensive catalogue of guarantees and favours" and almost a commitment was assumed with the abolition of the "unjustifiable primacy of the individual's interest over that of social protection. We cannot continue to temporise with pseudo-individual rights to the detriment of the common good." That is why, as it was still clear from the exposition of motives that well confessed the purposes of the diploma that followed it, the "application of the in dubio pro reo" was restricted.

In terms of the parties' action in the process, it was the same exposition of motives that predicted that "no defendant, even if absent from the district of guilt, fugitive or hidden, can be prosecuted without the intervention and assistance of a defender." What was named as "the insidiousness of an accusation without the correlative of the defence" was forbidden, and the ex officio criminal procedure, insofar as—according to the exposition of motives—"demands the complete separation between the judge and the prosecution body, the initiative of the criminal action should belong exclusively to the latter."

The portico was followed by the Code still in force today, with the secular prestige of the police investigation (Arts. 4 and ss.), an investigative procedure that already opened to the investigated (rectius: "indicted") to request "any diligence" to be carried out at the discretion of the police authority, according to the terms of

[51] (1935), p. 9.

Article 14. In the scope of the criminal action, the expert evidence was treated in the terms of Article 159 of the Code of Criminal Procedure.[52]

The system of interrogation was completely redone more than once, since the advent of the new and already old Code of Criminal Procedure in force. First, because until the advent of Law No. 10,792/2003, the old provision of Article 186 of the Code of Criminal Procedure still allowed the judge to observe the defendant that, "although he is not obliged to answer the questions that are asked of him, his silence may be interpreted to the detriment of his own defence."[53]

Regarding the collection of witness evidence, Article 217 of the Code of Criminal Procedure, in its original wording, simply provided that:

If the judge verifies that the presence of the defendant, by his attitude, may influence the spirit of the witness, in such a way that it prejudices the truth of the testimony, he will have him removed, continuing with the inquiry, in the presence of his defender. In this case, the occurrence and the reasons that determined it must be recorded in the minutes.

In the systematic treatment given to the parties in the Brazilian criminal process, particularly with regard to the Public Prosecutor's Office, the original wording of the Code stated, in Article 257, that "The Public Prosecutor's Office will promote and supervise the application of the law." As for the accused, although it was provided that "no accused, even if absent or fugitive, will be prosecuted or judged without a defender,"[54] his coercive conduct to the hearing that depends on his presence to take place is admitted, which affronts the prohibition of using the defendant as an object of evidence production in the process (Art. 260).

Regarding the plan of procedural equality, in the original wording of the Code, the rule was the prompt receipt of the complaint or accusation without the possibility of a defensive reaction to the terms of the complaint itself to avoid the beginning of the criminal action (Art. 394, CPP[55]).

As to that original wording of the Code of Criminal Procedure, both possible global reforms—Hélio Tornaghi Project and Frederico Marques Project—and punctual changes that modified in many aspects the structure of the law in place, are discussed in the following topics.

[52] "The examinations of the body of the crime and other expertises will generally be done by official experts. § 1° If there are no official experts, the examination will be done by two trustworthy people, preferably those who have technical qualifications. § 2° Non-official experts will pledge to perform the task well and faithfully."

[53] Only in 2003, with the advent of Law No. 10.792/2003, was it safeguarded, in the same Article 186, the "right to remain silent and not to answer questions that are asked." According to the sole paragraph of the article, "silence, which will not imply confession, cannot be interpreted to the detriment of the defence."

[54] Article 261 of the Criminal Procedure Code.

[55] And more: the preliminary defence of then was, according to Article 395 of the Code, filed *after* the interrogation. The forensic practice established that such a piece was merely procedural, just so that the defence, at the dawn of the instruction, would not display its... arms!

2.4 Equality in the Hélio Tornaghi Project

The draft Code of Criminal Procedure presented by Professor Hélio Tornaghi to the then Minister of Justice and Interior Affairs, João Mangabeira, contained terminological and systematic precisions regarding the equality of rights of those involved in the process.[56]

If right at the beginning of the police investigation "acts of accusation or defence" were prohibited, there was already (Art. 11) the provision for compliance with requests, by the police authority, aimed at "the objective investigation, of the fact or authorship."[57] Later, in the so-called procedural relationship, the draft provided that it united "each of the parties and the State, through its judicial body" (Art. 43). The document also dealt with the reply in the criminal process, made necessarily before the acceptance or rejection of the accusation by the judge (Art. 549).[58]

Such evolution in the treatment of the subjects of the process was reflected in a chapter of the draft specifically for the parties. There it was defined, in the first section, the Prosecutor's Office as the "accuser," being certain that, as "organ of the accusation," it was "main party" in the public criminal action and "secondary party" in the so-called private criminal action (Art. 67, I, "a" and "b").[59]

As far as the accused and the defenders (treated together in section II of the same chapter pertaining to the parties), there was equivalence between the first ("the one to whom the practice of a criminal offence is imputed in a complaint or charge accepted," ex vi of Art. 77) and the "almost-accused." This was the so-called accused by equivalence, given that, although not the target of a complaint or charge accepted, he suffers acts of coercion, "real or personal, before the complaint or charge" (Art. 78).[60]

---

[56] Professor Hélio Tornaghi (1963).

[57] Marta Saad (2004) p. 79, footnote no. 156, recalls the lesson of João de Deus Cardoso de Mello, according to whom, in the inquiry, "it is strictly forbidden to practice acts of accusation or defence. The direct intervention in the inquiry of any interested party is proscribed, whether it is the offended, the indicted, or the Prosecutor's Office. The prosecutors will no longer be able to interfere in the activity of the judicial police, attending declarations, re-questioning witnesses, guiding diligences. Therefore, all the norms of judicial organisation or of the Prosecutor's Office, which allow this anomalous intervention of the accusing party in the police process, are revoked. It is certain that the final part of the article in question allows the delegate to attend requests that aim at the objective investigation of the fact or authorship. It will be allowed to suggest diligences or indicate witnesses: but the attendance of such requests does not authorize, in any way, the presence of the applicants in the act of producing the evidence, since the inquiry is confidential."

[58] "When the complaint or accusation is presented to him and before pronouncing on its acceptance or rejection, the judge will order the accused to reply to the accusation within three days."

[59] There was a noticeable hypertrophy—which leads to functional distortion—in the attributions to the Prosecutor's Office, because, in the preliminary draft (Art. 67, II), it was the responsibility of the Prosecutor's Office to "act as a body defence of the defendants who, being poor, cannot constitute lawyers."

[60] In the preliminary draft, there was no distinction as to whether the accused was or was not a defendant or fugitive, for the purposes of prohibiting processing and trial without a defender (Art.

It is noted, in the parameter of the judge's evidentiary appreciation, with emphasis on the contradictory, that the judge was prohibited from "basing his conviction on evidence that have not been subjected to the scrutiny of the contradictory or that have been refuted by the contrary evidence collected in court" (Art. 247). Still in the evidentiary field, the draft dealt with the interrogation, placing it before the taking of the witnesses' statements (Art. 248), being that the act was eminently judicial—except for questions of order that could be raised by the parties, defenders, or curators, after the closing (Art. 249, § 2°). It also prevailed, the rule that the silence could be interpreted against those who made use of it (Art. 251).[61] In any case, the judge was prohibited from formulating "vague, obscure, equivocal or insidious questions"[62] and neither was it allowed to "promise of reward of any nature."[63]

In the collection of witness evidence, the rule was to follow the presidential system, in which the parties asked questions to the judge, who addressed them to the witness. As a rule, the refusal of questions was prohibited, "unless they have no relation to the case or imply repetition of another already answered" (Art. 287), being certain that it allowed the parties to give up the indicated witnesses (Art. 561).

2.5 Equality in the José Frederico Marques Bill (PL n° 633/1975) and in the 1981 Draft, Converted into Bill n° 1.655/1983

In terms of the evolution of systematic clarity with which the matter is exposed, in Bill n° 633, of 1975,[64] authored by Professor José Frederico Marques, an important treatment given to equality in the process is noted.

---

80). As for such acts of coercion, by the text of the preliminary draft, they were a cause of prevention (Art. 100).

[61] The rule still prevailed that "the silence of the accused, the flight, the concealment, the default or any other similar fact can constitute an element for the conviction of the judge, but does not entail a fictitious confession" (Art. 264).

[62] In Article 253, in addition to requiring that the questions flowed "one from the other in natural order," it was avoided "the making of questions in which facts that have not yet been admitted are taken as already admitted been or that indicate by name or any other means the participants sought."

[63] According to the provisions of Article 254, the use of threats, of "coercive means or processes to weaken the will of the accused" was prohibited.

[64] The bill was only presented to the Chamber that year, by presidential message 15.975, but the work of José Frederico Marques had been going on since 1967, when he was already part of the then-established Commission for Coordination and Revision of Codes, which was supposed to suggest changes and reforms within 3 years. In March 1970, by Order No. 32, the Minister of Justice Alfredo Buzaid appointed Frederico Marques, Benjamim de Moraes Filho, and José Salgado Martins to the Review Subcommittee of the Preliminary Draft of the Code of Criminal Procedure—a preliminary draft projected by José Frederico Marques. The preliminary draft was published on the 29th ***(edit: of what month?)*** of 1970, underwent a new review in 1974, this time

The conception imagined by the professor from São Paulo and used as a model for the 1981 draft[65] was largely maintained. As reported by the Minister of Justice Ibrahim Abi-Ackel, signatory of its presentation to the President of the Republic by the Exposition of Motives n° 212, of May 9, 1983, it was up to José Frederico Marques himself to technical-legal review of the work carried out by the Commission and its modifications were incorporated into the text (Exposition of Motives, item 7).

That is why here we deal together with the two bills: the oldest, in the main text; the one that followed it, presented as a draft in 1981 and converted into a bill in 1983, with footnotes throughout this presentation.

The first judicial duty imagined in the project was to direct the process "in a way that ensures respect for the principle of contradiction and equality of arms" (Art. 66).[66] The passage of the text that was then imagined to be published is full of meanings, either because it presupposes the notion of parties in the criminal process, or because, from this, it presupposes and imposes on the judge respect for equality between them.

From the explanatory memorandum of Bill No. 1,655/1983, in fact, not only is the treatment of the Prosecutor's Office itself as a "party" (item 41) noted, but also precautions are imagined so that the "balance between the prosecution and the defence, a basic assumption of the administration of criminal justice" (item 43) is not broken.

---

with the replacement of Salgado Martins (deceased) by Hélio Tornaghi, and the works were then presided over by José Carlos Moreira Alves. This is reported by Edilenice Passos [n.d.], pp. 4–5.

[65] Re-examined by the Commission composed by Professor Rogério Lauria Tucci, by then Deputy Attorney General Francisco de Assis Toledo, and by the consultant of the Ministry of Justice Hélio da Fonseca, in which also collaborated Professors Manoel Pedro Pimentel, Miguel Reale Júnior, Sérgio Marcos de Moraes Pitombo, and Ricardo Antunes Andreucci, in addition to José Paulo Sepúlveda Pertence (by the Brazilian Bar Association), Roberto Joacir Grassi (Prosecutor's Office), Antonio Acyr Breda, Fernando Newton Bittencourt Fowler (UFPR), and other entities.

[66] The provision generated criticisms of the most diverse, as was seen in a cycle of lectures promoted in 1971 by the Association of Lawyers of São Paulo (1971). The first to criticize the important point was Judge Dinio de Santis Garcia, who likened to the accusatory system what he called "absolute equality of rights and powers, between accuser and defendant" to, subsequently, say that, "as for absolute equality between the parties, in terms of rights and powers, it is completely non-existent in the Preliminary Draft" (pp. 16–17). But the speaker who generated more in-depth theoretical expositions on both sides was Canuto Mendes de Almeida. The professor, present on the occasion when Frederico Marques' preliminary draft was being discussed, among many passages that reflect not only the technical complexity of the theme, but also its centrality in criminal procedure, said that "the adversarial principle is indisputable in criminal procedure, although it is discretionary and should be discretionary in civil procedure, because in civil procedure the parties are interested in the private law relationship, and personally interested, and the interest is theirs and, therefore, the process is theirs. But, in criminal law, the parties are not parties, they are a relationship of law penal. Therefore, there are no parties, except the defendant, in a way, and the individual offended because of the civil nature of the criminal sentence, and nothing more" (p. 50). The text of the 1981 draft went beyond what was imagined in the first project, by providing, in its Article 61, that the judge will direct the process to: "I - ensure respect for the adversarial principle, to the equality of the parties and the possibility of a full defence of the accused."

The systematic advance, therefore, and the approach to the topic here developed are notable, as was also notable the structuring of an entire title in the projected Code to deal with the "parties" in the criminal process (Title III). In that title, the Prosecutor's Office, the defendant, and the victim were divided, according to the chapters. From there, a line of possible equality between the parties[67] of preemption from the proposal to pay a fine made by the Prosecutor's Office to the defendant, whose acceptance would imply the extinction of punishability (Arts. 90 and 230 of the draft).[68]

When dealing with the beginning of the criminal action, that draft provided that, in preliminary defense, the one named as defendant would offer his response to the accusation in ten days (Art. 277[69]). Such a piece opened, according to the language of Rogério Lauria Tucci, the possibility for the "judgement according to the state of the process," as happened in the civil process innovated with the new Code of 1973. According to the author, this possibility, which resulted from an authentic criminal contestation, would open one of three alternatives to the judge—scattered between Articles 289 to 294 of the project—"judgement according to the state of the files, equivalent to the extinction of the process without resolution of the merit; b) anticipated judgement of the criminal dispute; and c) process sanitation."[70]

On the other hand, the draft persisted in a course of procedural inequality, insofar as it imposed on the defendant the duty to, under penalty of default and as a means of "collaborating with Justice for the discovery of the truth" (Art. 299, caput and §

[67] Regarding the Prosecutor's Office, the draft strictly took it as *party*, except when, by the linguistic aspect of specific forecasts, it treated it as a law enforcer—namely, in the case of processes for crimes of private criminal action (Arts. 88, II, and 92; in project 1.655/83, Art. 81, II); enforcer of execution of the sentence (Art. 88, III; in project 1.655/83, Art. 81, III). In the 1981 draft, the tripartite division of the parties in the criminal process is the same, and the allusions to the Prosecutor's Office when it does not play the role of party are found in Articles 82, II and III, and 86.

[68] Article 90: "Instead of returning the police inquiry for new diligences, the Prosecutor's Office may, before offering indictment, hear the indicted, the offended and the witnesses. The indicted will be summoned to attend the testimonies, which will be taken without his presence, if he fails to appear. § 1°. If any witness does not appear, the organ of the Prosecutor's Office may propose to the police authority coercive conduct. § 2°. When appropriate, the Prosecutor's Office, in the indictment, may propose, as an alternative, immediate conviction in fine, as disciplined in art. 230, §§ 1° and 2°. § 3°. If the judge deems it appropriate, and the indicted agrees with the immediate conviction in fine, the punishability will be considered extinct, by peremption. Otherwise, the process will continue its legal course. § 4°. In the procedure provided for in this article, the indicted may be assisted by a lawyer." Article 230: "The process, in cases of private criminal action, will be extinguished by peremption, when: [...] § 1° In the case of a public criminal action process, peremption will occur in cases expressly provided for in this Code, when the defendant, by accepting the fine imposed, tacitly gives up exercising the powers and faculties inherent to his right of defence, so that the procedural relationship is extinguished [...]." The theme is of the order of the day, as will be discussed later when addressing PL n° 8,045/2010. In the 1981 draft, the provisions are in Article 85 and paragraphs, as well as in Article 264. Such forecasts were not repeated in project 1.655/83.

[69] In the 1981 draft, Article 251.

[70] Tucci (1978), pp. 162–164. The forecasts, in the 1981 draft, are found in Articles 263 to 266.

2°),[71] submit to the expertises or examinations deemed necessary. A possible reading that separated the passive and active attitudes of the defendant, in this detail, could justify the provision here treated and its coexistence with that of Article 300, which provided that it was the defendant's prerogative to refrain from "presenting evidence that incriminates him."[72]

Still on the detail of the conceptual indefiniteness of the *nemo tenetur se detegere*, and in what this has to do with the treatment of the defendant as a procedural party, Article 307[73] provided for an interpretation unfavorable to the defendant if he chose to remain silent in the interrogation; in sequence, Article 315[74] dealt with other procedural situations that could weigh against him.[75] In terms of procedural equality, the draft dealt with the prohibition of the *reformatio in pejus* resulting from a defensive appeal (Art. 583)[76] and, unprecedentedly, a special criminal review for those defendants who had been convicted in absentia (Arts. 748 and ss.),[77] in addition to a specific incident of allegation of falsehood in the citation of a defendant convicted in absentia (Art. 751 and ss.).[78]

Presented to the Chamber of Deputies, after being forwarded by its president, Deputy Sérgio Murilo, the project was approved and directed to the Senate, where, however, it was never voted on. The explanatory memorandum of what later became

---

[71] In the 1981 draft, Article 270. In the 1983 project, Article 260.

[72] In the text of the 1981 draft, Article 272, and in the 1983 project, Article 262. From the current perspective, the petty separation between passive or active intervention in the exercise of the defendant's defensive activity is no longer justified. It may still be reasonable, to achieve a better interpretative result, to separate the impositions of the indicated articles between those that are directed to the offended and those that concern the defendant, with the latter not being subjected to the expertise. After all, the device (Art. 299 of Bill No. 633/75, Art. 270 of the 1981 draft, and Art. 260 of the 1983 project) is directed to the "defendant and the offended," in that order. In the same sequential order, it deals with the appearance in court whenever ordered and, afterwards, the submission to the expertise. It can be considered that the first part is directed to the defendant and the second to the offended. The paragraph "c" of the devices (299 in one text, 270 in the other, and 260 in the third), this one, can be directed to both: "perform the legal act that is determined."

[73] Article 279 of the 1981 draft. In the 1983 project, the projected legislation was limited to saying that, "if the accused refuses to answer, the fact will be recorded" (Art. 267, § 3°).

[74] Article 287 of the draft bill of 1981. The forecast was not repeated in project 1.655/1983.

[75] "The silence of the accused, the flight, the concealment, the default, or any other similar fact, can constitute an element for the conviction of the judge, but does not entail fictitious confession."

[76] Article 539, draft bill of 1981, and Article 501, § 2°, of project 1.655/83.

[77] One cannot forget the passages of Dínio de Santi Garcia—with which one does not agree—to recall even the tension of the debates in such lectures promoted by the Association of Lawyers of São Paulo: "the Draft gave undue emphasis to the defence of the absent defendant. It showed, moreover, more rigorous with the defendant who does not repudiate the bonds of social coexistence and remains in the district of guilt, than with the fugitive defendant. Incomprehensible concern since, in almost all cases, the absent will either be a marginal, whose life clandestine is necessary assumption of criminal habituality, or is person who has means to escape the action of Justice and the Police" (1971, p. 21). The provision was not repeated in the draft bill of 1981.

[78] Articles 688 and following of the draft bill of 1981, and Articles 639 and following of the project presented in 1983.

Bill No. 1,655/83 presents the following justifications for the withdrawal of Frederico Marques' draft:

> revocation of the Penal Code of 1969, even before its entry into force. Thus, the project became inadequate in many of its conceptions, given its relationship with the postulates of the Penal Code revoked. The incorporation of the list of amendments approved by the Chamber affected its systematic structure. Finally, the modifications introduced in the penalty system by Law no. 6.416, of 24-5-1977, imposed on the legislator by the increasing pressure of crime rates.

From its revision, as already mentioned, the draft of the Code of Criminal Procedure was born, later converted into Bill No. 1.655/83, which we also talked about here and which, however, was withdrawn from the process—when it was already in the Senate, filed under PL No. 175/1984—by the Executive Power.[79]

2.6 Equality in the Code of Criminal Procedure of 1941 and the Legislative Changes up to Law No. 12.403/2011

Regarding expert evidence, in 1994, the wording of Article 159 of the Code of Criminal Procedure was changed, which removed the escape valve of the expression as a rule previously provided to make it essential that the expertise was always carried out by official experts.[80]

From the advent of Law No. 11.690, of June 10, 2008, it was opened to the Prosecutor's Office, the assistant to the prosecution, the offended, the plaintiff, and the defendant "the formulation of questions and indication of technical assistant" (Art. 159, § 3°, with wording given by Law No. 11.690/2008). With the new wording of the device, it was opened to parties the opportunity to request the hearing of experts in hearing with the consequence of, eventually, provoking written responses to new questions, or to indicate assistants to present opinions, or, still, to request the custody of the material that served as the basis for the expertise for examination by the assistants (Art. 159, §§ 5° and 6°).[81] On the other hand, and with novelty, Law No. 11.690/2008 brought to Brazilian criminal procedural law the figure of the tech-

[79] Passos (n.d.), p. 6.

[80] The Summary No. 361 of the STF, approved in plenary session of 13 December 1963, provided that, "in criminal proceedings, the examination carried out by a single expert is null, considering the one who has previously worked in the seizure diligence as impeded."

[81] Law No. 11.690 results from one of the proposals of the Ada Pellegrini Grinover Commission, established by the Ministry of Justice through Ordinance No. 61, of 21 January 2000, and chaired by that professor of Procedural Law and president of the Brazilian Institute of Procedural Law, which resulted, after discussions held among its members, in the submission of seven legislative proposals for topical changes in the Code of Criminal Procedure. The mentioned law was the result of the legislative process resulting from the presentation of PL No. 4.205/2001. Antonio Magalhães Gomes Filho (2008), p. 276, is right when, regarding the legislation now in force, he points out that the "observance of the adversarial principle" is what he calls the "most significant feature of the procedural reform in relation to expert evidence."

nical assistant, until then provided exclusively for the field of civil procedural law (Art. 422, CPC).[82]

The interrogation system was completely redone more than once, since the advent of the new and already old Code of Criminal Procedure in force. First, because until the advent of Law No. 10.792/2003, the wording of Article 186 of the Code of Criminal Procedure was drastically changed. If before the silence of the accused could be interpreted to his detriment, the single paragraph inserted in that article provided that "the silence, which will not imply confession, cannot be interpreted to the detriment of the defense."

That same law also dealt for the first time, by changing Article 188 of the Code of Criminal Procedure, with the possibility of the judge, if he considered it "pertinent and relevant," to formulate, after the interrogation, new questions because some party understood that there was "some fact to be clarified." The criterion for a new interrogation, previously exclusive to the judge, was also eliminated, opening it to the free request of the parties, which can be seen from the change of Article 196 of the Code of Criminal Procedure.[83]

Then, with the advent of Law No. 11.900/2008, the form of interrogation of the defendant in custody was reshaped in Brazil (Art. 185, § 1°[84]), as well as the conduct of the interrogation using the apparatus of videoconferencing "or other technological resource of sound and image transmission in real time" (Art. 185, § 2°), providing the cumulative requirements for its occurrence.

Regarding the collection of witness evidence, the 2008 criminal procedural reform significantly changed the Code of Criminal Procedure. The so-called direct examination of witnesses was inaugurated (Art. 212[85]), with the inquisitorial activ-

---

[82] There is a certain incongruity in the treatment of the parties in the process, given that, in the wording resulting from Law No. 11.690, of 2008, while Article 159, § 3°, provides that not only the Public Prosecutor, the complainant and the accused can indicate a technical assistant, but also the offended and the assistant to the prosecution, in paragraph II of § 5°, it reads that in the judicial phase of criminal prosecution only the "parties" can "indicate technical assistants who can present opinions." When mentioning the word *parties*, it does not speak of an offended, nor of an assistant to the prosecution. After all, if—contrary to what Antonio Magalhães Gomes Filho teaches (2008), p. 278—one could imagine technical assistance in the preliminary phase of the accusation, one would have to admit that a larger number of legitimates could plead for the intervention of the *expert* in that phase, which did not happen with the legislative change.

[83] In the original wording: "At any time, the judge may proceed to a new interrogation." In the wording given by Law No. 10.792/2003: "at any time the judge may proceed to a new interrogation of his own accord or at the substantiated request of any of the parties."

[84] The aforementioned 2003 law had already altered the original wording of Article 185 of the Penal Procedure Code. From 2003 to 2008, therefore, the rule was that "§ 1 The interrogation of the accused prisoner will be done in the prison establishment where he is located, in a proper room, provided that the security of the judge and assistants, the presence of the defender and the publicity of the act are guaranteed. If security is not available, the interrogation will be done according to the Penal Procedure Code. § 2 Before the interrogation, the judge will ensure the right of private interview of the accused with his defender."

[85] In the wording of Law No. 11.690/2008: "The questions will be formulated by the parties directly to the witness, the judge not admitting those that could induce the answer, have no relation to the

ity of the judge being provided as supplementary, made only if there are "points not clarified" (Art. 212, single paragraph). The wording of Article 217 was also changed with the advent of Law No. 11.690/2008. From such a change, the removal of the defendant from the courtroom became the last of the consequences provided in case of presence that causes humiliation, fear, or serious embarrassment to the victim or the offended.[86]

In the systematic treatment given to the parties in the Brazilian criminal process, a modification was provided for the treatment of the Public Prosecution Service. This is because originally (Art. 257 of the Penal Procedure Code) the "Public Prosecution Service will promote and supervise the application of the law," with the advent of Law No. 1,719/2008,[87] the attribution was divided to separate, in the new wording of the same article, the function of, on the one hand, "promoting, exclusively, the public criminal action, in the manner established in this Code" and, on the other hand, that of "supervising the execution of the law." Such a change makes the two-faced action of the Public Prosecution Service in the criminal process ostensible.[88] As for the accused, Law No. 10,792/2003 added a single paragraph to Article 261 of the Penal Procedure Code.[89] In any case, the interrogation was defined as a means of defense, providing it as the last act to be carried out in the so-called hear-

cause or imply the repetition of another already answered. Single paragraph. On the points not clarified, the judge may supplement the inquiry."

[86] Which presupposes, including, the impossibility of the hearing being done by videoconference with the witness outside the courtroom and the accused inside it.

[87] Also, this constant of the set of legislative propositions of the aforementioned Ada Pellegrini Grinover Commission, instituted by Minister José Carlos Dias when he was in charge of the Justice Department. The bill that originated it was number 4.207/2001.

[88] For Gomes et al. (2008), p. 316, this was the procedural change that gave concreteness to the constitutional provision of Article 129, I, of the Republican Text. Even though there is the authors' analysis regarding the bifrontal performance of the Public Prosecutor's Office, one cannot agree with them when they affirm that the partial performance of the MP would make it "healthy and, before, even necessary, that the judge may disagree with the request for archiving (invoking art. 28 of the CPP), or convict the defendant in the face of a request for acquittal formulated by the Public Prosecutor's Office" (Art. 385 of the CPP). It is not agreed here that the impartial subject (judge) disagrees with the decision of the party that decided *not to accuse* and provoke the internal administrative instance of the accusing body to review the position of those who requested the archiving of the inquiry. There seems to be no escape from such a position in the light of the requirement of impartiality of the magistrate and respect, on the procedural level, to the rule according to which those who *judge* cannot *accuse*. For greater reason, if throughout the procedural arc the accusing body requests acquittal, it is not up to the judge to value such a plea to replace those who could exclusively plead for conviction and, with that, convict the accused. Nor is it said, although the authors did not touch on the point, that the assistant to the Public Prosecutor's Office could behave as a litisconsort, so as to, in disagreement, take the front of any criminal actions or even appeals. This will be dealt with later. Specifically on the point of Article 385 of the Penal Procedure Code, Aury Lopes Júnior's position is correct (2012), p. 359, which preaches that this possibility is nothing less than an "inquisitorial setback."

[89] The insertion seems to be of questionable constitutionality, as it seems to start from premises of qualitative valuation of effective defence if practised by appointed lawyers, on the one hand, or by public defenders or appointed lawyers, on the other.

ing of instruction and judgment, which occurred with the new wording to Article 400 of the Criminal Procedure Code, according to Law No. 11,719/2008.

If before it was imagined that the accused could be in the dark to respond to the terms of the indictment—that is, even before knowing what the details of the accusation were and, in this measure, on what oral evidence it was based—he began to be respected with the legislative change of 2008 (Law No. 11,719), as he began to be heard when all the evidence was collected, which, if the legal dictation is to be respected, is carried out in a single act.[90]

As far as the plan of procedural equality is concerned, it is still worth mentioning that, if in the original wording of the Code, as indicated, the rule was the prompt receipt of the indictment or complaint without the possibility of defensive reaction to the terms of the indictment itself to avoid the beginning of the criminal action (Art. 394, CPP[91]), Law No. 11,719/2008 brought significant changes in this respect. As it was regulated by Articles 396 and 396-A of the Criminal Procedure Code,[92] the formal response of the accused to the accusation[93] was a requirement of validity of the criminal action (Art. 396-A for the ordinary and summary procedure; Art. 406 for the jury procedure).

Also in 2008, an important novelty was brought to the jury system, as, according to Article 474, § 3°, with the wording given by Law No. 11,689/2008, it was, for the

---

[90] Article 400: "In the hearing of instruction and judgement, to be held within a maximum period of 60 (sixty) days, the statements of the offended will be taken, the witnesses listed by the prosecution and the defence will be questioned, in this order, except for the provided for in art. 222 of this Code, as well as the clarifications of the experts, confrontations and the recognition of people and things, interrogating, then, the accused." In the specific procedures of the jury, the deadline for the holding of such a hearing is not 60 days, but more than 10 (Arts. 410 and 411).

[91] In addition, the preliminary defense was, in the terms of Article 395 of the Code, filed *after* the interrogation. The forensic practice established that such a piece was merely procedural, precisely so that the defence, at the dawn of the instruction, would not display its… arms!

[92] Article 396: "In ordinary and summary procedures, once the complaint or accusation is offered, the judge, if not outright rejecting it, will receive it and order the accused to respond to the accusation, in writing, within 10 (ten) days. Single paragraph. In the case of summons by notice, the deadline for the defence will start to run from the personal appearance of the accused or the appointed defender." Article 396-A: "In the response, the accused may argue preliminaries and allege everything that interests his defence, offer documents and justifications, specify the intended evidence and list witnesses, qualifying them and requesting their summons, when necessary."

[93] Although this point is not central to the work developed, the controversy is known regarding the *moment* of receiving the complaint, given the confusion made by the reformist legislator (Law No. 11,719/2008) in Articles 396 ("if the judge does not reject it outright, he will receive it"—before the written response) and 399 ("received the complaint or accusation"—after the written response), it seems to us that Gustavo Badaró (2009), p. 152, is right when he states that "the moment of receiving the complaint, or rather, of the admissibility of the accusation, will be that of art. 399 of the CPP, and, therefore, after the response of the accused, the judge will have, at such an opportunity, three possibilities: (a) reject the complaint, in the cases of art. 395 of the CPP; (b) summarily absolve the accused, in the cases of art. 397 of the CPP; (c) receive the complaint and schedule the instruction and trial hearing."

first time, forbidden to use handcuffs on the accused "during the period in which he remains in the jury room" (Art. 474, § 3°).[94] It was also, for the first time in the scenario of Brazilian criminal procedural law, forbidden to make value-laden references for the conviction of the jurors, such as:

> decision of pronouncement, subsequent decisions that admitted the accusation or determination of the use of handcuffs as an argument of authority that benefit or prejudice the accused; silence of the accused or absence of interrogation due to lack of request, to his detriment.[95]

Recently, with the publication on May 5, 2011, and effectiveness from July 4, 2011, in the specific plan of the precautionary measures of the criminal process, the entire Title IX of Book I of the Penal Procedure Code was changed. Where before only "arrest and provisional freedom" was provided, it is now detailed "on arrest, precautionary measures and provisional freedom."

Thus, while Article 282, in force until July 2011, began the treatment of personal precautionary measures by the opposition between arrest in flagrante and the others, now it deals, in general, with "precautionary measures," with particular emphasis on the new § 3°, related to the prior contradictory to the decree of the precautionary measures, except for "urgency" or "danger of ineffectiveness of the measure."[96]

---

[94] It is striking that, even in the face of the current provision and even also in the face of the content of Binding Precedent No. 11, of the STF ("Only the use of handcuffs is lawful in cases of resistance and of founded fear of escape or danger to one's own or others' physical integrity, by the prisoner or third parties, the exceptionality justified in writing, under penalty of disciplinary, civil and criminal responsibility of the agent or authority and of nullity of the arrest or of the procedural act to which it refers, without prejudice to the civil responsibility of the State," as decided in the plenary session of August 13, 2008), the Supreme Court, in judgments of complaints, softening the rigours of the prohibition here remembered. In this regard, from recent judgments, see Rcl 9468 AgR, full, Rel. Min. Ricardo Lewandowski, published on 11th April 2011. It is pertinent, in this sense, the passage of vote repeated in the following terms: "It is not possible to admit, in a complaint, any doubt about the issues of fact pointed out by the magistrate to determine the use of handcuffs during the conduct of the hearings" (Rcl 6,870, reported by Justice Ellen Gracie, monocratic decision published on November 6, 2008).

[95] Article 478, I and II, also in the terms of Law No. 11,689/2008.

[96] "§ 3 ° Except in cases of urgency or danger of ineffectiveness of the measure, the judge, upon receiving the request for a precautionary measure, will order the notification of the opposing party, accompanied by a copy of the request and the necessary parts, keeping the files in court."

2.7 Equality in the Penal Procedure Code Project (Bill No. 8045/2010)

After Opinion No. 1,636 of the Temporary Study Commission for the Reform of the Penal Procedure Code, of December 7, 2010, which gave the final wording to PLS No. 156/2009,[97] the project was forwarded to the Chamber of Deputies and is currently under consideration there under No. 8.045/2010.[98]

From the outset, obedience to what is called "constitutional due process" (Art. 2) is adopted in relation to all forms of criminal intervention, to then deal with the adversarial system and the broad defense in guaranteeing the "effective manifestation of the technical defender in all procedural phases," being certain that the judge was prohibited from taking investigative initiative and also from substituting the evidentiary action to the prosecution body (Art. 4). Regarding the rights of the investigated, above all, access to the material produced in the investigation Art. 11)[99] and the right to be heard by the authority before the end of this (Art. 12).

A fundamental novelty, inspired by the Italian Code of Criminal Procedure, consists of the defensive investigation. This is a procedure according to which, by the proposed Brazilian law, it is allowed to the investigated, under the terms of Article 13, "through his lawyer, public defender or other agents with express powers, to take the initiative to identify sources of evidence in favour of his defence, being able to even interview people."[100] Also unprecedentedly, it was provided for the exclusively public criminal action, with a single exception related to the private subsidiary initiative, in case of negligence on the part of the prosecution body (Art. 45).

Another important innovation was the treatment of the "subjects of the process" (Title IV), which systematized the placement of the Prosecutor's Office as prosecution body ("is the holder of the criminal action," ex vi of Art. 57) and of the accused as deserving of the technical defense in "all acts of the process" (Art. 60). The

---

[97] The PLS n° 156/2009 deals with the project of a new Code of Criminal Procedure in Brazil. Such PL resulted from the works of a commission established by Request No. 227, of 2008, added by Requests No. 751 and 794, of 2008, authored by Senator Renato Casagrande, and designated by Acts No. 11, 17, and 18, of 2008, by President of the Senate José Sarney. The commission was composed of Hamilton Carvalhido (coordinator), Eugenio Pacelli de Oliveira (rapporteur), Antonio Correa, Antonio Magalhães Gomes Filho, Fabiano Augusto Martins Silveira, Felix Valois Coelho Junior, Jacinto Nelson de Miranda Coutinho, Sandro Torres Avelar, and Tito Souza do Amaral. Of the criticisms that can be made to PLS No. 156/2009 and PL No. 8.045/2010, the most forceful is not directed at the work of the members of the Commission of Jurists, but at the proposed amendments made in the committees established by the chairman of the Criminal Procedure Code Reform Commission. Some of them distort the purpose clarified by the members of the Commission of Jurists.

[98] PL No. 8.045/2010 has identical wording to Opinion No. 1636, from the Federal Senate. Therefore, the references to the articles of the projected Criminal Procedure Code are valid for both.

[99] In the final part of that provision, it reads: "except strictly concerning ongoing proceedings."

[100] The paragraphs of that law article explain the breadth of powers and the deontological commitments of the so-called defensive investigation.

matter was also addressed with unprecedented detail, because, in addition to the specific provisions for the judge, the Prosecutor's Office and the accused (process as *actum trium personarum*), it also dealt with the Public Defender,[101] the assistant, the civil party[102] and the experts and interpreters.

An entire distinct section for the interrogation as an act of defense (Art. 64) was included; it is worth highlighting the rule of the prohibition of its realization without the presence of the defender[103] and respect for the capacity of understanding and discernment of the interrogated, with the prohibition of illicit methods or techniques, of any form of "coercion, intimidation or threat against the freedom of declaration, being irrelevant, in this case, the consent of the person interrogated." It also prohibits the promise of advantages without legal support (Art. 65, caput and § 1). The performance of the act, in fact, is preceded by a list of instrumental information of which the interrogated must be aware (Art. 66).

In the hearing, in addition to the direct examination, it advanced to the cross-examination, either in the interrogation (Art. 74), or in the collection of testimonies (Art. 179), being certain that the premise in the production of any and all evidence is the freedom in the initiative of the parties (Art. 165), so much so that, for example, the party can give up its witness regardless of the consent of the opposite party (Art. 184, single paragraph). It is also worth highlighting the exclusive and anachronistic legitimacy that was conferred, exclusively, to the Attorney General of the Republic to initiate the incident of displacement of competence,[104] provided for in Article 119 of the proposed diploma.

Without prejudice to all these innovations, which are nothing more than an introduction to the theme of procedural equality, the so-called summary procedure is an eloquent example in which the presumption of equality of positions of the parties in the process draws attention.

In such provision (Art. 283), in a few lines, it is imagined the request for immediate application of penalty in certain crimes (those that have a maximum abstract

[101] Article 59: "The Public Defender's Office is an essential institution to the jurisdictional function of the State, being responsible for legal guidance and defence, at all levels, of the needy. § 1 With the aim of ensuring the adversarial process and the broad defence within the scope of criminal proceedings, it will be up to the Public Defender's Office to sponsor the defence of the accused who, for any reason, has not appointed a lawyer, regardless of their economic situation, reserving the right to, at any time, appoint another of their trust, or to defend themselves, if they have qualification. § 2 The accused who has economic condition and does not appoint a lawyer will bear the fees resulting from the technical defence, whose values will be reverted to the Public Defender's Office, according to the law."

[102] The participation of the latter takes place "without expanding the matter of fact contained in the indictment, [...] to request the civil reparation of the moral damage caused by the infraction, in the terms and limits of the criminal charge, for which it will be notified after the filing of the accusatory initial" (Art. 81).

[103] Reason for which the proposal contained in § 1 of Article 64 of the preliminary draft should be criticised, which opens the possibility of, with the consent of the person caught in the act, taking his interrogation without the presence of a defender.

[104] Piovesan and Vieira (2005), pp. 8–9.

sanction less than or equal to eight years), after agreement in this sense between the accused—through his defender—and the Prosecutor's Office.[105] At one time, the controversial provision speaks of the adversariality that can be imprinted on the Brazilian criminal process and, at another, induces reflection on the equality of arms in the criminal process.

From what has already been advanced so far, it is important to deal with the notion of parties, doing it first in the field of civil procedural law, then, and precisely due to the nuances of the criminal process, address the concept within the scope of such process. This is what the next chapter will consist of.

References

Almeida, F. S. (2021). *Codigo do Processo Penal do Estado do Amazonas*. Thoth Editora.

Almeida, J. C. M. d. (1973). *Princípios fundamentais do processo penal*. Revista dos Tribunais.

Almeida Júnior, J. M. d. (1901). *O processo criminal brasileiro*. Laemmert & C.

Andrade, M. F. (2021). *Código de Processo Penal do Estado do Rio Grande do Sul*. Juruá.

Associação dos Advogados De São Paulo. (1971). *Ciclo de palestras sobre o Anteprojeto do Código de Processo Penal*. Editora Unidas Ltda.

Badaró, G. (2009). *Rejeição da denúncia ou queixa e absolvição sumária na reforma do Código de Processo Penal: atuação integrada de tais mecanismos na dinâmica procedimental*. Revista Brasileira de Ciências Criminais.

Barbosa, M. G. V., & Mota, Á. F. d. R. (2021). *Codigo do Processo Penal do Estado do Piauhy. Lei n. 962 de 4 de julho de 1919. Texto legal e breves apontamentos históricos*. Thoth Editora.

Caiuby, J. S. (1927). *Novas linhas sobre o processo criminal*. C. Teixeira & Cia.

[105] "§ 1 The requirements of the agreement referred to in the *caput* of this article are: I - the confession, total or partial, in relation to the facts charged in the accusatory piece; II - the request that the custodial sentence be applied at the minimum provided for in the legal penalty, regardless of the possible incidence of aggravating circumstances or causes of increase of the penalty, and without prejudice to the provisions of §§ 2 and 3 of this article; III - the express manifestation of the parties in the sense of dispensing with the production of the evidence indicated by them. § 2 The substitution of the custodial sentence will be applied, when appropriate, in the terms of the provisions of art. 44 of the Penal Code, as well as the conditional suspension provided for in art. 77 of the same Code. § 3 Upon request of the parties, the penalty applied according to the summary procedure may also be reduced by up to 1/3 (one third) of the minimum provided for in the legal penalty, if the personal conditions of the agent and the lesser severity of the consequences of the crime indicate it. § 4 The provisions of § 3 of this article do not apply if another cause of reduction of the penalty, which will be expressly indicated in the agreement, applies to the concrete case, except in the case of attempted crime. § 5 If there is a cumulative penalty of a fine, this will also be applied at the legal minimum, and the value must be included in the agreement. § 6 The accused will be exempt from expenses and court costs. § 7 In the approval of the agreement and for the purposes of applying the penalty in the form of the summary procedure, the judge will observe the formal fulfilment of the requirements provided for in this article. § 8 For all purposes, the approval of the agreement is considered a conviction sentence. § 9 If, for any reason, the agreement is not approved, it will be removed from the records, and the parties are prohibited from making any references to the terms and conditions then agreed, nor the judge in any decision-making act. Art. 284. If there is no agreement between the prosecution and the defence, the process will proceed in the form of the ordinary rite."

Costa, P. B. F. M. d. (1997). *Inquérito policial e a investigação dos fatos que antecede a ação penal no ordenamento jurídico instaurado pela Constituição de 1988*. Revista Brasileira de Ciências Criminais.

Espínola, E. (1916). *Código do Processo do Estado da Bahia. Annotado por Eduardo Espínola*. Revista dos Tribunais.

Gomes, L. F., Cunha, R. S., & Pinto, R. B. (2008). *Comentários às reformas do Código de Processo Penal e da Lei de Trânsito*. Revista dos Tribunais.

Guimarães, R. R. C. (2021). *Codigo do Processo Penal do Estado do Paraná. Lei n. 1916 de 23 de fevereiro de 1920, com as emendas da Lei n. 2.012 de 21 de março de 1921. Texto legal e breves apontamentos históricos*. Thoth Editora.

Lopes Júnior, A. (2012) Por que o juiz não pode condenar quando o Ministério Público pedir a absolvição? Um diálogo com James Goldschmidt, Binding e Guasp. In: Greco, Luís, Martins, Antonio (Orgs.). *Direito penal como crítica da pena*. Estudos em homenagem a Juarez Tavares por seu 70° Aniversário em 2 de setembro de 2012. Marcial Pons.

Marinho, G. (1917). *Consultor criminal*. [s.n.], Pelotas

Marques, J. F. (2000). *Elementos de direito processual penal* (Vol. I, 2nd ed.). Millennium, Campinas.

Moura, M. T. R. de A. (Coord.) (2008) *As reformas no Código de Processo Penal*: as novas leis de 2008 e os Projetos de Reforma. Revista dos Tribunais.

Oliveira Filho, J. d. (1927). *Código do Processo Penal de Minas Gerais: notas*. Casa Duprat e Casa Mayença Reunidas.

Passos, E. *Código de Processo Penal*: notícia histórica sobre as comissões anteriores [n.d.]. Senado Federal; Secretaria de Informação e Documentação.

Paula Pessoa, V. A. de(1899). *Código de Processo Criminal de Primeira Instancia do Brazil com a lei de 3 de dezembro de 1841, n. 261 e regulamento n. 120 de 31 de janeiro de 1842*. Jacintho Ribeiro dos Santos Livreiro-Editor, Rio de Janeiro

Pierangeli, J. H. (2004). *Processo penal: evolução histórica e fontes legislativas*. Thomsom Iob.

Pimenta Bueno, J. A. (Marquis of São Vicente) (1910). *Apontamentos sobre o processo criminal brasileiro*. Livraria Clássica Editora de A.M. Teixeira & Cia.

Piovesan, F., & Vieira, R. S. (2005). *Federalização de crimes contra os direitos humanos: o que temer?* Boletim do Instituto Brasileiro de Ciências Criminais.

Ráo, V. (1935). *Código de Processo Penal (exposição de motivos)*. Revista Forense.

Saad, M. (2004). *O direito de defesa no inquérito policial*. Revista dos Tribunais.

Siqueira, G. (1917). *Curso de processo criminal*. Livraria e Officinas Magalhães.

Tucci, R. L. (1978). *"Habeas Corpus," ação e processo penal*. José Bushatsky Editor.

Chapter 3
Of the Parties in the Criminal Process

The fact that the doctrine of civil procedure itself is attentive to the observation that "the concept of party is one of the most problematic of procedural law,"[1] evidences the necessary care when considering who the *parties* are in criminal procedural law.[2]

To deal with *parties* in the criminal process, the scientific advancement of civil procedure is of great value. Civil procedure is more accustomed to dealing with antagonistic parties (the notion that the *duality of the parties* is one of its characteristics insofar as it does not admit that someone litigates with oneself). It is possible to take as a principle the if not equal, at least symmetrical (obeying the innate rules of justifiable inequality) distribution of chances[3] procedural to the claimants of judicial protection. It is spoken about the *equality of arms* in civil procedure[4] precisely in view of the footing of equality in which, as a rule, plaintiff and defendant are found.

If in civil procedure there is a distribution of duties, powers, and procedural subjections among the parties from the thought of a cooperative structure linked to the notion of procedural relationship[5] (hence talking about obligations of the parties as

---

[1] Marinoni and Arenhart (2011), p. 162.

[2] The notion of *parties* here appears on its subjective side, that is, it refers to those involved from the rights *sub judice*, under penalty of not falling into the confusion between *part* and *whole* or, in other words, *container* and *content*.

[3] From here on, a different notion of process follows. As a procedural legal relationship, which is consecrated by the cultivators of the general theory of the process, given the peculiarities of the criminal process when compared with the civil process. The further development and explanations of this position, with which we align ourselves with the observations of authors, in Brazil, such as Aury Lopes Júnior and Ricardo Jacobsen Gloeckner, will be explained later.

[4] Dinamarco et al. (2020), pp. 85 and 130. Nery Júnior (2016), pp. 279–280.

[5] Or, in summary, *risks* and *chances* with a view to the prospects and expectations of a favorable judicial sentence, in the lesson of Goldschmidt and in the doctrine of the legal situation, which will be discussed later.

R. S. Vieira, *Equality of Arms in Criminal Procedure*,
https://doi.org/10.1007/978-3-032-03663-6_3

one of the links of the so-called *legal relationship*[6]), such a division, at least in this way, does not exist in criminal procedure. In this, inequality is innate to the birth of the opposition of interests, which is even a reflection of a pre-existing factual situation incomparable to that which motivates the birth of the civil claim. In addition, the beginning of the civil claim is distinct from that seen in criminal procedure, in which a two-phase prosecution is noted (pre-procedure aimed at the formation of the *opinio delicti* and, then, the beginning of a criminal action).

In criminal procedure, different interests are attended to than those at stake in the civil procedural field, which is also perceived in the distinct method of collection of information elements to precede the judicialization of conflicts and in the way the procedural position of the defendant is presented in civil procedure and in criminal procedure. In the latter, one commonly went through an investigation procedure, in charge of an organ supervised by the Prosecutor's Office[7]—the accusing party—in which the participation of the then investigated is problematic,[8] which motivates some temperament, even if, to some extent, the civil procedural doctrine will be used for the construction of the concept of criminal procedural party.

There are, as will be seen here, with extensive explanations of a historical and ideological nature, embodied in positive law norms, including prevalences in favor sometimes of the accusing party, sometimes of the accused, which makes the distribution of *burdens* of civil procedural law even further from the criminal procedural scenario[9] and makes it irrelevant—from the assumed initial equality in the process from party to party in the civil claim and its problematic aspect in criminal procedure—the considerations of distribution of probative burdens in the latter.

In addition, it is necessary to mention the scholars of the concept of party in civil procedure, insofar as, as will be seen, from such a concept is extracted the connection with the contradictory and, therefore, the treatment that is given to the contenders involved in the process. From there will develop, here, the concern with the temporal arc in which the guarantee of the contradictory will accompany, or not, the application of the concept of equality of arms in criminal procedure.

Such an argumentative course is justified, also, because, if in criminal procedure it was more stormy than in civil procedure, the problematic of the very existence of *parties* (or, at least, of some other besides the accused[10]), it is impossible to advance

[6] This relationship does not exist according to Goldschmidt, especially because there are no obligations of the parties in the process.

[7] The dispensability of the inquiry in the formation of the *opinio delicti* (Art. 12, CPP) does not invalidate the reasoning, but only serves as a general rule to accommodate exceptions.

[8] For it is prodromic to its consideration of *part* in the process, and such an investigation procedure has the predisposition to determine, for the future accusing body, whether the investigated should come to be denounced to justice.

[9] In Brazil, see, for all, Badaró (2003).

[10] Aury Lopes Júnior, reported, in previous editions of his *Direito Processual Penal* (2025), currently in its 22nd edition, from Editora Saraiva, the existence of a doctrine that understood that the only party in the criminal process would not be the accused, but the accuser, considering that the accused would be a mere object of the process insofar as, because it is—the criminal process—of development of public function, part could only be the accuser, given the imperiousness of fulfill-

to equality of arms if the methodological premise is not achieved that, from a criminal procedural concept of party, one begins to imagine if the prosecution body (usually, the Prosecutor's Office, given the prevalence adopted by the law of public initiative for the criminal prosecution in court) has the position of party in the criminal procedure. Hence follows the establishment of the necessary antagonism of interests to determine the application and limits of equality of arms in criminal proceedings, with highlights for the initial opposition of interests between prosecutor and defendant.

For the ideas of this chapter to be concatenated with those that will follow, it is necessary to reflect on the very nature of the criminal process, given that it is the adversarial system that fits, among the models historically and ideologically already consecrated of process, with greater accuracy to the study of equality of arms. It is important, therefore, to say why it deviates from the notion of process as a procedural legal relationship.

3.1 The Criminal Process: From Legal Relationship to Legal Situation

Whether one imagines the decanted general theory of the process, whether one clings to the notions of civil procedural law, whether one focuses the research on the criminal process, it is essential, even if one is not going to dare to conceptualize *the process* (as a legal relationship, legal situation, institution or legal relationship animated by the contradictory), to treat it, at least, under two consecrated currents: that of the legal relationship and that of the legal situation. This is due, methodologically, to two reasons.

The first of them is that, even in order to construct the critique, these two currents were responsible for building notions dear to civil process and criminal process. Each of the two areas of law owes, today, much to the studies of those responsible for the doctrines of the legal relationship and the legal situation.

The second reason is that it is already time in Brazil, in critical assumption to the mercurial spread of the lessons of the so-called *general theory of process*,[11] to open one's eyes to the lessons of authors who, privileging the doctrine of James Goldschmidt (legal situation), direct the analysis of criminal procedural law to a point propitious to the debate on equality of arms.

In the plan of the development of ideas, therefore, still without the specific cut of the criminal process, one owes to Oskar von Büllow, among many, the notable

ing the state duty of criminal repression and nothing more. Check, for this historical mention (2009), p. 2.

[11] On the first page of the presentation of *Criminal Prosecution, Imprisonment and Freedom*, Tucci (1980) considers criminal procedural law an "equally important branch of procedural science, totally uprooted from conventional positions, suitable for a *general theory of process* that, over time, for him, is left without a reasonable number of plausible explanations."

evolution in the general theory of law that gave the process the feature of a legal relationship. The importance of the author's lessons, dictated in 1868 in the famous work *Theory of Procedural Assumptions and Dilatory Exceptions*, lies in the treatment that, from it, began to be given to the parties of the process.

At the beginning of the well-known work, von Büllow said:

> It has never been doubted that civil procedural law determines the powers and duties that link the parties and the court. But, in this way, it has also been affirmed that the process is a relationship of reciprocal rights and obligations, that is, a *legal relationship*.[12]

The study of the procedural phenomenon (and it is very important to highlight the own conceptual separation between the *process* and the *procedure*) based on the ties that unite its subjects (among themselves and before the judge) gained unprecedented attention from the work, which had an influence on modern Western civil procedural law. The great point of attention, however, is that the widespread lesson jumped from civil process to criminal process.

Indeed, from the separation of the material and procedural planes and from the reflection on the nature of the ties that unite the procedural subjects (the *parties* and the *judge*[13]), the theory of von Büllow, in addition to building the development of the chained links between those involved in the procedural scene, was, in the language of Aury Lopes Júnior, the "most relevant milestone for the study of the concept of parties."[14]

According to the words of the professor from Rio Grande do Sul, it was through the theory of the process (criminal, inclusive) as a legal relationship that the defendant began to be considered not just as a mere object, but as a subject of rights. In the ties resulting from the procedural relationship he maintained with the accusing party, he began to be able to claim favorable jurisdictional protection. Indeed, to affirm the existence of a *legal relationship* between plaintiff and defendant in the criminal process implies no longer treating the latter as an object, but rather as a claimant, that is, aspiring to a jurisdictional protection. This was already a notable advance.

In this regard, a confessed adherent of such theory—albeit recognizes, in the approach, that it was imagined for the field of civil process—reminds that,

> unlike what happened in the old ordinances, the relations between the accused, the accuser and the judge are regulated by law, they become legal relations in which the rights, powers, charges and obligations of each one are seen. Thus, the accused is no longer a mere object of the process, but appears in it as a true subject of rights, linked to the determinations of the law and not to the discretion of the judge.[15]

---

[12] von Büllow (1964), p. 1.

[13] For that German author (1964, p. 2), such a legal relationship is public exactly because the bond of reciprocity not only unites the parties among themselves, but also guarantees the cooperation of the parties before the state, dressed as a judge.

[14] Lopes Júnior (2008), p. 178.

[15] Tornaghi (1985), p. 13.

According to von Büllow, "the process could be characterised as a progressive legal relationship that involves the parties"[16] from the claim to the obtaining of the final judgement. Such a legal relationship—which is based on the "link between people, by virtue of which one of them can claim something, to which the other is obliged"[17]—is supported by the existence of reciprocal obligations and rights, in the context of the process.

In a passage from well-known authors of the general theory of the process, it is taught:

> it is undeniable that the State and the parties are, in the process, interconnected by a very large and significant series of legal ties, being holders of legal situations by virtue of which each one of them is required to practice certain acts of the procedure or allows them the legal system this practice; and the legal relationship is exactly the link that connects two or more subjects, attributing them powers, rights, faculties, and the corresponding duties, obligations, subjections, burdens.[18]

The most fruitful contributions to the concept of the process (in its subjective sense) were given by scholars of civil procedure. From the lines of the authors of that legal area, the criminal procedural doctrine—and it is likely that Vincenzo Manzini was its precursor[19]—ended up incorporating them.

From the perspective of the scientific division between criminal procedure and civil procedure, although the theoretical influences of the latter are very useful to the former, it is impossible not to mention Francesco Carnelutti.

In a masterful text, the author compared the areas of criminal law, criminal procedure, and civil procedure to three sisters who would have as a link only paternity. Among them, the criminal procedure would be the *Cinderella*, and, if on the one hand it would have a connection of the same cohabitation with criminal law (crime

---

[16] von Büllow (1964), pp. 2–3.

[17] *Ius et obligatio correlata sunt*, in a lesson updated by Del Vecchio and translated by Tucci (2002), p. 159. In the words of Tornaghi, "there is a legal relationship between two people when one of them has the right to demand something from the other, who in turn has the legal duty to do what is demanded (or when someone has the power to subject another to his will. [...] The subjects of the legal relationship are always in correlation: to the right of one corresponds the duty of the other: to the power of one, the subjection of the other" (1985), pp. 52–53.

[18] Dinamarco et al. (2020) p. 344. In the work, a page ahead, the authors conclude that "the dominant theory affirms the existence of obligations and subjective rights of a procedural nature."

[19] In a critical passage, Gloeckner (2013), p. 62, anticipating a value judgment about the legal relationship as irrelevant to criminal procedure because it promotes authoritarianism, recalls that "it is not for nothing that Manzini will choose it as the theory that best explains the criminal process. And here it is very important the conception that the Italian proceduralist has of the criminal process: it is, for him, a process '*a Parte unica*', which arises in the relationship between Prosecutor's Office and judge, not producing any effects on the accused." Tornaghi (1985), p. 12, reminds that the peninsular author called the theory of the procedural relationship transposed to the criminal process of *our theory*. Alonso (1979), p. 53, argues that the adaptation of the theory of the legal relationship to the criminal process was made by von Kries in 1892, followed by Birkmeyer and von Hippel.

and punishment are, in Carnelutti's words, the two sides of the same coin), on the other it also suffered notable influence of civil procedural law.[20]

Among us, among those who criticized the prevalence of the lessons of civil procedural law in criminal procedure as if this meant the construction of the so-called *general theory of the process*, is Jacinto Nelson de Miranda Coutinho. This author reminds us that the general theory of civil process,

> riding on the general theory of the process, penetrates our criminal process and, instead of giving it a general theory, reduces it to a poor cousin, a parcel, a slice of the general theory. In short, general theory of the process is deception; the general theory is that of civil process and, from it, the others.[21]

Among the civil proceduralists who, in open cultivation of the so-called general theory of the process, deal with the process (continent) linked to the legal relationship (content, its subjective side), is also Cândido Rangel Dinamarco, who, in *Institutions of civil procedural law*, decodes the structural components of the concept. Thus, *relationship* is a link, a connection between two elements; it is *legal* because it is governed by law and, therefore, implies obligation of conduct or abstentions or inevitability of a submission; and *procedural* because it takes place in the process. The concept, according to Dinamarco, unites "*relationship* (link) *legal* (governed by law) *procedural* (that takes place in the process)" and, therefore, is the "system of links governed by law that interconnects the subjects of the process."[22]

As it is not the purpose of this work to deal with the details of von Büllow's theory, but only its diffusion in the criminal procedural field, it seems relevant to summarize that, from the procedural relationship (thought for the field of civil procedure, it is repeated) emerges the existence of reciprocal rights and duties (in the process, between the parties, and of both—clearly for cooperation purposes—before the state, represented by the judge).

From this, it is possible to move on to a new perspective, as it seems to be criticizable the opinion spread according to which "the theory of the procedural relationship, which arose with a view to civil procedure and in the theory of this was developed, discussed and consolidated, has equal validity for criminal procedural law."[23]

The main inadequacies of the theory of the process as, subjectively, a legal relationship, are presented by James Goldschmidt, who takes the process as a set of *legal situations*.[24] The critical turn is, from the point of view of the treatment of the parties in the criminal process (and also the theoretical accommodation in one of

---

[20] Carnelutti (1960), pp. 15–17, spoke of a *leading position* of civil procedural law in relation to criminal procedural law. According to him, more than 90% of the criminal process was influenced by civil procedural law.

[21] Coutinho (1989), pp. 118–119.

[22] Dinamarco (2024)), p. 226.

[23] Dinamarco et al. (2020), p. 346.

[24] Goldschmidt was a prolific thinker, also for civil process, as seen from his work (1936).

such *criminal procedural systems*, about which we will talk in the next chapter), fundamental and deserves attention.

It was Goldschmidt who, in 1925, in the work *The process as a legal situation*, most vividly fought the said conception of the process as a legal relationship. The criticisms there were repeated, later, to the criminal process in lectures given at the University of Madrid, between 1934 and 1935, and summarized in the work *General Principles of Criminal Process*.[25]

Both regarding the work of 1925, which celebrated the criticisms of Goldschmidt to von Büllow (and which, therefore, repeats the theoretical prevalence of civil procedural law when compared to the *Cinderella* that was the criminal process), and regarding the lectures of 1934 and 1935, the German author makes an analogy between the process and war. This is particularly important to the adversarial criminal process model, and it is emblematic to think about the equality of arms when imagining the process as a war.

Goldschmidt said:

> when war breaks out, everything is at the tip of the sword; the most intangible rights become expectations, possibilities and obligations, and every right can be annihilated as a consequence of not having taken advantage of an occasion or neglected an obligation; as, on the contrary, the war can provide the winner with the enjoyment of a right that does not correspond to him.[26]

Therefore, Aragoneses Alonso refers to the war metaphor to say that, once it is declared, the rights are "at the tip of the sword."[27]

The paradigm for the study of the process is another: it is adversarial. It is guided by the defense and the prosecution, that is, by the contenders, carriers of antagonistic interests, and the connection between them is not given by obligatory links (to the judge), but before the taking advantage of the *occasion* or, as Aury Lopes Júnior wants, *chance*.

From the occasion or chance, arise, in the words of Goldschmidt, the *expectations* ("of a favourable sentence") or *prospects* ("of an unfavourable sentence"). In this sense, "the expectations of a favourable sentence generally depend on a previous procedural act by the interested party, which is successful. On the contrary, the expectations of an unfavourable sentence always depend on such a procedural act by the interested party."[28]

In continuity:[29]

[25] There is a Brazilian edition, and this was the one consulted: *Princípios gerais do processo penal* (2002).

[26] Goldschmidt (2002), p. 49.

[27] Goldschmidt's phrase is in Alonso (1979), p. 57, footnote no. 14.

[28] Goldschmidt (2002), p. 50. Lopes Júnior (2008), p. 184, reminds us that "faced with a *chance*, the party can free itself from a procedural burden and move towards a favourable sentence (expectation), or not free itself and, with this, increase the possibility of an unfavourable sentence (perspective)."

[29] It seems that when the translator alluded to the procedural *obligation*, he was referring to the *burden*, since there is no procedural obligation in Goldschmidt's theory. In his *Civil Procedural*

> the party that is in the situation of producing an advantage by an act has a possibility or occasion or procedural opportunity. On the contrary, when the party has to perform an act to avoid a procedural disadvantage, ultimately, for an unfavourable sentence, it has a procedural obligation.[30]

Being non-existent, the notion of legal obligation (given that there is no immediate state sanction as a consequence of non-compliance, but rather an increase in expectation of a final unfavorable decision) of the parties in the process,[31] the construction made by the German professor is, for the defense, the assumption of risks (proven or not his allegation, carried out or not such diligence, arises the expectation of favorable sentence or prospect of an unfavorable one) and, for the prosecution, the discharge of procedural burdens (in the criminal process, the burden is of the prosecution, all of it; and to the defense remain the risks of the process).

The doctrine of the legal situation clings to the taking advantage of *chances*, of *opportunities*, of the process,[32] with a view to obtaining the favorable decision of the party that best takes advantage of its opportunities. Thus, the so-called "legal situation" is "the state of a person with respect to his right from the point of view of the judicial sentence that is expected based on the laws."[33]

Law (1936), Goldschmidt (2002), p. 8, said: "The litigants as such are not generally reached by any procedural obligation." By the way, for those—as was the case with Schmidt (1957), p. 36—who followed James Goldschmidt's theory, "just as there are no specific procedural duties, neither can we speak of rights of the same class."

[30] Goldschmidt (1936), p. 50. Lopes Júnior (2008), p. 184, recalls: "Neither do obligations fall to the parties, but rather *procedural burdens*, understood as the performance of acts with the purpose of preventing a procedural prejudice and, consequently, an unfavourable sentence. Such acts translate, essentially, into the proof of their assertions." Shortly thereafter, he concludes: "the procedural obligation (burden) is seen as an imperative of the party's own interest, before which there is no right of the adversary or of the State" (p. 185). The same lesson is posited by Gloeckner (2013), pp. 69 and 73–74.

[31] Also, in this sense is the lesson of Schmidt (1957), pp. 37–38, in the forceful criticism he makes of the assimilation of the criminal process into the civil proceduralist doctrine of the legal relationship. In addition to saying that the existence of such a relationship in the criminal process is "very doubtful" and taking the legal relationship itself, in the process, as a "false concept," the author recalls that in the criminal process, unlike what is seen in the civil process, "The Prosecutor's Office can 'proceed' sometimes for a long time until it is possible to direct the procedure (the 'process') against a certain person. But even then it is usually necessary, a series of procedural acts before with the promotion of the action the matter is brought to the court. But the criminal process begins with the first measures of persecution of the Prosecutor's Office, practiced even by the police. That is why the image used for the civil process of bilateral or trilateral procedural relations, does not fit the criminal process as a whole."

[32] Lopes Júnior (2008), p. 184

[33] Goldschmidt (2002), p. 51. In the field of civil process, and in more detail: "The legal ties that arise here between the parties are not properly 'legal relations' ('static' consideration of Law), that is, they are not powers or duties in the sense of powers over imperatives or mandates, but 'legal situations' (dynamic consideration of law), that is, situations of expectation, hopes of judicial conduct that is to occur and, ultimately, of the future judicial ruling; in a word: expectations, possibilities and burdens. Only those are rights in procedural sense—the same right to legal protection (procedural action) is, from this point of view, nothing more than a legally founded expectation—

In James Goldschmidt's conception, there is also no duty of cooperation between the parties, given that each one takes advantage—in procedural situations that trigger expectations or prospects of a favorable or unfavorable judicial sentence—of the chances of discharging the *burden* or assumption of the *risk* of the process with a view to obtaining a final sentence.[34]

In the process thus imagined—that is, in which the connections of the parties do not arise from a legal relationship (which presupposes obligations and duties procedural, even if not between the parties, but at least between them and the judge[35]), but from a complex of legal situations (with the use of procedural chances in search of a favorable decision)—there is no cooperation for the pronouncement of a sentence.[36]

The links that connect one party to another, says Aragoneses Alonso, "are only expectations or prospects of a favourable or unfavourable sentence. Therefore, a series of categories specific to the world of the process, such as burden, discharge of burden, possibility, etc." must be created.[37]

Conceiving the process as a legal situation provides, therefore, a model closer to the adversarial system (remember that Goldschmidt himself compared the process

---

and the latter—the burdens—'imperatives of own interest', occupy in the process the place of obligations" (Goldschmidt, 1936, p. 8). Alonso (1979), pp. 53–54.

[34] Tornaghi (1985), p. 11, an author who understands that the doctrine of the legal situation would not be incompatible with that of the legal relationship, without mentioning Goldschmidt, privileges his points of view in scattered passages. This is what is seen, for example, when Tornaghi says that "from the beginning both parties are in the procedural field. And for both the principle applies: whoever fails to make use of the faculties (the possibilities of acting) that belong to him, does so at his own risk. He may not recover the possibility despised (the action despised) and then suffers the loss that he could have avoided, which the law allows in consideration of the interest of the adversary in the continuation and termination of the process" (p. 26). And still: "Really the use by any of the parties of their faculties produces effect on the adversary and the purpose of the procedural activity is the achievement of this effect" (p. 27).

[35] For if the connections of obligation were between the parties themselves, it would be very difficult to escape from the dependence, still, of the private process, of the Roman *litiscontestatio* (TornaghI, 1985, p. 23).

[36] Here, an important distinction is noted between the ideas of Goldschmidt and those of Grinover (1990), p. 3. The author from São Paulo, in a very influential doctrinal article that directly touches on the *par condicio*—which will be discussed later—takes as a premise for the application of procedural equality the process—from lessons by Claudio Faranda—as a cooperative structure. Thus, there is "collaboration between parties and judge. The participation of the subjects in the process not only allows each one to increase the possibilities of obtaining a favourable decision, but it means cooperation in the exercise of jurisdiction. Above and beyond the selfish intentions of the parties, the dialectical structure of the process exists to revert in favour of the good quality of the jurisdictional provision and the perfect adherence of the sentence to the underlying material law situation." Also, to see Goldschmidt's conception: Schmidt (1957), p. 38.

[37] Alonso (1979), pp. 56–57. It is also from Alonso (1960), p. 190, the following enlightening passage: "the expectation of a procedural advantage and, ultimately, of a favourable sentence, the dispensation of a procedural burden, and the possibility of reaching such a situation by the performance of a procedural act constitute the rights in the procedural sense of the word. In reality, these are not rights properly said, but situations that could be called with the French word: 'chances'."

to a war) and, thus, to the dispositive power of its object by the contenders, placing them as protagonists of the litigation, and not the judge.

The lesson that can be drawn from this, in the words of Ricardo Jacobsen Gloeckner, is that

> the theory of the legal situation allows and provides theoretical support for the construction of a criminal process in the mould of the adversarial system. Without the omnipresent action of the magistrate, a legacy of the theory of the legal relationship and whose predilection for the sustenance of a criminal system founded on the foundations of the ideology of social defence is notorious, Goldschmidt perceives the importance of procedural dialectics. And within this perspective, it is easy to glimpse the greater adequacy of the theory of the legal situation to the moulds of a democratic regime.[38]

We do not give here wings to the pretension of reviewing in detail the many and successive[39] theories that sought to explain the process and, particularly, the criminal process. Not only because, as Montero Aroca said, "process is process, lacking sense all reference to different concepts,"[40] but also because the temptation could be, at the limit, not very fruitful, insofar as one would run the serious risk of trying to fit the *process* into one of the predefined categories (whether legal relationship, whether legal situation, whether, still, the older and already outdated conceptions of process as contract or quasi-contract, and so many others).[41]

Even if it is not done this way, it follows from the two highlighted theories and here briefly studied, that of the legal situation. Its study seems appropriate and useful from the warnings of Pedro Aragoneses Alonso,[42] Aury Lopes Júnior and Ricardo Gloeckner. In addition, from the extraction of the fundamental points of the

---

[38] Gloeckner (2013), p. 68.

[39] Among the many criticisms that Goldschmidt's theory suffered, those that had the most echo were those of Calamandrei (1950), pp. 23–51, who took the theory as sociological and sceptical, with the risk of the conception of the process as a legal situation leading to the degeneration of procedural science at the whim of the strategies of the litigants. But it was Calamandrei himself who, in a later writing (1951), pp. 1–8, took Goldschmidt for "a maestro of procedural liberalism." In the last article, the Italian professor not only focused on the fertility of Goldschmidt's ideas to non-authoritarian systems, contrary to the inquisitive process, but also stopped subscribing to the criticisms then made, insofar as "la aleatorietà dell'esito finale, dipendente dal giuoco dialettico dell'attività nelle parti, non è da considerarsi una degenerazione patologica ed. eccezionale Che possa esser trascurata in uma riscostruzione degli istituti processuali *secundum jus*, ma è proprio una espressione essenziale e caratteristica del principio dispositivo, secondo Il quale Il giudice deve giudicare '*secundum allegata et probata*'." And, repeatedly, he emphasized, in the wake of Golschmidt's theory, that "per aver giustizia non basta aver ragione, ma bisogna farla valere, cioè conoscere e saper manovrare la tecnica per farla valere."

[40] Aroca (1976), p. 191.

[41] Jardim (1984), p. 106.

[42] "The concept of the legal situation forms the synthesis of the abstract consideration, procedural assumption, and of the concrete, material assumption, of judicial law, namely: it reduces to a common denominator the abstract demand of the citizen, that the State administer justice and the concrete one of the holder, according to the material law that the State grants him legal protection through a favourable sentence" (1960), p. 192.

Goldschmidtian conception, one can get closer to the notions of equality of arms and adversarial criminal process.[43]

Therefore, here we take the position of the non-existence of (a) obligations and duties that, if they existed, would qualify the link between the parties as a procedural relationship,[44] and of (b) cooperative duty of the parties towards the judge to reach a sentence on the merits. Having done this, we move on to deal specifically with the parties, which is the object of this chapter.

3.2 The Party and the Third Party in Civil Process

The lesson of Cândido Rangel Dinamarco is well known, according to which the parties are the "interested" subjects[45] of the (accepted by him) procedural relationship. Still, for him, and in decoding the generic concept:

> They are said to be *interested* because they are always there in defence of any claim of their own or of others, in preparation to receive the effects of the final provision of the process. They participate in the battles inherent to this and will benefit from its substantial direct or indirect effects, or they will bear them: the jurisdictional protection to be granted will address one of the parties, imposing on the other the sacrifice of a claim (winning party and losing party).[46]

---

[43] Which is not immune to criticism. The main ones and the reactions that followed, either from Goldschmidt himself, or over time, from various authors, can be consulted in the work of Gloeckner (2013), pp. 77 and foll.

[44] Moreover, the theory of the procedural relationship is also not accepted here because, as Schmidt (1957), p. 36 reminds us: "To see in the criminal process a legal (procedural) relationship is very doubtful, as here - unlike in the civil process, which begins with the promotion of the action and immediately the court and the parties are put in relation - only successively do the parties enter the procedure. The Prosecutor's Office can 'proceed' sometimes for a long time until it is possible to direct the procedure (the 'process') against a certain person. But even then it is usually necessary a series of procedural acts before with the promotion of the action the matter is brought to the court. But the criminal process begins with the first measures of persecution of the Prosecutor's Office, practiced even by the police. That is why the image used for the civil process of bilateral or trilateral procedural relations, does not fit the criminal process as a whole."

[45] Dinamarco (2024), p. 287. In the same work and on the same page, the author continues the construction of the concept with a reference to Liebman's doctrine, reminding that parties would be the "subjects of the contradiction instituted before the judge." The very adjectivation of *interested* already motivates doctrinal divisions. Silva (2005), p. 84, for example, in the *Comments on the Code of Civil Procedure*, understands that the mere mention of the simple *interested* refers to the idea of voluntary jurisdiction and, hence, to the absence of requests that configure the positions of plaintiff and defendant.

[46] Dinamarco (2024), p. 287. The reasoning is resumed in *Fundamentos do direito processual civil moderno* (2000a). There, Dinamarco says: "reality shows that personal interest is always the most efficient spring of the life of rights and their effectiveness. Whoever comes to court to claim or resist is moved by the aspiration to the good of life in dispute, either to obtain it (author, claimant), or to preserve it (defendant, defendant)" (p. 125).

Next, the professor develops the exposition from the connection of those involved in a dual perspective: the fact of being someone involved in the demand and, more than that, being there to try to satisfy a claim. From there, the notion of *warrior* of the process is rescued, repeated by Calamandrei: "the parties are the protagonists of a real duel, in which each one has the right to strike according to the pre-established rules with a view to the desired profit."[47]

Civil procedural technique also separates the so-called concepts of the *material* and *procedural* parts. This is an attempt to avoid taking the one who is subject to the contradiction established by the judicial authority as the one who is the holder of right and obligation (to follow the dictates of the theory of the procedural relationship) or the one who participates in the division of chances and opportunities in the process (to follow the theory of the legal situation).

Thus, if the subject who exercises in the process the activities that are attributed to him with a view to obtaining the judgement on the merits coincides with the holder of the debated good, it is said that there is an identity between the *part in procedural sense* (the "subject of the process," in the language of Humberto Theodoro Júnior[48]) and the *part in material sense* (the "subject of the dispute," also in the language of the professor from Minas Gerais).

Athos Gusmão Carneiro says, based on extensive bibliographic research, that although the "classics" dealt with the concept of part from the relation of material right, "current doctrines seek the concept of part only *in the process*, not in the substantial relation deduced in court."[49]

The construction of the concept of part in the process, therefore, does not necessarily result from the relation of the subject to the desired good of life, but from the law—because it is the civil procedural law that traditionally says whether the legitimation *ad processum* is of an ordinary nature (defense of own interest in own name) or extraordinary (defense of someone else's interest in own name), just as it is itself that deals with procedural substitution in its various possibilities.

Hence, it does not matter the connection between the part (procedural) and the good of life—even though, as a rule in civil process, both coincide with each other—to try to reach an operative concept of part in the civil process. Pontes de Miranda said that "the concept of part is of formal law, and usually coincides, but does not need to coincide, with that of the holder of the right in the disputed legal relationship, or with that of the passive subject of this relationship."[50]

Arruda Alvim, in a current passage, recalls that the concept of part is "eminently procedural, resulting from the simple assertion of the action. It results from the fact of the proposition of the action."[51] With this, once again in the language of

[47] Dinamarco (2024), p. 288.

[48] Theodoro Júnior (1997), p. 76.

[49] Carneiro (2010), p. 4.

[50] Pontes de Miranda (1974), p. 241.

[51] Alvim (2008), p. 34.

Dinamarco, except for the non-uniformity of doctrine regarding nomenclature,[52] the so-called *pure concept of part* is reached. For the author, the relation of material right does not matter, because only the procedural relation counts (here again, the remnants of the *legal relationship* designating the subjective side of the process): "to be part in the process means to be the holder of the faculties, burdens, powers and duties inherent to the procedural legal relationship, in a state of subjection to the judge."[53]

In other words, "it matters little, for the determination of the concept of part, whether these subjects debate in the process a right they claim to be theirs, or even if it is concluded that this right does not exist. It does not matter, in other words, for this definition, whether the part is legitimate."[54] Pontes de Miranda said, in his time, that part is, "therefore, whoever enters, as a subject, active or passive, in the procedural legal relationship. Parts are procedural figures; there are parts that are not the subjects of the legal relationship, object of the dispute."[55]

A party is, therefore, whoever requests judicial protection (active party; plaintiff), or the one against whom protection is requested (passive party, defendant), regardless of the existence of a material right invoked by one or the other side. The notion clings purely and simply to the process: who requests and against whom it is requested. In this regard, Donaldo Armelin points out that, precisely because the concept of a party depends on the request for judicial protection and this implies the initial petition as a "typically procedural act," the concept of a party "is exclusively procedural."[56]

This is what comes from Giuseppe Chiovenda, in civil procedure: "a party is the one who demands in his own name (or in whose name is demanded) the enforcement of a will of the law, and the one against whom this enforcement is demanded."[57] In criminal procedure, it can be said that a party is who requests or against whom it is requested, both being interconnected by the legal situations dictated by the chances that the law assigns to each of the parties to discharge evidentiary burden (prosecutor) or procedural risks (accused). Both have initial opposing interests: to

---

[52] On this subject, besides the cited, see: Bueno (2006), p. 3.

[53] Dinamarco (2024), p. 290.

[54] Marinoni and Arenhart (2011), p. 164. There is a certain doctrinal division insofar as Dinamarco establishes, in the concept of part, the consequence of the exercise of the contradictory, something that is criticized by Bueno (2006), p. 3, by Marinoni and Arenhardt (2011), pp. 163–164, and by Alvim (2008), pp. 34–36, even if implicitly, because, by removing from the concept of part the connection with the contradictory, we arrive at the more restricted notion of part in the civil process. In any case, there is no disagreement at all that the concept of part is eminently procedural, detached from material law, with which we return to Dinamarco (2009), p. 25: "it is methodologically legitimate to assert that 'the notion of part is a strictly procedural notion'—or, in other words, this is a *pure concept of part.*"

[55] Pontes de Miranda (1974), p. 242.

[56] Armelin (1979), p. 81.

[57] Chiovenda (2000), p. 278.

obtain a judicial ruling that upholds the claim (prosecuting party) or, on the contrary,[58] to obtain a sentence that dismisses the initial claim.[59]

This is close to—and let us stick to the construction of civil procedure, which, as will be seen, remains relevant to the field of this work—the notion of third party taken by Dinamarco, in rare linguistic beauty, as "specular refraction" of the party, since the concept of who is "third party" is constructed negatively and symmetrically to that of a party.[60] Thus, a third party is one who does not get involved—or does not *yet* get involved—in the relationship (or situation) procedural. Returning to Pontes de Miranda: who is not—or is not *yet*—a "procedural character."

In this particular case, a new doctrinal dispute is seen, because, while Dinamarco, strong in the notion of attachment to the contradiction established before the judge, understands that the *third party* who *intervenes* in the process acquires the quality of *party* precisely by intervening in it,[61] Luiz Guilherme Marinoni and Sérgio Cruz Arenhardt assert that the *intervention of the third party* does not denature it as such and therefore does not transform it into a *party*.[62] In an intermediate position, separating the type of *intervention* and, hence, the acquisition of the quality of party, are Cássio Scarpinella Bueno[63] and Ovídio Baptista da Silva.[64]

Notwithstanding the particularities of each approach and taking as a pertinent example the *assistance* as a typical form of third-party intervention (even because, in criminal procedure, there is no *denunciation of the lawsuit*, *opposition*, *nomination to authorship* or *call to the process*), the treatment given by the law indicates that it is the interest—the so-called legitimating interest to act in favor of one of the parties involved in the pre-existing demand—that gives place to such subjective expansion of the demand.

[58] Armelin (1979), pp. 101–102, argues, based on Liebman's doctrine, that the right to defend oneself is not confused, in particular, with passive legitimacy in the process. For him, while the former stems from the objective of removing from the defendant's rights the consequences of an unfavourable decision—and there it is even admitted, the warning to defects of the legal-procedural relationship for this—the passive legitimacy in the cause, as a consequence of the right of action, aims to achieve a favourable merit sentence for the defendant.

[59] In the case of the Prosecutor's Office, the situation is special: in the interests it represents.

[60] Dinamarco (2000b), p. 18. It is important to nuance, without prejudice to linguistic beauty, that while refraction is a physical phenomenon that implies a change in the direction of light or sound by changing the medium in which it propagates, the notion of reflection could better serve the idea, given that it is the deviation that the ray of light or sound suffers when, in the same medium in which it propagates, it encounters an obstacle. Thus, while reflection returns light to the medium in which it propagated, without surpassing it, refraction is the passage of light through an obstacle, causing a deviation in its propagation.

[61] Dinamarco (2000b), p. 18. Athos Gusmão Carneiro, moreover, deals with admission as a third-party intervention for the acquisition of party status (2010), p. 6.

[62] (2001), p. 65.

[63] Bueno (2006), pp. 12–13. An example of a third party becoming a party comes from opposition, and of a third party who never loses such quality would be that of assistance.

[64] Silva (2005), p. 84.

It is from the *legal interest*, therefore, that the admission of the third party in the process arises. This notion, that of *interest* in acting in favor of the plaintiff or the defendant (or against both, as is known with the news of the nomination to authorship) in civil procedure, can be one among many indices of how controversial the treatment of the parties in criminal procedure is, especially from the lessons of Giuseppe Sabatini. It is that, in criminal procedure, as it is often said, the official accuser does not have a *legal interest* of his own or of a defined third party, but purely an objective and social interest, hence the opinion that, among other arguments, does not consider him as a *party* in the process.

Although the fallibility of the argument is easy to prove—if it were not *part* it would not fit, logically or legally, the *assistance* to the Prosecutor's Office in criminal prosecution, and, as it is known both from the legal and logical plan, the assistant assists the *part* principal, hence the accusing body being *part*—provokes the evolution of this work. This is because the criminal process does not constitute a one-party process, in which the only party defending *interest* (in this case, self-interest) is the accused. The interest is the driving force of the procedural activity of the parties, whether on one side—the accuser—or on the other—the accused.

Once the notion of the opposing position in the process is established, even if not necessarily coinciding with the facts of life and with the connection to the good of material law over which it is disputed in the process, one can move on to the treatment of the parties in criminal proceedings.

3.3 The Concept of Part in Criminal Proceedings

If, on the one hand, the subsidies of civil procedural law assist in the theme when transposed to criminal proceedings, on the other hand, they permeate it with further difficulties arising from the distinct initial connection between those involved with a view to obtaining jurisdictional protection. After all, in criminal proceedings, there is the entrenched principle of the obligation of criminal action linked to the no less consecrated notion of official accusation. This, in turn, is accompanied by the unavailability of the object of the process as a dogma of criminal proceedings.[65]

The fundamental premise, as it comes from the doctrine of Giuseppe Guarneri and Giuseppe Sabatini, is that the concept of part in criminal proceedings also defines itself from a purely procedural perspective.[66] They are parts—here is the

[65]The idea of the unavailability of the object of the process, even before the news of PL n° 8.045/2010, was not unanimously celebrated. Coutinho (1989), p. 127, already in a study from the end of the 80s of the last century, not only reminded that "the unavailability, as it is seen, is not total," but also took his argument (that of unavailability) as "fallacious, poor."

[66]There are those who, like Schmidt (1957), p. 74, categorically deny the existence of the very concept of part in the criminal process, notably in view of what that revered German author Schmidt (2006), p. 74, understood to be the non-existence of any dispositive power as to the object of the process. The doctrine evolved in the sense of not tying the notion of *part* to another, affecting

lesson, still, from Chiovenda—the one who asks for jurisdictional protection, on one side, and the one against whom it is asked, on the other; in other words, and also for the criminal proceedings, the accuser and the accused.[67]

Brazilian doctrine, not without mentioning that it is a concept "of undeniable Chiovendian nature," points out that the part, in criminal proceedings, is the "qualifier given to people who ask or against whom jurisdictional protection is requested."[68]

It matters for criminal proceedings, as it is settled in the wide majority doctrine,[69] the notion of the initial request for opposed jurisdictional protection. In the language of Jorge de Figueiredo Dias—although with him one does not agree on the particularity of the treatment given to the Prosecutor's Office, as will be discussed later—the parties in criminal proceedings are the

> holders of opposing interests that are discussed in the process and are concretely at stake; accuser and accused will then be true contenders, in whose procedural activity opposing interests confront and whose procedural rights concretely come into conflict.[70]

In Brazil, the doctrine of Frederico Marques is eloquent, according to which "it is a nameless nonsense to talk about criminal proceedings, without there being parts. Only those who do not understand the function of the process in the realization of the punitive activity of the State can deny the Prosecutor's Office and the defendant the quality of parts."[71] Hence why it is denied, with emphasis on Guarneri, the concept that was then spread by Manzini, extracted by Romano-Di Falco, of part in a non-procedural sense, but only and solely *formal*. To such *formal part* would be who deduces the thing in court and the one against whom the thing is deduced in court, that is, the one who asks the judge for an application of the law in his own

---

the principle of disposition of the object of the process, which could configure the so-called *process of parts*. This is what Figueiredo Dias (2004), pp. 251–252, says when he recognizes the existence of the *parts*, but because there is, according to him, in Portuguese law, the freedom of disposition of the object of the process, a legitimate and authentic *process of parts*.

[67] Guarneri (1949), p. 23; Sabatini (1943), p. 159.

[68] Zanoide de Moraes (2000), pp. 237–238 and footnote no. 94.

[69] It is said to be the majority because one cannot disregard the lesson of Sabatini (1943), pp. 159 and foll., according to whom what qualifies the party in the process is not the opposition of interest, but the very procedural relationship animated by subjections and duties. Precisely for this reason, the peninsular author assumes that: "The notion of part, as it has been seen, is not in itself neither material nor formal, but a notion 'relational'" (p. 165). In the most recent Brazilian doctrine, also disagreeing with the very existence of the *interest* in criminal process, Oliveira (2013), pp. 102 and 444–446, denies not only such theoretical construction, but also the existence of the so-called *punitive claim* in the sense that the state can demand the subordination of a foreign interest to its own. For the author, the criminal procedural relationship is structured from a *state duty*, a *duty of action*: "in our opinion, and as it happens with jurisdiction, in which it is recognized to the holder of a materially allegedly injured or threatened right the right to move the Public State Power (Judiciary) for the resolution of the controversial situation, it is to recognize the community, in general, and the offended (holder of the legal good at risk or affected), in particular, the *right* to demand from the State the criminal action, when public, this becoming the position of debtor, then, of the addressing of the criminal case to Justice, for the purpose of applying the norms of Criminal Law."

[70] Figueiredo Dias (2004), pp. 245–246.

[71] Marques (2000a), p. 40. Consult also Lopes Júnior (2005), pp. 1–4.

interest or in the interest of the one he represents or substitutes, as well as the one against whom this same application is requested.[72]

Such a perspective, among us, followed by Eduardo Espínola Filho,[73] is relevant to the discussion because it privileges the treatment of part, notably with regard to the official accuser body and with regard to form. Still, it is imprecise from a procedural perspective, as it does not admit the opposition of positions between accuser and accused before the judge, insofar as it understands that the accuser's body acts with impartiality by representing the state,[74] i.e., *society*.

It is precisely with such impartiality that contradicts the procedural concept of part that we do not agree here. The part, for being so, is partial.[75] If it is impartiality that is dealt with, one may even be facing one of the procedural subjects—for example of the judge—but not a part. In addition to this, Manzini starts from the premise that, in criminal proceedings, only two concepts of part would be dealt with: a formal (external) and another material, "ontological, intrinsic."[76] It is, therefore, a perspective dissonant from the one adopted here.

Moreover, it is also Manzini's understanding that the Public Prosecutor, when acting in criminal proceedings, even if it is to deduce the accusation, part is only in a formal sense, since it asks for nothing in its own name. The action stems from being a state body in the exercise of the public function for the enforcement of objective law.

Now, when an accusation is made against the accused, the impartial side of the state is not pronounced,[77] and the very creation of the Public Prosecutor as a public

---

[72] Manzini (1996), p. 5. It is true that Marques (2000b), pp. 443–444, also took the Public Prosecutor as a "party in a formal sense," but there he wanted to refer only and solely to the subjection to the "procedural relationship," complemented by a party in a material sense, "for representing the State in the material relationship between this and the defendant." Such opinion was followed by Gomes Filho (1997), p. 150, who, in a doctrinal article, pondered that in the criminal process the activity of the Public Prosecutor as a party has two characteristics: "party in a formal sense, as a subject of the procedural relationship, and also in a material sense, because it represents the State in the substantial legal relationship between this and the accused."

[73] Despite the author having stated that the Public Prosecutor is part of the criminal action, it was said that "it is, however, only in a formal aspect, not losing its character as an organ of public power, whose interest is solely the rigorous investigation of the truth and punishment" (1965), p. 242.

[74] Guarneri (1949), p. 16.

[75] Guarneri, in at least two passages, spoke what is defended here. About this, it is enough to remember, from his work, that the accusing party is, for that very reason (that is: for being accusing), partial (1949, p. 145, footnote no. 3, and p. 165). In Brazil, authors like Oliveira (2013), pp. 460–461, argue that at least one of the parties in the criminal process (the Prosecutor's Office) is impartial. On the other hand, Ubertis (2008), p. 62, reminds us that such reasoning—the impartial party—even becomes an oxymoron.

[76] Manzini (1996), p. 5.

[77] The state, a person, or the entity that wants to stick to another established term, the *claim* (or interest) to punish someone, does it only because it has already valued the conduct, has already said that it does not agree with it, and wants, therefore, in the process, to impose a sanction. In this intention to punish, and for so operating with one of its official arms, there is absolutely nothing

and official body of criminal prosecution acts as a purposeful contradictor to the accused.[78] Hence, why to repudiate the existence of criminal proceedings as a single part (the accused or even the accuser[79]), as well as the structure of the criminal process is not based on the bipolarity of positions between who accuses and who defends against the accusation.

Indeed, if Guarneri said it was "unacceptable" for any theory that denied the existence of opposing parties in criminal proceedings,[80] among us and in a specific work, Hélio Tornaghi came to, when he mentioned the substantial conception of the concept of part, treat criminal proceedings as a process of a single part (the accused). Even so, when examining the widespread consecration of the procedural concept of part, the professor of the National Law School (current Law School of the Federal University of Rio de Janeiro) recognized that the parties in criminal proceedings are two and antagonistic: the accuser and the accused.[81]

It follows, therefore, a strictly procedural notion of part[82] also in criminal proceedings, especially because, if it were to recognize some coincidence between the satisfaction of material interest and the procedural, both would only coincide in the ownership of the defendant.[83] This shows the uselessness of adopting such a criterion not only in civil proceedings, but also in criminal proceedings.

It is assumed in the text that it is about the equality of arms when looking at the specific activity of the *party* in the process, and not that of the *subject* of the process.

---

impartial. And strangely, the same state is the persecutor of the punishment and the one that, there, yes, with an aura of impartiality, determines if it will be applicable or not. The state that accuses, but not the one that judges, has absolutely nothing, not a single tear, of impartiality.

[78] Guarneri and Dominioni take the Prosecutor's Office as a "natural contradittore dell'imputato" Guarneri (1949), p. 17; Dominioni (1985), p. 14.

[79] Tornaghi (1985), p. 161 and footnote no. 36, besides reminding those who admitted that in the criminal process there would not even be parties ("the accused is not a party but rather means of proof and the Prosecutor's Office is also not because it must act also in favour of the accused, when appropriate"), also reminded those who understood that the party would only be the accused, like Otto Mayer, or even, in an important footnote, dealt with the widespread conception that Manzini would have advocated for part in the process as only the accused when, in fact, he wanted to say that the Prosecutor's Office is part "in merely formal sense."

[80] Guarneri (1949), p. 16. It is worth mentioning, also, the exception of Sabatini (1943), pp. 141–146.

[81] Tornaghi (1985), pp. 161–163. As "parties in a procedural sense," there are, according to Tucci (2002), p. 186, the Prosecutor's Office and the accused.

[82] Deu (2007), p. 81, also follows a procedural notion of party in the criminal process, but formulates a broader concept, thus cast: "who acts in the process asking the jurisdictional body for a resolution jurisdictional; and who brings allegations, evidence, and material, as well as participates in the contradiction" (our translation).

[83] It is Figueiredo Dias (2004), pp. 242–243, who reminds us of the inappropriateness of transposing the "criminal-legal relationship in everything analogous to the private legal relationship," even because, if it were to follow the material notion of part, the relationship would not be between accuser and accused, but between state and accused, which is unthinkable. The same critical warning—but from a point of view with which we do not agree here because it seems to establish a relationship between *victim* and perpetrator of the crime and not between the *accuser* and the *accused*—is made by Tourinho Filho (2012a), p. 533.

This is because, as is known, if the judge is an impartial third party in the dispute that is brought to him to decide, he gets involved in the triangular relationship as a *subject*, but not as part.

The topographic exposition of the current Code of Criminal Procedure indeed makes it difficult to specifically address the parties in criminal proceedings.[84] And this has led the doctrine to, without greater foundations, treat those involved in the process who are not parties sometimes as "occasional and secondary subjects of the procedural relationship,"[85] sometimes as "secondary or accessory subjects," considered as those who "intervene in incidental procedural relations due to non-criminal order interests."[86]

The relationship that antagonizes accusation and defense is of interest, as this is where the parties in criminal proceedings are located. More than the subjection to contradiction in the process (with which, on the one hand, the dependence of the notion of the parties on the bilaterality of the knowledge of the acts of the process would be sharpened and, on the other hand, it would necessarily be taken as part who does not formulate a request for jurisdictional protection), the request and the reaction matter, both with a view to jurisdictional protection in criminal proceedings: who makes it and against whom it is made.

3.4 The Accuser

Historically, overcoming private revenge, in which the material parts were also the parts in the procedural sense, and it was up to the offended to deduce the accusation, the state arrogated to itself the monopoly[87] (or almost a monopoly[88]) of the prosecution.

[84] In Title VIII of Book I of the current Code, only the treatment of "judge, Prosecutor's Office, accused and defender, assistants and auxiliaries of justice" is provided.

[85] Aquino and Nalini (2009), p. 289. In the work, the authors separate the so-called "occasional subjects of the procedural relationship" (who posted bail in favor of the prisoner, the third party harmed, the assistant to the accusation) from the "secondary subjects of the procedural relationship" (witnesses, experts, assistants, translators, auxiliaries of justice).

[86] Marques (2000b), p. 445. The professor understands that the offended and the third party harmed are parties due to incidents of civil indemnification; the defendant's guarantor can be a subject if the bail incident is at stake.

[87] Tucci (2002), p. 63, recalls that the phase of *accusatio* in Rome—whose duration basically coincided with the republican period and declined along with it, when the principate was established in 27 BC—was characterized "precisely by granting the formulation of the *accusation* to any person, then considered representative of the public interest of the community."

[88] Given the reminiscence, in the Brazilian criminal procedural system, of the private criminal action of the offended, even with constitutional foundation, subsidiary to the public initiative (Art. 5°, LIX, of the Federal Constitution, and Art. 29 of the current Code of Criminal Procedure). Once again, we see how *partial* the state's action is when it accuses someone: if there is negligence by one of its representatives, the door is opened for the individual to reassume the *claim*, that is, to keep alive the *interest* in punishing someone. If the initiative of the official accusation were a dem-

As seen, also through the Brazilian historical review, that gradually the overcoming of the penal prosecution ex officio was achieved here. With this, we can anticipate a topic to be addressed in the next chapter: the presence of the accuser (notably official[89]) is indicative of the presence of the accusatory system in criminal procedure. Thus, at least one of its core characteristics is represented: the separation between *accusing* and *judging*.

The criminal accusation is, therefore, as a rule, an official task entrusted to a body of legal professionals for this purpose. In Brazil, just look at the current constitutional wording, which assigns to the Prosecutor's Office the promotion, in a private capacity, of public criminal action (Art. 129, I).[90]

As already seen, the constitutional exception of the criminal action initiated by the offended party subsidiary to the public initiative (Art. 5°, LIX), as well as the scattered provisions throughout infraconstitutional legislation about the hypotheses in which the criminal prosecution in court is deduced from the filing of a complaint (i.e., Articles 30–39 of the Code of Criminal Procedure of 1941 and, in the current Penal Code, the general rule of publicity of the initiative of the action criminal in Article 100 and its exceptions, for example, in Articles 145 and 225, without prejudice to reminiscences also in scattered laws, such as the case of Law No. 9.279/96, according to its Article 199).

The accuser is the one who initiates the lawsuit, who proposes the criminal action, and, therefore, on whom the entirety of the evidentiary burden falls. Upon initiating the judicial phase of criminal prosecution—and this is what is linked to the legal possibility of the request in the field of criminal procedure—he deduces a generic request for conviction. It is not required, in the criminal process of a condemnatory nature,[91] the success with a request for conviction to the payment of

onstration of the state's impartiality, there would be no room for the *punitive interest* to be safeguarded with the *reserve soldier*, who is the individual who enters the field when those who would have the aptitude to accuse do not accuse improperly.

[89] The accusation developed by a specific body is not, however, essential to the accusatory system. Tourinho Filho (2012b), pp. 102–106 and 113–114, gives an example of this, both in the passages about the Roman system, and, notably, when dealing with the "type of criminal process" he envisaged.

[90] The configuration was not always like this, and it is useful to evoke the lessons of Canuto de Mendes de Almeida. If, on the one hand, the professor pointed to an "artificial revival" of public power—given "a civic duty, by imposing penalties on offenders, or a duty of public officials, under penalty of civil and criminal liability. These officials, when specialized, constitute bodies of the so-called representatives of the Prosecutor's Office"—on the other hand, he recalled that the first mention of the necessary official accusation came from the already mentioned Law No. 261, of 1841, and Regulation No. 120, of 1842. According to Article 222 of the cited decree, "in cases where it is incumbent upon the prosecutor to denounce, it is also incumbent to promote the accusation and all the terms of the process, in which, as well as in the granting and arbitration of bail, he should always be heard." According to Almeida (1938), pp. 59 and 162–163, "the official action ceased to be supplementary to the inertia of individuals."

[91] After all, there are distinct protections in criminal procedure, not necessarily all condemnatory. Think, for example, of habeas corpus aimed at deconstructing a certain legal situation (indictment or precautionary arrest); also think of criminal review, which also has the power to declare-decon-

fines, to the annulment of acts, or even to the declaratory request, all plausible hypotheses in civil procedure. In criminal procedure, the success of the request (at least in criminal actions of condemnatory nature) always generates the conviction, with the judgment of the suitability, from there—to be modulated by the procedural subject who is the judge—among the penalties provided for the hypothesis, which one is applied and in what measure.

The empirical observation that the public or private accuser can, at the end of the criminal action moved by him, plead for the acquittal of the accused does not disqualify the procedural activity as being part of it.[92]

The final provision, moreover, is not given ex officio, but is the result of an activity that requires judicial pronouncement after the knowledge of the evidence, that is, of the arguments and explorations about facts brought to the contradictory and debated in it. Such activity is, necessarily, a party activity.[93] The peremption as a cause of the extinction of punishability resulting from the request for acquittal of the complainant (or the mere non-request for conviction). And this observation does not denature the action of the private accuser as a party.

Because it is commonly invoked a dual action of the official accuser in criminal procedure (Prosecutor's Office), namely, the accusation and the zeal for observance of the law, it is good to remember the pertinent lesson of Tornaghi:

> It may happen that during the process the MP is convinced of the innocence of the accused and asks for his acquittal. But the initial contrast, born with the complaint, remains, since the law does not exempt the judge from finding out the truth about the accusation and to condemn, if he understands that the defendant is guilty. [...] there is, therefore, no conflict between the impartiality that the MP must observe and its character as a party. Impartial he must be only in supervision, vigilance, zeal for the law. But this is just one of his functions and it is not the one he has as a party. As such, it is up to him to promote the application of the criminal law to the accused, to persecute him, to bring to the process all the evidence of

---

struct. When dealing, in this text, with criminal prosecution and the antagonism between accuser and accused, the general rule of public criminal actions is condemnatory, with exceptions running in each explanation ahead.

[92] Again, the criticism of Coutinho (1989), p. 133: "It is so incoherent and not advisable to request a conviction in the indictment, under penalty of altering the situation in the course of the process and, later, having to go back, a measure not very easy for some insecure, always hidden behind a curtain of inflexibility, of rigidity. Everyone knows that there is no demerit in this; the vast majority even confirms; but not everyone executes it in practice and, that initial request for conviction, generating a race to the necessary elements to enable conviction, ends up conditioning the agent - who is an organ and, therefore, a state, but is still a person - not to recognise, in the face of legal provisions, especially that translator of the *in dubio pro reo*, that the best decision is acquittal. Much of this comes from that unrealistic and unacceptable mentality of Leone, copied generally in our traditional doctrine without pruning its excesses, that the official accusation (the only one known today, in Italy), to a certain extent is blind, robotic, accusing even without reason, because that is its mission. Fortunately, lucid minds transformed - still under resistance - our Prosecutor's Office into a promoter of justice."

[93] Any jurisdictional provisions given ex officio, by nature, are exceptions to the consideration of party activity.

> his guilt, to draw the attention of the judges to the circumstances that may burden him, aggravating the penalty or qualifying the crime.[94]

This is linked to a distinct consideration: it is not by virtue of defending own or alien interest—or, perhaps, metaindividual—that the activity of the author of the demand is qualified as if it were part.

The issues related to procedural representation and specific to active legitimacy are not linked to those of the exercise of party: if the Prosecutor's Office offers a complaint in a case that is processed upon complaint, the indictment is received and, in the end, it is recognized that it lacks active legitimacy, part, however, it will have been throughout the entire arc of the criminal action. Even if, hypothetically, the eventual sentence that did not perceive the serious mistake of legitimacy is annulled, on appeal, the court cannot deny that, despite being part *illegitimate*, part will have been the Public Prosecutor's Office. And so, it will be because it has brought an accusation against someone.

Maurício Zanoide de Moraes is right to point out, in criminal proceedings, the distinctions between "procedural party," "legitimatio *ad causam*" (while the first is linked to the position in the process, the second refers to the power given to someone to occupy such a position) and, in his words, "from the combination of these two conceptions," the notion of "legitimate party," which

> merges, in a single institute, the structural need for the person reachable by the effects of the decision to appear in one of the procedural poles and, concurrently, for the effectiveness of the process, that that person is the one legally authorised to bear the jurigenic effects of the requested protection.[95]

Again, and to stick to the doctrine of Chiovenda brought to criminal process, it is said that "the parties are the one who formulates and the one against whom the accusatory claim object of the criminal process is formulated, according to the forms provided for in the criminal procedural norm and having as recipient the jurisdictional body."[96]

It is in the procedural situation and in the antagonism dictated by the rules of process—on one side, who imputes; on the other, who reacts to the imputation—insist that the criteria are established to say whether the public or private accuser is

---

[94] Tornaghi (1985), pp. 171–172.

[95] Zanoide de Moraes (2000), p. 240. The "legitimacy, in the process, is eminently bilateral, so that the author is legitimized, as a rule, to propose the action against that defendant, and not against another" (Armelin, 1979, p. 103). In criminal procedure, although there is a position that also separates between ordinary and extraordinary legitimacy (the Prosecutor's Office would be an ordinary legitimized in the case of public initiative criminal actions and the complainant, an extraordinary legitimized), it follows understanding according to which, being the actions of public or private initiative, the legitimations would be, in the cases, ordinary. The extraordinary legitimation in criminal procedure would exist only in the case of exercise of criminal action by the complainant, subsidiary to the Prosecutor's Office (when the ordinary legitimized would not have activated the jurisdiction). Even so, the case, according to Badaró (2025), pp. 204–205, would better fit in the category of subsidiary legitimacy, and not extraordinary.

[96] Lopes Júnior (2009), p. 5.

a party. And this raises another problem, namely: the presumption of advantage of the accusing party, be it public, as usually happens, or private, which is increasingly rare. The issue of equality of arms has already been raised, which will be dealt with in detail later.

The idea is widespread that the accusing party represents the state in criminal prosecution. Hence why, sometimes, under the conviction of enforcing the will of the law, under the one of making the return of or to prevail social peace, or under the repeated conception of seeking the truth, various coercive powers are established, varying between each criminal procedural system.[97]

In Brazil, if there was a time when the Public Prosecutor's Office, as accuser, was nothing more than representation led in the process by person directly appointed by the Head of the Executive Power and had contiguous attributions to those of the Judge of Law (Arts. 37 and ss. of the Code of Criminal Procedure of 1832), today the situation is very different.

Currently, the idea of requisition powers of the Public Prosecutor's Office (Law No. 8.625/93, Art. 26; Complementary Law No. 75/1993, Art. 7), as well as investigative powers in the criminal sphere (on which the plenary of the Supreme Federal Court has not yet spoken, but has already agreed with it more than once by a fractional body[98]).

Just look at the following attributions: to request a wiretapping measure (Law No. 9.296, Art. 3, II); to request preventive detention (Arts. 311 and ss., CPP); to request the initiation of a police inquiry (Art. 5, II, CPP); to offer an indictment (Arts. 40 and ss., CPP), to add to it (Art. 384, CPP) and even to add to the complaint if it deems it appropriate (Art. 45, CPP); to request property precautionary measures (seizure, *ex vi* of Art. 127, CPP, and, in specific cases, also the request for registration in legal mortgage and the arrest of movable property, under the terms of Arts. 134 and 137, combined with Art. 142, all of the CPP).

Logically, the attribution of such procedural opportunities results from the defense of the collective and transindividual interest in the criminal process, as it is important to society that the state has means as effective as legally possible to pursue and punish crimes and those who commit them. It is therefore justified that the accusing body is attributed a wide range of attributions so that the accusation can be brought in court in the best possible way.

From this, it can be seen, from the occurrence of the possible criminal act, that although technically one can only consider a party to exist with the proposition of

[97] To get an idea of how problematic and difficult it is to divide situations of advantage in criminal procedure, just remember the thinking of Andrade (2008), p. 173, with which this text does not agree. That scholar starts from the premise that the commission of the crime means an inequality of arms in favour of the accused. From this, then, according to him, an inequality of arms in the investigation *in favor of the State* is justified to "neutralise the initial advantage that the alleged criminal has in relation to the State itself."

[98] See, among the precedents of the STF on the matter, the *HC* No. 93.930, judged by the second chamber, under the rapporteurship of Minister Gilmar Mendes. There is extensive doctrinal research from both the rapporteur and Minister Celso de Mello, and a wide reference to other precedents of the Court on the matter.

the demand, the attributions to whoever will exercise the accusation are available even before the formalization of the procedural activity. After all, in the general rule of the officiality of the criminal action, the recipient of the information from any preliminary investigations is the Public Prosecutor's Office.[99]

With this, it is possible to anticipate a problematic point: the typical powers of the accusing party exist before it is formalized in the process, or in other words, they are prodromic. They exist even before it is constituted as part of the judicialization of the demand. This is what is often seen, in the Brazilian case, with police inquiries initiated and supervised by representatives of the Public Prosecutor's Office, administrative procedures in which there are even claims for the production of evidence search measures, now of personal or property precautionary measures.[100]

If the equality of arms is justified not only tied to the formalization of the party's activity in the process, but also by the idea of the consequence of procedural equality, it applies even before the party's activity is formalized.

Thus, it applies from the moment the antagonism of the interests at stake is qualified, that is, not only between accuser and accused, but between investigated and investigator, and even accuser. The result coming from the prodromic activities of the party, before the judicialization of the demand, can justify or remove the initiation of the criminal action. That is, at the moment when the concrete activity of accusing someone, of indicating someone as a target of investigation, or of precautionary measures during the preliminary phase, there is activity (atypical, considering that formally there is no accusation in court) of the party.

The equality of arms, which would be better implemented if there were the so-called process of parties, dispenses with this, to some extent,[101] because it detaches, at least in the scope of one of its premises, from the dependence on the beginning of the judicial phase of the criminal prosecution, given that it draws the first foundations of the constitutional distribution of opportunities in the process in a broad sense.

---

[99] Which, in our opinion, as long as the notion of equality of arms does not develop in the field of positive law and in the practical consequences of criminal investigation, makes it problematic to understand that there is no, according to Binding Precedent No. 234, of the STJ, impediment or suspicion of the prosecutor who has participated in the investigative phase and then comes to offer the indictment. By making his investigation, the Prosecutor's Office, before the process, not only approaches the investigative side typical of police authorities (behaves almost like a deputy delegate), but also anticipates, in the role of part of the criminal process, since it will be the same body to, in the future, initiate criminal action. In the field of bifrontal action (Art. 257, CPP), indeed, it is certain that such activity is not that of a law inspector, but that of a prodomal part.

[100] There is a detail that is intended to be studied in the course of this work: when requests for precautionary measures or others, in investigation, come from the Prosecutor's Office, their admissibility is not questioned. On the other hand, depending on the request, if it is the case of having come from the offended party, whether or not he was the formulator of the request for instigation of the inquiry, it is usually answered negatively in front of the a priori argument that, as there is no part in the inquiry, assistance is not considered. The argument, in light of the exercises of the activities of the part, makes no sense.

[101] In the sense of the text, see Sandermann (1975). pp. 43–44.

Observed the logical and ethical limits of the exercise of the accusatory and defensive activity, it is content with the definition of the roles of the involved, before and after they are formally established with their respective opposing interests.

3.4.1 The Public Accuser: Prosecutor's Office and Its Two-Faced Action in the Criminal Process

It is necessary to insist on the treatment of the theme in the light of the concept strictly procedural, without giving wings to variations of nomenclature (formal party, procedural party, material party).[102] Marcellus Polastri dealt with the theme in the Brazilian context: the Prosecutor's Office has the quality of a party depending on "the phase or act to be practised." For the author,

> the position of the Prosecutor's Office will vary, sometimes accentuating the quality of party and at other times that of *custos legis* or fiscal of laws. Therefore, the identification of the nature of the intervention of the *parquet* presupposes the verification of the phase of the criminal prosecution in which it acts.[103]

Hence, it can be noted that the two-face (or hybrid, as termed by Giulio Ubertis[104] and Carlo Taormina,[105] for context particularly like the Brazilian) Prosecutor's Office in the criminal process is not a harbinger, but, in fact, problematic.[106]

This is something that, moreover, results from the provision of Article 257 of the current Code of Criminal Procedure, which bifurcates the action of the Prosecutor's Office: while paragraph I provides for the private promotion of "public criminal action, in the form established in this Code," paragraph II determines the action with a view to "supervising the execution of the law."

If, on the one hand, here is repeated the lesson that one type of action does not inhibit the other,[107] on the other hand, the issue deserves to be deepened. After all,

---

[102] Abade (2005), pp. 56–57, without explaining, sometimes uses the concept of the Prosecutor's Office as "part in the legal relationship procedural" and sometimes as "material part in the criminal process." Oliveira (2013), p. 448, admits that the "procedural" part is the "procedural position" of someone in the process, while the "material" part is the one that would come with partiality in the manifestations of a certain subject.

[103] Lima (2007), p. 30.

[104] That author (2006), pp. 62–63, refers to the distinction of the Prosecutor's Office, in the Italian criminal procedural regime, as "institutional and professional placement"—to which its approximation with the magistracy and the duty of impartiality—and as "part activity" in the criminal process.

[105] The Italian professor spoke of an "ambiguous organisation of the function of the public prosecutor" (1992), p. 450.

[106] A similar criticism was made by Guarneri (1949), p. 149, when he looked at the scenario of the old Rocco Code. There, from the bipartite division of the performance of the Prosecutor's Office, the author advocated that the Prosecutor's Office should be invested in the activity of part and nothing more.

[107] Zanoide de Moraes (2000), pp. 281 and foll.

although organically one can imagine the coexistence of the two activities of the Prosecutor's Office in the criminal process (that of party and that of law supervisor[108]), functionally and in the development of each procedural situation, the defense of the two-faced action may prove impossible or at least legally inconvenient.[109]

On a practical level, it is worth considering the impossibility of action by the same body now as holder of the criminal action, now as *custos legis* in public criminal actions. Similarly, it is strange to issue an opinion in ongoing investigations in which there is the action of the same body (Prosecutor's Office) with anticipation of accusation acts, such as requests for personal and property precautionary measures.[110]

On the level of party activity, therefore, even if one strives to treat the Prosecutor's Office as an impartial party—which was done notably by Carnelutti[111]—the contradiction in terms cannot be underestimated.[112] Indeed, Rubens Casara emphasizes that

> the very origin of the Prosecutor's Office, an institution essential to justice, which emerged to remove the judging body from the accusatory functions and thus ensure the impartiality of the Judicial Agency, demonstrates the mistake of those who argue that the accusing body boasts the quality of impartiality. If the Prosecutor's Office arises to, in a qualitative leap, make the judging body equidistant from the interests at stake in the criminal case, that is, it is born to guarantee the impartiality of the Judicial Agency, how can it be expected that this body, with the constitutional assignment to accuse, also be impartial?[113]

---

[108] Double function that, moreover, there are no strong arguments enough to deny being also exercised by the opposing party: the defence. In the sense of what is exposed here, see: Casara (2011), p. 753.

[109] Toron (2003), p. 101, pointed out that the Public Prosecutor cannot *speak last* not even for the offering of oral opinion in courts, when one wants to convince that the accusing body only and solely acts as if *custos legis* was, nor by Cruz (2002), p. 98, nor by Casara (2011), p. 754. The criticisms of the authors cited still do not have acceptance in jurisprudence, which can be perceived from the judgment of STJ, in Habeas Corpus No. 825.180, in which the reporting minister Ribeiro Dantas, from the fifth Chamber, understood that the performance of the Prosecutor's Office as *custos legis* does not occur as a party, not giving rise to the contradictory (judgment published on August 31, 2023). The Supreme Federal Court, moreover, in the Appeal in Habeas Corpus No. 107.584, judged by the first Chamber under the rapporteurship of Minister Luiz Fux also understood that the dichotomy (between party and law enforcement) has justifications and that, therefore, "the performance of the Prosecutor of Justice from São Paulo, as *custos legis,* after the offering of counterarguments to the appeal by the Prosecutor, does not violate the principles of due process and the contradictory" (*DJe* 28.09.2011), a position that remains to this day, see *ARE* No. *1459568*, from the second Chamber, under the rapporteurship of Minister Gilmar Mendes, who followed the same understanding (judgment published on 12/11/2023).

[110] Note the example of, in a preliminary investigation, the Prosecutor's Office requests the suspension of the telephone secrecy of the investigated (Art. 3, Law No. 9.296/96), and this is the means of research of evidence, if obtained without a reasoned judicial decision that has supported the proof of materiality for the purposes of indictment. In this case, there is no reasonableness in taking the indictment as based on illegitimately obtained evidence (Art. 5, LVI, CF), to collect the opinion of the Prosecutor's Office as a law enforcer.

[111] Carnelutti (1953), pp. 257 and foll.

[112] Also, in the sense of this text, Aroca (2008), pp. 122–123.

[113] Casara (2011), p. 753. In the same critical sense of the approximation, even figurative, including between Prosecutor's Office and Magistracy, see: Taormina (1992), p. 451, last paragraph.

In this regard, a quick digression indicating the historical evolution of the Prosecutor's Office in Brazil is justified, at least since our first Code of Criminal Procedure.

If, on the one hand, Magalhães Noronha reminds us that the Prosecutor's Office, as it is outlined close to what is known today, is an institution contemporary to the Republic (Law No. 1.030, of 14 November 1890),[114] on the other hand, we cannot lose sight of the fact that the touted "impartiality of the party" was linked to the justification that, in the past, the Prosecutor's Office was part of one or more of the state powers.

Thus, while in the Constitution of 1891 the Attorney General of the Republic was "appointed" by the President of the Republic from among the members of the Supreme Federal Court (Art. 58, § 2), in 1934 the Prosecutor's Office was imagined as an anomalous body, entrusted with the "cooperation in government activities" (Chap. VI of the Federal Constitution of that year, Arts. 95–98[115]). In observation of the context of 1934, Pontes de Miranda took the Prosecutor's Office as "one of the heterotopic branches of the Executive Power."[116]

In the Constitution of 1937, the inclusion of the Attorney General of the Republic was repeated in parallel to the ministers of the Supreme Federal Court, of "free appointment and dismissal by the president of the Republic" (Art. 99), having been observed in doctrine, once again, that the institution was "tied to the Executive."[117]

With the Constitution of 1946, the Prosecutor's Office was dealt with in the chapter dedicated to the Judiciary (Arts. 125–128). In fact, for that reason, Walter Acosta said that the "Prosecutor's Office is an institution composed of agents of the Executive Power, who are part of the Judiciary, without, however, being subordinate to the hierarchy of the magistracy."[118]

Then, in the Constitution of 1967, subsequently amended in 1969, the Prosecutor's Office was again treated as a mere section inserted in the Constitutional Chapter addressed to the Executive Power (Arts. 94–96).[119]

Hence, for a long period, as inconceivable as it may be today, the Prosecutor's Office was housed as an arm of either the Judiciary or the Executive. In other words, as Hélio Tornaghi explained in a work about that time, "the Prosecutor's Office is a

[114] Noronha (1972), p. 133. In a similar sense, see: Gomes Filho (1997), p. 140.

[115] In that Constitution, if on one hand the dismissal *ad nutum* of the Attorney General of the Republic was perpetuated, equated, by the way, to the Ministers of the Supreme Court in the form of appointment and in earnings, for the so-called "members of the Public Prosecutor's Office created by federal law and serving in the common court" it was already foreseen the appointment preceded by competition and loss of positions after judicial sentence or administrative process with safeguard of broad defence (Art. 95, § 3°).

[116] Pontes de Miranda (1973), p. 407.

[117] Gomes Filho (1997), p. 141.

[118] Acosta (1957), p. 95. Strangely, in that context, as the author reports, in the Federal District, the initial position of the Public Prosecutor's Office in the Federal District was that of public defender, and one acceded to the position of public prosecutor by seniority and merit (p. 97, footnote no. 78).

[119] Antonio Magalhães Gomes Filho reports that, in the Constitution of 1967, the Public Prosecutor's Office was linked to the Judiciary; in that of 1969, to the Executive (1997), p. 141.

link between the Executive and the Judiciary, it is a representative of the former next to the latter."[120]

That is why, as Magalhães Noronha reminds us, the Prosecutor's Office "in the criminal process is a party, as master of the action: it proposes it, enumerates and provides the evidence, fights and strives for the final triumph of the punitive claim, which will be proclaimed by the Judge against the accused. It participates, therefore, in the Judgement—*actum trium personarum*—where there are author, defendant and Judge"; on the other hand, it is only an impartial party, since it represents "the State-Administration, exposes to the State-Judge the claim based on the *jus puniendi*."[121]

With a focus on the current placement of the Prosecutor's Office from the constitutional dictation and in the recovery of the equality of arms, the double ministerial performance in the process is unfeasible: one as author and another as guardian of the law.

There is even a more subjective perspective of assimilation of the (false) idea that the Public Prosecutor's Office, given the aura of impartiality, can often be seen as endowed with the same reason that guides judicial reasoning. Thus, "by believing in the impartiality of the Public Prosecutor's Office, the judge's equidistance from the parties disappears and, consequently, the very impartiality of the Judicial Agency."[122]

At the same time, advancing a little in what will be discussed later, the very act as a *custos legis* should disappear from the context of criminal actions that are not typically of private initiative of the offended. Hence, the assumption of the representative's action as *part* and the knowledge that those involved will bring to the jurisdictional bodies.

In the accusatory criminal process, insofar as the activity of judging separates from that of accusing, it makes no sense to consider the Public Prosecutor's Office either as *an organ of justice* or as *an assistant to the judge*.

It is salutary to the complementary notion of the accusatory process that separating who accuses from who judges implies separating, also, who *judges* from who *accuses*, that is, if the judicial activity cannot disguise itself as an accuser, the reciprocal is also true, and, among the auxiliary bodies of the court, the Public Prosecutor's Office is not included.

Moreover, it has already been said that the exercise of the activity of party—and this applies both to the Public Prosecutor's Office and to the complainant in criminal actions brought by private initiative—implies partiality.[123]

---

[120] Tornaghi (1985), p. 141.

[121] Noronha (1972), p. 133.

[122] Casara (2011), p. 746. The procedural situation becomes—frankly, inequality—the following: on one side, the judge and the prosecutor bearers of the same ideal *impartial* representation of the state against crime; on the other, the accused of the practice of the crime that it is up to the state to punish.

[123] It is true that Marques (2000a), p. 41, is more cautious when dealing with this and remembers that what "characterizes the concept of part is not partiality or impartiality, but the ownership of own rights in relation to the content of the process, and the opposition to the function of resolving

Impartiality, even in the activity of *custos legis*, does not fit with the connection, in the records, of activity in judgment or that has resulted from an act performed by the same accusing body.

It is necessary to avoid the partial residue in the activity of *custos legis* in criminal actions that are not handled, privately, by the offended. After all, if there is no controversy about the activity as *part*,[124] regarding the other, as *custos legis*, there is a risk of favoring the old understanding that the body of the Public Prosecutor's Office could behave as *an organ of justice*,[125] or, in the language of Figueiredo Dias, "an administration body," "with the particular function of collaborating with the court in the discovery of truth and the realisation of law."[126]

The position of Figueiredo Dias, followed by authors such as Julio Maier,[127] is read with reservations, because it does not follow the line according to which the action of the Public Prosecutor's Office in the criminal process can be considered as an adjacent part of the Judiciary.

The action of the Public Prosecutor's Office as an annex to the Judiciary for the prosecution of the same ends[128]—even though what is called impartiality for judges is referred to as objectivity for prosecutors—is unnecessary, technically incorrect (there are express provisions, in any criminal procedural order, of who are the auxiliary bodies of the court) and, contrary to what is imagined, implies a *capitis deminutio*: it places the Public Prosecutor's Office as a mere helper of a procedural subject who is the judge.

In the words of Frederico Marques, the thought here criticized barely hides a "*bis in idem* entirely dispensable and useless." For that proceduralist, in what seems to be right, "in the accusatory procedure, the prosecutor must act as a party, because, if not, the repressive function of the State will be weakened."[129] And as Tornaghi affirms, the same reasoning would not disguise a "useless duplication."[130]

In addition to the duplication without reason to be, there seems to be, behind the defense of the action of the Public Prosecutor's Office as *custos legis*, a temptation to act even as *amicus curiae*, something that is unknown in the criminal process and that is not justified in the light of the non-specificity of the matters that claim such

---

the conflict of interests and judging." Taormina (1992), p. 460, points out: "*there is no act of the public prosecutor or the judicial police that does not arise with a predisposition to assume full evidentiary relevance.*"

[124] Like Tornaghi, Frederico Marques (2000a), pp. 41–42, understands that it does not denature the attitude of part the mere possibility of a request for acquittal or even the non-appeal against an acquittal decision.

[125] Expression, by the way, in the lesson of Chiavario (1971), p. 718, is nothing more than a *slogan* that can serve both positions said to be democratic, as well as conservative or reactionary in criminal procedure.

[126] Figueiredo Dias (1988), pp. 25–26.

[127] Maier (2004), pp. 581–582.

[128] Opinion that was, to some extent, esteemed by Espínola Filho (1965), p. 242.

[129] Marques (2000a), p. 41.

[130] Tornaghi (1985), p. 172.

action. If it were to emerge from there, the activity of the Public Prosecutor's Office, distinct from that of the party, would necessarily have to admit the intervention of other legitimate bodies as *amici*.

It is argued, at this stage, that the recognition of the Public Prosecutor's Office's action in the criminal process is typical[131] or primarily,[132] as being part of, and not as, additionally, a tutor of the supervision of the application of the law.[133]

3.4.2 *The Private Accuser: The Offended in the Criminal Action of Strict Private Initiative and in the Criminal Action of Private Initiative Subsidiary of the Public*

Reminiscence of times of the criminal process dictated by private interests,[134] with the private accusation, it is about the other accusing party: the private one, sometimes associated with the offended party, sometimes to whoever takes his place.

Even if some distinction is noted in the matter at the doctrinal level—while Tornaghi does not necessarily link the offended to the "passive subject of the crime,"[135] Tourinho says exactly that, "offended, or victim is the passive subject of the criminal offence"[136]—the fact is that, in criminal actions of private initiative of the offended, a new accuser is opened: the private accuser. In the words of Tucci, the most notable distinction of this category before the previous one rests on the difference of the subjective criterion: "while this is moved by the Public Prosecutor's Office, in that the holder of the action (*action of the party*) is a private individual, that is, the exercise of the right to act and to accuse is transferred to the passive subject of the crime."[137]

For the present work, it matters that, with the exercise of the criminal action by the offended party (whether it is a criminal action typically of private initiative, or

---

[131] What is otherwise seen in comparative criminal procedural law, notably the Italian (on this subject: Conso and Grevi, 2008, p. 59), and also in the peninsular criminal process (Chiavario, 2007, pp. 12–13). Also: Taormina, Carlo. The process of parts in front of the new regime of contests and trial readings, cit., p. 460, last paragraph. Of course, the suggestion indicates the need to, in Brazil, remove the possibility of impediment or suspicion of members of the Prosecutor's Office, which is seen from the final part of Article 258 of the current code.

[132] Tornaghi's lesson (1985), p. 171, is: "this last [the function of accusing] is its main attribution, since the process is organized in a contradictory form."

[133] Nor is the broad notion of part in the criminal process of the Prosecutor's Office accepted, even though in procedural criminal action, of "organ of protection of constitutional public freedoms, of defence of individual or collective rights and the guarantee of the very criminal contradiction" defended by Abade (2005), p. 65.

[134] Tucci (2002), p. 135.

[135] (1985), p. 178.

[136] Tourinho (2012a), p. 543.

[137] Tucci (2002), p. 133.

subsidiary resulting from the inertia of the state body), the range of procedural chances is expanded, given the acquisition of the quality of *party* in the process. Accusing party, as much as the official of whom was previously spoken of.

It is important to highlight, also, situations in which the exercise of the private accusation is shown in the criminal process, which should be done with the same attention already indicated, that is, without clinging to the form of the criminal action initiated with the complaint, but rather to the content of the determination of the attribution of a criminal fact to someone.

It is worth mentioning, in this regard: the request for the initiation of the police inquiry (Art. 5, II, CPP); any and all requests that may to be formulated before the police authority in the case of existing police inquiry (Art. 14, CPP), in the typical forms of private criminal action (the private one of the offended, in the terms of Art. 30, CPP, and the subsidiary of the public, in the terms of Art. 29, CPP); the specific applications of institutes of forgiveness (Art. 49, CPP) and renunciation (Art. 50, CPP); the cases of peremption (Art. 60, CPP); the requests for measures securities (seizure, Art. 127, CPP; specialization of legal mortgage legal, Art. 134, CPP; arrest, Arts. 137 and 142, CPP); the request for the execution of search and seizure (Art. 242, CPP); and even the request for the decree of preventive detention measure (Art. 311, CPP).[138]

3.5 The Accused

With fidelity to the premises of his own work, which are useful to this text, Guarneri, when dealing with the accused, once again resorted to Chiovenda to remember that, if the party is the one against whom a declaration of right is requested in court, the accused is, undoubtedly, a party in the process.[139] The accused is, in the language of Tourinho Filho, "the procedural subject against whom the application of Criminal Law is requested."[140]

It is the other side of the coin, in the polarized and necessary[141] connection there is with the accuser: to the accuser corresponds who bears the accusation; the accusation needs the subject to impute a certain conduct and, only thus, to request the protection jurisdictional. After all, one does not just accuse someone *of*

[138]As mentioned, there are precautionary measures in the criminal process that are exclusive to the Prosecutor's Office, such as the request for telephone interception. The dissonance of legitimacy to move them is strange, given the possibility that, in a private criminal action of the offended, the search for evidence may also be necessary.

[139]Guarneri (1949), p. 177.

[140]Tourinho Filho (2012a), p. 549. In this regard, Armelin (1979), p. 102, says: "The passive legitimacy comes from the circumstance of being situated as obliged, that is, in the passive pole of the material right obligation that is intended to be enforced in court."

[141]Deu (2007), p. 91, in this sense, reminds us that the accused is the "necessary passive party against whom the criminal action is exercised and, definitively, the criminal process is directed."

something; one accuses *someone* of having committed or failed to commit a certain penal relevant conduct. Accused and accuser are the two sides—equal, to the best extent that can be justified—of the set of legal situations that occur in the process.

In this regard, Tornaghi reminds us that the accused is the so-called "weaker party"—the reason "the ordinances that love justice try to surround him with all guarantees." Hence, still in the words of the professor from Rio, "a Penal Procedure Code is made, above all, to guarantee the accused."[142]

In the opposition of interests protected between the accuser and the accused is where the relevance of the study of the principle of equality of arms manifests, as both act in the sense of trying to convince the magistrate of the correctness of their respective theses.

It is in the polarity of the relationship, therefore, that not only the distribution of procedural chances and opportunities is shown, but, particularly for the activity of the party with a view to equality of arms, the possibility of convincing the magistrate. To deal with this presupposes, as was done with the accusation, making a technical distinction between the phases in which there is formally an accused in the criminal process and that other, preliminary, in which only an investigated person is considered.

3.5.1 Accused (Strict Sense) and Imputed (Broad Sense)

Based on the notion of party as the active or passive side of the demand—that is, the one who brings the accusation against someone or the one on whom the accusation falls—in the strict sense, there is only an accused once the procedural legal relationship is defined, with the receipt of the complaint or charge.

In the language of Frederico Marques, "accused or defendant is the name given to the person to whom the practice of a crime or misdemeanour is attributed, in a complaint, charge or order with which the criminal procedure is initiated before an authority invested with jurisdictional functions."[143] Only then is the subjective side (active and passive) of the criminal cause stabilized.

But the strict concept of the accused in the criminal process, as thus presented, in the strict connection of the activity of the party with the characteristic of being placed as the passive side of the imputation,[144] does not meet the demands to give to

---

[142] Tornaghi (1985), p. 181.

[143] The professor's lesson echoes, with the caveat that there has been no judicially formed procedure in Brazil since 1988 (provided for in the rite of the old so-called summary process, Articles 531–540, of the Code of Criminal Procedure, later entirely reformulated by Law No. 11.719/2008) considered as the mentioned one that started with an ordinance and ran before authorities other than judges. In the sense of the text, see: Gomes Filho (1997), p. 145.

[144] Greco Filho (2009), p. 237, follower of this direct link between party and imputation, reminds us that the "accused is the natural person, over 18 years old, to whom the practice of a criminal infraction is imputed." The lesson does not seem accurate to us. It is possible for someone—a legal

the passive subject of the criminal prosecution all the range of guarantees constitutionally provided. And, for this work, such a concept neither justifies the incidence of equality of arms in the best possible way, as will be seen later.

Given that the accusation has as its essential core, as stated by Antonio Scarance Fernandes, the "attribution of a criminal offence to someone," it is necessary to think about this attribution from another perspective, namely, that based on a precarious judgement—and not addressed to the court—of such attribution of the alleged crime to someone. That is why we talk about imputation,[145] which technically differs from the act of accusing, not only because of the recipient of the judgement (in one case, the judge; in the other, the authority presiding over the preliminary investigation), but, as it is taught, also due to the escalation of degrees of legal certainty about the authorship of a certain crime.[146]

That is why, in criminal process, we talk about the accused—with reference to the strict notion already mentioned—and about the investigated or, in the language of the code itself, indicted (e.g., Art. 6°, V, and Art. 14, CPP). While the first word—*accused*—is technically linked to the criminal cause brought to court with a received complaint or charge, the latter words are directed to the concept of imputation, broader than that of accused.[147]

Indeed, the criminal prosecution is carried out in two phases and guarantees are provided to the investigated not only depending on the initiation of the so-called procedural phase—that in which the demand is formalized with a complaint or charge—but also during the phase that precedes it: that of the investigation itself.

If the very Article 14 of the still valid Penal Procedure Code would argue against the thought, as repeated as it is retrograde that "the investigation phase develops without the participation of the defence,"[148] only an exaggerated attachment to the formula allows the exercise of defensive and reactive activity to the burden of the

---

entity included, as in the case of the practice of a possible environmental crime, under the terms of Law No. 9.605/98—to face the accusation, even if later it is said to have been unwarranted, as in the case of the unimputable and the minor under 18 years old. Here, Dinamarco's didacticism (2024), p. 289, seems to have relevance, once the teratology of the example of civil process to criminal is transposed: "a case that is almost caricature, but illustrates well the distinction, is that of the mother-in-law who, displeased with the son-in-law, proposes against him a judicial separation action. But she is not a party in the conjugal society that the separation sentence would dissolve. Consequently, she is not a legitimate party. Even so, having taken this absurd initiative, *she is a procedural party* and as such will be treated." Absurd indictment made against the unimputable, or the teenager? Yes. But if they are a party, while the situation lasts, they will be manifestly illegitimate.

[145] Fernandes (2002), p. 105.

[146] This is the understanding of Marta Saad (2004), p. 237.

[147] "The accusation is not confused with the imputation, because before the accusation is formulated, with the complaint or complaint, there was already imputation during the investigation, considering that in the indictment the fact investigated was attributed to someone as its probable author" (Fernandes, 2002, p. 153).

[148] Oliveira (2013), 446.

criminal prosecution, depending on the initiation of the procedural phase of criminal prosecution.

It is because there are, as is known, preferably in the investigative phase, not only various activities that indicate that the involved person is already suffering the effects of the criminal procedural coercion,[149] as notably precautionary measures that indicate a certain person to be the target of the allegation to be deduced, at an imminent moment, in court.[150]

Thus, it is seen, for example, with all measures of a patrimonial nature—sometimes anticipatory of future damage repair, supported in *fumus comissi delicti* and *periculum in mora* without the connection with such repair.

Also, with personal precautionary measures—in which, as exemplified by preventive detention, a "sufficient" indication of authorship is required (Art. 312, CPP); with various means of evidence search (searches and seizures, when, for example, a "founded suspicion" of the concealment of something, cf. Art. 240, § 2°, CPP; measures of telephone interception, in which the presence of "reasonable indications of authorship or participation in criminal offence," according to Art. 2°, I, of Law n° 9.296/96).

The exercise of the reactive activity to the ongoing allegation (activity of defendant in the strict sense, if after the criminal action has begun, with the formalization of an accusation) or to the charge already formulated in preliminary investigation (activity of defendant in the broad sense, given the scenario of mere investigation) does not depend, therefore, on the offering of the indictment or of the complaint. And not even on the declaration in the records of the formalization—exclusive to the act of the authority presiding over the preliminary investigation—of the legal situation, from a certain procedural moment, of the situation of someone being indicted.

Hence, it is commendable that the proposal, then formulated by Professor Hélio Tornaghi, in the Code of Criminal Procedure, projected the figure of the *almost-accused*. There, with the care of, on the one hand, evidencing the inquisitiveness of the investigation (accusation or defense acts would not be allowed, except for requests that would facilitate "objective investigation, of the fact or authorship"—Art. 11), on the other hand, he dealt, in Article 78, single paragraph, with a character

[149] The criminal prosecution, whether in the first or second phase, contains acts of "criminal procedural coercion," which are, in the language of Pitombo (1973), pp. 108–109, "those of restrictions to rights, practiced in the interest of the process, or as to the assurance of instruction, or as to the guarantee of possible and useful future judgment, or, still, as to the safeguarding of execution." They are, according to the professor, those of personal physical coercion (of which prison is an example) or psychic (as evidenced by the notification), real physical coercion (seizure) and psychic (order of display), restrictive criminal procedural coercion of the physical inviolability of the person (search) and criminal procedural coercion of other rights (censorship of correspondence and violation of secrets) (phase typically police as a later decision-making basis, see, in comparative law, article by Andrade (2009), p. 529.

[150] Fernandes (2002), p. 153.

equated to the accused insofar as he came to suffer "any act of coercion, real or personal, before the indictment or complaint."[151]

Even though the current Code of Criminal Procedure has not been so clear about this important matter, it is worth remembering that, in addition to the idea of the Rio de Janeiro professor, in comparative law there is a fruitful example of equating the activity of a party (therefore, in the assumption of a lawsuit filed in court) to the first phase of criminal prosecution (therefore, typically investigative), especially with the Italian Code of Criminal Procedure.

The author said that, in cases of *almost-accused* or, as stated in *The criminal procedural relationship*, *almost imputatus*, "the procedural relationship only exists *pro reo*. In other words: it is to reap the benefits of the legal relationship that he is attributed the quality of accused."[152]

In the current Italian Code of Criminal Procedure (Decree n° 447, of 22 September 1988), as can be seen from Article 61, the "rights and guarantees of the accused" are equated to the person who is placed in the preliminary investigation.

And this is explained by Ubertis in the sense that, although one could even say that someone is *accused* of a criminal practice when the object of the criminal settlement is fixed (that is, when the indictment is offered), it is necessary to safeguard the right to defense even in the preliminary phase, to what in Italy is called *indagato*.[153]

The accused in criminal proceedings, according to the broad notion that follows, is, therefore, whoever suffers the proper accusation and poured into the narrative in the indictment or complaint (narrow sense, hence being *formally accused* of the practice of a certain offence, as it is communicated to the court), or who, in the preliminary phase, suffers the accusation directed at it, either with investigative measures devoid of precautionary nature (for example, determination of indictment), either with measures of evidence search (searches, seizures, interceptions), or with personal or real precautionary measures (broad sense, which encompasses the notion, strict, of investigated and indicted, since these two figures technically only exist in the first phase of criminal prosecution).

In this regard, Scarance is right when he states:

> before the formal accusation, there can be an identical judgement, attributing to a certain person the responsibility for the fact ascertained and subjecting it to restrictions, sometimes severe such as imprisonment. There is no sense in limiting the accusation to the procedural phase, it being of utmost importance, in a democratic state, to ensure the person considered the probable author of the criminal offence means to act in his defence. Therefore, it is

[151] Tornaghi (1985), p. 185, said: "when the indictee suffers a restriction of a legal good (freedom, property or any other), the law allows him to defend it immediately, thus equating him to the accused for this effect." He disagreed with the professor because he understood that the conceptual construction of the accusation is something to be achieved from the escalation of degrees of legal certainty to link an author to a fact, Saad (2004), p. 237.

[152] Tornaghi (1985), p. 186.

[153] Ubertis (2008), pp. 64–65.

essential that we work with an expanded concept of accusation and admit there is an accused (indicted, investigated), with rights and duties, from the investigation phase.[154]

3.6 Third-Party Intervention in Criminal Proceedings: The Prosecution Assistant

The third party, while not *intervening* in the pending case, *is not a party*. However, as this happens, they can become *a party*; this depends on the possibility that the law grants them to sue or, on the contrary, to suffer the effect of passive subjection in the case. These are therefore more than speculative concepts: as indicated by Dinamarco's passage, such concepts are antithetical at least insofar as *a third party*, while not intervening, *is not a party*.

The intervention known in criminal proceedings is that of assistance to the prosecution, a spontaneous third-party intervention,[155] which was equated by Frederico Marques to the joinder of parties provided for in the old Civil Procedure Code of 1939[156] and, more specifically, taken by Hélio Tornaghi as "joinder assistance" given that the intervention occurs *ad coadjuvandum tantum*.[157] Here, we partially agree with Tornaghi.[158]

Firstly, we disagree with Frederico Marques' position because it is based on the equivalence that the Civil Procedure Code of 1939 (Decree-Law No. 1608, of September 18, 1939), in its Article 93, made between assistant and joinder.[159] Such difference ceased to exist with the Civil Procedure Code of 1973, which, although it dealt with both figures in the same chapter (Book I, Chap. V), discussed them in separate sections (to joinder was reserved in sect. I, Arts. 46–49; to assistance, in sect. II, Arts. 50–54).

---

[154] Fernandes (2002), p. 104. It is worth mentioning, still in the wake of what the author preaches, that "not always the judgment of external attribution is expressed by a certain and determined act, being able in the investigation to show itself by the way the suspect person is treated in various manifestations of police authority" (p. 102). Thus, it is the empirical observation (e.g., if so-and-so is the *target* of wiretapping, if against such-and-such a precautionary prison measure is pending), and not the way the investigation presents itself—since it can, eventually, camouflage acts of attribution behind the non-ostentatious documentation of such a value judgment—that indicates the existence of an act of attribution. This is also the opinion of Saad (2004), pp. 261–265.

[155] Xavier de Albuquerque (1966), p. 91. The author understood, in the doctrinal article, that, "as a form of third party intervention, the assistance in the civil process does not fundamentally differ from the assistance in the criminal process."

[156] Marques (2000b), p. 304.

[157] Tornaghi (1985), p. 175.

[158] The prosecution assistant is neither one thing nor another: neither litisconsort, nor litisconsortial assistant. The assistance is *simple*.

[159] Article 93: "When the sentence is to influence the legal relationship between any of the parties and a third party, this one may intervene in the process as an assistant, equated to the litisconsort."

The technique of civil procedural law justified the separation of institutions also because in the joinder there is a "communion of rights or obligations in relation to the dispute," or the same factual or legal root of the existence of rights, connection between causes or, still, "affinity of questions by a common point of fact or law" (Art. 46). Hence, if in the joinder there is an accumulation of parties in the exercise of main activity in the process, this is unthinkable in assistance.

Indeed, whether in simple assistance (Art. 50), or in joinder (Art. 52), the assistant *assists* the *main party*. They are, therefore, a supporting actor in the procedural relationship (and if we are using the terminology of civil procedure, given its consecration in that scope) already established, but not expanded with the intervention in the pending (civil) dispute.

The doctrine of civil procedure, once again, helps in understanding the assistance, even for criminal proceedings. This is because, in the lessons of Dinamarco,

> the admissibility of the joinder presupposes the legitimacy of each of the co-litigants (or of all, jointly, when it comes to necessary joinder), which is nothing more than an elementary imposition of the general rule of legitimacy *ad causam* contained in art. 6 of the Civil Procedure Code.[160]

In a word, only those who have the *legitimacy* to act as *a party* in the process are co-litigants.

Now, the reasoning applied to criminal proceedings leads to rejecting the view of assistance as something equivalent to joinder, especially because the intervention only fits in *public action* and by those who would not have the legitimacy to move it, since it is an attribution of exclusive legitimacy to the Public Prosecutor's Office (Art. 129, I, CF).

There is no possibility for expanding active legitimacy in the criminal case, and, for this reason, one cannot consider the assistance to the accuser as equivalent to that of a party.

That is why we should partially agree with Tornaghi, in the sense that the *assistance* in criminal proceedings neither confuses nor approaches the *joinder*. In fact, the joinder—"necessary" active joinder, in the words of Antonio Magalhães Gomes Filho[161]—in criminal proceedings, only exists in the case of Article 29 of the current Brazilian Procedural Code.

There is only active joinder of parties (and it will be necessary), then, in a criminal action of private initiative subsidiary to that of public initiative in the extent that it allows the Public Prosecutor not only to "amend the complaint, reject it and offer a substitute indictment," but, notably, "resume the action as the main party."[162]

---

[160] Dinamarco (2000b), p. 50. Strictly in the same sense, in civil procedural doctrine, see Bueno (2006), pp. 161–163, and Carneiro (2010), pp. 195–196.

[161] Gomes Filho (1997), p. 151.

[162] The legislative treatment given to such behaviour of the Public Prosecutor helps to reinforce the conclusion that the body cannot act as a two-headed entity in the criminal process: when (re) assuming the ownership of the criminal action—which has always been of its exclusive exercise, but only managed by the offended due to the unreasonable initial inaction—as a party, there is no sense in supposing that, until the moment of the resumption of the ownership of the criminal action

Hence, it is fundamental, once again, to work with the procedural notion of the party: the concept is detached from the material claim or, in other words, from the concrete proximity between the imputed conduct and the request made in court.[163]

This is noticeable on the active side of the criminal action, where, as already seen, being the criminal action initiated by the victim or by public initiative, there is no consideration of dependence on the material relationship with the crime for the provocation of jurisdiction. The remaining cases of criminal action, typically of private initiative, are exceptions that confirm the rule here repeated.

And, unlike the civil procedural plane, in which active legitimacy is treated in its eminently procedural aspect with a view to the interests at stake,[164] in criminal proceedings, the guidance to the legitimacy of the action is constitutional: the rule is the exclusive ownership of the Public Prosecutor's Office (Art. 129, I).

Consequently, the reasoning of civil procedural law that admits the bifurcation of the assistance modality (simple or joinder) cannot apply to criminal proceedings. The lesson speaks too much: in the case of joinder assistance, the assistant

> can confront the will of the assisted, appealing when this one does not want the appeal, proving when this one dispenses the proof, excepting the forum or the judge when he accepts the competence or considers absent any cause of suspicion or impediment. In addition, those powers of disposition of the main party referred to in art. 53 (recognition, transaction, renunciation, withdrawal), which will depend on the concurrence of the will of the joinder assistant for the dispositive acts to have effectiveness.[165]

It is unthinkable to distinguish the figures of assistance to the prosecution in criminal proceedings, because the ownership of the public criminal action derives not from procedural technique (which occurs in the scope of civil procedural law), but from the constitution, which attributes it in a private character to the state, represented in the procedural plane by the Public Prosecutor's Office.

---

the body acted as *custos legis* and, from the event provoked by the offended, should act, just for that, as *party*. The Public Prosecutor is a party. *Party* inactive as it was, resumes the case as a result of the natural exercise of the constitutional function of accusing. It seems, still, and therefore, from *joinder*, strangely, one could only consider in the case of amendment of the complaint (Art. 29, CPP). The others there provided (reject, offer indictment, provide evidence, appeal and reassumption as main party) are either unintelligible (What is a *rejection* of a complaint by part of the author of the public criminal action? What procedural consequence does such manifestation have? What is the judge to decide, if this is the case?), or are natural consequences of the substitution of the active pole of the criminal action.

[163] Regarding this, Badaró (2009), pp. 138–139, says, "The Public Prosecutor is not the holder of the right to punish, which belongs to the State. The Public Prosecutor has been given, only, the ownership or legitimacy for the proposal of the criminal action. Such power, however, simply derives from the law, regardless of the ownership of the 'material right' debated in court, in this case, the 'right to punish'. Thus, only in the sense of being the holder of the procedural claim put in court, can the Public Prosecutor be considered an 'ordinary legitimated'."

[164] Just remember, in the evolution of the related doctrine, of notions like *adequate representation* and the various and always more varied situations provided for in scattered laws of extraordinary legitimation in the field of civil procedural law.

[165] Dinamarco (2000b), p. 61.

There is no room, therefore, for the exercise of criminal action or its consequences (e.g., filing of appeals, request for application of precautionary measures) exclusively by the assistant or, on the contrary, by the position of the assisted body.

And for this reason, it is that, as already anticipated, we agree, but only in part, with Tornaghi.

Adopting the premise, in the activity of simple assistance in criminal proceedings, it is noted that, in doctrine, sometimes the reason for the intervention in aid of the Public Prosecutor, as the main party (position of Tornaghi,[166] Frederico Marques[167] and Espínola[168]), or it is indicated that the motive is in guarantee of indemnification of the damage *ex delicto* (firm position of Tourinho Filho[169]), or, still, in both situations jointly (lesson of Vicente Greco Filho[170]).

There is also another position, which is not followed here, according to which the reason for the assistance to the prosecution in criminal proceedings would be, given to be the performance as *custos legis*, in function of the particular perspective of the civil claim brought to the criminal process,[171] with which the intervention would be justified on the plane of equality of arms between the accused and accuser.

As we adopt an abstract perspective of the treatment of the assistant in criminal proceedings as a supporter of the official accuser, such a process does not take care of the remote interest of the assistant, be it civil reparation, be it the soundness of the jurisdictional provision. This is especially true because, if the second hypothesis is admitted, the assistant to the Public Prosecutor's Office would behave as an uninterested subject in aid of an interested subject, which would not make sense.[172]

Now, whoever assists the one who represents the ownership of the exercise of the power to punish someone has no other motive than to aim, also, to punish him, even if the indirect interest of the assistant is not purely and simply the exercise of punitive pretension, but moral or economic. The first, and what he brings to the process, is to assist the main, that is, to punish.

---

[166] The "legitimate party in the public action" is, for the author, the Public Prosecutor. The assistant is an intervening *ad adjuvandum tantum* (1985), p. 175.

[167] Marques (2000b), p. 304.

[168] Espínola Filho (1965), p. 269.

[169] Tourinho Filho (2012a), p. 610.

[170] Greco Filho (2009), p. 241.

[171] Oliveira (2013), pp. 483–485. There is no agreement with the conception of an assistant for the body that is understood to be *custos legis*. There is no *custos legis* in the second degree; that is, there is no assistant to the *custos legis*.

[172] It is interesting to remember that Xavier de Albuquerque (1966), pp. 91–92, having formulated in a doctrinal scope the *vexata quaestio*, concludes for the existence, in the criminal process, and even if the wording of the Code is tight, of the two types of assistance. In the author's reasoning, "simple assistance should be spoken of, in the criminal process, in those cases where the accusatory coadjutancy of the offended does not intend nor can it exceed, in its motivation, the mere moral satisfaction that the punishment of the offender provides him." And, on the other hand, "qualified assistance can be spoken of, in the criminal process, in all cases in which the crime causes compensable damage in favour of the assistant."

From the provisions of Articles 268 and following of the current Penal Procedure Code, it can be seen that assistance results from a contingent and ancillary activity to the main one in the criminal process. But, just like the main activity of accusing, it is an *interested* activity.

Again, the doctrine of civil process assists in positioning, because, for the criminal process, the intensity with which the assisted is exposed to the effects of the sentence to be pronounced does not matter.[173]

The active procedural legitimacy in criminal law is not a two-way street: the public accuser can reassume the criminal action initiated by the private individual if the hypotheses provided by law occur (case of procedural substitution); but the opposite does not occur.[174]

Therefore, the considerations of Sérgio Demoro Hamilton are pertinent, who does not admit that the assistant is taken as a supporting or secondary part of the criminal procedural relationship. According to him, "the assistant is not a party, because he does not ask," but only proposes, according to the terms of Article 271 of the Penal Procedure Code.[175]

In addition, to indicate the limitation of assistance in criminal process not as a party but as its auxiliary, in scattered laws, it is enough to mention the striking intervention of defensive assistance *defensive*, from the Brazilian Bar Association (Art. 49, sole paragraph, Law No. 8.906/94[176]), within the Securities and Exchange Commission and Central Bank of Brazil, according to Article 26, sole paragraph of

[173] Dinamarco (2000b), p. 61.

[174] Hence, it seems to be unconstitutional the provision of Article 598 of the current Criminal Procedure Code, given that it affronts the privativeness of the exercise of criminal action by the state, represented in the process by the Prosecutor's Office, according to Article 129, I, of the Federal Constitution. Contrary to this position, adopting the procedural substitution depending on the closure of what was named procedural instance, Zanoide de Moraes (2000), pp. 327–329.

[175] Hamilton (2007), p. 84. In fact, for the author, "the verb to propose is well used because who asks or requires, as the case may be, is the party, in this case, the Prosecutor's Office, this in the initial (Art. 41 of the CPP) or later (Art. 499 of the CPP). In fact, the assistant only suggests a means of proof that seems useful to him in the criminal process and that, only, will be admitted after a double judgment of valuation, of the Prosecutor's Office and, finally, of the judge." In the same sense, from the same author, see the article titled "O recurso do assistente do Ministério Público" (2002), pp. 22–29. Precisely, and in the opposite pole, for taking the assistant improperly as a party (be it secondary, be it adjacent, but, in any case, *party*) in the criminal process is that Lima (2000), pp. 153–163 understands unconstitutional the provisions of the Criminal Procedure Code that touch the matter.

[176] Article 49: "The presidents of the Councils and Subsections of the OAB have legitimacy to act, judicially and extrajudicially, against any person who infringes the provisions of this Law. Single paragraph. The authorities mentioned in the *caput* of this article also have, legitimacy to intervene, including as assistants, in inquiries and processes in which those registered in the OAB are indicted, accused or offended."

Law No. 7.492/86,[177] within the scope of consumer criminal law (Arts. 82, III and IV, c.c. Art. 80, Law No. 8.078/90[178]).

On the other hand, the Penal Procedure Code project (Bill No. 8.045/2010), in what affects the *assistance* (Chap. V, Book IV, Book I), makes a distinction between the *civil party* that comes to use criminal jurisdiction to support a claim for compensation and the typical assistance, in which such discussion is not carried out.

Hence, the idea, with a view to the projected legislation, that the assistance, not without criticism as to the lack of technicality of the legislative provision, could be bifurcated into simple assistance (which is discussed here) and assistance combined with a civil compensation claim (the projected one, from the civil party).

A perspective that privileges assistance as a supporting activity of the accusation closes the doors, including, to the controversy waged in the scope of the Supreme Federal Court during the trial of the Habeas Corpus No. 102.085, in which the Full Court, led by Minister Carmen Lúcia, apparently mistakenly, signaled the possibility of the assistant assuming the protagonism of the exercise of the procedural claim to punish in cases of acquittal request by the main party who, due to a first-degree acquittal decision, did not appeal.[179]

---

[177] "Without prejudice to the provisions of art. 268 of the Criminal Procedure Code, approved by Decree-law 3.689, of October 3, 1941, the assistance of the Securities and Exchange Commission - CVM will be admitted, when the crime has been committed within the scope of activity subject to the discipline and supervision of this Autarchy, and of the Central Bank of Brazil when, outside that hypothesis, it has been committed in the orbit of activity subject to its discipline and supervision."

[178] Article 80: "In the criminal process pertaining to the crimes provided for in this Code, as well as to other crimes and contraventions that involve consumer relations, those legitimized indicated in art. 82, III and IV, may intervene as assistants to the Prosecutor's Office, which is also allowed to propose a subsidiary criminal action, if the indictment is not offered within the legal deadline." It jumps to the eyes, there, the confusion between the institutes: the assistant and the subsidiary complainant, treated improperly in the same legal provision.

[179] Reason assists ministers Marco Aurélio and Cezar Peluso, who, each in their own way, rejected the constitutionality of Article 598 of the Penal Procedure Code due to the public ownership of the criminal action and, particularly by the voice of the first, for not admitting that the public initiative criminal action can be transformed, given the appeal recourse, into *relay race*. To this we add: neither a relay race, nor atypical provision of succession of parties in criminal process, nor, as mentioned in the text, comparison of assistance to the litisconsortial assistance of the civil process, as the assistant could never be a party. And, it should be said, there is no coherence in the edition of two summaries of the Supreme Federal Court regarding the matter, namely, numbers 208 (it prevents the extraordinary appeal by the assistant in the event of granting a habeas corpus) and 210 (it allows the extraordinary appeal of the assistant, including under the terms of Articles 584, § 1°, and 598 of the CPP). Well, if the performance is *ad coadjuvandum tantum*, legitimacy would fail in both cases; and if not, given the patrimonial claim brought to the criminal process, conversely, in both cases it would be the case to admit the assistance appeals, depending mainly on the imputation then made in the action blocked by habeas corpus. The unconstitutionality of the aforementioned article of the Code of Criminal Procedure—Article 598—is also argued because there it is admitted, even, appeal even by someone who, in favour of an accusatory thesis, decides to appeal even if they have not been qualified as an assistant. The provision, in the last interpretation, seems to constitute an inappropriate exercise of criminal action by someone who not only would not have legitimacy if they were an assistant, but, worse, by someone who would never have it in any case

References

Abade, D. N. (2005). *Garantias do processo penal acusatório: o novo papel do Ministério Público no processo penal de partes*. Renovar.
Acosta, W. P. (1957). *O processo penal: teoria, prática, jurisprudência, interpretação gráfica*. [s.n.].
Almeida, C. d. M. d. (1938). *Ação penal: análises e confrontos*. Livraria Acadêmica Saraiva & Cia.
Alonso, P. A. (1960). *Proceso y derecho procesal: introducción*. Aguilar.
Alonso, P. A. (1979). *Instituciones de derecho procesal penal* (Vol. 1, 2nd ed.). Gráficas Encinas.
Alvim, A. (2008). *Manual de direito processual civil, volume 2: processo de conhecimento*. Revista dos Tribunais.
Andrade, M. d. C. (2009). Métodos ocultos de investigação (plädoyer para uma teoria geral). In M. F. Monte et al. (Eds.), *Que futuro para o direito processual penal?* Coimbra ed., Coimbra.
Andrade, M. F. d. (2008). *Sistemas processuais penais e seus princípios reitores*. Juruá.
Aquino, J. C. G. X. d., & Nalini, J. R. (2009). *Manual de processo penal* (3rd ed.). Revista dos Tribunais.
Armelin, D. (1979). *Legitimidade para agir no direito processual civil brasileiro*. Revista dos Tribunais.
Aroca, J. M. (1976). *Introducción al derecho procesal*. Tecnos.
Aroca, M. (2008). *Proceso penal y libertad*. Tecnos.
Badaró, G. H. R. I. (2003). *Ônus da prova no processo penal*. Revista dos Tribunais.
Badaró, G. (2025). *Direito Processual Penal*.
Bueno, C. S. (2006). *Partes e terceiros no processo civil brasileiro*. Saraiva.
Calamandrei, P. (1950). *Il processo come giuoco*. Rivista di Diritto Processuale.
Calamandrei, P. (1951). *Un maestro del liberalismo processuale*. Rivista di Diritto Processuale.
Carneiro, A. G. (2010). *Intervenção de terceiros*. Saraiva.
Carnelutti, F. (1953). *Mettere il Pubblico Ministero al suo posto*. Rivista di Diritto Processuale.
Carnelutti, F. (1960). *Cuestiones sobre el proceso penal*. El Foro.
Casara, R. R. R. (2011). *A imparcialidade do Ministério Público no processo penal brasileiro: um mito a ser desvelado*. Lumen Juris.
Chiavario, M. (1971). *Il Pubblico Ministero organo di giustizia?* Rivista Italiana di Diritto e Procedura Penale.
Chiavario, M. (2007). *Diritto processuale penale: profilo istituzionale*. UTET.
Chiovenda, G. (2000). *Instituições de direito processual civil, v. II: as relações processuais; a relação processual ordinária de cognição*. Bookseller.
Conso, Giovanni; Grevi, Vittorio (Orgs.) (2008) *Compendio di procedura penale*. Cedam.
Coutinho, J. N. d. M. (1989). *A lide e o conteúdo do processo penal*. Juruá.
Cruz, R. S. M. (2002). *Garantias processuais nos recursos criminais*. Atlas.
Deu, T. A. (2007). *Lecciones de derecho procesal penal*. Marcial Pons.
Dinamarco, C. R. (2000a). *Fundamentos do direito processual civil moderno*. Malheiros.
Dinamarco, C. R. (2000b). *Intervenção de terceiros*. Malheiros.
Dinamarco, C. R. (2009). *Litisconsórcio*. Malheiros.
Dinamarco, C. R., Badaró, G. H. R. I., & Lopes, B. V. C. (2020). *Teoria geral do processo*. Malheiros.
Dominioni, O. (1985). *Le parti nel processo penale: profili sistematici e problemi*. Giuffrè.
Dinamarco, C. R. (2024). *Instituições de direito processual civil*. v. 2 JusPodivm.
Espínola Filho, E. (1965). *Código de Processo Penal brasileiro anotado* (Vol. III, 6th ed.). Borsoi.
Fernandes, A. S. (2002). *Reação defensiva à imputação*. Revista dos Tribunais.

---

or circumstance. It is noted, in any case, the prestige of the cited judgment as can be seen, even if it was not the main reasoning of the decision, in the result of the R *HC* No. 106.710, second C., under the rapporteurship of Justice Gilmar Mendes (publ. 13th April 2011).

Figueiredo Dias, J. (2004). *Processo penal*. Coimbra.
Figueiredo Dias, J. (1988). *Sobre os sujeitos processuais no novo código de processo penal*. Almedina.
Gloeckner, R. J. (2013). *Nulidades no processo penal: introdução principiológica à teoria do ato processual irregular*. JusPODIVM.
Goldschmidt, J. (1936). *Derecho procesal civil*. Ed. Labor.
Goldschmidt, J. (2002). *Princípios gerais do processo penal*. Líder.
Gomes Filho, A. M. (1997). *Ministério Público e acusação penal no sistema brasileiro*. Revista Latinoamericana de Política Criminal.
Greco Filho, V. (2009). *Manual de processo penal*. Saraiva.
Grinover, A. P. (1990). Defesa, contraditório, igualdade e *par condicio* na ótica do processo de estrutura cooperatória. In *Novas tendências do direito processual de acordo com a constituição de 1988*. Forense Universitária.
Guarneri, G. (1949). *Le parti nel processo penale*. Fratelli Bocca.
Hamilton, S. D. (2002). *O recurso do assistente do Ministério Público*. Revista Síntese de Direito Penal e Processual Penal.
Hamilton, S. D. (2007). A taxatividade das atribuições do assistente do Ministério Público. In *Estudos de processo penal* (3rd ed.). Lumen Juris.
Jardim, A. d. S. (1984). *Reflexão teórica sobre o processo penal*. Revista Justitia.
Lima, M. P. (2000). A assistência ao Ministério Público e a Constituição de 1988. In *Temas controvertidos de direito e processo penal*. Lumen Juris.
Lima, M. P. (2007). *Ministério Público e persecução criminal*. Lumen Juris.
Lopes Júnior, A. (2005). *Direito processual penal e sua conformidade* (Vol. I).
Lopes Júnior, A. (2008). *(Re)pensando o processo penal desde uma análise da sua natureza jurídica (ou quando finalmente vamos compreender a superação de Büllow por Goldschmidt)*. Revista da Associação Brasileira de Professores de Ciências Penais.
Lopes Júnior, A. (2009). *Direito processual penal e sua conformidade* (Vol. II). Lumen Juris.
Lopes Júnior, A. (2025). *Direito processual penal*. Saraivajur.
Maier, J. (2004). *Derecho procesal penal II: parte general: sujetos procesales*. Editores Del Puerto.
Manzini, V. (1996). *Tratado de derecho procesal penal* (Vol. II). El Foro.
Marinoni, L. G., & Arenhart, S. C. (2011). *Curso de processo civil, v. 2: processo de conhecimento*. Revista dos Tribunais.
Marques, J. F. (2000a). *Elementos de direito processual penal*. (vol. I, 2nd ed. rev. e atual. por Eduardo Reale Ferrari). Millennium.
Marques, J. F. (2000b). *Elementos de direito processual penal*. (vol. II, 2nd ed. rev. e atual. por Eduardo Reale Ferrari). Millennium.
Nery Júnior, N. (2016). *Princípios do processo na Constituição Federal: processo civil, penal e administrativo*. (12th ed. rev., ampl. e atual. com as novas Súmulas do STF (simples e vinculantes) e com o novo CPC). Editora Revista dos Tribunais.
Noronha, E. M. (1972). *Curso de direito processual penal* (5th ed.). Saraiva.
Oliveira, E. P. d. (2013). *Curso de processo penal*. Atlas.
Pitombo, S. M. d. M. (1973). *Breves notas em torno da coação processual penal*. José Bushatsky.
Pontes de Miranda F. C. (1973). *Comentários à Constituição de 1967, com a emenda n. 1, de 1969. Tomo IV*. Revista dos Tribunais.
Pontes de Miranda, F. C. (1974). *Comentários ao Código de Processo Civil*. (Tomo I (Arts 1–45). Forense.
Saad, M. (2004). *O direito de defesa no inquérito policial*. Revista dos Tribunais.
Sabatini, G. (1943). *Il Pubblico Ministero nel diritto processuale penale*. v. 2.
Sandermann, A. (1975). *"Waffengleichheit" im Strafprozess*. Zu den rechlichen Grundlagen dieses Rechtsinstituts. Inaugural. Dissertation zur Erlangung der Doktorwürde einer Hohen Rechtswissenchaftlichen Fakultät der Universität zu Köln.
Schmidt, E. (1957). *Los fundamentos teóricos y constitucionales del derecho procesal penal: comentario doctrinario de la ordenanza procesal penal y de la ley orgânica de los tribunales*. Ed. Bibliográfica Argentina.

Schmidt E. (2006). *Los fundamentos teóricos y constitucionales del derecho procesal penal*. Lerner.
Silva, O. B. d. (2005). *Comentários ao Código de Processo Civil, volume 1: do processo de conhecimento, arts. 1° a 100*. Revista dos Tribunais.
Taormina, C. (1992). *Il processo di parti di fronte al nuovo regime delle contestazioni e delle letture dibattimentali*. La Giustizia Penale.
Theodoro Júnior, H. (1997). *Curso de direito processual civil: teoria geral do direito processual civil e processo de conhecimento*. Forense.
Tornaghi, H. (1985). *A relação processual penal*. Saraiva.
Toron, A. Z. (2003). O contraditório nos tribunais e o Ministério Público. In *Escritos em homenagem a Alberto Silva Franco*. Revista dos Tribunais.
Tourinho Filho, F. d. C. (2012a). *Processo penal v. 2, 34. ed. rev. de acordo com a Lei n. 12.403/2011*. Saraiva.
Tourinho Filho, F. d. C. (2012b). *Processo penal* (Vol. 1, 34th ed.) (rev. de acordo com a Lei n. 12.403/2011).
Tucci, R. L. (1980). *Persecução penal, prisão e liberdade*. Saraiva.
Tucci, R. L. (2002). *Teoria do direito processual penal: jurisdição, ação e processo penal (estudo sistemático)*. Revista dos Tribunais.
Ubertis, G. (2008). *Il processo penale: la verifica dell'accusa*. Giuffrè.
Von Büllow, O. (1964). *La teoria de las excepciones dilatorias y los presupuestos procesales*. Ediciones Jurídicas Europa-America.
Xavier de Albuquerque, F. M. (1966). *A assistência no processo penal brasileiro*. Revista Brasileira de Criminologia e Direito Penal.
Zanoide de Moraes, M. (2000). *Interesse e legitimação para recorrer no processo penal*. Revista dos Tribunais.

Chapter 4
Criminal Procedural Systems: The Equality of Arms and the Adversarial System

It is common to read, in judgments and doctrine, passages about the criminal process from what is known as criminal procedural systems.[1]

Without prejudice to this analysis that separates the system from the principle (even so that one word is not taken for the other), another theoretical prism matters. Recently, some authors, of whom it is worth mentioning Montero Aroca,[2] began to emphasize that, in the criminal process, it would not be possible to consider distinct systems.

For the Spanish author, the procedural method presupposes the accusatory and, therefore, the inquisitiveness makes the word *process* not go beyond, even, a

[1] In the criminal process, in an attempt to separate the concept of what would be the *accusatory* from the *inquisitive*, Prado (2006), p. 104, distinguishes the *principle* from the accusatory *system*. For the author, while the system is a body of "fundamental norms and principles orderly arranged and oriented from the main principle, that is, the one from which it inherits its name: *accusatory*," the principle holds, in itself, characteristics that vary from doctrine to doctrine, but which would have as a common core the separation of tasks of accusing, judging, defending. For Grinover (1999), p. 71, the word *system* is taken as an "*accusatory model* to say that in it the functions of accusing, defending and judging are attributed to different bodies." Mauro Fonseca Andrade (2008), p. 254, touches on the distinction between *accusatory principle* and *accusatory system* in the following terms: "the most secure and correct definition of accusatory principle is that which reflects the necessary presence of an accuser distinct from the judge in the process. More than that, this identification of the accusatory principle also raises it to the condition of one of the elements fixed of the accusatory system." Scholz (1999), p. 464, also argues as the first of the striking features of the accusatory system "the exercise by different bodies, of the functions of accusing, defending and judging."

[2] It is true that Marques (1960), p. 23, recalls, before the publications of Montero Aroca, the lessons of Alcalá-Zamora (for whom the inquisitive procedure would be a "self-defensive form of the administration of justice") and Sentís Melendo, according to whom in the aforementioned system there would always be nothing more than a police investigation, even if the official who directed it was called a judge, but never a judicial process.

R. S. Vieira, *Equality of Arms in Criminal Procedure*,
https://doi.org/10.1007/978-3-032-03663-6_4

contradictio in terminis.[3] Thus, the accusatory process would be a pleonasm or a vicious redundancy of words: "el calificativo acusatorio no añade nada a la palabra proceso, por lo menos si ésta se entiende correctamente."[4]

Montero Aroca, moreover, is not only critical of the rhetorical optimism that surrounds the *accusatory system*, but also, in at least one of his passages, he dealt with the adversarial system not as a synonym, but as complementary to it. For the Spanish author, the adversarial system assumes that the accusatory system only refers to the method of oral judgment, in which the parties should convince the court of the truthfulness of each statement.[5]

Even if briefly, it is necessary to consolidate the opposition between the systems, because, if the notion of equality of arms does not seem to be conceptually dependent on any of them (read: accusatory or inquisitive), it also does not depend on what is intended to be taken for a *mixed* criminal procedural system.[6]

Indeed, and once again from the lessons of Montero Aroca, but with an echo in the jurisprudence that was established in the European Court of Human Rights, Lorena Bachmaier Winter understands that it is time to overcome the dichotomy between the terms *accusatory* and *inquisitive*.[7]

According to her lessons, with which we agree here,

> at a time when international treaties, constitutional texts and the doctrine of courts, both national and international, have achieved a broad understanding of the meaning of procedural guarantees, and specifically of the guarantees that must be respected in the criminal process, it is probably of little interest to resort to the term 'accusatory' as an icon of all advances. The term 'accusatory' becomes a political slogan.[8]

As Richard Vogler says, by the rhetorical use of the term *accusatory* as a reflection of everything respecting the guarantees of the process and as a presupposition of the framework of the Rule of Law, and, on the opposite side, by the unfortunate doctrinal career that was made with the term *inquisitive*, it is noted, in the studies of the

---

[3] The author (2008a), pp. 97–99, mentions his point of view in several known writings but here it is important to consider the text *The uselessness of the so-called accusatory principle for the shaping of the criminal process*, in which, in addition to saying that "the so-called 'inquisitive process' never was and, obviously, could not be today, a true process," he states: "the so-called criminal procedural systems are concepts lacking all technical procedural rigour, so it is necessary to make it very clear that in certain historical periods the Criminal law was not applied exclusively by the courts and that in other times it was applied by the courts, yes, but not through the process, and it must be proclaimed as an irrenounceable conquest of civilisation the jurisdictional guarantee, understood in its original sense, that is, assumption of the monopoly of the ius puniendi (right to punish) by the courts and procedural exclusivity of its exercise." From the same author, see Aroca (2008b), pp. 19 and foll. And still: Aroca (1997), pp. 25 and foll.

[4] Aroca (2008a), p. 99.

[5] Aroca (2008a), p. 100.

[6] As it has settled to deal with *systems* from the Napoleonic Code of Criminal Instruction of 1808.

[7] Armenta-Deu (2016), pp. 57/75, also advocates for a strict overcoming. Deserves special mention, in the same volume, the deep and particular approach of Langer (2016), pp. 273/99.

[8] Winter (2008), p. 46.

opposition between the two systems, a certain temptation of an "appropriation of the term 'accusatory'."[9]

Here, it is assumed that the fertile field for the development of the principle of equality of arms is the adversarial criminal process, which, moreover, is not confused with either of the two commonly studied. The assumption of this point of view also does not mean that the adversarial system is *better*, or *more guarantor* than any other that is wanted to oppose it. It only facilitates the development of the principle, and hence also follows its natural risks of overlapping the interests of one party or another. It is, therefore, not worse or better, but more functional for the deepening of the equality of arms in the criminal process.

It is necessary to remember that the doctrine of the legal situation is linked to the adversarial system and that, for such a doctrine, the process is seen as a war; a war in which not necessarily the one who is right wins, but the one who makes better use—and of the best—of the weapons available in the process.

We return, therefore, to think of the process (adversarial) as a set of *opportunities and burdens* that entail *expectations and prospects*, each one to be taken advantage of in the best possible way to achieve a favorable judicial decision.

The conclusion of the differentiation of the adversarial system from those classically and repeatedly studied is only reached if one can separate such a model from the one that is taken, by certain doctrine, as close (according to some, as synonymous): the accusatory. Similarly, it is necessary to separate it from what is studied as its antithesis: the inquisitive.[10]

4.1 Two Criminal Procedural Systems: Inquisitive and Accusatory

History is the most used tool to separate one criminal procedural system from another. Sometimes, in fact, it is the only instrument accepted for the study of a given phenomenon.

From the passage of the centuries and how a system was shaped to a certain political context (and possibly religious, in the case of the inquisitive), its differentiation from the other followed. It is, therefore, with eyes on the succession of events in the West, from the Roman Republic,[11] that the characteristics of such systems are imagined.

---

[9] Vogler (2001), p. 252.

[10] Which has been translated into English, sometimes, as *inquisitorial*, implying that *adversarial* would be opposed to *inquisitorial*, which is also not true.

[11] We know the lesson of Andrade (2008), p. 51, according to which the inquisitive criminal process historically preceded the accusatory, as there would be signs of inquisitiveness already in the times of Draco. Such an approach, although it is also given by Vélez-Mariconde (1986), p. 21, seems solitary and has no proven connection with the characteristics of the system that came to be established in the European Middle Ages.

The accusatory system is erected on two pillars: the functional separation between judging and accusing; and the procedural characteristic of being the accusation the triggering source of the criminal process, and not the judge.[12] Its model was reached in the "twilight of the Republic"[13] (Roman), when the state assumed the ownership of the criminal repression previously spread among the citizens.[14]

In a didactic passage by Luiz Carlos de Azevedo, which dates to the *quaestione perpetuae*, the remote origin of the accusatory system, it is remembered that the name *quaestiones* comes from

> quaestio, inquiry, procedural investigation. These true courts, with delegated and special function for the trial of causes of criminal nature, becoming permanent, completed their denomination to 'quaestiones perpetuae'. Their members, chosen first among the senators, and then from the laws that gradually were expanding the prerogatives of the other social classes, by knights and tribunes of the treasury, knew highlighted importance in the trial of criminal causes, in the context of the republican period; these processes were developed *coram populo*, in the presence of the people, carrying in their procedure the right of accusation, defence and judgement, publicity and contradiction.[15]

In the words of Rogério Lauria Tucci, if the *quaestio* started only as temporary commissions to investigate possible crimes committed by magistrates, they ended up becoming perpetual, or permanent, given the stretched competence, with judgment of crimes, also, of embezzlement, poisoning, sicarii, false judgment, parricide, perjury, and adultery. The *quaestio*, according to Tucci, would not only be the embryo of the ordinary Roman criminal process, but also the germ of "a fixed and permanent jurisdiction in Rome."[16]

The matrices of the accusatory system, of Roman origin, which would have as its core the "clear separation between the functions of accusing, judging and defending,"[17] remained until the twelfth century, when they gave way to the inquisitive system, which, in the words of Aury Lopes Junior, changed "the face of the process in a radical way."[18]

---

[12] Andrade (2008), p. 259. It is true that Marques (1960), p. 23. understood as "basic concepts" of such a system not only this, but the fact that, (a) from the separation between the bodies of accusation, defence and judgement one could reach, he thought, a "process of parties"; (b) similarly, he imagined that from the freedom of defence would result in the "equality of position of the parties"; that (c) the rule of contradiction would be innate, (d) the free presentation of evidence by the parties and, also, the (e) rule of autonomous procedural impulse or initial activation of the cause by the interested parties. As will be seen in this text, to a large extent, what the author linked to the accusatory system is pertinent to the adversarial system.

[13] Expression of Scholz (1999), p. 463. There are repeated passages of doctrine that originally place the accusatory system in a period prior to the high Roman Republic, but still, the consecration of the system took place in that period, and it was from there that its fundamental elements arose.

[14] Tucci (2002), pp. 145–146; Malan and Saad (2005), p. 4.

[15] Azevedo (2004), pp. 49–50.

[16] Tucci (1976), p. 73.

[17] Badaró (2003), p. 108.

[18] According to the author (2008), pp. 10/12, "what was a fair and frank duel between accuser and accused, with equality of powers and opportunities, it turns into an unequal dispute between the

The transition from the Roman matrix accusatory system to the inquisitive, also on continental European soil, in which the Church played a great role, is painted with vibrant colors by Jacinto Nelson de Miranda Coutinho in reference to the Fourth Lateran Council, taken as

> historical landmark of the new system.[19] From there the notion of Bulgarian (*actus trium personarum: iudiciis, actori et rei*[20]) tends to disappear in criminal process. Everything is consolidated with the Bull of Gregory IX (*Ex Excomuniamus*), from 1231, where the technical framework is outlined; and with the Bull *Ad extirpanda*, by Innocent IV, in 1252, extended to the world in 1254. [...] Excluding the parties, in the inquisitorial process the defendant becomes a *sinner*, therefore, holder of a 'truth' to be extracted. More importantly, apparently, than the crime itself, he becomes the *object of investigation*.[21]

Pedro Alonso Aragoneses' synthesis about the inquisitive system is as follows:

> The State, through its justice organs, when it becomes aware of the existence of a fact that may be punishable, proceeds ex officio to the investigation of such fact and the collection of the necessary elements, in order to verify the existence of the crime. The instruction that determines the subsequent accusation is put in the hands of the subject, who, ultimately, has to impose the penalty; and as the accused is the best source of knowledge of the facts, he is required to declare, or coercive means are used to achieve that result.[22]

It is curious to note history: while in the inquisitiveness that followed the accusatory system, the accused went from subject to object of investigation,[23] the adversarial

---

inquisitor-judge and the accused. The former abandons his position of impartial arbitrator and assumes the activity of inquisitor, acting from the beginning also as accuser. The activities of the judge and accuser are confused, and the accused loses the condition of procedural subject and becomes a mere object of the investigation."

[19] Slightly dissonant in time, the historical landmark of the inquisitive system, in the lesson of Azevedo (2004), p. 51, would be another, namely, the renewal of Roman law studies with the consecration of canon law, especially by edicts of Pope Innocent III about the so-called three ways of initiating criminal prosecution: "in three ways it is possible to initiate criminal proceedings: by accusation, denunciation and inquisition."

[20] This is Ada Pellegrini Grinover's synthesis for the accusatory model (1999), p. 71, as seen from the article here, so often inspiring (the judge's instructive initiative in the accusatory criminal process).

[21] Coutinho (2009), p. 105. In fine irony, the author also says: "the model is brilliant, were it not, before, diabolical, although born, as seen, within the Catholic Church." It does not go unnoticed, here, the reminder of Ennio Amodio, who joins the more acidic warning of Aroca (2008c), p. 195, according to whom the opposition between accusatory and inquisitorial has an "emotional significance" in the measure in which the first model is presented as "the place of guarantee, territory in which freedom and the defence of the accused find the most ample spaces; and the second is on the other hand characterised by a markedly negative connotation" (our translation). From a point of view that deviates, in history, from the initial landmark defined by Jacinto de Miranda Coutinho, the Professor Luiz Carlos de Azevedo (2004), p. 51, took as the landmark of the inquisitive process the *Decretals* of Pope Innocent III, which provided, for the first time, the three admitted forms of initiating criminal prosecution: by accusation, by denunciation and by inquisition. In this last sense, also: Pezzotti (2020), p. 78.

[22] Alonso (1979), p. 59.

[23] In the synthesis of Marques (1960), p. 23, the so-called main rules of the inquisitive system are: "a) concentration of procedural functions in the judicial body, in order to make it the main accuser

system, centuries later, and through the parity between defensive and accusatory action, takes him out of the position of object of criminal prosecution. And this happened mainly due to the change in treatment given to the performance of his defender, which obviously reflects on the treatment given to the accused.

4.2 Adversarial System: The Paradigm of the Criminal Process of Parties

The adversarial system[24] (without italics and pronounced as it is written[25]), is not confused, historically or legally, with the accusatory system or with the inquisitive one. In it, the criminal process of parties is fruitful.

If the notions of accusatoriness (obligation of accusation and functional separation of the activities of the subjects of the process) and of inquisitiveness (secrecy of investigation, procedure ex officio, and confusion between accusing and judging activities) are linked to continental Europe, it was in England that the adversarial model of process was born.

According to Stephan Landsman's lesson, one could even go back to the *trial by battle* to shade, still in the eleventh century, the remote origin of the adversarial

---

and also judge of its own accusation; b) restriction of the rights of the defence, with the duty to the judge to supplement the activity of the defendant, according to the principle of Carpsovio, that *judex supplere debet defensiones rei* ex officio; c) suppression of the contradictory; d) inquisitive judicial instruction with the duty to the judge, to 'gather, by his own activity, the material of the dispute'; e) procedural impulse ex officio."

[24] About the adversarial system as a *system*, see the critical understanding of Taruffo (2008), p. 5.

[25] The few Brazilian authors who addressed the adversarial procedural system highlighted the adjective in italics because there is no exact translation in Portuguese. In this text, some premises are taken that can justify the choice not to do so. Here, adversarial is written without quotes and without italics. The *adversativity* is innate to the procedure, and the word *adversative* is, according to the dictionary *Houaiss*, an adjective that indicates "opposite, contrary to; adverse; that expresses opposition." In turn, also according to *Houaiss*, the suffix *al* is used in the use of words in Portuguese brought from other languages, like English and French (*facial*, *individual*, *musical*, *sentimental*, *tribal*, *editorial*), and its use is admitted, exemplarily, "in voc. With more specific meanings, gen. Marked by the idea of qualifying the 'that is based on or that uses (base)': [...] note that all adj. in *-al* potentiate or even visualize abstract subs. in *-ity* (*manual: manuality, sexagesimal: sexagesimality*)" (Houaiss, 2012). In Portuguese, there is no expression *adversarial*, and, although here it could be taken as indicative of its meaning, the translations *adversative* or *adverse*, it still seems to justify the neologism. The risk is assumed, exposed by Segismundo Spina, of inviting the text to a language "exquisitely precious, sometimes pedantic - not to say pernicious," but it is proposed to achieve with such linguistic construction the opposite of. It is not wanted, in obedience to the same lesson from Spina (2003), p. 57, to seem "pompous, solemn, rhetorical, inadequate to the expression of the truth that is wanted to demonstrate," nor even "mannerist, visible in the voluptuousness of the exotic vocabulary, which often is empty of meaning." It was preferred to accept the consecrated term, simple and of immediate association by jurists, to escape from mannerism, from the pedantic aspect, and, finally, unnecessary to the communication of the message that is wanted to pass.

system. The *trials by battle* would have given the first impulse to the adversarial system and to its resemblance, as it is repeated in doctrine, to fight rituals or duels.[26]

After the judgment of *trial by battle*,[27] other modes of justice application in the process followed, of which three are worth highlighting, as indicated by Landsman: the *wager of law*,[28] the battle itself, and the ordeals.[29] In any of them, divine intervention was notable, as "the system did not make much use of evidence, it was not oral, it was not contentious and the research of evidence was not even necessary because the facts were not deduced from the evidence."[30]

Still, according to the same author, even if one could recognize that none of these systems were even remotely adversarial, they caused their development because they made the role of the parties become prominent in the process (the idea of *active party participation* was developing as a reaction to the atrocities).

In addition, they provoked the limitation of judicial activity in controlling the process. According to Landsman's research, in summary, it was precisely from the decline of the medieval customs in progress in England that new practices began to be imagined between the thirteenth and seventeenth centuries, practices that ended up shaping the English adversarial system consecrated in the eighteenth and nineteenth centuries.

It was on English soil, after all, as Landsman points out once again, that in 1577 the *attorney-client privilege* was recognized, and that the judicial action and its passivity meant independence from the central organs of government. Then, in the sixteenth century, oral testimony in the process was honored, and rules of evidence production began to be discussed.

---

[26] Landsman (1983), p. 717. The author is critical of the origin of the system and affirms that, remotely, the *trials* served the rich class of medieval society, given the possibilities of better technical manoeuvres in battles.

[27] "Trial by combat. A trial that is decided by personal battle between the disputants, common in Europe and England during the Middle Ages; specif., a trial in which the person accused fought with the accuser, the idea being that God would give victory to the person in the right. This method was introduced into England by the Normans after 1066, but it was a widely detested innovation and was little used. It became obsolete several centuries before being formally abolished in 1818, having been replaced in practice by the grand assize and indictment. Also termed *trial by battle*; *trial by wager of battle*; *trial by duel*; *judicial combat*; *duel*; *duellum*; *wager of battle*; *ornest*; *vadiatio duelli*; *wehading*" (Garner, 2009, p. 1645).

[28] "A method of proof in which a person defends against a claim by swearing that the claim is groundless, and by enlisting others (compurgators) to swear to the defendant's credibility. Also termed gager del ley; vadiatio legis" (2009), p. 1717.

[29] "A primitive form of trial in which an accused person was subjected to a usu. Dangerous or painful physical test, the result being considered a divine revelation of the person's guilt or innocence. The participants believed that God would reveal a person's culpability by protecting an innocent person from some or all consequences of the ordeal. The ordeal was commonly used in Europe until the thirteenth century, but only sporadically after 1215, when the Fourth Lateran Council forbade the clergy from participating in ordeals. Also termed *trial by ordeal; judicium Dei; vulgaris purgatio*" (2009, p. 1205).

[30] Landsman (1983), p. 719 (our translation).

According to the historical outline presented by the already mentioned Harvard professor, not only from 1640, when the rules of the *Star Chamber*[31] were repealed, but more than a century later, with the advent of the American and French Revolutions, the adversarial system initially in force in England reached the shores of the United States of America. Today, it is widely understood that it is an *Anglo-American* system.[32]

Such historical development, distinct and unmistakable in relation to those of the accusatory and inquisitive systems, is a parameter of differentiation of the adversarial system. After all, it seems clear, as Richard Vogler wants to nuance, that an initial development of the system, by the origins that have been outlined here, was indeed due to its affirmation on English soil, especially in the eighteenth[33] and the nineteenth centuries.

After that, observing the reaction that Vogler took for "inquisitive practices carried out in the Stalinist penal systems, Nazi Germany, Vichy France and Latin American totalitarianism," one can note another adversarial wave, this time under the ideological baton of the United States of America. Vogler does not seem to be wrong when, in another text, he states that the adversarial system, from an ideological and historical point of view,

> has its origins in the development of England's capitalist economy and it is no mere coincidence that the adversarial system was created by the same *common law* lawyers who represented the businessmen in the country that led the Industrial Revolution. It is essentially a plan of a penal system from the conceptions of the free market, based on individual negotiation, freedom to contract and on the concept of an individual bearer of rights.[34]

It is no coincidence that the idea—today widely disseminated from the North American model of criminal procedure—of consensual justice or negotiated justice is in line with the theoretical approximation that is given to it, namely, to the adversarial system.

If before there was a certain appropriation of the term *accusatory*, given the rhetorical charge that its meaning carried, now, as has been noted from comparative criminal procedural law, there is a "temptation of Anglo-American adversariality."[35]

---

[31] "An English court having broad civil and criminal jurisdiction at the king's discretion and noted for its secretive, arbitrary, and oppressive procedures, including compulsory self-incrimination, inquisitorial investigation, and the absence of juries. The Star Chamber was abolished in 1641 because of its abuses of power. Also termed *Court of Star Chamber; Camera Stellata.* Any secretive, arbitrary, or oppressive tribunal or proceeding" (Garner, 2009, p. 1537).

[32] We must not lose sight of the fact that another important historian of the adversarial system, John H. Langbein, takes the *Treason Act of 1696* as the most fundamental document in the configuration of the English adversarial system. Particularly, the preamble of that document, as Langbein (2003), p. 88, recalls, establishes for the defence the "procedural equality with the prosecution." A similar position, in the sense of defensive arms, is that of Shapiro (1993), pp. 215–255.

[33] This is what Malan (2009), p. 7, points out.

[34] Vogler (2008), p. 182.

[35] Vogler (2005), pp. 180–181.

4.3 The Adversarial Criminal Procedural System: Characteristics

Unmistakable concepts and realities make the accusatory and adversarial systems not to be taken as interchangeable[36] and prevent seeing in their relationship something similar to the relations of gender (accusatory) and species (adversarial). The distinction is, currently, even more important when taking into account the radicalization of some measure of availability of the process—*plea negotiation*—especially from the second half of the twentieth century. This characteristic, not innate to the adversarial system, is entirely unthinkable in the accusatory system.

About this, and in the plan of conceptual distinctions, besides the historical ones[37] about which we have already spoken, one among many merits of the already mentioned work of Ada Pellegrini Grinover lies in the effort to try to distinguish the accusatory system from the adversarial one.

For that professor, the two concepts do not touch because the accusatory system depends on the constitution of public and official accusation and the separation between functions of accusing, defending, and judging in the assumption of the development of the process in contradiction before a natural judge.[38] On the other hand, the *adversary system* is analyzed in perspective of its parallel with the *inquisitorial system* in terms of the judge's instructional activities in the criminal process and the demand of the parties.

As it is only in the last of the criteria (that of probative freedom and of demand in the criminal process) relevant the mention to the adversarial system (impulse of the parties) when compared with the inquisitorial (of the judge), Ada Pellegrini Grinover asserted:

> The term inquisitive process *inquisitorial*, in opposition to the accusatory, does not correspond to the *inquisitorial* (in English), which is opposed to the adversarial. An accusatory system can adopt the *adversarial system* or the *inquisitorial system*, a term that could be translated as 'official development process'. That is, the principle of demand remains firm, by which it is up to the party to propose the action, the process develops by official impulse.

---

[36] Vogler (2005), p. 177. In another text, the same professor, when dealing with what he names as "accusatory fallacy," teaches that: "this particular confusion seems to have arisen in relation to the lack of understanding of the dominant mode of trial in the Anglo-American world, which is not accusatory but rather *adversarial*. The terms are not, as is often assumed, interchangeable. Adversariality, as a form of trial, has almost nothing to do with the old accusatory tradition and was, in contrast, a radically new procedure developed in England in the eighteenth century" (2005, p. 188).

[37] Langbein (1995), p. 551: "Legal procedures do not exist in the abstract. A procedural system bears the most intimate relation to the institutions that operate the procedures. It is difficult to carry insights from Continental to Anglo-American procedure, because the different procedures presuppose different institutions. There is a deep relationship between *how* we proceed and *who* does the proceeding. This nexus between procedure and institutions materially complicates the task of those who would derive practical insight from the study of comparative procedure."

[38] Grinover (1999), pp. 71–72, item 2.

> [...] Accusatory-inquisitorial and *adversarial-inquisitorial* are different categories, in which the terms must be used correctly.[39]

While in the accusatory model the notion of opposition between the state and the citizen is shaped, in the adversarial one the idea of a dispute between equals is worked on, whether in civil proceedings, or, later and with nuances, in criminal proceedings.[40]

The adversarial system took to the extreme the role of the parties in the collection, selection, presentation, and proof of evidence.[41]

Hence, Gustavo Badaró is right to affirm that, in countries that privilege the procedural activity of the parties, the role of the lawyer prevails "as an effective participant in the procedural dynamics,"[42] as well as Diogo Malan in arguing that "the central idea is to distance the judge from the management of evidence in the dispute, forcing the procedural parties to investigate and propose the elements of proof they find most persuasive."[43]

One can see, therefore, the relevance of the equality of arms and, particularly, for the adversarial criminal process of James Goldschmidt's doctrine about the legal situation. According to Ricardo Jacobsen Gloeckner, it is in the adversarial system that

---

[39] Grinover (1999), p. 72, item 3. Of the same understanding of the author, Andrade (2008), p. 227, and also Zilli (2010), p. 19. It is curious that *Black's Law Dictionary* (2009), p. 62, says that "the term *adversary system* sometimes characterises an entire legal process, and sometimes it refers only to criminal procedure. In the latter instance, it is often used interchangeably with an old expression of continental European origin, 'accusatorial procedure' and is juxtaposed to the 'inquisitorial', or 'nonadversary' process. There is no precise understanding, however, of the institutions and arrangements denoted by these expressions." In the scope of dictionaries, it is also noteworthy that the *Oxford Dictionary of Law*, in addition to ordering a referral from *adversarial* to *accusatorial*, goes so far as to say that, in the latter, "Common-law systems usually adopt an accusatorial procedure" (2003), p. 7. Adopting a different premise, Winter (2008), p. 31, reminds us that what exists is, effectively, an *inquisitive* trait that links the notions of accusatorial system to the adversarial when one thinks about the investigative function assigned to the state in the first phase of criminal prosecution. It is close to the lessons, finally, of Ada Grinover and Kai Ambos; from this last (2005), p. 162.

[40] Damaška (1986), p. 3, at one point, reserves only superficial clarity in separating one thing from the other, and at another, points out: "The resulting policy-implementing perspective on criminal justice managed to survive, essentially intact, the nineteenth-century reign of laisser-faire ideology on the Continent. The classical liberal concept of the criminal process as a dispute between the individual and the state was obviously far less plausible in the institutional Continental milieu than in the environment of Anglo-American countries: civil-service judges did not fit the role of neutral arbiters in this dispute as well as ordinary citizens enlisted in jury service" (1997, pp. 119–120).

[41] Langbein (1995), p. 1.

[42] Coutinho (2009), p. 127. The professor also says, in another passage: "In the *adversary system* it is up to the parties to produce the evidence, the judge, as a rule, does not have probative initiative" (pp. 127–128).

[43] Malan (2009), p. 19. In this sense, the understanding of Olavo Evangelista Pezzotti, in his *Awarded Collaboration...*, cit., pp. 80/92, also follows.

> the parties debate, bring evidence, request others and finally, wage a battle that consolidates the process as an agonistic and dialectical activity. The first step to project an adversarial conception of the process is the renunciation of the main characteristic of the theory of the legal relationship. As glimpsed in the preceding topic, it is possible to synthesize that the theory of the legal relationship was characterized basically by aggregating, within the procedural relationship, a set of rights and obligations between the parties, including the duties and rights of the magistrate. Not only does the punitive claim appear as a consolidated and imbricated accessory in the theory of the legal relationship.[44]

For Mirjan Damaška, in the adversarial system,

> the procedural action is controlled by the parties and the judge remains essentially passive. In the field of fact-finding, this implies that the litigants and their lawyers decide which facts should be submitted to proof. This consequently implies that the litigants and their lawyers are entrusted with the research of evidentiary materials, their preparation for use in the trial and presentation to the court.[45]

This is linked, still according to Damaška's lesson, to the circumstance of there being, in the adversarial system, distrust in relation to the collection of sources of evidence by official bodies.

There is a distrust and fear of the occurrence of abuses by the state, so in such a system, the idea of the "*evidentiary barriers limiting the search for the truth*" is tolerated.[46] That is why, still, the *privileges against* are expressions traditionally connected to the adversarial system, not being so to the accusatory and, obviously, much less to the inquisitive.[47]

This very idea disseminated from the adversarial system as attentive to state limits in prosecution is understood, by the doctrine, as a typically liberal characteristic, in the Lockean model—therefore, enlightenment and liberal—of conception of the state,[48] even because it does not demand from the parties (particularly from the accused) cooperation with the state.

---

[44] Gloeckner (2013), pp. 67–68. A page later, the author from Paraná concludes: "Entering the core of the relative importance to the criminal process, the theory of the legal situation allows and supports the theoretical construction of a criminal process in the moulds of the adversarial system. Without the omnipresent action of the judge, inheritance of the theory of the legal relationship and whose predilection for the foundation of a criminal system based on the foundations of social defence ideology is notorious, Goldschmidt perceives the importance of the dialectical process. And within such a perspective it is easy to glimpse the greater adequacy of the theory of the legal situation to the moulds of a democratic regime."

[45] Damaška (1997), p. 74, our translation. From the same author, also see Damaška (1973), p. 506. Taking, like many, the terms *adversarial* and *accusatory* as synonymous in particular, Amodio states: "accusatory is the system in which the procedural and evidentiary initiative is entrusted to the parties: party-prosecution and party-presentation of evidence are characteristics that place the judge in the position of arbitrator of a conflict that falls entirely on the shoulders of the accuser the task of defending society by repressing criminal acts" (2003, p. 198).

[46] Damaška (1973), p. 583.

[47] In this sense, see: Fedorova (2012), p. 94.

[48] Fassler (1991), Grande (2000), pp. 230–231; Fedorova (2012), p. 110.

There is, therefore, no relationship of submission between the representative of a state power (judge) and the one who is, or can be, at the end of the criminal process, submitted to him as a subject (the accused).

The adversarial system is concerned with the relationship between the parties. It gives them the leading role in obtaining and presenting the evidence they can obtain to then have the expectation (or perspective, in the language of James Goldschmidt) of a favorable (in the first case) or unfavorable (in the second) sentence. And it has also been said that, from its radicalization at the end of the twentieth century started in the United States of America, such a system works even with the assimilation (which is not seen in the accusatory, nor in the inquisitive) of civil process rules,[49] of which the agreement between the parties to end the process is an example.[50]

The notion of dispositivity[51] of the object of the process, innate to civil process and brought cum *granum sallis* to the criminal process in the adversarial system[52] (in radicalization of which, the examples are the *guilty plea* of the American criminal process and the *patteggiamento*[53] Italian), is proof of distancing from the models in comparison. It is also a central characteristic point of the adversarial criminal process, as it has been outlined since the second half of the twentieth century.[54]

Therefore, the observation of a certain temptation of adversariality in the criminal processes studied by certain institutes does not allow it to be taken as if it were

---

[49] This is what Langbein says in more than one passage of his text, especially in the initial part, when he defines his object of study: "To some extent, the development of adversary criminal procedure can be depicted as the absorption into criminal procedure of a model already operating in the civil trial. [...] The adversary model came from the civil side, where the parties routinely engaged counsel to shape the course of litigation to partisan advantage, but the significance of the adversary system expanded greatly when transposed to crime. [...] the development of adversary criminal trial raised an acute theoretical challenge, which has never been satisfactorily resolved in the Anglo-American tradition: how to justify the truth-impairing tendencies of a procedure that remits to partisans the work of gathering and presenting the evidence upon which accurate adjudication depends. Civil litigation arises from private interests, which is why the law encourages the parties to settle their case without regard to any public interest. The purposes of criminal law, by contrast, are prevailingly those of the public interest, which is why in the European legal tradition the work of investigating and adjudicating cases of serious crime is treated as a public responsibility assigned to neutral professionals who bring the resources of the state to bear both for and against the accused" (1995, pp. 1–8).

[50] Malan and Saad (2005), p. 4.

[51] Badaró (2003), p. 133: "In the *adversary system* prevails the possibility of the accuser, whether public or private, to dispose of his own punitive claim, either by not formulating the accusation, or by using the mechanisms of *bargaining*."

[52] "An adversarial prosecution pattern exists in all forms of litigation whether in civil or criminal cases in order to expose the evidence in the case" (Gabbay, 1990, p. 13).

[53] This also occurs with the Italian *patteggiamento*, in the lesson of Illuminati (2008), pp. 159–160. For a critical view of this radicalisation of a possible facet of the adversarial system—since it is neither historically innate to it nor essential to it, despite being currently widespread especially from lessons of criminal procedural law of the United States of America—see, in addition to the authors so far referred to: Schünemann (2013), pp. 240 and foll.

[54] Langer (2004), p. 259. From legal transplants to legal translations: the globalization of plea bargaining and the Americanization thesis in criminal procedure.

synonymous with accusatory. Nor can we consider the adversarial system as a part (affecting the evidentiary regime) of distinct criminal procedural families: the accusatory and the inquisitorial.

While the accusatory system is concerned with the division of functions with a focus on the prohibition of the judge in the formation of evidentiary elements, the adversarial system is forged with prevalence to the performance of the parties in the process and, indirectly, affects the judge in his instructive power.

From the perspective of this work, it is conceived that the first is concerned with the judge and his activities to safeguard the functional tripartition, while the latter focuses on the parties, notably from the defensive performance and their reaction to the accusatory attack.[55]

If this distinction is important for the study of equality of arms, it cannot get there, yet, without recognizing critical points that are directed at the adversarial system, especially in its current radicalization regarding the consequence—which affects both sides of the contest, that is, the accused and the accuser—from a certain dispositivity of its object.

As already seen in a previous chapter, the adversarial criminal process can be much more *risky* to the defense, given that, if the accusation is foreseen the burdens of proof, to the defense is foreseen the taking advantage of chances and the risks of assuming more passive or active postures in the process, hence its perspectives (of unfavorable sentence) or expectations (of favorable sentence).

In the adversarial criminal process, the one who argues better wins, given the weapons available to the contenders. The rules of the game are directed at the parties. The one who plays better wins.

4.4 Criticisms of the Adversarial System

From the lessons of John H. Langbein and Michelle Taruffo, it is possible to address criticisms of the adversarial system.

In the words of the first, the points susceptible to questioning are the "*combat effect*" and the "*wealth effect*."[56] Such criticisms do not stem from the opposition between accuser and accused in the criminal process, but from the inequality

[55] As Langbein (2003), p. 67 and foll. reported, especially from the *Treason's Act* of 1696. In this regard, McEwan (1992), p. 6, says that "the increased importance of the judicial role correspondingly diminishes the Power and function of the advocate." On this matter, see: Malan (2009), p. 16. For Fedorova (2012), p. 110, "the adversarial process encompasses procedural equality between two parties to the proceedings."

[56] Right on the first page of Langbein's work (2003), p. 1, it reads: "By the combat effect, I refer to the truth-impairing incentives of the adversary system. By the wealth effect, I refer to the enormous advantage that adversary procedure bestows upon persons who can afford to hire skilled trial counsel, and to pay for party-conducted factual investigation. Because most persons accused of serious crimes are indigent or near indigent, the wealth effect is a profound structural flaw in adversary criminal procedure."

between the accused themselves, since socioeconomic inequalities external to the criminal process are reflected in it.[57]

The criticisms problematize even the constitutional ideal of justice from the search for material equality, insofar as it is said that the adversarial system does not take care of such a concept of equality. According to this criticism, for the process, formal equality is enough; that is, what matters is how the parties present themselves before the judge.[58] The model built under the molds of the liberal Rule of Law does not take care of the procedural reflections of extraprocedural inequality. And it is precisely for this reason that Taruffo says that, in the current socioeconomic context, the prestige of the adversarial system in search of substantial justice does not go beyond a "profession of faith."[59]

Hence, from the combat effect (*combat effect*) can arise the problematic wealth effect (*wealth effect*): the combatant who can afford a technically better equipped defense can go in search of more effective sources of evidence to introduce them into the criminal process.[60]

The same difference echoed in the criminal process from the economic disparity between the accused (the rich and the poor) appears in another case in which it radicalized in association made, from the second half of the twentieth century, to the adversarial mechanism of the process, although it is not a historical or technically innate notion: the agreement with a view to reducing the sentence or extinguishing the process (*guilty plea* or *plea bargaining*).

The example of agreements in criminal proceedings, incidentally, is analyzed with quite severity by Taruffo, who sees in them not only the violation of the very adversariality of the criminal process, but the eruption of other principles dear to the current criminal process.

In the study he made from the observation that the American criminal process is about 90% resolved in agreements, Taruffo criticizes the injury to the rights of the accused to appreciate their defensive theses and the precariousness in the knowledge of the facts by the magistrates.

Hence why it is the Italian professor's understanding, once again,

> the typical effect of the guilty plea is to completely eliminate the adversary nature of the procedure leading to the sentence, as the preliminary admission of guilt implies the waiver

[57] In Brazil, and from this perspective (without prejudice to others) of introjection of socioeconomic inequalities into the process and with reflections precisely on the possibility of coercion of the accusation to accept plea bargain proposals in criminal proceedings, see: Prado (2011), p. 312, item 77.

[58] Taruffo (2008), pp. 55 and foll. Also in the same work, at p. 100: "the adversary system not only does not eliminate inequality between the parties, which derives from factors external to the procedural situation, but it works as a multiplier of such inequalities, increasing the differences in defensive chances between 'strong' and 'weak' parties."

[59] Taruffo (2008), p. 51.

[60] Aware of this is Winter (2008), p. 47.

of the trial (also the discovery phase that precedes it), and allows the judge, once the plea is accepted, to provide only with reference to the determination of the sentence.[61]

Under this bias, an internal inconsistency of the system is exposed: it is said that the adversarial works in the United States, but, according to Taruffo, it works precisely, and paradoxically, by (and not *for*) not working.[62] And as for the *plea bargain*, the criticism can still reach another point.

That is, if Maximo Langer is right when he states that one of the definitions of the inquisitive system could be the system or mechanism that has the function of coercively obtaining recognition of guilt,[63] the very agreements in the criminal process can be seen as inquisitive traits within one of the main characteristics of the supposed adversariality of the system.[64] The accused who is better equipped within the process will suffer pressure—even if psychological—less than the other, who, due to a worse economic situation, will bear less skilled technical defense.

To draw attention to the word, the same *weapons* available to one or another accused can be used more or less effectively, depending on the presentation of the defense in the process.

Hence, it is inevitable and more perceptible, in the adversarial criminal process, that "from a perspective of confrontation of parties, of struggle between them, the most skilled or clever party triumphs, not necessarily the party that is right."[65]

Hence, also, that the *combat effect* can translate into a consequence of the very inequality in the distribution of justice, and that, as Michelle Taruffo aptly says, "equal justice under the law" ends up transforming into "unequal justice under the lawyers."[66]

From the perspective of achieving the inquiry of the facts motivating the criminal prosecution, the *wealth effect* can privatize the investigation and the presentation of the evidence.[67] In turn, the *combat effect* is capable of distancing the criminal

---

[61] Taruffo (2008), p. 218.

[62] In Brazilian doctrine attentive to this problem of comparative law, see: Badaró (2003), p. 134.

[63] Langer (2004), p. 246. The author also says: "from this perspective, it does not matter what the elements of the system and the subsystem or mechanism are—as it is central in pure or ideal types –. That is, it does not matter if the coercive guilt recognitions are obtained by an inquisitor judge torturing the defendant, by a prosecutor on a plane of formal equality with him, by a policeman asking him questions before informing him of his rights, by a grand jury during its secret proceedings or, even, by a judge-psychiatrist using hypnosis."

[64] Schünemann (2013), pp. 242–3.

[65] Badaró (2003), p. 131. Hence, the heightened deontological concern that the doctrine points out should be a fundamental part of the adversarial criminal process. Regarding this, not only footnote n. 259 of the cited page of the Brazilian author's work, but also the text by Comoglio and Zagrebelsky (1993), p. 461. In the sense that the prosecution should *lay all the evidence on the table*, including those that favor the accused, see: Babcock (1981-1982), p. 1134. Already in the sense that the system would even privilege good professional ethics, see: Landsman (1983), p. 716.

[66] Taruffo (2008), p. 94.

[67] "Such a procedure is intrinsically skewed to the advantage of wealthy defendants, who can afford to hire the most skilled counsel and to pay for the gathering and production of defensive evidence" Langbein (2003), p. 102.

process from the objective of achieving the truth. After all, from the partial activity of collecting and presenting the evidence that best interests, each party may be encouraged to suppress or distort elements of evidence that are unfavorable to them.[68]

4.5 The Contribution of the Adversarial System to the Equality of Arms in the Criminal Process

Even though the critical points of the adversarial system are noted, one of its characteristics is what justifies taking it as conducive to equality of arms: this is the process model that, potentially, takes the idea of equality of positions between accused and accuser most seriously.[69] Here is the aspect that justifies its importance for the equality of arms in the criminal process.

Indeed, and given that the *party presentation* and the *party prosecution* are two central ideas in the adversarial process, it is Taruffo himself who indicates that a "fundamental condition of the functioning of the adversarial method" is the need to guarantee to the parties a relative equality of defensive capacity within the scope of the process.[70]

It is in the adversarial criminal process that the idea of a criminal process of parties can be realized, nonexistent, at least in the core, in the accusatory criminal process. After all, it is assumed in such a process—and only in it—that the action of the parties is "motivated by interests of an individual character. When the party has to perform an act in order to avoid any kind of procedural damage, at its maximum degree embodied in the experience of the unfavourable sentence, it incurs a procedural burden."[71]

The adversarial criminal process is an environment in which a so-called *dispute model* takes place. In it, according to Maximo Langer,

> the parties are on a plane of complete formal equality. Both have the same procedural powers which include, among others, the possibility of conducting their own investigation into the facts, the power to present witnesses and experts, to question their own and the other party's witnesses and experts, to argue about the evidence produced and about the law, etcetera.[72]

In the words of Taruffo,

---

[68] Langbein (2003), p. 103. Geraldo Prado concludes: "while the accusatory and inquisitorial models touch on the search for truth, consensual criminal solutions deal with something different and therefore do not fit directly into any of these models" (2011), p. 310, item 57.

[69] Interestingly, its distortion—clearly facilitated by the very disregard for the equality of arms—is what can undermine the notion of equal treatment of the parties in the process.

[70] Taruffo (2008), p. 53.

[71] Gloeckner (2013), p. 74.

[72] Langer (2004), p. 264.

> the equality of the parties is an indispensable prerequisite for *procedural justice*, especially as the adversarial process depends in its multiple aspects on the way the parties manage it. This is equivalent to saying, moreover, that the adversarial process can function fairly only when there is no appreciable inequality of power (economic) and defensive capacities.[73]

Therefore, even if attention is paid to the criticisms, the characteristic of procedural equality as innate to the adversarial system makes it significant for the equality of arms in the criminal process. The main rule of the procedural game becomes the observance of the equality of the parties, and the favorable result to one side or the other ends up becoming a contingency of the most effective argument of one side or the other.

To say that the one who plays better wins is complemented by saying that the one who plays better wins, observing the procedural equality between the contenders.

Recognizing the criticism addressed, perhaps with good arguments that support it, particularly in relation to the radicalization of agreements in criminal process, does not denature the privilege of studying the adversarial criminal process with eyes on the equality of arms.

Even Taruffo's criticism about mere formal equality can be seen from another perspective, as is that of Maximo Langer. According to this author, in what he calls the *dispute model*, the mere formal equality between the adversaries in the procedural scene is not enough. It must also be observed that the parties have

> not only the same formal powers, but also similar material powers that allow them to prove their own hypotheses and refute those of others. This means, fundamentally, that both parties have similar human and material resources to carry out their own factual - and legal - investigations and thus be on an equal footing during the trial. For the same reasons, it is also necessary for there to be equality not only formal but also material so that the accused is an authentic subject of rights and so that, in case of negotiations, the material inequality between the parties does not make every threat from the accuser coercive.[74]

The main contribution of the adversarial criminal process to the equality of arms, therefore, is the concern with equality in the treatment of the subjects of the process and in the distribution of opportunities for the manifestations with a view to convincing the judge. The adversarial criminal process is concerned with the beginning of everything: the equality of the parties.

References

Alonso, P. A. (1979). *Instituciones de derecho procesal penal* (Vol. I, 2nd ed.). Gráficas Encinas.

Ambos, K. (2005). *¿Es el procedimiento penal internacional "adversarial," "inquisitivo" o misto?* Revista Brasileira de Ciências Criminais.

Amodio, E. (2003). *Processo penale, diritto europeo e common law: dal rito inquisitorio al giusto processo*. Giuffrè.

---

[73] Taruffo (2008), p. 54.

[74] Langer (2004), p. 265, our translation.

Andrade, M. F. (2008). *Sistemas processuais penais e seus princípios reitores*. Juruá.
Armenta-deu, T. (2016). Beyond accusatorial or inquisitorial systems: A matter of deliberation and balance. In *Visions of justice. Liber Amicorum Mirjan Damaška*. Duncker & Humblot.
Aroca, M. (1997). *Principios del proceso penal: una explicación basada en la razón*. Tirant lo Blanc.
Aroca, M. (2008a). *La inutilidad del llamado principio acusatório para la conformación del proceso penal*. Ara Editores.
Aroca, M. (2008b). Principio acusatório y prueba en el proceso penal: la inutilidad jurídica de un eslogan político. In J. L. Gómez Colomer (Ed.), *Prueba y proceso penal: análises especial de la prueba prohibida en el sistema español y en el derecho comparado*. Ara Editores.
Aroca J. M. (2008c). *Proceso penal y libertad*. Ensayo polémico sobre el nuevo proceso penal. Civitas.
Azevedo, L. C. d. (2004). *Sistemas processuais penais: acusatório, inquisitivo, misto; origens distorções, atualidades*. Revista do Advogado.
Babcock, B. A. (1981-1982). Fair play: Evidence favorable to an accused and effective assistance of counsel. *Stanford Law Review, 34*, 1133.
Badaró, G. H. R. I. (2003). *Ônus da prova no processo penal*. Revista dos Tribunais.
Comoglio, L. P., & Zagrebelsky, V. (1993). *Modello accusatorio e deontologia dei comportamenti processuali nella prospettiva comparatistica*. Rivista Italiana di Diritto e Procedura Penale.
Coutinho, J. N. d. M. (2009). *Sistema acusatório: cada parte no lugar constitucionalmente demarcado*. Revista de Informação Legislativa.
Damaška, M. (1973). *Evidentiary barriers to conviction and two models of criminal procedure: A comparative study*. University of Pennsylvania Law Review.
Damaška, M. (1986). *The faces of justice and state authority: A comparative approach to the legal process*. Yale University Press.
Damaška, M. (1997). *Evidence law adrift*. Yale University Press.
Fassler, L. (1991). The Italian penal procedural code: An adversary system of criminal procedure in continental Europe. *Columbia Journal of Transnational Law, 29*, 245.
Fedorova, M. (2012). *The principle of equality of arms in international criminal proceedings*. Intersentia; School of Human Rights Research.
Gabbay, E. (1990). *The English adversarial system*. E. & J. Gabbay.
Garner, B. A. (Ed.). (2009). *Black's law dictionary* (9th ed.). West Group.
Gloeckner, R. J. (2013). *Nulidades no processo penal: Introdução principiológica à teoria do ato processual irregular*. JusPODIVM.
Grande, E. (2000). Italian criminal justice: Borrowing and resistance. *The American Journal of Comparative Law, 48*, 227.
Grinover, A. P. (1999). *A iniciativa instrutória do juiz no processo penal acusatório*. Revista Brasileira de Ciências Criminais.
Houaiss, A. *Great Houaiss dictionary of the Portuguese language*. Available at: http://houaiss.uol.com.br/. Accessed 20 Dec 2012.
Illuminati, G. (2008). *El sistema acusatório en Italia*. Barcelona.
Landsman, S. (1983). Brief survey of the development of the adversary system. *Ohio State Law Journal, 44*, 713.
Langbein, J. H. (1995). The influence of comparative procedure in the United States. *The American Journal of Comparative Law, 43*, 545.
Langbein, J. H. (2003). *The origins of adversary criminal trial*. Oxford University Press.
Langer, M. (2004). From legal transplants to legal translations: The globalization of plea bargaining and the Americanization thesis in criminal procedure. *Harvard International Law Journal, 45*, 1.
Langer, M. (2016). *In the beginning was fortescue: On the intellectual origins of the adversarial and inquisitorial systems and common and civil law in comparative criminal procedure*. Duncker & Humblot.

Lopes, A., Jr. (2008). *Direito processual penal e sua conformidade constitucional* (Vol. I, 3rd ed.). Lumen Juris.

Malan, D. (2009). *Direito ao confronto no processo penal*. Lumen Juris.

Malan, D., & Saad, M. (2005). *Origens históricas dos sistemas acusatório e inquisitivo*. Revista dos Tribunais.

Marques, J. F. (1960). *Do processo penal acusatório*. Forense.

Mcewan, J. (1992). *Evidence and the adversarial process: The modern law*. Blackwell Business.

Oxford (Ed.). (2003). *Paperback reference: A dictionary of law* (5th ed.). Oxford University Press.

Pezzotti, O. E. (2020). *Colaboração Premiada. Uma perspectiva de direito comparado*. Almedina.

Prado, G. (2006). *Sistema acusatório: a conformidade constitucional das leis processuais penais* (4th ed.). Lumen Juris.

Prado, G. P. (2011). *Poder negocial (sobre a pena), common law e processo penal brasileiro: meta XXI, em busca de um milhão de presos!?* Lumen Juris.

Scholz, L. R. (1999). *Sistemas processuais penais e processo penal brasileiro*. Revista dos Tribunais.

Schünemann, B. (2013). *Estudos de direito penal, direito procesual penal e filosofía do direito*. Marcial Pons.

Shapiro, A. A. (1993). *Political theory and the growth of defensive safeguards in criminal procedure: The origins of the treason trial acts of 1696*. Cambridge University Press & Assessment.

Spina, S. (2003). *Normas gerais para os trabalhos de grau: um breviário para o estudante de pós-graduação*. Ateliê Editorial.

Taruffo, M. (2008). *El proceso civil adversarial en la experiencia americana: el modelo americano del proceso de conotación dispositiva*. Temis.

Tucci, R. L. (1976). *Lineamentos do processo penal romano*. José Bushatsky.

Tucci, R. L. (2002). *Teoria do direito processual penal: jurisdição, ação e processo penal (estudo sistemático)*. Revista dos Tribunais.

Vélez-Mariconde, A. (1986). *Derecho procesal penal* (Vol. I, 3rd ed.). Marcos Lerner Editora.

Vogler, R. (2001). *La dicotomia acusatorio-inquisitivo y la importación de mecanismos procesales de la tradición jurídica anglosajona: algunas reflexiones a partir del procedimiento abreviado*. Editores del Puerto.

Vogler, R. (2005). *Adversarialidad y el dominio angloamericano del proceso penal*. Universidad Externado de Colombia.

Vogler, R. (2008). *El sistema acusatorio en los procesos penales en Inglaterra y en Europa continental*. Barcelona.

Winter, L. B. (2008). *Acusatorio versus inquisitivo: reflexiones acerca del proceso penal*. Barcelona.

Zilli, M. (2010). *Os atores e seus papéis*. Boletim do Instituto Brasileiro de Ciências Criminais. Boletim do Instituto Brasileiro de Ciências Criminais.

Chapter 5
The Concept of Equality of Arms in Criminal Proceedings

5.1 Resumption of Starting Points and Methodology of Work

To arrive at a useful concept of equality of arms in criminal proceedings, it is necessary to revisit what has been seen so far regarding the constitutional extract of the principle and the procedural system in which such a principle can be applied.

The constitutional premise for the application of equality of arms in criminal proceedings is equality, particularly equality of treatment in the process between the accused (in a broad sense) and the accuser.[1] Because of this, Chap. 1 discussed the evolution of the constitutional concept of formal and material equality. There, it was necessary to explain to what extent a principled rule is realized in criminal proceedings in opposition to other fundamental rights rules, which are the *rules*.

In Chap. 2, the legislative oscillations in each Brazilian Criminal Procedure Code were seen, including the current one. It also dealt with the scenario of the projected Code in terms of procedural equality.

In Chap. 3, it was assumed that the process can be focused by the doctrine of the legal situation (Goldschmidt) to perceive the conflict between the accuser and the accused. According to this theory, the role of the judge is more distant than what is seen in the concept of process as a procedural relationship, when the judicial figure hovers over the relationship that animates everyone.

In this way, the main problems were dealt with, sometimes from one side (the accuser and the issues arising from following the tradition of considering him an

[1] Fedorova (2012), pp. 105–106, understands that equality of arms does not derive from equality. For her, equality of arms is an expression of the ancient principle *audi altera paretem* or *audiatur et altera pars*. Marczak (2000), pp. 18–20, understands that the equality of arms originates from the principle *audiatur et altera pars* and, in current German positive law, it distinguishes itself from equality and is linked to the guarantee of the Rule of Law. Cassese (2008), p. 384, on the other hand, considers that the principle integrates the guarantee of the *fair trial*, in the wake of the doctrine of the European Court of Human Rights (ECHR), without, however, a focus on equality.

R. S. Vieira, *Equality of Arms in Criminal Procedure*,
https://doi.org/10.1007/978-3-032-03663-6_5

impartial representative of the state and part), sometimes from another (the accused and the possibilities of defensive reaction, dispensing him the arms to face the accusation), or even, concerning the particularity and the limits of the intervention of third parties in criminal proceedings.

In Chap. 4, the work first dealt with criminal procedural systems as separate and distinct models (inquisitive and accusatory), to then advance in the treatment of the adversarial system, fertile for the development of equality of arms.

This journey made it possible to approach the judgments and comments of doctrine that, in this chapter, will be brought as guides for the concept of equality of arms in criminal proceedings.

This methodology (of comparative law and even of international criminal procedural law[2]) was also adopted because there is almost no study in Brazil about equality of arms in criminal proceedings.[3] After all, either due to the little attention that the current Code gives to the distribution of possibilities of accusatory and defensive arguments in criminal proceedings, or, correlatively to this, because the national doctrine and jurisprudence are resistant to the lessons that international law—including in the field of criminal procedure—can give to the subject, it lacks theoretical reflections that, at least, deal with questioning the application of the concept to Brazilian criminal procedural law.

It seems that there is still a clear opposition between authoritarian and libertarian conceptions of criminal proceedings. It is a recent understanding that the state should not only and simply condemn the guilty (and, for this, have resources in favor of the accusations), but also provide procedural guarantees to the accused (and spend resources on the defense). Thus, it is rightly said that "a reconsideration of the application of procedural rules in the light of the principle of equality of arms is a key to the complete and effective realization of procedural equality and fair trials."[4]

For such circumstances, in an attempt to reach such a useful concept of equality of arms, judgments of the European Court of Human Rights (hereinafter, ECHR[5]) are

[2] Cole (2010), p. 35, says that "though the principle has flourished and gained acceptance as the bedrock of procedural fairness in the jurisprudence of the European Court of Human Rights as well as international and internationalized tribunals, its scope and application is somewhat constricted and contextualized in the latter."

[3] There is a work by Welton Roberto, published in 2011, which is dedicated to equality of arms in criminal proceedings, and an article by Karam (2009), pp. 394–406. Apart from that, there are no direct focuses. Andrade (2008), p. 159, states that "the principle of equality of arms has not received specific attention from the doctrine, as we rarely find really complete studies on the theme."

[4] Cole (2010), p. 36.

[5] The European Convention on Human Rights, signed in Rome on 4 November 1950, in its Article 6 °, when dealing with the so-called *fair trial*, provides that: "1. Everyone has the right to have their case examined fairly and publicly, within a reasonable time by an independent and impartial court, established by law, which will decide, either on the determination of their civil rights and obligations, or on the basis of any criminal charge against them. The trial must be public, but access to the courtroom may be prohibited to the press or the public during all or part of the process, when in the interest of morality, public order or national security in a democratic society, when the interests of minors or the protection of the private life of the parties in the process require it, or, to the extent deemed strictly necessary by the court, when, under special circumstances, publicity could

used—interpretation given to Article 14 of the International Covenant on Civil and Political Rights (hereinafter, ICCPR) by the UN Human Rights Committee (HRC)[6]—and judgments of the Inter-American Court of Human Rights (IACHR).[7] To some

be detrimental to the interests of justice. 2. Anyone accused of an offence is presumed innocent until their guilt has been legally proven. 3. The accused has, at least, the following rights: a) to be informed in the shortest possible time, in a language they understand and in detail, of the nature and cause of the charge against them; b) to have the time and the necessary means for the preparation of their defence; c) to defend themselves or to have the assistance of a defender of their choice and, if they do not have the means to pay a defender, to be assisted free of charge by an official defender, when the interests of justice require it; d) to question or have the prosecution witnesses questioned and to obtain the summoning and questioning of the defence witnesses under the same conditions as the prosecution witnesses; e) to be assisted free of charge by an interpreter, if they do not understand or do not speak the language used in the process" (The Portuguese version of the Convention is the one found in the work of Barreto (2005)).

[6]The Covenant, adopted by Resolution No. 2.200-A (XXI) of the United Nations General Assembly on 16 December 1966 and ratified by Brazil on 24 January 1992, provides, in its Article 14, the following: "All persons are equal before the Courts and the Courts of Justice. Every person shall have the right to be heard publicly and with due guarantees by a competent, independent and impartial court, established by law, in the investigation of any criminal charge formulated against them or in the determination of their civil rights and obligations. The press and the public may be excluded from part or all of a trial, either for reasons of public morality, public order or national security in a democratic society, or when the interest of the private life of the parties requires it, or to the extent that this is strictly necessary in the opinion of justice, under specific circumstances, in which publicity may prejudice the interests of justice; however, any sentence pronounced in criminal or civil matters must become public, unless the interest of minors requires the opposite procedure, or the process relates to matrimonial disputes or the guardianship of minors. 2. Every person accused of an offence shall have the right to be presumed innocent until their guilt has been legally proven. 3. Every person accused of an offence shall have the right, in full equality, to the following minimum guarantees a) to be informed, without delay, in a language they understand and in detail, of the nature and reasons for the charge against them formulated; b) to have the time and the necessary means for the preparation of their defence and to communicate with a defender of their choice; c) to be tried without undue delays; d) to be present at the trial and to defend themselves personally or through a defender of their choice; to be informed, if they do not have a defender, of the right they have to have one, and whenever the interest of justice so requires, to have a defender appointed ex officio free of charge, if they do not have the means to pay them; e) to question or have the prosecution witnesses questioned and to obtain the attendance and questioning of the defence witnesses under the same conditions as those of the prosecution; f) to be assisted by an interpreter, if they do not understand or do not speak the language used during the trial; g) not to be compelled to testify against themselves, nor to confess guilt" (The Portuguese version used is from a document published by the Centre for Studies of the State Attorney General's Office of São Paulo, 1997).

[7]The Convention, ratified by Brazil on 25 September 1992, in its Article 8, provides that: "1. Everyone has the right to be heard, with due guarantees and within a reasonable time, by a competent, independent and impartial judge or court, established previously by law, in the investigation of any criminal accusation made against her, or in the determination of her rights and obligations of a civil, labour, tax or any other nature. 2. Every person accused of a crime has the right to be presumed innocent, until her guilt is legally proven. During the trial, every person has the right, in full equality, to the following minimum guarantees a) the right of the accused to be assisted free of charge by a translator or interpreter, if they do not understand or do not speak the language of the court or tribunal; b) prior and detailed communication to the accused of the accusation made; c) granting the accused the time and means necessary for the preparation of their defence; d) the right of the accused to defend themselves personally or to be assisted by a defender of their choice and to communicate freely and privately with their defender; e) the inalienable right to be assisted by

extent, judgments of the Tribunal ad hoc of the former Yugoslavia (ICTY[8]) and the Tribunal ad hoc of Rwanda (ICTR[9,10]).

---

a defender provided by the State, paid or not, according to domestic law, if the accused does not defend themselves, nor appoint a defender within the deadline established by law; f) the right of the defence to question the witnesses present in the Court and to obtain the attendance, as witnesses or experts, of other people who can shed light on the facts; g) the right not to be forced to testify against herself, nor to confess guilty; and h) the right to appeal the sentence to a judge or higher court" (The Portuguese version is from the same document published by the Centre for Studies of the Attorney General's Office of the State of São Paulo, cited in the previous footnote).

[8] Article 21 of the Statute of the Tribunal, established by Resolution 827 of 25 May 1993, by the United Nations, provides, as rights of the accused, the following: "1. All persons shall be equal before the International Tribunal. 2. In the determination of charges against him, the accused shall be entitled to a fair and public hearing, subject to article 22 of the Statute. 3. The accused shall be presumed innocent until proved guilty according to the provisions of the present Statute. 4. In the determination of any charge against the accused pursuant to the present Statute, the accused shall be entitled to the following minimum guarantees, in full equality: (a) to be informed promptly and in detail in a language which he understands of the nature and cause of the charge against him; (b) to have adequate time and facilities for the preparation of his defence and to communicate with counsel of his own choosing; (c) to be tried without undue delay; (d) to be tried in his presence, and to defend himself in person or through legal assistance of his own choosing; to be informed, if he does not have legal assistance, of this right; and to have legal assistance assigned to him, in any case where the interests of justice so require, and without payment by him in any such case if he does not have sufficient means to pay for it; (e) to examine, or have examined, the witnesses against him and to obtain the attendance and examination of witnesses on his behalf under the same conditions as witnesses against him; (f) to have the free assistance of an interpreter if he cannot understand or speak the language used in the International Tribunal; (g) not to be compelled to testify against himself or to confess guilt" (The English version of the Statute of the Tribunal consulted is updated until September 2009 and is available at: http://icty.org/x/file/Legal%20 Library/Statute/statute_sept09_en.pdf)

[9] Article 20 of the Statute of that Tribunal established by Resolution 955 of 8 November 1994, by the United Nations, provides, as rights of the accused, the following: "1. All persons shall be equal before the International Tribunal for Rwanda. 2. In the determination of charges against him or her, the accused shall be entitled to a fair and public hearing, subject to Article 21 of the Statute. 3. The accused shall be presumed innocent until proven guilty according to the provisions of the present Statute. 4. In the determination of any charge against the accused pursuant to the present Statute, the accused shall be entitled to the following minimum guarantees, in full equality: (a) To be informed promptly and in detail in a language which he or she understands of the nature and cause of the charge against him or her; (b) To have adequate time and facilities for the preparation of his or her defence and to communicate with counsel of his or her own choosing; (c) To be tried without undue delay; (d) To be tried in his or her presence, and to defend himself or herself in person or through legal assistance of his or her own choosing; to be informed, if he or she does not have legal assistance, of this right; and to have legal assistance assigned to him or her, in any case where the interest of justice so require, and without payment by him or her in any such case if he or she does not have sufficient means to pay for it; (e) To examine, or have examined, the witnesses against him or her and to obtain the attendance and examination of witnesses on his or her behalf under the same conditions as witnesses against him or her; (f) To have the free assistance of an interpreter if he or she cannot understand or speak the language used in the International Tribunal for Rwanda; (g) Not to be compelled to testify against himself or herself or to confess guilt" (The consulted version, in English and French, is updated until the Resolution 1.901, of 16 November 2009, and is available at: http://www.unictr.org/Portals/0/English/Legal/Statute/2010.pdf)

[10] In this regard, the uniform lessons of what can be understood as a minimum of procedural guarantees to the accused are provided even in the International Criminal Court, which can be seen

What is used from comparative law for the research of the concept of equality of arms in criminal proceedings is not, topically, the study of its treatment in certain countries. This is because there is consensus in the sense that its development is due, much more than to the treatment in positive law of each state, to what is given to it by international organizations.

Thus, as a justification for the limitation of the sources of the law comparative criminal procedure, it is possible to affirm that the conceptual matrix of the principle is not reached from the plane of the procedural law comparative criminal law of each country, but its application is what can vary in each of them.[11]

From the matrix derived from precedents and doctrinal studies, it can be said that, from country to country, the incidence of the principle is noted with greater or lesser clarity, given the vicissitudes of each criminal procedural order.[12]

from reading its Article 67: "1. In the determination of any charge, the accused shall be entitled to a public hearing, having regard to the provisions of this Statute, to a fair hearing conducted impartially, and to the following minimum guarantees, in full equality: (a) To be informed promptly and in detail of the nature, cause and content of the charge, in a language which the accused fully understands and speaks; (b) To have adequate time and facilities for the preparation of the defence and to communicate freely with counsel of the accused's choosing in confidence; (c) To be tried without undue delay; (d) Subject to article 63, paragraph 2, to be present at the trial, to conduct the defence in person or through legal assistance of the accused's choosing, to be informed, if the accused does not have legal assistance, of this right and to have legal assistance assigned by the Court in any case where the interests of justice so require, and without payment if the accused lacks sufficient means to pay for it; Rome Statute of the International Criminal Court; (e) To examine, or have examined, the witnesses against him or her and to obtain the attendance and examination of witnesses on his or her behalf under the same conditions as witnesses against him or her. The accused shall also be entitled to raise defences and to present other evidence admissible under this Statute; (f) To have, free of any cost, the assistance of a competent interpreter and such translations as are necessary to meet the requirements of fairness, if any of the proceedings of or documents presented to the Court are not in a language which the accused fully understands and speaks; (g) Not to be compelled to testify or to confess guilt and to remain silent, without such silence being a consideration in the determination of guilt or innocence; (h) To make an unsworn oral or written statement in his or her defence; and (i) Not to have imposed on him or her any reversal of the burden of proof or any onus of rebuttal. 2. In addition to any other disclosure provided for in this Statute, the Prosecutor shall, as soon as practicable, disclose to the defence evidence in the Prosecutor's possession or control which he or she believes shows or tends to show the innocence of the accused, or to mitigate the guilt of the accused, or which may affect the credibility of prosecution evidence. In case of doubt as to the application of this paragraph, the Court shall decide" (The Treaty that established the International Criminal Court was adopted on 17th July 1998 and has been in force since 1st of July 2002. The English version of the Statute of the Court is available at: http://www.icc-cpi.int/NR/rdonlyres/ADD16852-AEE9-4757-ABE7-9CDC7CF02886/283503/RomeStatutEng1.pdf)

[11] "In this context, it is crucial to understand that the interpretation of equality of arms in the human rights context does not depend on the different domestic criminal procedural models. However, the application of this principle can only be understood having regard to the contextual features of one reticular model. in other words, although the human rights case law provides a general minimum understanding of the values and norms involved, it can only guide the application *in concreto*" Fedorova (2012), p. 18.

[12] "The legislative power is subordinate to the constitutional order; the executive and judicial powers obey the law and the right" (Germany, 1996). Kohmann (1974), pp. 311–321, does not deal with the constitutional basis of the application of the principle, but is prolific in listing the concep-

For this very reason—that is, due to the configurations specific to each criminal process—it would be fruitless, as well as random, to approach the principle not from the international organizations that gave it its current configuration, but from its manifestation in each country.

From the uniform matrix, one can see, for example, the distinctions that the German and Colombian criminal procedural law give to the matter: while the German criminal procedural doctrine defines as the internal basis of the equality of arms the clause of the *Rule of Law* (Art. 20, III, Basic Law of 1949[13]), in Colombia, it is known that the principle of equality of arms applies from the *equality* (Art. 13, Colombian Constitution of 1991).[14] Already in a study directed to the civil process in Portuguese doctrine, it is noted that the "original foundations" of the equality of arms are "human dignity itself, the democratic rule of law, the equitable process and the principle of equality."[15]

Peter-Alexis Albrecht, in addition to saying that equality of arms means that the accuser and the accused should be seen at the same "eye level" ("*Dass sich Staatsanwaltschaft und Beschuldigter auf gleicher Augenhöhe begegnen*"), recalls that Article 1 of the Preamble of the French Code of Criminal Procedure already dealt with the principle: "la procédurale pénale doit être equitable et preserver l'équilibre des droits des parties."[16]

tual root in Article 6, 1, of the European Convention on Human Rights. Hartmann and Schmidt (2012), pp. 33–34, approached the equality of arms from the same root (Art. 6, 1, ECHR) to say that the principle is provided for in Article 20, III, of the Basic Law. Volk and Engländer (2013), p. 97, understand that the principle derives from the guarantees of the Rule of Law and Procedural Justice. Schroeder and Verrel (2011), p. 30, deal with the principle only from the direct link with the Art. 6, I, of the ECHR.

[13] González (2010), pp. 29–33. In the precedent research done by the author, it is noted that the Colombian Constitutional Court sees in the equality of arms the concretization of the constitutional rule of equality and that the concept of the principle is extracted from Article 6, 1, of the ECHR. The precedent cited is the judgment by the Plenary Chamber of the Constitutional Court, sentence C-396, of 2007.

[14] Costa (2012), p. 37.

[15] Costa (2003), p. 133 and endnote no. 154. Kohlbacher (1978), pp. 22 and foll., also saw the equality of arms directly linked to the guarantee of *fair trial*, in the terms of Article 6°, I, of the ECHR. From the same perspective of linking to the guarantee of *fair trial*, see: Sandermann (1975), p. 17 and following. In strict connection with the *fair trial* (*Who came first? The egg or the chicken?*) and with a slightly different conception of the principle ("parity of knowledge"—*parität des Wissens*), see: Hies (2009), pp. 64–65.

[16] Trechsel (2005), p. 94). In the author's words, who was a judge of the Tribunal ad hoc of the former Yugoslavia and President of the European Commission on Human Rights, as well as Professor of Criminal Procedure Law at the University of Zurich: "It is an essential element of a fair Trial." The same professor, on another occasion, took the topic as "complicated and complex," and placed the equality of arms as linked to the "cradle" of the notion of justice. See: "Equality of arms is a rather complicated and complex issue. Again, the closeness to 'fair proceedings' is obvious, a specification of the right to be heard—namely under the same conditions as the opposing party. Here we are confronted with a metaphor which recalls one of the cradles of the very notion of fairness—sports" (2018), p. 28. Zapater (2004), p. 475, when he was a member of the Supreme Court of Spain, said that the principle of equality of arms is the "fundamental and structural principle of the process with all guarantees." Rainey et al. understand that since the judgment of *Neumeister v. Austria* (*Application* no. 1936/63) the principle has been connected to the interpretation of Art. 6, I, of the European Convention on Human Rights (2014), p. 263.

The usefulness of the study of comparative law for this work, therefore, is not to think about the conformation of the principle of equality of arms in each country, but rather to delimit the concept from the international organs that gave it attention.

The centrality of this chapter for the work requires that one try to distinguish between what equality of arms *is not* and what it *is*. Then, it is hoped to say *to whom* (only to the defendant in criminal proceedings, or also to the investigated in the pre-judicial phase of criminal prosecution, or to those who are in the executive phase of the criminal process) the application of the principle is intended.

It is clear that dealing with the *who* means answering the *when* of the application of the principle—that is, if it covers only the arc of the judicial phase of the criminal process or if, on the contrary, it also covers the investigative phase and, after the judgement has become final, the execution of the sentence—and to the *where* it also applies—that is, what are the *situations* of incidence of the principle.

In addition to allowing the separation of what equality of arms *is not*, it is necessary to think about the *recipient* of the norm, as well as in the *moment* and in the *situation* of its application. This helps to define it even from the point of view of its treatment as a fundamental law norm, because in this way one can reach its factual support (broad) in the criminal process. And only in this way is it possible to consider, later, justifiable restrictions.

With the caution of dealing with the theme from the premise of theoretical and practical construction that was reached *outside* of the Brazilian criminal procedural scenario, the matter is focused on to try, in sequence, to construct a scientifically justifiable concept.

5.2 General Approaches from the Judgments of the TEDH

Since the earliest precedents of the ECtHR, the principle of equality of arms has been consecrated, in the words of Stefan Trechsel, as an "essential element of the fair process."[17] There are those who today take it as "sacrosanct"[18] and as "one of the great aporias of the modern criminal process."[19]

Currently, by the precedents of the Court and by the authors who have addressed the subject, the importance that equality of arms has reached is so great that it is seen both as the starting point of any examination of specific guarantees of Article 6, 1, of the ECHR,[20] as well as the gateway for any criminal process to be considered fair and consistent with human rights parameters,[21] or, still, as one of the significant

[17] Cole (2010), p. 38.

[18] Rodrigues (1991), p. 77.

[19] Summers and Jackson (2012), pp. 83/4.

[20] Negri (2005), p. 514.

[21] Wąsek-Wiaderek (2000), p. 23; Ubertis (2006), p. 15; Fedorova (2012), p. 30. In a footnote no. 38, the author cites the understanding of Nowak, according to whom the equality of arms is the most important criterion of a *fair trial*. Apparently, placing the equality of arms only as a consequence of the right to be heard: Harris et al. (1995), p. 202. Official publication of the Council of Europe (1994). p. 41, states that the concept of *fair trial* requires respect for the principle of equal-

elements of the fair process.[22] It was not always like this, however, and the application of the principle as it is known today did not properly start in the criminal procedural field.

While Trechsel[23] and Stefania Negri[24] take the case of *Dombo Beheer v. Netherlands*, judged by the Court in 1992,[25] as the first precedent of what later came to be consecrated as the principle of equality of arms, Sarah J. Summers reports that, as early as 1959, in the case *X v. Sweden* (*Application* n° 434/58),[26] equality of arms was brought up in a civil process.

Regarding the different approaches, it is opportune to remember that, in civil process, the notion of opposing parties is more widespread than in criminal process, as the parties that contend in the civil procedural scope, as a rule, defend private interests. In addition, it is easier to affirm the relevance of the principle of equality of arms[27] in civil process, as the plaintiff and defendant are equidistant and have abstractly the same argumentative potential.[28]

---

ity of arms, that is, the principle of "procedural equality between the parties." Prado (2024), p. 385, places the requirement that the state guarantees that "prosecution and defence can present their arguments and evidence in equality of arms and equality of treatment, orally and publicly," as inherent to the notion of a fair or equitable process.

[22] Wąsek-Wiaderek (2000), p. 96.

[23] Trechsel (2005), p. 515.

[24] *Application* no. 1.448/88, judged on ninth September 1992. Ubertis (2006), p. 15, footnote no. 4, takes as the first precedents in which the Court would have pronounced on the equality of arms the case *Delcourt v. Belgium* (*Application* no. 2.689/65, judged on 17th January 1970) and the case *Neumeister v. Austria* (*Application* no. 1.936/63, judged on 27th June 1968). In the same sense of the Italian author, Fanego (2009), p. 455, footnote no. 10, cites the two cases mentioned as the first precedents in the criminal procedural scope of the equality of arms. In truth, however, even in these precedents, the Court already alluded to previous confrontations of the matter. This is seen, for example, in the mention made in *Delcourt* to the cases *Ofner*, *Hopfinger*, *Pataki* and *Dunshirn* (*Delcourt*, § 15) and even to *Neumeister* (*Delcourt*, § 28) and in the case *Neumeister*, to previous confrontations either of the Court, or of the European Commission of Human Rights on the matter (*Neumeister*, §§ 22 and ss.).

[25] Negri (2005), p. 105, footnote no. 35, reports that, in that case, the applicant could not participate personally in the trial that involved his right to see his own son, as he was forbidden to enter Swiss territory. When deciding the case, it was understood that there had been a violation of Article 6, 1, of the ECHR.

[26] In this work, it is asserted that the equality of arms stems from equality, not from contradiction. In the sense that the principle is linked to contradiction, not equality, see: Roberto (2011), pp. 93 and 99; Fedorova (2012), pp. 105–106. da Costa (2012), p. 29, does not clearly separate the equality of arms and the contradiction. On the contrary, he points to the remote origin of the former as dependent on the latter.

[27] In this regard, Wasek-Wiaderek (2000), p. 50, notes that the counterclaim is only admitted in civil proceedings, not in criminal proceedings, as well as in criminal proceedings, the accused can be convicted if the criminal action is judged to be valid, but if it is judged to be invalid, the accuser is not convicted.

[28] Grevi (2000), p. 160. In this regard, also see: Rodrigues (1991), p. 87. Ferrua (2007), p. 49, notes that a "levelling of subjective situations would be unachievable in criminal proceedings where the public prosecutor exercises authoritative powers unthinkable by the defender. Nor can one think of a perfect symmetry on the ground of evidence production." Also: Wąsek-Wiaderek (2000), p. 50;

Because of the distinction between criminal process and civil process, finally, the authors who have delved into the theme of equality of arms see with reservations its unrestricted and unconditional application in the criminal process. Among the most recent, it is worth mentioning Vittorio Grevi, who recalls that there is in the criminal process a natural inequality of positions between prosecution and defense, which denotes, in his words, the impossibility of achieving within the process a rigid and absolute condition of *parity* between the parties.[29]

Regarding the focus of the principle for the criminal process, there are even those who say that, since the accused has broken the law—insofar as he is attributed the practice of a crime—equality of arms implies granting the state a certain privilege so that it can *repair* the breach of the legal order due to the crime attributed to someone.[30]

Back to the proper field of the criminal process, Sarah J. Summers refers to two precedents of the ECtHR that, at the end of the 1950s, would have been the first two specific cases of criminal process to challenge the position of the Court. They are: *Ofner and Hopfinger v. Austria* (*Applications* n° 525/59 and 617/59[31]) and *Pataki*

Roxin (2000), pp. 80–81. With a similar understanding, Giostra (2020), pp. 75/7. Rainey et al. (2014), p. 263, establish a distinction, but with a different bias: "in the context of civil cases between private parties, 'equality of arms' does not have to be absolute. There is no duty on the State, for example, to provide legal aid to an impecunious litigant to such a level as to bring him or her into total parity with a wealthy opponent. What matters is that parties are afforded a reasonable opportunity to present their case—including their evidence—under conditions that do not place them at a substantial disadvantage *vis-à-vis* the other side."

[29] This point of view is not endorsed in this work. However, for Mauro Fonseca Andrade, the equality of arms would allow the inequality of forces between prosecution and defense because it would serve to "neutralise the initial advantage that the alleged criminal has in relation to the State itself" (2008), p. 173. In our opinion, the reasoning of such an author does not hide disregard for the presumption of innocence of the accused, especially in the cited example, in which the inequalities between prosecution (public) and defense occur at the beginning of the criminal prosecution.

[30] In this case, the role of part or of *custos legis* of the prosecuting body was debated. It is true that, in the precedent—which, it seems, deserved criticism from the author precisely because of what is only remembered here in this footnote—the role of the prosecuting body was distinguished if acting in one way or another and, when it only *rubber stamped* at a certain procedural stage, it was understood that there was no violation of the principle Andrade (2008), pp. 106–107. The expression *rubber stamped* appears in the referenced work in the following passage: "He had simply 'rubber stamped'." Pages ahead, the author cites the precedent *Borgers v. Belgium* (*Application* no. 12.005/86, judged on 30 November 1991), in which, according to her own words, "things looked rather different." There, the author said, "those affiliated with the prosecution cannot logically be seen, particularly on the institutional level, as impartial, and thus cannot be permitted to communicate privately with the judiciary" (pp. 109–110).

[31] In this case, the prosecution was allowed, on appeal from conviction, to plead—successfully—for an increase in sentence, and the defendants were not allowed to counter-argue the prosecution's plea. The concrete result was that the conviction of *Pataki* went from 3 to 6 years in prison, and of *Dunshirn*, from 14 months to 54 months in prison. In the precedent, it was even understood that it would not even be necessary to demonstrate the damage, since—in the author's words—"In order for a violation to be found it was sufficient if one party was afforded an opportunity to influence the court that was not awarded to the other party" Summers (2007), p. 104, footnote no. 24, and p. 106. This same understanding, that the offense to the protective rule is enough, regardless of the

and Dunshirn v. Austria (*Applications* n° 596/59 and 789/60).[32] In the last precedent cited, moreover, the Court would have stated:

> the equality of arms, that is, the procedural equality between the accused with the public accuser, is an inherent element of the 'fair trial'. Whether such equality has its legal basis in paragraph 3 depends on the interpretation given to subparagraphs (b) and (c). The commission does not need to express a definitive opinion on this issue, since in any case it is beyond doubt that the broad and generic concept of a 'fair trial', contained in paragraph 1 of article 6, involves the notion of equality of arms.[33]

Thus, both in the case of *Dombo Beheer* and in the more remote precedents of *Ofner* and *Pataki*, in civil justice and in criminal justice, the central issue of equality of arms was seen as the reasonable opportunity given to each party to present their case, including their evidence,[34] under conditions that do not put them at a substantial disadvantage vis-à-vis their opponent.[35]

From his analysis of the precedent *Bulut v. Austria*,[36] Stephan Trechsel drew a parallel between the application of the precept in civil justice and in criminal justice. While in the first, there is concern with equality in the presentation of evidence, this

proof of damage, was repeated in other judgments of the ECHR: *Sharomov v. Russia* (*Application* no. 8.927/02, judged on 15th April 2009; particularly § 44). Also, in *Lanz v. Austria* (*Application* no. 24.430/94, judged on 30th April 2002), the proof of damage was waived to see the violation of the principle of equality of arms. Regarding this, in § 58: "As regards the contents of submissions filed by the prosecution, the Court recalls further that the principle of the equality of arms does not depend on further, quantifiable unfairness flowing from a procedural inequality. It is a matter for the defence to assess whether a submission deserves a reaction. It is therefore unfair for the prosecution to make submissions to a court without the knowledge of the defence" (Bulut v. Austria judgment, op. cit. § 49). Elisa Toma believes that the first precedent of equality of arms was another one, faced only by the Human Rights Commission of the ECHR, and not by the Court: *Szwabowicz v. Sweden, opinion of* 30.06.1959, *Application* no. 434/58 (The principle of equality of arms: part of the right to a fair trial. *Law Review Judicial doctrine and case-law online quarterly publication*, v. II, issue 4, Oct./Dec. 2012, p. 9). As the first precedent faced by the Court, Elisa Toma cites *Neumeister v. Austria* (*Application* no. 1.936/63, judged on 27th June 1968).

[32] Wąsek-Wiaderek (2000), p. 23; in the original: "The equality of arms, that is the procedural equality of the accused with the public prosecutor, is an inherent element of 'fair trial.' Whether such equality has its legal basis in paragraph 3 depends upon the interpretation of subparagraphs (b) and (c). The commission needs not express a definitive opinion on this question, since in any case it is beyond doubt, that the wider and general provision of a 'fair trial', contained in paragraph 1 of art. 6, embodies the notion of 'equality of arms'."

[33] "Finally, it is worth remembering that the main procedural moments in which the equality of arms must be protected can be identified in those corresponding to the acquisition (distinguished in its moments of admission and assumption) of evidence, the presentation of arguments aimed at persuading the judge and the deliberation" Wąsek-Wiaderek (2000), p. 15.

[34] "Finally, it is worth remembering that the main procedural moments in which the equality of arms must be protected can be identified in those corresponding to the acquisition (distinguished in its moments of admission and assumption) of evidence, the presentation of arguments aimed at persuading the judge and the deliberation" Ubertis (2006), p. 15.

[35] The period is a literal translation of the passage from Trechsel (2005), p. 96, and from Negri (2005), p. 515.

[36] *Application* no. 17.358/90, judged on 22nd February 1996.

does not exist in the criminal procedural sphere precisely because there is no defensive burden of proof.

Moreover, in the author's opinion, while in civil justice one works with the notion of *substantial* disadvantage between the opponents, in criminal justice it does not go that far, given the functional differences between accuser and accused.[37]

Regarding this distinction, Masha Fedorova, in addition to dealing with the burden of proof of the accusation, believes that the omission of the term *substantial* would be intentional because, in criminal proceedings, *any* disadvantage to the defense should be avoided.[38]

In a landmark case in the field of civil procedural law, two activists from London *Greenpeace* were sued by *McDonald's* for distributing offensive and harmful leaflets about the business practices of the corporation. In the precedent, the ECHR saw an offense to the principle of equality of arms because, among other factors, while the defendants had successive defenders appointed and always complained about the lack of resources—from extracting copies of the process, to paying costs and general expenses of resources—the multinational conglomerate, which was defended by the best law firms, did not see itself hindered in any particularity of the right of action.[39]

Although the generic notion of equality of arms is an idea of "certain equivalence" between accusation and defense,[40] in criminal proceedings (hence the understanding that the principle has its seat in Article 6, 1, of the European Convention on Human Rights),[41] this does not prevent the perception of its particularities depending on concrete situations. Thus, even if one sees the matrix of the principle in that provision, there are developments in its referred paragraphs (Art. 6, 3, of the ECHR).[42]

---

[37] Trechsel (2005), pp. 96–97.

[38] Fedorova (2012), p. 37. "However, the omission of 'substantial' could imply that *any* disadvantage for the defence must be avoided."

[39] *Steel and Morris v. United Kingdom* (*Application* no. 68.416/2001, judged on 15th February 2005). In that case, over 130 testimonies were collected, and the appeal trial lasted 28 days, which would be easily manageable by *McDonald's*, but not by the two applicants, who, moreover, were unemployed at the time. In this regard, see: Cole (2010), p. 49.

[40] Trechsel (2005), p. 96. The author reminds us that it is only in theory that the public prosecution is impartial and the defense is not. He also recalls the well-known imbalance of forces inherent in the criminal process, as coercive measures such as arrest warrants, telephone interceptions, searches and seizures, and the availability of a large technological apparatus are typical of the public prosecution, while none of this, as a rule, is available to the accused. In the author's words, "one might recall fights of gladiators in ancient Rome where one was in armour and equipped with a sword, whilst the other was unprotected and equipped with a net and a trident."

[41] In this sense, see: Harris et al. (1995), p. 207.

[42] The Court understands that the principle of equality of arms is just one of the contributions to a broader concept of "fair trial" in criminal proceedings and, therefore, in cases where the state allegedly violating the precept can present in its defense its non-violation, the Court concludes that there is an offense to Art. 6, §1, of the European Convention on Human Rights on other grounds (Deliktaş v. Türkiye, *Application* no. 25852/18, judged on 12th March 2024, § 54).

From the premise—repeated both in doctrine and in ECHR precedents—that equality of arms equates to a reasonable opportunity for each party to present their case under conditions that do not put them at a disadvantage vis-à-vis their opponent, corresponding to a condition of verification of whether or not one is facing a fair process,[43] and even being read as "just one element of the broader concept of

[43] *Neumeister v. Austria* (*Application* no. 1.936/63, §§ 22 and ss.); *Kennedy v. United Kingdom* (*Application* n° 26.839/05, judged on 18 May 2010; from § 184, in addition to outlining the general line of the principle of equality of arms with quotations from other precedents, it deals with focusing on exceptional measures, given the balancing that could make the principle not applicable in some concrete case); *Pishchalnikov v. Russia* (*Application* n° 7.025/2004, judged on 24 December 2009; from § 68, it deals with the equality of arms in relation to the right not to incriminate oneself and its observance dependent on the participation of a lawyer in the police interrogation) *Huseyn and others v. Azerbaijan* (*Applications* n° 35.485/05, 45.553/05, 35.680/05, 36.085/05, judged on 26 October 2011; in § 188, one can read, with quotations from other precedents of the ECHR, the general notion of equality of arms and its application in both criminal and civil proceedings); *Ali v. Romania* (*Application* n° 20.307/02, judged on 9 December 2010; here, the mention of equality of arms is in §§ 101 to 104 and the theme was about the distinctions between an undercover agent and an agent provocateur to conclude that even the use of the technique of an undercover agent cannot annihilate the defensive rights to have the evidence produced in the opposite direction valued and to be able to count on the judicial impartiality to demand that the infiltrators be, if necessary, heard in court); in Yakhymovych v. Ukraine (*Application* n° 23,476/15, j. 09.05.2022), by majority, the Court understood as violating the principle in question, also, of an agent provocateur; *Zhuk v. Ukraine* (*Application* n° 45.783/05, judged on 21 October 2010; the mention of the principle is in §§ 25 to 35, centred on not having guaranteed the presence of the accused or defender in a hearing in which the prosecutor was present and produced evidence in favour of the accusation); *Dolenec v. Croatia* (*Application* n° 25.282/06, judged on 26 February 2010; in § 207 the Court was confronted again with a citation of the general rule of the principle and applied it in a situation in which the defensive access to documents from the files was questioned; in the precedent, it also dealt with possible exceptions to the incidence of the principle, depending on contrary justifying situations). In a case in which the Court also confronted documents to which the defense did not have access—and even had a connection with Brazil, given that the accused had left Mato Grosso heading to London with a view to international drug trafficking—the matter was addressed, namely: *Atlan v. The United Kingdom* (*Application* no. 36,533/97, judged on 19th September 2001; see §§ 36 to 46). *Lazoroski v. the former Yugoslav republic of Macedonia* (*Application* no. 4922/04, judged on eighth January 2010; in §§ 68 to 70, the Court confronts the equality of arms from the recognized violation of access to written evidence that were brought to the Judiciary); *Rasmussen v. Poland* (*Application* no. 38,886/05, judged on 28th July 2009; a violation of the equality of arms was recognized both in terms of the general rule discussed here, in § 42, and in the recognition, which was stamped in § 51, of the violation of the principle due to the failure to present to the accused the documentary evidence that concerned him, this in the face of the argument that the documents would be confidential as they were produced during the dictatorial period of that country). Similar to the last judgement cited: *Luboch v. Poland* (*Application* no. 37,469/05, judged on 15th April 2008; relevant, in this judgement, are §§ 59 to 73). Also: *Matyjek v. Poland* (*Application* no. 38,184/03, judged on 24th April 2007, §§ 55 to 65); *Natunen v. Finland* (*Application* no. 21,022/04, judged on 31st March 2009; in the specific situation, the police had selected the evidence collected and then separated what was of interest to the prosecution and forwarded it to the prosecution, but not to the accused; the evidence that the police did not consider relevant was simply destroyed. In §§ 39 and 41, the equality of arms was discussed in relation to the adversarial criminal process). In *Abbasov v. Azerbaijan* (*Application* no. 24,271/05, judged on 17th April 2008), it was understood, in §§ 26 to 34, that the failure to notify the accused and neither the lawyer for the session in which the defensive and accusatory appeals were judged violates the

fair trial,"[44] one arrives at specific situations where the principle has already been put to the test.

---

equality of arms. Particularly in this case, the principle was focused in light of, including the adversarial system. In *Stoimenov v. The Former Republic of Macedonia* (*Application* no. 17,995/02, judged on fifth June 2007), it was understood that the denial of a defensive request for indication of new experts to enable him to counter the official expertise violated the equality of arms. See, in this regard, §§ 41 and 42. In a similar vein to this judgement, but with the particularity of it being an accusation of paedophilia committed against relatives, in a process in which the experts who would determine the mental sanity of the accused after receiving new documentation from the prosecution ended up preparing a new report more damaging to the defense, which could not hire expertise to counter the new expert report prepared in a short space of time, *G.B. v. France* (*Application* no. 44,069/98, judged on 2nd January 2002; Particularly §§ 37, 45, 56 to 59 and 64 to 70). In *Salov v. Ukraine* (*Application* no. 65,518/01, judged on 6th December 2005), it was understood that the arrival of a protest from the Public Prosecutor's Office at the prison where the accused was serving his sentence, without him being able to have prior knowledge of the document to comment on it, constituted a violation of the equality of arms. Again, both as a general rule of the principle referred to by the ECHR, and by the connection that is commonly seen between the equality of arms and the adversarial system, §§ 87 and 88.

In a case where there was apparent persecution against a journalist in Azerbaijan, with the accusation that he had committed bodily harm to a third person, the Court reiterated the main understandings about the equality of arms (Zayidov v. Azerbaijan, *Application* no. 60824/08, j. 19.04.2023, particularly §§ 90, 92, 108). In the scenario, an opposition journalist to the regime would have been offended and assaulted by a woman in public, and, in an altercation with a third party who intervened in the case, would have ended up injuring him. The Court understood that there was an ambush to silence the freedom of the journalistic press in the case in question, with the curtailment of the journalist in question producing evidence in his defense (of not having injured such a third person on the street). Also against the backdrop of perceived persecution against a journalist from Azerbaijan, the Court understood there had been a violation of the principle in a situation in which drugs would have been "planted" with a journalist, and there would, consequently, have been an unlawful search and seizure, with the prohibition of his contact with family members and lawyers, in addition to the denial of the production of counter-evidence in his favour (Fatullayev v. Azerbaijan. N. 2, *Application* no. 32734/11, j. 07.02.2022, §§ 79, 81, 96, 104).

[44] *Delcourt v. Belgium* (*Application* no 2.689/65, judged on 17th January 1970, § 28, our translation). Franz Matcher made an interesting approach to the principle of equality of arms from the judgments of the ECHR, taking it as a central principle of the equitable process. In this regard, the right to a fair trial is recognized in the case law of the organs of the European Convention on Human Rights. In: *The Right of a fair trial.* Collection Science and Technique of Democracy, no. 28. Strasburg: European Commission for Democracy through Law. Council of Europe Publishing, 2000, pp. 12 and foll. Strictly in the lesson that the principle is directly related to the adversarial criminal process and is one of the elements of the broader concept of an equitable process, including in the sense of giving each party a reasonable opportunity to present the case under conditions that do not put it at a substantial disadvantage vis-à-vis its opponent: Gracia Gonzalez v. Spain (*Application* no. 65107/16, j. 06.01.2021, § 68). Also: Zanin v. Russia (*Application* no. 54339/09, j. 09.06.2021).

5.2.1 *Judgments of the ECtHR: Moment of Incidence of the Principle*

Before addressing the particularities of concrete situations that have led, as doctrine has pointed out, to a certain catalogue of application of the principle, it is important to make a warning and deal with the application from a temporal determination.

The warning is that, since the late 1980s, as already mentioned in a footnote and as Sarah J. Summers points out, the idea of equality of arms has been commonly linked to what is understood by adversarial process.

The adversarial criminal process, although conducive and fruitful to the application of the equality of arms, is not an absolute condition of its application. In other words, the equality of arms does not presuppose, necessarily, that the criminal procedural model is the adversarial one.[45]

Thus, in chorus with the doctrine of Sarah J. Summers, if on one hand it is noted how "increasingly common" it has been to find the concepts "cited together,"[46] something particularly noticeable because the notions can be close (especially in the evidentiary field), on the other hand, as the author points out, "equality of arms means that there must be a balancing of procedural opportunities between defence and prosecution, while the adversarial process guarantees the right of the defence to be informed about and be able to question the claims of the prosecution."[47]

The adversarial nature of the process is not dependent on the observance of the principle of equality of arms; and nor is the reverse true, even because it is not agreed with the idea that the incidence of the principle of equality of arms depends on the existence of *parties* in a strict sense, nor that it depends unconditionally on the configuration of the so-called *party process*.

Having made the warning, we move on to the precedents of the ECtHR that highlighted the equality of arms in temporal application. The analysis takes into account the coercion suffered by the person and the nature of the acts (considered indicative of criminal conduct) that are attributed to him, but not the formal aspect of having parties in the criminal process.

---

[45] Fedorova (2012), pp. 47–49.

[46] "With the development of the case law it becomes increasingly common to find the concepts cited together" (2007), p. 110. It is interesting to note that Cole (2010), pp. 34–38, states that the principle of equality of arms dates back to *trial by battle* and recognizes that it has roots in both the *common law* and *civil law* systems. Mauro Fonseca de Andrade, to discuss the origin of the principle, cites two currents (one of Germanic law and another of Anglo-Saxon law) and denies the application of both. He defends the idea that the origin of equality of arms dates back to the Roman period. What is uncontroversial among all authors is that the notion of equality of arms brings with it the idea of ritualization of a war, "where there is regulation not only of the time or place of its acts, but also of the weapons that can be used by the contenders. This would be, therefore, the explanation for the reference to arms in the principle of equality, when specifically applied to criminal procedural law" (2008), p. 160. Also see Rainey et al. (2014), p. 264.

[47] (2007), p. 112.

Since the late 1970s, with the judgment of *Engel and others v. The Netherlands*,[48] the Court understands that the concept of criminal charge is independent of the legal qualification given to it by each state that accepts its jurisdiction. Thus, whether by the consequence on the freedom of the accused, or by the very gravity of the acts committed—and both circumstances are analyzed by the ECtHR—it is deduced that the criminal or non-criminal nature of the acts is assessed by each national court.

It can be said, in this regard, that the ECtHR has, from *Engel*, a three-phase methodology to define the autonomy of the concept of *criminal charge*. It is as follows: (i) classification given by the signatory state of the ECHR; (ii) nature of the conduct practiced by the investigated person who comes to the doors of the ECtHR; (iii) severity of the punishment. The three criteria are successive. If the classification of the state coincides with that of the ECtHR by the affirmative of the existence of a criminal issue, the other two are dispensed with.[49]

And in determining the issue to be of a criminal nature—so that the application of the equality of arms in the criminal process is not lost sight of—the ECtHR has been attentive to the impositivity of the principle from the moment there is a criminal charge.

Hence, it is possible, even, to distinguish the *nature* of the issue (whether criminal or not and, with that, the incidence of the protective norms of the European Convention on Human Rights) from the *coercion* directed at the citizen. After all, the expression debated in the ECtHR and about which we are talking here is composed of two words: *criminal* and *charge*.

As for the charge (i.e., *charge*), it materializes at the moment when there is "official notification to the individual by a competent authority about an allegation that he committed a crime or some other act that implies such an allegation and that, likewise, substantially affects the suspect's situation."[50] The *criminal charge*, therefore, can arise either with the signaling of an investigation against someone, or—as is most common—with the measure of arrest, or even with other acts, such as the decree of property precautionary measures.[51]

---

[48] *Application* no. 5.100/71; 5.101/71; 5.102/71; 5.354/72; 5.370/72, judged on 8th June 1976.

[49] Harris et al. (1995), p. 166. If the ECHR did not have its construction, say the authors, rightly, it would be very simple for a certain signatory state to breach the convention by prevailing the particular legal classification that *does not* treat a conduct as a crime, but that it is either by gravity, or by consequence. A crucial point about the autonomy achieved by the ECHR at this point was seen in *Ozturk v. Germany* (*Application* no. 8.544/79, judged on 23rd October 1984). There, the consequence of an act of dangerous driving, no longer considered a crime in Germany, but which was understood as justifying the incidence of the protective norms of the ECHR due to its consequences to the applicant.

[50] Harris et al. (1995), p. 171, our translation. The authors refer to *Deweer v. Belgium* (*Application* no. 6.903/75, judged on 27th February 1980, § 42) and to *Corigliano v. Italy* (*Application* no. 8.304/78, judged on 10th December 1982, § 34).

[51] *Funke v. France* (*Application* no. 10.828/84, judged on 25th February 1993, §§ 41 and ss.), in which a request was made to freeze a bank account. In that precedent, the issue was discussed, including whether the confidential information provided by the person investigated for a tax crime can be considered—and to what extent—as a violation of their right not to produce evidence

Thus, when imagining the nature of the issue (*criminal*) or when referring to the moment when coercion is noted (*charge*), what is seen from the precedents of the ECtHR is a prevalence of material interpretation—and not merely formal—of the act that, if theoretically committed by someone, may trigger the protective norms of the ECHR.[52] And still, in the explanation of Malgorzata Wasek-Wiaderek's monograph, the criteria used by the ECtHR derive, including, from the observation that the criminal process must be fair as a whole and that it would be impossible for the judge to assess its legality with a mere partial view of its events.[53]

As none of this depends on the technicality of having an official accusation brought to court, it has been understood, unquestionably and correctly, that the principle is independent of the formal qualifier of the investigated as *part*. This understanding seems to be irreproachable even in light of the need to, once the existence of a criminal charge is verified—which is independent of the procedural stage in which the criminal prosecution is found—give the opportunity for defense.[54]

5.2.2 ECtHR Judgments: Cases of Incidence and Doctrinal Cataloguing

In addition to the distinction between equality of arms and adversarial criminal process and the concern with the moment of the principle's onset,[55] one can deal with a certain *catalogue* in which its application has already been established.

While some link the principle of equality of arms to the right to evidence in criminal proceedings—particularly to the so-called *right of confrontation* and to situations of witness anonymity, expert witness *expert* and *hearsay*[56]—others

---

against themselves. In Beuze v. Belgium (*Application* no. 71409/10, judged on 9th November 2018), the Court endorsed the understanding that it violates the principle of equality of arms, the prohibition of contact between the arrested person and their lawyer.

[52] Contrary to the claim made in this text, stating that the equality of arms would only be applicable in the judicial phase of criminal prosecution, see: Andrade (2008), pp. 164–165.

[53] Wąsek-Wiaderek (2000), p. 21.

[54] In line with the text and with rich bibliography and extensive jurisprudential repertoire, see: Ambos (2006), particularly pp. 426–427. See also: Negri (2005), p. 520; and Cole (2010), pp. 44–45. Also: Rainey et al. (2014), p. 248.

[55] It was preferred to treat these two critical points in conjunction exactly because, as Malgorzata Wasek-Wiaderek points out, while in systems of *common law* the first phase of criminal prosecution can even be adversarial, in systems of *civil law* the first phase is traditionally inquisitorial. Hence, the affirmation that the system in which the equality of arms flourishes is not necessarily adversarial is not inseparable from that according to which the principle also does not start to apply only in the judicial phase of the criminal issue (*The principle of "equality of arms"* ..., cit., p. 21).

[56] Masek-Wiaderek (2000) pp. 27 and foll.

understand there are distinct and specific established applications of the principle in the criminal procedural field.[57]

According to the classification of Roger Gamble and Noel Dias, even if the application of the principle to the evidentiary field is focused, the equality of arms manifests itself in the following five main aspects:[58] (i) right to be brought to the presence of the judge who will judge the case;[59] (ii) right to self-defense;[60] (iii) right to free choice of lawyer;[61] (iv) right to be aware of having a lawyer for the defense;[62] (v) right to receive free assistance.[63]

Without prejudice to this classification,[64] it seems to be more sustainable the list of cases presented by Stefania Negri. Even though the evidentiary side is the most focused on visualizing the equality of arms, dealing with the most relevant points already faced and established by the ECtHR allows going beyond the aspects raised by the previously mentioned authors. According to the lesson of the aforementioned Italian professor, one can arrive at the following and broader catalogue:

(i) witness evidence: observance of the right to confront the witnesses listed by the prosecution and to question them freely, whether they are witnesses in the strict sense of the term, or experts indicated by the prosecution;[65]

---

[57] Gamble and Dias (2009). As already mentioned here, Harris et al. (1995), p. 207, have a restrictive notion of equality of arms. In any case, in the authors' view, the fields would be the right to be heard by a judicial authority, the observance of the position of the representative of the prosecuting body in appeals as one who opposes their theses to the defensive ones and not as an impartial body and, finally, the equal treatment that the experts appointed by the accused must have when compared with the experts appointed by the prosecution.

[58] Gamble and Dias (2009), p. 189.

[59] Gamble and Dias (2009), pp. 192 and foll., with citations of judgments.

[60] Gamble and Dias (2009), pp. 194 and foll., with citations of judgments.

[61] Gamble and Dias (2009), pp. 198 and foll., with citations from judgments.

[62] Gamble and Dias (2009), pp. 201–202.

[63] Gamble and Dias (2009), pp. 201 and foll., with citations from judgments.

[64] As is also useful, moreover, that other one, proposed by Mustafa (2007), p. 15, according to whom the rights are the following: i) to be promptly informed of the charge; ii) to have time and facilities for the preparation of the defense; iii) to defend oneself or through a lawyer; iv) to confront the witnesses; v) to have free assistance from an interpreter. For Fedorova (2012), p. 19, there are four themes on which the principle focuses: preparation for the trial and the purpose of the investigations; access to mutual information between the parties thanks to the *disclosure regime*; availability of funds and facilities for the defense from its institutional position; presentation of the case itself by the parties.

[65] Negri (2005), pp. 518–519. Within the precedents, the well-known *Barberà, Messegué and Jabardo v. Spain* (*Application* no. 10.590/83, judged on 6th December 1988, § 78), when not only the adversarial side of the oral instruction was focused on, but the equality of conditions in which the defense witnesses must be heard, when compared with those brought by the prosecution. Also cited is *Bonisch v. Austria* (*Application* no. 8.658/79, judged on 6th May 1985), a precedent in which the Court emphasized that, having been the expert himself listed by the prosecution, he should be given the treatment of a common witness so that the defense can question him on an equal footing with the other prosecution witnesses. This was particularly said in §§ 29 to 35. Also, regarding the collection of defense witness evidence under the same conditions attributed to the

(ii) documentary evidence: observance of the duty of the prosecution to show the defense all the materials it holds and relate them against or in favor of the investigated or accused;[66]
(iii) right to be present before the judge throughout the evidentiary arc, including in the appeal trial;[67]
(iv) in the event of precautionary arrest,[68] the right to be quickly heard by a judge and to orally present—or at least in writing, and, for that, in a reasonable

prosecution: Škoberne v. Slovenia (*Application* no. 19920/20, judged on 15th May 2024); Vasaráb and Paulus v. Slovakia (*Applications* nos. 28,081/19 and 29,664/19, judged on 15th March 2023, § 50); Lilian Erhan v. The Republic of Moldova (*Application* no. 21947/16, j. 05.10.2022, §§ 16 and 21); Faysal Pamuk v. Turkey (*Application* no. 430/13, judged on 09th May 2022), in which the Court found a violation of the equality of arms in a situation in which a person's conviction was based on written statements from witnesses who were not heard in court, but rather, submitted written statements. Also: Olga Kudrina v. Russia (*Application* no. 34313/06, judged on 06th July 2021).

[66] Negri (2005), p. 519. The precedent cited was *Edwards v. United Kingdom* (*Application* no. 13.071/87, judged on 16th December 1992). In § 36 of that judgment, there is a reference to the equality of arms. In *Jasper v. United Kingdom* (*Application* no. 27.052/95, judged on 16 February 2000), however, the ECHR, faced with the argument—unlikely in the sense that *there is, logically, no way to prove it in the opposite direction*—that there are no absolute rights, understood that under certain circumstances the right to publicity of information elements must yield. Thus, even if they may incriminate the applicant, the ECHR understood that there was no violation in not displaying a significant part of the documents unfavourable to the defense (see: §§ 52 and 53). Nevertheless, there is an interesting dissenting opinion from Judge Zupančič, according to whom "non-disclosure, that is, secrecy concerning some aspects of the prosecution's case, is of course a problem in itself. However, compared to the predominantly inquisitorial Continental systems of criminal procedure in which the ex officio investigation used to be entirely secret, the partial non-disclosure in an adversarial system cannot be seen as a breach of a fundamental procedural standard. Still, for me, this is not a minor technical consideration because it affects the whole philosophy of criminal procedure." Even when considering the limited applications of the principle of publicity of investigation documents, that judge also pondered that not just any arguments could validly dismiss it, but only "insurmountable difficulties." As can be seen, here is an interesting criterion for consideration: not the mere existence of a counterposed right, but rather the considerable evidentiary difficulty, which is distinct.

[67] Negri (2005), p. 520. As cited in *Belziuk v. Poland* (*Application* no. 23.103/93, judged on 25th March 1998), even if the representative of the prosecution did not appeal, his mere presence at the appeal trial in the absence of the defendant-appellant signified an offense to the equality of arms. The argument that the representative of the prosecution would be seated in the trial session as a representative of the public interest, but rather as an active spectator of the maintenance of the conviction against which the defense had appealed, was not agreed with (see, in this regard, § 39).

[68] The precedents consulted are faithful to the premise of imprisonment as a precautionary measure, and not to others, because Article 5, § 4, of the ECHR provides for the application of its precepts in the event of "any person deprived of their liberty by arrest or detention has the right to appeal to a court, so that it can rule, in a short period of time, on the legality of their detention and order their release, if the detention is illegal."

time[69]—arguments that can rebut the grounds for the precautionary measure requests.[70]

In view of this, it can be said that, in the synthesis of the TEDH's position, if on the one hand the equality of arms is linked to the evidentiary aspect (witness, expert and documentary evidence, above all) during the instruction, on the other hand, it also encompasses the right to be present and to be heard regardless of the stage of criminal prosecution (the examples of the TEDH go back to investigations, or to the trials of accusatory or defensive appeals).

In this second aspect, therefore, the equality of arms does not manifest as pertaining to criminal procedural evidence, but as a norm of treatment of one of its involved. And this rescues a generic side of the conceptualization, namely, the one that demands equality in the presentation of the case, in a broad sense, not only in the evidentiary aspect, in order to avoid that one side is in an unfavorable situation—also in a broad sense—when compared to its antagonist.

Therefore, it can be concluded that equality of arms not only means distribution of opportunities for evidence production, but also involves the type of treatment given to the accused and the accuser when considering the presentation of each party's case, in a broad sense. This assumes, evidently, not only equal treatment in the matter of evidence, but the rule of treatment before and after criminal procedural instruction, that is, in the investigative, appeal, and execution phase.

Ultimately, it is not only from the distribution in the possibility of evidentiary aptitude that the greater or lesser possibility of influence in a judicial decision arises; it also arises from the way in which—abstractly—the system treats (giving, there,

---

[69] Negri (2005), pp. 520–521. In *Frommelt v. Lichtstenstein* (*Application* no. 49.158/99, judged on 24th September 2004), the ECHR saw a violation of the equality of arms because the lawyer who was going to rebut the arguments used for the procedural arrest was not given a reasonable time for its preparation and presentation to the court (§ 33). In the concrete situation, even the acceptable hypotheses of renunciation of the exercise of the procedural faculty allowed by the principle were considered.

[70] Negri (2005), pp. 520–521. Regarding this, *Megyeri v. Germany* (*Application* no. 13.770/88, judged on second May 1992, § 22), which dealt with procedural imprisonment, however treated as a security measure. In the concrete case, there were periodic reviews of the mental situation of the citizen confined in a psychiatric hospital, and, as the ECHR sees a judicial aspect in decisions concerning imprisonment and also saw in the situation the comparison to such psychiatric treatments, the possibility for the applicant to present his arguments is demanded so that he could leave the place. In *Frommelt v. Lichtstenstein* (*Application* no. 49.158/99, judged on 24th September 2004), it was understood in the same way, although here it was properly about typical detention of criminal prosecution of an accountable citizen (about this, see § 29). The work of Rowland James Victor Cole, although it can be read as a distinct classification, sometimes goes back to the core of Stefania Negri, and sometimes goes beyond the strict field of the principle. Note the list envisaged by the author: "i) right to be afforded a reasonable opportunity to present the facts of his case to the court; ii) right to present his legal arguments to the court; iii) right to respond to evidence; iv) right to comment on legal arguments of the prosecution; v) right to disclosure of evidence in the possession of the state that is necessary for preparation of the defence cause; vi) right to legal representation; vii) right to be presumed innocent" (*Equality of arms and aspects of the right to a fair criminal trial in Botswana*, cit., p. 39).

greater or lesser possibility of being present in decisive acts) its involved, regardless of the evidence to be produced.

5.3 Conceptual Contributions Brought by the ICTY and the ICTR

The International Criminal Tribunal for Rwanda (Art. 20 of the Tribunal's Statute) and that of the former Yugoslavia (Art. 21 of the Tribunal's Statute) follow almost literally the provisions contained in Article 6 of the ECHR.[71] In this text, however, although doctrinal approaches are known that focus on precedents from the Rwanda Tribunal, preference will be given to the treatment of the principle of equality of arms given by the Tribunal of the former Yugoslavia, considering its lessons to be more frequent and influential.

In any case, both tribunals (Rwanda and Yugoslavia) specify the principle of equality of arms in matters related to the evidence regime insofar as they put *on the same footing* the prosecution and the defense.

The main aspects perceptible from the rules of evidence that each of them has and that can be remembered as indicative of the equality of arms are: prohibition of evidentiary advantages for the prosecution (ICTY, rule 41 and 66; ICTR rules 66 to 68); right to defense by a lawyer in the investigative phase (ICTY, rule 42; ICTR, rule 45); right to a public hearing (ICTY and ICTR, rule 78); right of the accused to test the prosecution evidence and present their own witnesses (ICTY and ICTR, rule 85); presumption of innocence (ICTY and ICTR, rule 87); and right to protect against self-incrimination (ICTY and ICTR, rule 90).[72]

An illustrative case in which the ICTY applied the principle of equality of arms and in which consonance with the criteria already seen by the TEDH was *Prosecutor v. Tadic*.[73] There, the defense had alleged a violation of the principle of equality of arms insofar as one of the states that recognized the jurisdiction of the Tribunal had made it difficult to present a witness to be heard.[74] According to the defensive

[71] Negri (2005), p. 543, footnote no. 94.

[72] Negri (2005), p. 543. In our view, both the presumption of innocence and the protection against self-incrimination are more linked to other favors, which allow procedural imbalance in favour of the accused, than to the equality of arms, in the aspect here exposed. The updated version of the ICTR was consulted, up to the modification of first October 2009 of its rules of evidence, adopted since 29th June 1995. From the ICTY, the version updated up to the amendment of 20th October 2011 was consulted.

[73] *Case* no. IT-94-1-A, judged on 15th July 1999.

[74] The ICTR faced a similar question in *Prosecution v. Nahimana* et al. (ICTR-99-52-T, *decision on the motion to stay the proceedings in the trial of Ferdinand Nahimana*, judged on 05th June 2003). In that case, Nahimana's defense argued a violation of the equality of arms between the accused and the accuser because it had insurmountable difficulties in gathering witness and documentary information in Rwanda to face the accusation made. From the precedent, it can be seen that the

claims, such a situation prevented the enjoyment of adequate time for the preparation of defensive arguments.

When faced with the principle (especially as done in §§ 46 to 48), the Tribunal pondered—not without referring to some of the precedents just referred to in this text of the TEDH—that, in matters of evidence production, a "more liberal interpretation" should be given to the application of the principle than that given by the Courts of each state that recognizes its incidence.[75] It was in this precedent, indeed, that the ICTY mentioned that the equality of arms between the prosecution and the defense in a criminal trial goes to the heart of the guarantee of a fair process.[76]

Then, in *Prosecutor v. Oric*,[77] the ICTY analyzed the principle of equality of arms in light of the right of the defense to have or not, strictly, the same time granted to the prosecution to produce its evidence. In the new approach, the Tribunal understood that the principle of equality of arms, although covered with all the density that the ECHR has already given it (cited in the precedent), would not yield between prosecution and defense an absolute equality of time to present the arguments. According to the ICTY's reasoning,

> the prosecution has the burden of telling a whole story, of putting a coherent narrative and proving all the elements of the crimes beyond reasonable doubt. The defence strategy, in contrast, usually focuses on pointing out chosen holes in the prosecution's case, a challenge that may require less time and fewer witnesses. This is a sufficient reason to explain why a principle of basic proportionality, and not a strict principle of mathematical equality, generally governs the relationship between time and witnesses available to both sides.[78]

ICTR clearly adopts as a decision rule the line set by the ICTY in *Tadic*. About this, in the consulted decision, see §§ 4 to 6.

[75] *Prosecutor v. Tadic*, § 52. The text in quotes is a translation of the expression "a more liberal interpretation." The ICTY, in that case, gave precedence to the principle with a view to respecting all the defensive possibilities—even if it had to face resistance from states that recognize the jurisdiction of the ICTY—to present their evidence to be appreciated. In this case, according to Stefania Negri, the ICTY even came to favour a so-called *material concept*, and not merely *procedural* of equality of arms (The principle of "equality of arms" and the evolving law of international criminal procedure, cit., p. 545).

[76] *Prosecutor v. Tadic*, § 44: "[...] The principle of equality of arms between the prosecutor and accused in a criminal trial goes to the heart of the fair trial guarantee." In this precedent, there was another interesting discussion: that of the defense showing in advance to the prosecution any testimonies of the witnesses it wanted to indicate to be heard in the Court. The rule that applied at the time of the trial (Art. 67 *ter G* of the rules of procedure and evidence of the ICTY) determined, in what was called *reciprocal disclosure*, that the parties would advance, reciprocally, the witnesses they wanted to bring to the court to testify and, also, the line of testimony that would be used (if to prove alibi etc.). By a majority of votes, the ICTY decided that there was no such reciprocity and that the accused "need not afford the prosecution any assistance in making out the Prosecution case" (FEDOROVA, Masha. *The principle of equality of arms in international criminal proceedings*, cit., pp. 279–280). The ICTR also faced this principle in *Prosecutor v. Renzaho* (ICTR-97-31-T, judged on 14th July 2009, particularly in §§ 59 and 62).

[77] *Case* no. IT-03-68-AR73.2, judged on 20th July 2005.

[78] *Prosecutor v. Oric*, Interlocutory Decision on Length of Defence Case, § 7. In this case, despite the Court having started the restrictive approach to the application of the precept—given that *it compared the defensive ease to the accusatory*—it concretely went down to the minutiae that

In another trial, *Prosecutor v. Simic*,[79] the ICTY reiterated what had already been stated by the ECHR in determining that the prosecution should provide the defense with the elements of information to which it had access; otherwise, it would be penalized for not applying a fair process.[80]

In a critical view of these precedents, one can perceive two distinct doctrinal approaches, both in relation to the trials themselves, as well as in relation to the illustrative configurations of the equality of arms in the criminal process.

According to Stefania Negri, the three main manifestations in which the ICTY has encountered the equality of arms are those concerning the (i) indictment of the investigated; to the (ii) analysis of means and facilities for the preparation of the defense; and (iii) to the attention to the disclosure of evidence or information elements that are in the possession of the prosecution.[81]

---

proved there had been a violation of the principle. Among other reasons, because while the defense had 27 days to hear 30 witnesses, the prosecution enjoyed no less than 100 days to hear the 50 it listed. In the same trial and still according to the premises that, in theory, would allow the flexibility of the principle—because it is a *principle* and not a *rule* that is being dealt with—the Court understood there had been a violation because, also, so noticeable was the disparity in the time granted to the prosecution and the defense that, in that case, it would not even be necessary to demonstrate the prejudice.

[79] *Case* no. IT-95-9, judged on 28th February 2000. "Decision on (1) application by Stevan Todorovic to re-open the decision of 27 July 1999, (2) motion by Icrc to re-open scheduling order of 18 November 1999, and (3) conditions for access to material."

[80] *Prosecutor v. Simic*, § 22: "[…] It was clear to the Trial Chamber that not only equality of arms but also common fairness demanded that he should have such access for that purpose, and that the confidentiality presently accorded to the whole of that material should be lifted so far as he is concerned, just as the prosecution had access to the whole of it for the purposes of the motion which led to that decision, subject to redaction to protect the identity of the witness. The Trial Chamber believed that it could not reasonably be argued to the contrary." In the configuration of the equality of arms from the perspective of *disclosure*, Masha Fedorova, in addition to comparing the provisions of the rules of evidence and procedure of the ICTY and the ICTR, recalls the recommendation adopted within the European Community. According to Rec (2000) 19 of the Committee of Ministers of the Council of Europe of 6 October 2000, "public prosecutors should seek to safeguard the principle of equality of arms, in particular by disclosing to the other parties—save where otherwise provided in the law—any information which they possess which may affect the justice of the proceedings" (*The principle of equality of arms in international criminal proceedings*, cit., p. 251, footnote no. 89). As a possible solution adopted, within the ICTR: *Prosecutor v. Bizimungu* et al. (ICTR-99-50-T, judged on 30th September 2011, *Judgment and Sentence*). As reported in the precedent, the prosecution withheld, for a period between 9 and 14 months, relevant case information that could have favored the defense. The solutions given by the ICTR were: the immediate availability of the information that the prosecution had and improperly did not expose to the defense; the reopening so that testimonies could be heard again in the light of the documentation shared with the defense; the valuation *pro reo* of much of the material segregated with the prosecution (*Prosecutor v. Bizimungu*, §§ 170–175). Within the ICTY, see the precedent of *Prosecutor v. Karadžic* (IT-95-5/18-T, T. Ch., judged on second November 2010, *decision on the accused's eighteenth to twenty-first disclosure violation motions*). In the case, in the face of the violation of the *disclosure* rule, the Court postponed the testimony of witnesses who would be affected by the accused's ignorance of the content of the segregated material and granted a new deadline for the defense to comment on the documents (*Prosecutor v. Karadžic*, §§ 40–41).

[81] Negri (2005), p. 545.

Thus, if on the one hand there is concern about the prior communication of the grounds for the indictment, on the other hand, an attempt is made to achieve a parallel between an *effective prosecution* (given the relevancies and characteristic complexities of the humanitarian offenses that give rise to the jurisdiction of the ICTY) and an *effective defense*.

It is in this particular that the difficult question of how to contemplate financial resources for the defense to produce the evidence it deems relevant to the proof of its thesis(es).[82] Finally, the disclosure of evidence, in the ICTY's lesson, as seen in relation to the ECHR, coexists with the exceptions that would justify the ignorance, until a reasonable time, of the elements of information on the part of the accused.[83]

Alongside this, some analyze the incidence of the principle under the plan of reasonableness in light of each concrete situation.[84] This is because the ICTY would also have the following criteria for applying the equality of arms: as said in

[82] The point is, as can be easily seen, of delicate balance, because even from what we have already seen here, the financial issue is ordinarily treated as if it were outside the process. Introducing it to concretize the application of the principle of equality of arms does not dispense with the valuation on the need to provide funds so that the defensive evidence can be produced, which, as is not uncommon, makes the application of the principle unfeasible. Particularly complex is the situation in cases involving humanitarian crimes, those that cause revulsion in common sense, which often confuses notions of fair trial (aptitude of the request for the production of defensive evidence and, consequently, imagined granting of financial aid for this, observed the criminal process as a means to achieve justice, and not as an end in itself) with that of summary justice. About this, see: Knoops (2004-2005), p. 1577. The author himself, in fact, is sceptical about equality of arms when the issue reaches the equality of resources available for the defense and for the prosecution. From a comment on the precedent *Prosecutor v. Milutinovic* (Case no. IT-99-37), in which the Court denied a request for supplementary fund grant on the argument that it would lack exceptional justification, he concludes that there is no equality of arms when the issue involves sources of resources (p. 1581). From the same critical bias, see also the thesis of Rowland James Victor Cole, according to whom "the lesson to be learnt from these tribunals is that resources are a fundamental Pillar of the equality of arms principle." The author, with a focus on the ICTY, ponders: "while equality of arms does not mean precise equality of resources, it is clear that there is substantial inequality in the allocation of resources to the prosecution and defense in international tribunals. This is inevitable as they depend on the goodwill and financial contributions of states and are usually under pressure to wrap up proceedings. With limited budgets, they are obviously compelled to employ judicial economy, with the result that equality of arms is compromised. The situation is similar on the domestic front. As the fight against crime is seen as a pressing social demand, state machineries established for this purpose attract funding, whereas the importance of allocating funds to protect individual human dignity is relegated to the background" (2010, p. 52).

[83] The author cites the so-called *primary interests,* such as the protection of victims, witnesses, national security, and ongoing investigations, as justifications (in light of Arts. 66, 67 and 69 of the ICTY's rules of procedure) for not immediately providing the information held by the prosecution to the accused (Negri, 2005, p. 561). Fedorova (2012), pp. 250–251, agrees, with the caveat that, when it comes to *exculpatory evidence*, the content of the material must, unconditionally, be shared with the accused. Specifically regarding *exculpatory evidence*, see: Zappalà (2004), pp. 620–630; Ambos (2009), pp. 543–568.

[84] Knoops (2004-2005). This researcher is critical of what he names a direction of *civil law* in evidence issues of the ICTY, ordinarily tailored for the assumption of the *common law* model of knowledge of the facts. Thus, alongside more investigative powers granted to judges, as portrayed in the rules of procedure, there would also be a limitation, in favour of expressions like procedural

Prosecutor v. Tadic, (i) there is not "precisely the same amount of time or the same number of witnesses" available to the defense and the prosecution, because, as already mentioned, (ii) a criterion of basic proportionality prevails and not one of mathematical equality in the relationship of time available for the witnesses on both sides,[85] which makes the ICTY analyze this issue (iii) from the conjunction between Article 73 *ter* of the Tribunal's rules of procedure[86] and Article 21 of its Statute.

Thus, at the same time as it is perceived that references to the ECHR's judgments are common, there is concern with the use of proportionality as a limiter of the effectiveness of the principle of equality of arms, particularly with the allocation of financial resources for the production of evidence and investigative facilities. Until these financial issues are resolved, there will be no equality of arms.[87]

Thus, if there is already not a mathematical division, but a proportional division of the ICTY regarding the distribution of abilities conferred to the parties for the presentations of theses, by precedents and doctrinal comments one can see another important step towards the conceptual delimitation of equality of arms: the distribution of financial resources made available to the prosecution and the defense, regardless of the severity of the case.[88]

---

economy, of the exercise of defense rights before that Tribunal. This is what is seen, from the author's warning, for example, in rule 73 *ter* of the ICTY's procedures.

[85] Knoops (2004-2005), p. 1578.

[86] Rule 73 *ter* Pre-Defence Conference: "(A) Prior to the commencement by the defence of its case the Trial Chamber may hold a Conference. (B) In the light of the file submitted to the Trial Chamber by the pre-trial Judge pursuant to Rule 65 *ter* (L)(ii), the Trial Chamber may call upon the defence to shorten the estimated length of the examination-in-chief for some witnesses. (C) In the light of the file submitted to the Trial Chamber by the pre-trial Judge pursuant to Rule 65 *ter* (L)(ii), the Trial Chamber, after having heard the defence, shall set the number of witnesses the defence may call. (D) After commencement of the defence case, the defence may, if it considers it to be in the interests of justice, file a motion to reinstate the list of witnesses or to vary the decision as to which witnesses are to be called. (E) After having heard the defence, the Trial Chamber shall determine the time available to the defence for presenting evidence. (F) During a trial, the Trial Chamber may grant a defence request for additional time to present evidence if this is in the interests of justice."

[87] Knoops (2004-2005), pp. 1590–1591. In the same vein, see: Cole (2010), pp. 50–52.

[88] A detail of the trial of the former president of Liberia by the Special Court for Sierra Leone (SCSL) may elucidate the final sentence. On 4 June 2007, the trial of Charles Taylor began. On that occasion, the accused did not have adequate contact with his until then only lawyer. While Taylor was imprisoned in the Netherlands, the lawyer officiated in Sierra Leone, and no funds were made available for the cost of the trip. In the session of 4 June, after several warnings from the presiding judge of the Court, the lawyer read a letter from the client with the explanations for which he could not be present at the trial and, for considering the trial as unfair (among other reasons, the prosecution team was composed of nine professionals, while the defense had only one), he resigned from the case and left the courtroom. The trial proceeded in that session, but was interrupted at the end. It was determined to suspend it until the Court ensured direct contact between the client and his lawyer. Thus, 7 months later, with a team of lawyers, the trial was resumed. In a comment about that episode, Richard Wilson pondered: "The right to equality of arms is a deeply established, and particularly apt, precept in the European system for protection of human rights, and one which has been imported into each of the international and hybrid criminal tribunals. While that guarantee does not mean dollar-for-dollar parity with prosecution funding, the defence must be provided with resources—time, space, library, staff, and compensation—sufficient for the task. The actions of the

5.4 Conceptual Contributions from the UNHRC

At the 19th session of the United Nations Human Rights Committee, held between 9 and 27 July 2007 in Geneva, Comment No. 32 to the ICCPR was formulated. This comment was intended to analyze Article 14 of the document, which dealt with the equality of arms.

The general rule, according to the Committee's interpretation, is that the right to equality before courts and tribunals and to a fair trial is a "key element of human rights protection and serves as a procedural means of safeguarding the rule of law."[89]

From this general rule, the Commission now approaches the principles already analyzed by the ECHR, and deviates from them, albeit to a small extent. This approximates the spirit that each signatory country of the ICCPR should mold its legislation to the interpretation of Article 14, and not the other way around.[90]

The Committee's interpretation also approaches that of the ECHR when it rejects the possibility of each state dictating what comes to be a violation, to deal with matters that could not be discussed as offenses against human rights.[91]

The Human Rights Committee understands, in the Recommendation studied here, that

> the right to equality before courts and tribunals, in general terms, guarantees, in addition to the principles mentioned in the second section of Article 14, paragraph 1, those of equal access and equality of arms, and guarantees that the parties in ongoing proceedings are treated without any discrimination.[92]

---

court, although not explicitly acknowledging their grounding in the concept of equality of arms, implicitly recognized the premise by ultimately ordering significant additional funding for the defence, and by Nmehielle's appointment (2008), pp. 7–8, of a defence team more nearly adequate to the challenges posed by the trial of a former head of state." The transcript of the session referred to here can be consulted at: http://www.sc-sl.org/LinkClick.aspx?fileticket=SA/7CCB4VCc=&tabid=160.

[89] Comment No. 32, item 2, available at: http://daccess-dds-ny.un.org/doc/UNDOC/GEN/G07/437/71/PDF/G0743771.pdf?OpenElement. Accessed on: 8 Mar. 2012. It was with this generic formula that the Committee faced the delicate question posed by the family of the widow and children of Thomas Sankara, assassinated president of Burkina Fasso, who pointed out that there had been no public or effective investigation to clarify the authorship of the assassination of the then president. Regarding the equality of arms, the Committee understood it to be one of the principles implicit in the generic notion of equality (Art. 14, ICCPR). *Communication* No. 1.159/2003, *Sankara v. Burkina Fasso*, decision of the Committee of 28 March 2006, § 12.4.

[90] Comment No. 32, item 4: "Article 14 contains guarantees that states parties must respect, regardless of their legal traditions and their domestic law."

[91] This was said in the *Communication* No. 1.015/2011 (*Perterer v. Austria*, 20 August 2004, § 9.2), when the Austrian government intended, in response to the allegation that it was a matter of civil nature, to remove the issue from the scope of the UN Human Rights Committee, and also in the *Communication* No. 961/2000 (*Everett v. Spain*, § 6.4).

[92] Comment No. 32, item 8. It is true that, according to item 13 of the same Comment, one step down is taken to deal with the equality of arms as a requirement of procedural rights that must be made available to the parties, "unless there are distinctions based on law and that can be justified from objective and reasonable reasons." And it was exactly in this sense, even with repetition of the

Particularly, item 13 of the Comment outlines the general lines of the interpretation that is intended to give to the equality of arms according to that advisory body of the United Nations:

> the right to equality before courts and tribunals also ensures equality of arms. This means that the same procedural rights must be provided for all parties unless distinctions are made in the law and can be justified on objective and reasonable grounds, not bringing actual disadvantage or other injustices to the accused.

As examples of the application of the principle presented by Comment No. 32, are cited: access to documents by the prosecution—which, necessarily, must also be guaranteed to the defense: access to the interpreter[93] and the availability of free professional action in favor of the most needy (*legal aid*—item 10 of Comment No. 32[94]).

In addition, the UNHRC also approaches the judgments of the ECHR because it follows a general rule in the sense of linking the equality of arms to the adversarial nature of the process. After all, it is understood that the principle should ensure that "each party is given the opportunity to contest all arguments and evidence brought by the opposing party."[95]

The reading of item 12 of the Comment, however, allows one to see a signal contrary to the repeated judgments of the ECHR in the sense that the principle of equality of arms applies not only at first instance, but also in appeal issues. This is because, although the ECHR is firm in understanding that the principle is applicable in situations before tribunals,[96] the aforementioned item of the Comment provides that "the right to equal access to a court, sheltered in Article 14, paragraph 1,

---

words that could bring the exception to the fore (justifications based on legal reasons and with objective and reasonable bases) that the Committee, in the case *Dudko v. Australia* (*Communication* No. 1.347/2005, 23rd July 2007), understood there to have been a violation of Article 14 of the ICCPR to a citizen to whom the rights of procedural equality were not assured. In this regard, in the decision, § 7.4.

[93] In a very limited way, as it seems that the permission is, as stated in Comment No. 32 (item 13), on an exceptional basis, so that the accused can participate in the hearings and understand the testimonies collected by oral evidence against him.

[94] Regarding the technical defense, in *J. Campbell v. Jamaica* (*Communication* No. 307/1988, 24th March 1993), the accused only found out the name of the lawyer who was already defending him after his appeal request was denied (cf. § 6.2). In *L. Simmonds V. Jamaica* (*Communication* No. 338/1988, 23rd October 1992), the accused did not even know the date of the trial, and therefore could not meet with the lawyer and prepare the defense. In this regard, the Committee said that what was at issue was: "What is at issue is whether he should have been notified of this assignment in a timely manner and given sufficient opportunity to consult with counsel prior to the hearing of the appeal, and whether he should have been afforded an opportunity to be present during the hearing of the appeal"—§ 8.4). In *Simpson v. Jamaica* (legal assistance must cover including the pre-judicial phase of criminal prosecution), the Committee understood there to have been a violation of Article 14 of the ICCPR (Gamble and Dias, 2009, p. 199).

[95] Comment No. 32, item 13, our translation. See, in this regard: *Äärelä and Näkkäläjärvi v. Finland*, *Communication* No. 779/1997, decided on 7 November 2001, § 7.4.

[96] See, in this regard, Kohlbacher (1978), p. 20.

concerns access to first instance proceedings and does not address the issue of the right of appeal or other remedies."[97]

Despite the UN Human Rights Committee's Comment No. 32 being synthetic when dealing with the equality of arms and providing few examples in this regard, one can note, in the evidentiary issue, the same Committee's action in favor of the implementation of the principle.

This was seen in *Larrañaga v. The Philippines* (*Communication* No. 1421/2005, decided on 24 July 2006), where the Spanish-Filipino citizen, along with others, was accused of committing more than one kidnapping—one of them resulting in the death of a victim—of Filipino citizens.

Initially, Larrañaga had received a life sentence, which was later converted into a death penalty. During the first-degree procedure, one of the accused took advantage of the plea bargain and, in court, admitted to having lied to incriminate Larrañaga. This prompted successive pleas from the defense for the witness's evidence to be recollected. Requests were denied, the lawyers left the case, and the Court appointed public defenders to the accused who were in prison and without a constituted defense.

In that case, abundant oral accusatory evidence was collected, and the collection of defensive oral evidence that even the constituted defenders tried to make was curtailed (as the alibi was brought to the case that, at the time of the events, Larrañaga and the other defendants would be in a city about 500 km away from the crime scene). The appointed lawyers also had difficulties in proceeding with the *cross-examination* due to the curtailment both in the hearing of the defense witnesses and in the questions they intended to ask, as listed by the prosecution. Thus, it was recognized, without prejudice to violations of other articles of the ICCPR, that there was a violation of procedural equality.[98]

Thus, even if the Committee's understanding is not so openly faithful to those followed so far by the ECtHR and the ICTY—mainly because the approaches seem to confine themselves to evidentiary issues—and nor to the rules of treatment of

[97] In any case, and for this reason the wording of the Commentary is literally transcribed, there is a precedent from the Committee in which a violation of equality was seen in the treatment of a citizen who ended up being extradited and who could not appeal the decision even though the prosecution was able to do so (*Weiss v. Austria*, *Communication* No. 1.086/2002, judged on 15th May 2003, § 9.6).

[98] For the case, see in detail §§ 3.1. and ss. (UN. *Selected decisions of the Human Rights Committee under the Optional Protocol*. v. 9. New York & Geneva: United Nations, 2008, pp. 266 and ss.). In another case, *Robinson v. Jamaica* (*Communication* No. 223/1987, judged on fourth April 1989), the Committee understood that there had been a violation of the equality of arms in a situation involving evidentiary issue: it was intended to maintain the death sentence of Frank Robinson, a citizen accused of murder, even though the trial, postponed six times at the request of the prosecution, had not been postponed even once at his request due to the non-appearance of his lawyer. Thus, the trial was held even with the refusal on the part of appointed lawyers—as they did not have sufficient contact with the case and would not bring witnesses to the act—the accused was prosecuted without defender, enlisted his mother as a witness and, in final oral defense, spoke for 3 min (mention to the equality of arms: § 10.4).

those involved, it is important to realize that the interpretation of the equality of arms in criminal proceedings stems from procedural equality.

Next, the influence of the IACHR's approaches on the construction of the concept of the equality of arms in criminal proceedings is questioned.

5.5 Conceptual Contributions from the IACHR

A particularity that is noted in the Inter-American system of human rights protection is that while the ECtHR (as seen) focuses on the application of the concept of equality of arms and domestic issues—read: in application to each practical case—the IACHR focuses on the application of the principle from the relationship between parties that demand before the Court.[99] Also, while the ECtHR focuses on the analysis of internal laws of each country to perceive a violation of the principle, in the IACHR, the approach of the equality of arms is based on the possibilities of access to the Court's own jurisdiction.

The equality of arms has fundamental importance in the sense of procedural balance between the claimant (citizen) and the defendant (state), notably with a view to guaranteeing the principle of access to the special jurisdiction of the IACHR.[100]

Also, for this reason, it is noted that the treatment given to the principle of the equality of arms is linked to equality (particularly to material equality, in which there is emphasis on access to the IACHR of humble people assisted by non-governmental organizations), and not to the adversarial principle.[101]

It was in this sense, for example, either for issues of form of sending petitions to the Court (via fax or telex), or for incorrect compliance with procedural formalities (how many copies of petitions should be sent to the Court), that the Court repeatedly (and, as seen in the ECtHR, to some extent self-referential) established the following understanding:

> The Court must maintain a fair balance between the protection of human rights, the ultimate end of the system, and legal security and procedural fairness that ensure the stability and confidence of international protection [because otherwise] it would result in the loss of authority and credibility indispensable to the bodies in charge of administering the human rights protection system.[102]

---

[99] Negri (2005), p. 531.

[100] Masha Fedorova shares this same perception (2012), p. 38.

[101] This is precisely the focus of an article by Vivanco and Bhansali (2004), p. 439, when they point out: "as regards issues of admissibility, exhaustion of domestic remedies and confidentiality, the Commission should review its rules and procedures with the purpose of reforming the system to ensure full respect for equality of arms and greater equity between the parties." In the same vein, see: Burgorgue-Larsen and Úbeda de Torres (2011), p. 666.

[102] Case *Cayara v. Peru*, judged on 3rd February 1993; preliminary exceptions, § 62. In this case, in which it was decided not to adhere to the formalism of the number of copies that the Human Rights Commission should send to the Court to have the demand accepted, since in the wording of the IACHR Statute prior to the demand twenty copies were required, and later ten were required—

The vote of Judge Cançado Trindade in *Castillo Petruzzi and others v. Peru* (judgment of 4 September 1998, preliminary objections, § 39) is emblematic of the IACHR's point of view on equality of arms regarding the citizen's right of access to the Court (or to the Human Rights Commission). There, in adherence to the votes of the other judges, there are references to the comparison between the European and Inter-American systems of human rights protection. It also dealt with the assimilation of the Inter-American system into the European one in terms of operation. Uninterrupted from the Court and the protection of fundamental rights from direct access of citizens to the Court.

In the vote cast in *Gangaram*,[103] Cançado Trindade made considerations about the interpretation that should be given to the binding nature of the opinion of the Inter-American Commission on Human Rights as a prerequisite for access to the IACHR in light of the "actual inequality of 'status' between the presumed victims and the governments sued in the procedure before the Court" (§ 6), to "procedural equality" and also to "a disparity between the parties" (§ 8).

The IACHR was quite direct, albeit generic, in addressing the equality of arms as a result of the principle of equality between litigants, and in Advisory Opinion No. 16/99, of October 1, about the right to information on consular assistance within the framework of guarantees of due legal process.

---

as in several other IACHR judgements, a balance is established not only between the parties in the demand, but, as the Court says, "between justice and legal security" (Case *Cayara v. Peru*, judged on third February 1993; preliminary exceptions, § 42). The understanding—whether of such *balance*, or of the measure of equality—predominantly of access to the Court, can be seen, *v.g.*, in the following cases: *Caballero Delgado & Santana v. Colombia* (judged on 21th January 1994, preliminary exceptions, § 44), in which it was discussed whether the deadline that the Commission had to analyze the feasibility of taking the case to the IACHR was peremptory or not; *Panel Blanca* (*Paniagua Morales and others v. Guatemala*; judged on 25 January 1996, preliminary exceptions, §§ 38, 42, 44), in which the first sending of a fax and then ten copies to the IACHR was dealt with, which was accepted. In addition to the *balance* between justice and legal certainty, it was said in the precedent that: "it is necessary to preserve the conditions necessary for the procedural rights of the parties not to be diminished or unbalanced, and for the purposes for which the different procedures have been designed to be achieved" (§ 42). In *Baena Ricardo and others v. Panama* (judged on 18th November 1999, preliminary exceptions), for example, the Court decided that, precisely in order not to exceed the 3-month period to deliberate on the referral of the case to the IACHR, the telephone conference held between the members of the Inter-American Commission on Human Rights could not be considered illegitimate. In that precedent, it was pointed out, among other things: "as far as the observance of certain formalities is concerned, it is essential to preserve the necessary conditions for the full validity of procedural rights and for the purposes for which the procedures in the Convention and the regulations of the Commission and the Court have been established to be achieved" (§ 41). On the other hand, if the defendant state unreasonably delays in complying with the deadline to respond, the imperative of "legal certainty and procedural equality" motivates the Court to firmly understand that the late state manifestations should not be received. Thus, for example, *Cantoral Benavides v. Peru* (judged on third December 2001, reparations and costs, § 31). Similarly, *Barrios Altos v. Peru* (judged on third September 2001, interpretation of the judgement on the merits, § 6).

[103] *Gangaram Panday v. Surinam* (judged on 4th December 1991, preliminary exceptions).

On the occasion, when dealing with the minimum contours of due legal process, the Court stated: "for there to be 'due legal process' it is necessary that a claimant can assert his rights and defend his interests effectively and on equal procedural terms with other claimants." More than that, the Court established that

> the process must recognise and resolve the factors of real inequality of those who are brought to justice. This is how the principle of equality before the law and the courts and the related prohibition of discrimination is met. The presence of conditions of real inequality requires the adoption of compensatory measures that help to reduce or eliminate the obstacles and deficiencies that prevent or reduce the effective defence of one's own interests. If these means of compensation did not exist, widely recognised in various aspects of the procedure, it could hardly be said that those who are in conditions of disadvantage enjoy true access to justice and benefit from due legal process on equal terms with those who do not have these disadvantages.[104]

Regarding the IACHR's position on the equality of arms, there are also cases where its similarity with the principle of contradiction, particularly with regard to the knowledge of each party about the admissibility of evidence. This is seen, from the outset, in Article 43 of the IACHR's rules of procedure, according to which only new evidence can be claimed if, before the decision, the opposing party can express itself about the claim.[105]

Even so, the prevailing approach is to treat the equality of arms from the perspective of equality. In the Inter-American scenario, there is the particularity of linking the equality of arms to overcoming inequalities between litigants. As Amaya Úbeda de Torres reminds us, such treatment prevails in the understanding of the IACHR, and it is worth mentioning the passage of Judge Sergio García Ramirez according to which Article 8 of the San José Pact of Costa Rica should be read in a way to

> project another radical principle of the democratic system in the exercise of the judicial function: the equality between the parties that demands that for the same standard of judgement, without prejudice to the singularities derived from the subject of the demand and with the inclusion of egalitarian elements when the controversy is between individuals with a natural 'inequality of arms'.[106]

[104] Advisory Opinion OC 16/99, of 1 October 1999, requested by the United Mexican States, "The Right to Information on Consular Assistance in the Framework of the Guarantees of Due Process of Law," §§ 117 and 119.

[105] Article 43: "After the receipt of the case submission brief, the petitions, arguments and evidence brief, and the answer brief, and before the opening of the oral proceedings, the Commission, the alleged victims or their representatives, the respondent State and, if applicable, the petitioner State may request the Presidency to carry out other acts of the written procedure. If the Presidency deems it appropriate, it will set the deadlines for the submission of the respective documents." The Portuguese version of the rules of procedure approved by the Court at the XXXV ordinary period of sessions, between 16 and 28 November 2009, was consulted (available at: http://www.corteidh.or.cr/reglamento.cfm). On this subject, *Maritza Urrutia v. Guatemala* (judgement of 27 November 2003, merits, reparations and costs, § 46). In the footnote of the cited decision, there are references to other decisions, in the same sense, taken by the IACHR. In the text of Negri (2005), p. 537, footnote no. 74, there are abundant references to precedents in the matter.

[106] Burgorgue-Larsen and Úbeda De Torres (2011), p. 666. The excerpt from Sergio García Ramirez that the author refers to was taken from: *Palamara Iribarne v. Chile*, Merits, Reparations and

This is because the focus of the IACHR stems not from possible offenses to the equality of arms in original processes of each country, but from the equality that is conferred on claimants before the Court, that is, in the relationship *citizen claimant* versus country, more than in the specific rules of criminal procedure of each state.

5.6 Distinction Between Equality of Arms and *Par Condicio* in Criminal Procedure

After the analyses on the main manifestations of the supra state bodies that dealt with the equality of arms in criminal procedure and on the prevalence that all give to the foundation of the principle in the aspect of equality, and not in contradiction—an option that was also followed in this work—it is necessary to distinguish between the equality of arms and the *par condicio.*

5.6.1 The Par Condicio *and Its Connection with the Doctrine of Procedural Relationship and with Contradiction*

In an influential monograph, Claudio Faranda, in the 70s of the last century, stated, right on the first page, that "*Il problema della* par condicio *non s'identifica con quello della cosiddetta 'parità d'armi'*."[107]

The Italian author built his theory on the *par condicio* in criminal procedure not only from the distinction (in fact, for him, an overcoming) of the equality of arms, but also based on the premise that, in criminal proceedings, there would be a cooperative structure between the parties and the judge aimed at reaching a fair decision.[108]

That is why it is important to say that Faranda recognized the connection that the equality of arms has with equality, as opposed to the *par condicio* and its connection

---

Costs. IACHR, 22.11.2005, *series* C n ° 135, Separate Concurring Opinion of Judge S. García Ramirez, § 10.

[107] Faranda (1968), p. 1. Hence, it is striking a bias of the reading that Welton Roberto made (2011), p. 96, of Faranda's work. According to the Brazilian author, the equality of arms would be synonymous with the *par condicio*. It does not seem to us that the best interpretation of the Italian work is this. On this subject, even Andrade (2008), p. 158, footnote no. 591, who assumes a position with which we do not agree (as he also takes as synonyms the equality of arms and the *par condicio*), quotes the work of Faranda and remembers that the Italian author did not equate one notion with the other, in which he is correct.

[108] Right at the beginning of the work, the distinction between *par condicio* and equality of arms is noted: "Il superamento di una concezione di 'parità d'armi'" would be the result of a "presa di conscienza del valore pubblicistico Che, particolarmente nel processo penale, assume la funzione di acceertamento giurisdizionale" Faranda (1968), pp. 2–3). The author reaffirms his link with the doctrine of the procedural relationship.

with the contradictory. It is also important to note that the construction was indeed composed of two pairs: on one side, equality and the equality of arms; on the other, the contradictory and the *par condicio*. Faranda's study refuted the first and privileged the second.

From the author's perspective, the cooperative structure between the parties and the judge aimed at reaching the sentence is achieved with strict observance of the contradictory, seen as a "method of truth-seeking based on dialogical opposition," by which "the performance of the *par condicio* among the parties to the process is considered an indispensable systematic requirement."[109]

The contradiction was taken by him as a requirement that goes beyond the need to confer procedural equality, as it is understood as a method of ensuring, in dialogical constructions between the parties, the procedural truth.[110] For this reason, for Faranda, the *par condicio*—linked to the contradictory—assumes autonomous prominence with respect to the said constitutional principle of equality.

Regarding this, the interpretation that Ada Pellegrini Grinover gave to the author's text is faithful in the sense that such a cooperative structure would be characterized by the "collaboration between parties and judge." In Grinover's words about Faranda's lessons,

> the participation of the subjects in the process not only allows each one to increase the possibilities of obtaining a favourable decision, but signifies cooperation in the exercise of jurisdiction. Above and beyond the selfish intentions of the parties, the dialectical structure of the process exists to revert to the benefit of the good quality of the jurisdictional provision and the perfect adherence of the sentence to the underlying substantive legal situation.[111]

Thus, the author deduces the proposition that "the parties are necessary for the development of the process. The contrary proposition, in the sense that the process serves the parties, is only valid in the narrow measure in which they have an interest in the provision."[112]

As can be seen, Faranda and Ada Pellegrini Grinover understand that the *par condicio* is linked to the contradictory. They also say that the process develops not from the sequence of legal situations, but as a complex and progressive legal

---

[109] Faranda (1968), p. 7.

[110] In Brazil, the study by Almeida (1973), pp. 82 and 107, on the principle of contradiction in criminal proceedings, if on the one hand obeys the author's theoretical reservations about the existence of parties in criminal proceedings, on the other hand focuses on the possibility of action and reaction and, thus, on the concrete possibility that this happens. Thus, if first we can see the always repeated passage according to which the contradiction is "bilateral knowledge of the acts and procedural terms and possibility to contradict them," specifically for criminal procedural law, the contradiction would manifest "by the timely knowledge given to the accused of all the charges judicially against him accumulable this means that the defendant should not be prosecuted without citation and without term for contradiction."

[111] Grinover (1990), p. 3. The idea, in other words, of treating the parties as assistants in the search for truth, and not as protagonists of the judicial scene, was also seen by Almeida (1973), p. 107. In the same sense, following this cooperative conception in the performance of parties in criminal proceedings is the study by Roberto (2011), p. 96.

[112] idem.

relationship in which the parties must have cooperative participation with the Judiciary in the settlement of the facts.[113] It is, therefore, a process with a cooperative structure.

The Italian author openly criticizes the equality of arms and its connection with equality in an attempt, in his own words, to *overcome it*. According to him, the equality of arms would be tied to the privatized notion of process, contrary to what should exist in the so-called *cooperative structure* of the process.

For her part, Ada Pellegrini Grinover, precisely because she privileges the procedural legal relationship to the detriment of the parties' interests, asserted that the adherence of the sentence to the debated factual situation matters more than the satisfaction of the parties' interests.[114]

Hence, the *par condicio* is linked to the contradictory as a procedural method tied to the idea of cooperation, typical of a procedural system shaped by the notion of procedural legal relationship. This distances the synonymy between *par condicio* and equality of arms in a process in which the legal situation of those involved matters, but not the relationship that animates them among themselves and, even less, before the judge.

5.6.2 The Equality of Arms, Its Separation from the Doctrine of the Procedural Relationship, and Its Consequence of Equality

It is assumed here that the equality of arms is a principle applicable in the field of criminal procedure and does not have the contradictory as its constitutional basis, but procedural equality, based on the constitutional provision.[115] It does not depend on the so-called cooperative structure of the process, which is alien to the conception of criminal procedure as a sequence of procedural situations in which each one of those involved takes advantage of the available opportunities, under penalty of not achieving a favorable decision.

What is meant by this is: while the *par condicio* depends on the consideration of the legal relationship between the parties and the judge in the search for truth, equality of arms is concerned with the relationship between the accused and the accuser with a view not to the attainment of truth, but to the set of legal positions and procedural means that each side may have in presenting the case to the judge.

---

[113] In the lesson of Canuto Mendes de Almeida, a *competition* between the Public Prosecutor's Office and the accused in the realization of justice is sought (1973), p. 107.

[114] Also, thus, before, Canuto Mendes de Almeida positioned himself (1973), pp. 100 and foll.

[115] With which we disagree with the position of Fawcett (1987), p. 154, according to whom "the principle of the equality of arms is an expression of the rule audi alteram partem, and implies that each party to the proceedings before a tribunal must be given a full opportunity to present his case, both on facts and in law, and to comment on the case presented by his opponent."

In both conceptions of the process, there is, naturally, subjection of the parties to the impartial subject (otherwise, the state would not regulate the conduct, nor would it impose its authoritative force in judicial provisions, whatever they may be).

But, on the one hand, the subjection arises from the premise of the search for truth as shaping the actions and reactions of the parties, with the parties themselves being contingent in the scope of cooperatively achieving the so-called fair decision. On the other hand, the subjection occurs from the procedural loyalty provided for in deontological norms that vary, in the plane of positive law, from system to system.

From this perspective, the participation of the parties is central, as what matters is the achievement of the objectives, given the rules of distribution of chances in the process, something very different from what the cooperative structure preaches, linked to the *par condicio*. In the second case, it is about equality of arms; in the first, about *par condicio*.

Furthermore, in a criminal process structured according to the constitutional guarantee of the presumption of innocence, with the particularity of respecting the right to silence—and the consequence of its exercise[116]—the cooperative structure of the criminal process is not favored to the extent that Faranda does.

From a different perspective, it can be said that the lesson of contradiction—although it is one of the most expensive in the criminal process—as well as its aspect of forming a synthesis from theses and antitheses, even though it is present both when there is observance of the *par condicio* and when it is about equality of arms, it is not nuclear in the latter case.

The contradiction refers to the "game of actions, reactions and reciprocal controls"[117] and, to some extent, it may even coincide with the result of having obeyed the equality of arms. But the consequence of such harmony, even if it results from equality of arms, does not therefore confuse it. In other words, because *there is* equality of arms, *there may*, *consequently*, be a guarantee of contradiction, but this equation is not infallible.

It is possible to exemplify the two sides involved: first, a case in which a different number of witnesses is provided for, if listed by the prosecution or the defense, means contradiction without equality of arms, as it allows the concretization of the idea of knowledge and reaction, but does not prevent disparate treatment of the parties.[118] On the other hand, there is equality of arms, but there is no contradiction,

---

[116] It does not seem possible to agree with such a *cooperative* structure if, in criminal proceedings, no one is obliged to incriminate themselves.

[117] Fazzalari (1966), p. 1074.

[118] This is the case of the current Brazilian Military Criminal Procedure Code (Decree No. 1.002/69): the prosecution can list six witnesses with the initial (Art. 77, CPPM), while the defense can initially list three (Art. 417, § 2°, CPPM). In addition, there is also a contradiction, with differentiated treatment between prosecution and defense in the situation where the Prosecutor's Office receives personal notifications (Art. 18, II, h, Complementary Law n° 75/93; Federal Law n° 8.625/93, Art. 41, IV). An interesting question arose in AP 470, as a lawyer for the co-defendants, faced with excessive mention of the name of the constituent when the public accusation was being orally sustained, had requested that the time for defensive oral argument be doubled (in a situation where the time for oral argument for the accusation was quintupled. The request was denied and

when neither of the contenders is given the opportunity to present their arguments before the Court on a document that is in the records and has been produced, for example, by a criminal expert or authority of the Brazilian Revenue Service by judicial order.[119]

From the point of view of the moment at which the principle of equality of arms can occur, it is understood here that it is a continent in which the contradiction is content (equality of arms occurs during a larger arc of the process than the contradiction). Likewise, the notion of contradiction to some extent presupposes equality in the treatment of opponents in the process; hence, its origin is close to that of equality of arms.

However, as the cases of manifestation of the two principles are not necessarily coincident, the relationship of continent and content is not inexorable. That is why it can be assumed, in this work, that the circle of incidence of equality of arms is larger than that covered by the contradiction,[120] but the incidences do not always occur in the same situations.

Equality of arms, which is structured on the broad notion of presentation of the case in a non-disadvantageous situation before the opponent, is not a procedural synonym for contradiction—*rectius, par condicio*—as it allows situations to be reached where there is no game of actions and reactions dealt with by Fazzalari and, in Brazilian criminal procedural law, by Joaquim Canuto Mendes de Almeida.[121]

Instead of being linked to contradiction, equality of arms in the criminal process is linked to equality because "it seeks to ensure that both parties in conflict enjoy the

---

exemplifies a situation in which the contradiction was exercised, but not the equality of arms (Supreme Federal Court, APn 470, under the rapporteurship of Justice Joaquim Barbosa, pp. 51909–11 of the records and, in the published judgment, pp. 294/6., published on 22nd April 2013).

[119] Elisa Toma (2012, p. 4) cites another example for the distinction: "The court states on the differences between the two principles in regards to the case where the miscommunication of a document from the cause's file affects only one of the parts, when the other part had access to that document. It is specified that in these situation we are confronted with a violation of the principle of equality of arms. The parts must be treated in an equal manner, without having one part enjoying a right to which the other didn't had access. Opposed to this case, if the both parts didn't have the possibility to study a useful information that already reached the judge, the violation concerns the principle of contradictory."

[120] Hence, the separation made by Roberto (2011), p. 93, seems correct when he states that equality of arms is "the core element for the realisation of the contradiction." For this reason, it is insisted, equality of arms separates from contradiction. Costa (2012), p. 31, builds a reciprocal link between equality of arms and contradiction: on one hand, he states that "the contradiction can be understood as a consequence of the principle of equality of arms, in the sense that this principle—of more comprehensive character—requires that the parties can pronounce on all the issues related to the dispute, under penalty of generating an imbalance of their situations in the process"; on the other hand, he indicates that "the equality of arms can be understood as a requirement of the contradiction, since this, as a right to be heard and to influence the final decision, requires an equal opportunity for exposure of reasons and arguments."

[121] The contradiction, for that professor, is the formal expression of *contrariness* (1938), p. 79. It has no connection with *equality*.

same means of attack and defence and the equality of arms to assert their allegations and means of proof."[122]

In the words of Mirjan Damaška, "all litigants should be treated as equals for the purpose of availability of procedural arms, just as all voters should be considered as equals for the purpose of regulating the election (one man, one vote)."[123]

In a subtle placement that assists in the separation adopted here, Elio Fazzalari takes care of situations of *dialecticity* and *parity* between subjects.[124] For him, such notions do not confuse: equality of arms is a result of equality, while the *par condicio*, based on the contradictory, is linked to dialecticity. Further, the first does not depend on the formal performance of a part; the second, yes. Thus, by Faranda's construction, the contradictory and the defensive and accusatory actions are limited until the decision of merit provision.

Also, for this reason, equality of arms is seen autonomously in relation to *par condicio*, since, as it has already been anticipated more than once here, it presupposes equality in the presentation of the cause, and not only in the distribution of the rules pertaining to proof or the dynamics of action and reaction in the criminal process.[125]

Thus, despite it being fruitful to think about the evidentiary aspects for the equality of arms (and for the *par condicio*), the first can be applied before the judicial phase of criminal prosecution is established (that is, before the *parties* exist), with typical investigative measures that indicate that someone may be considered as suspected of committing a certain infraction.

Equality of arms can also be applied in the appeal field with the observance of the right of presence of the accused and the right, if applicable, to be heard about the facts, being that this does not necessarily have relation to the notion of contradictory.

This argument, moreover, privileges the aspect of the broad factual support of the fundamental right norm, insofar as it does not exclude, aprioristically, some field of incidence of the principle of equality of arms in the criminal process. Thus, greater protection is granted to the fundamental right of the recipient of the protective norm.

Another exemplary situation of the distinction between equality of arms and *par condicio* is in criminal execution: there is still the right to freedom at stake, but there is no cooperative structure. This is because even the contours of the debate that takes place in criminal execution are distinct from those had in instruction of the criminal action that has become final, and because the very legitimacy to act, in criminal execution, is distinct.

The relationship established between the executed and the other bodies involved in the criminal execution—particularly the Prosecutor's Office—is unmistakable

---

[122] Moreno (2002), pp. 145–146. The same sentiment is the doctrine of Castañeda Paz (2001), pp. 571 and foll.

[123] Damaška (1986), p. 107, our translation.

[124] Fazzalari (1966), p. 1074.

[125] Vieira (2013), pp. 271 and foll.

with the one that animated opposing interests before the judge during the criminal instruction. This is because, in criminal execution, there is no longer controversy about the factual situation that motivated the criminal prosecution. The own procedural instruction that may exist in criminal execution results from incidents linked to the form of the regime of serving the sentence, to possible recalculations, remissions, incidences of faults, and calculations for progression of regime.

If one considers the application of equality of arms in this phase, and if one can even indicate the presence of contradictions in certain punctual manifestations, the fact is that it is not a cooperative structure, nor dialecticity with a view to the consonance of the judicial decision to the factual situation. In other words, one can say there is equality of arms, but not *par condicio* in criminal execution.

In criminal execution, there is no accusation of crime, but, punctually, manifestation of the Prosecutor's Office—even if disagreeing with the executed pleas—in incidents in the executive phase of the criminal process whose criminal action has become final. Both in the initial phase and in the final phase of the criminal process, there is no identity of possibilities of action between the accusation and the defense.[126] The incidence of equality of arms in these procedural moments separates the contradictory (and the *par condicio*) from the consequent lessons of *action and reaction* of what is exposed here as part of the concept of equality of arms.

In this regard, see the decision of the first Chamber of the Supreme Federal Court, which brought to the criminal process the lesson of the contradictory without the consideration of preventing the implementation of a double manifestation in the records of the accusing body to the detriment of one side only: the citizen who was denounced to public justice. In the precedent, it was understood to operate the contradiction in the sense that, from the joining of documentation from one of the parties, a view was opened to the opposing party.[127]

The reasoning developed there can even be explained by the premise of the adversarial principle, but it is not based on the equality of arms because, as the content of the judgement transpires, the notion of the adversarial principle was strictly followed, but not that of the difficult equation between the initial situation of the public prosecutor and the citizen who must defend himself from the criminal accusation.

After all, it is the accused who must know the elements and details of the accusation to address the defensive reaction to the Judiciary. To implement, to guarantee the adversarial principle, the opening of views to the accuser, depending on the

[126] "It is to be recognised that there is an initial inequality in criminal prosecution. The defence is placed in a position of disadvantages in the investigation phase, which is included in the right to investigate the sources of evidence. The prosecution's investigation is carried out by state bodies, structured for this purpose. On the other hand, the defence must develop its investigation with its own forces. The problem becomes even more sensitive when considering that the vast majority of the accused and investigated in the criminal process are poor and do not have the conditions to develop any investigative activity" Badaró (2024), p. 67.

[127] *HC* No. 105.739, under the rapportership of Justice Marco Aurélio, published on 28th February 2012.

content of the defensive response, is to allow a new accusatory manifestation, this time in rebuttal to the defense arguments.

Thus, the logic of the adversarial principle itself at the procedural moment of the defensive response is distorted: what is sought is for the defense to react to the accusation, but not the opposite. At this particular procedural moment, the protection rule guarantees the accused knowledge of the accusatory line, and it is not justified that the accusatory body rebuts the defensive arguments, especially since the point of controversy is the initial of the accusing body itself.

From the perspective of equality of arms, moreover, it is not just about the possibility of the accused rebutting defensive theses, but about preventing one of the parties from having more argumentative efficacy to convince the judge than the other. Such a conception implies seeing in the equality of arms not only the relationship between action and reaction, or parity manifestations whenever the opposing party manifests itself in the case.[128]

That this promise can be fulfilled with the implementation of the adversarial principle, there is no doubt, but the equality of arms is broader than the systematic action-reaction in criminal proceedings. As for the recipients, it does not depend on the conceptualization of part in a strict sense; as for the temporal scope, it is independent of the judicialization of criminal prosecution; as for the content, it is independent of the procedural dynamics, because it goes beyond the limits of the adversarial principle.

Thus, it is not correct to affirm that the equality of arms derives not from equality, but from the adversarial principle. Parity derives, in fact, from equality, and not from the adversarial principle. And such a mistake has visible consequences in criminal proceedings.

As seen from the precedents cited from the ECHR, the ICTY, the IACHR or the United Nations Human Rights Committee, the equality of arms goes beyond the systematic action-reaction, as it means guaranteeing rights that do not necessarily arise from the act of the opposing party (e.g., access to documents; the possibility of exercising the right to confrontation; presence at hearings and appeal trial sessions; the prohibition of accusatory manifestations disguised as a body *custos legis*; prior knowledge of indictment determination). The equality of arms, therefore, is a concept that is independent of the act or reaction of the opposing party.

[128] Because of this stance, we disagree with Manoel Monteiro Guedes Valente, who professes the idea that the equality of arms is an "unequivocal corollary of the principle of contradiction" and that it would also be an "accelerator" of the latter (2009), pp. 135 and 152, respectively. In our view, such acceleration of contradiction does not exist, as there is a justification, from procedural equality, for it to materialize in criminal procedure. Hence, also, contradiction is a corollary of the equality of arms, but not the other way around.

5.7 Distinction Between Equality of Arms and Presumption of Innocence

Similarly, the principle of equality of arms must be conceptually distinguished from another that is, to some extent, related: the presumption of innocence, in a broad sense, in criminal proceedings.

The so-called *broad sense of the presumption of innocence* is adopted here because it follows the understanding of Maurício Zanoide de Moraes, according to whom the presumption of innocence brings with it, as "aspects, meanings, projections or manifestations," the *favor rei* and the *in dubio pro reo*.[129] That is, in the language of fundamental law, the *favor rei* and the *in dubio pro reo* "integrate the normative scope of the presumption of innocence."[130] Thus, in the wake of the theory of fundamental rights, a broad factual support is given to the presumption of innocence.

That is why it is not adhered to, in this particular, to the understanding of Alexandra Vilela, for whom the *favor rei* would have a broader scope than the presumption of innocence because it could be taken as a "superior criterion of freedom and general principle informing modern criminal procedural law" which, therefore, "is always present in any rule or institution that, from any point of view, turns out to be favourable to the accused."[131]

Following the lesson according to which the *favor rei* and the *in dubio pro reo* are projections of the presumption of innocence requires that, first, both be analyzed separately and then return to dealing with their relationship with the presumption of innocence.

5.7.1 Favor Rei *and* In Dubio Pro Reo *in Criminal Proceedings: Distinctions*

While the *favor rei* implies a value choice of the interpreter from the "ideals of equality, human dignity and protection of the freedom and property of the citizen," the *in dubio pro reo* implies a choice based on criteria of doubt in the procedural

[129] Zanoide de Moraes (2010), p. 367. The mention of the components of the formula of the presumption of innocence is justified, because, as the author alludes, until times prior to those of international human rights treaties and the so-called constitutional theories of fundamental rights, the opposite was understood, that is, precisely from the *favor rei* would come the presumption of innocence and the *in dubio pro reo*. Also, for Bacigalupo (1992), p. 77, the *in dubio pro reo* is a component of the presumption of innocence.

[130] Zanoide de Moraes (2010), p. 369.

[131] Vilela(2005), p. 73. We also do not follow Bettiol (1966), p. 215, according to whom the presumption of innocence would be the consecration at the constitutional level of the norm of the European Convention on Human Rights, linked, according to him, to the *favor rei*.

plane, that is, in the factual doubt about the application of the law to the specific case.[132]

Due to the different valuation of the interpreter—regarding the *favor rei* and regarding the *in dubio pro reo*—it is that the *favor rei* can show itself as the meaning of the presumption of innocence not only in the jurisdictional plane (when the judge applies the norm in solving the case), but also in the legislative plane (because, in the broad factual support of the presumption of innocence, an interpretation that favors freedom should be adopted).[133]

In its turn, the *in dubio pro reo* has its own field for strictly procedural manifestation from the demand and the doubt that arise.[134] While the doubt that guides the application of the *favor rei* is an axiological doubt that does not depend on the procedural situation,[135] the one that motivates the application of the *in dubio pro reo* is concrete and necessarily is linked to factual uncertainty.[136]

In this regard, according to the lessons of Gilberto Lozzi, it is worth thinking about applications of the *favor rei* in the counting of votes of judgments when the tie favors the defense,[137] and in cases in which the defense is always guaranteed a manifestation after the accusation.[138]

[132] Zanoide de Moraes (2010), p. 365. At this point, we agree with Bettiol (1966), p. 214, who reminded, for the *favor rei*: "indeed, the judge cannot be *agnostic* with respect to the defendant." Gustavo Henrique Righi Ivahy Badaró, in an article, goes in the same line when distinguishing the *favor rei* from the *in dubio pro reo*. The author, in the text that dealt with the result to be expected in the trial of the original Criminal Action 470, which was processed in the STF, said that the *in dubio pro reo* applies in the case of "doubt about a fact legally relevant, as a rule of judgement in criminal procedure." Thus, in the wake of Lozzi, Badaró separated it from the *favor rei* (2012).

[133] Lozzi (1968), p. 178, when linguistically decoding the *favour of the king*, did so from the word *favour*. With this included in *favour of the king* were the phrases *favour of defence* and *favour of liberty*. In the same sense was Vilela (2005), p. 76. For Mario Chiavario, Carrara also linked the presumption of innocence to the idea of "favours for the defence" (1991), p. 359. Among us: Cruz (2002), p. 103; Fernandes (1999), p. 50.

[134] Zanoide de Moraes (2010), p. 366. For the author, the *in dubio pro reo* should be taken into account by the authority as a decisive guide in absolutely all phases of the criminal process. This position is agreed with and, therefore, the lesson of Vilela (2005), p. 77, is not accepted, according to whom the *in dubio pro reo*, in the aspect of evidentiary rule, "has its main moments of action in the context of accusation and judgement."

[135] What rule should the judge apply to the concrete case in which more than one interpretation is possible—in a situation where technically any decision would be axiologically justifiable from the ideology followed? Or, more abstractly, what rule should the legislator produce to achieve a certain procedural effect?

[136] What decision should be made in the face of a certain evidentiary scenario, that is, depending on the factual situation that presents itself for decision?

[137] Lozzi (1968), p. 54. Different and precisely on this point, Gustavo Henrique Righi Ivahy Badaró, for whom the question is not of application of the principle of *favour of the king*, but of pure non-overcoming of the initial state of innocence, states: "in the case of a tie in the voting of the collegiate body, there was no conviction The tie does not transform the innocent into guilty. The hypothesis to be corrected did not achieve the positive result necessary to change the *status* of innocent! If there is a tie, the condemnatory thesis did not win" (2012), p. 3.

[138] idem.

In Brazil, particularly in the context of some appeals and impugnatory actions, one can note the consecration of the *favor rei* principle.

Thus, for example, as Rogério Schietti Machado Cruz reminds us, the application of the *favor rei* is observed in the last of the items of Article 386 of the Code of Criminal Procedure,[139] which concerns the provisions of appeals and impugnatory actions of exclusive handling by the defense, such as the infringing appeals (and of nullity) and the criminal review,[140] the use exclusively in favor of the defense in an action of habeas corpus, the prohibition (even if indirect) of the *reformatio in pejus*.[141]

Brazilian authors such as André Nicolitt,[142] Paulo Rangel,[143] Ada Pellegrini Grinover, Antonio Magalhães Gomes Filho, and Antonio Scarance Fernandes deal with the infringing and nullity appeals as a result of the *favor rei*.[144]

Regarding specifically the criminal review as a result of the consecration of the *favor rei*, Ada Pellegrini Grinover, Antonio Magalhães Gomes Filho, and Antonio Scarance Fernandes take the constitutional revisional action as a result of the "*favor defensionis* (unfolding of that of the *favor rei*)."[145]

In this regard, as it is a decision favorable to freedom that can even surpass the final judgment of conviction, it is important to mention Gustavo Badaró. For the author, even though historically the current Federal Constitution does not provide for the fundamental guarantee of criminal review, the prohibition of the so-called criminal review *pro societate* derives from the notion of *favor rei* stamped in Article 8.4 of the CADH.[146]

Both the *in dubio pro reo* and the *favor rei*, in the lesson of Maurício Zanoide de Moraes, integrate the so-called normative scope of the presumption of innocence because each of them gives the presumption of innocence a wider range of application and, therefore, enables it to achieve greater effectiveness.[147]

---

[139] Cruz (2002), p. 103. It is to be thought: the *favour of the king* is seen by the abstract provision of the law; and the *in dubio pro reo* is seen in the judicial decision to use or not the norm of Article 386, VII, of the Code of Criminal Procedure.

[140] Cruz (2002), p. 104.

[141] Cruz (2002), p. 104. That is, the very provision aims to benefit exclusively the defense, hence why not speak of protection to the accusation against the *reformatio in pejus*.

[142] Nicolitt (2012), p. 575.

[143] Rangel (2012), p. 1017. The author is situated in the current understanding that the Prosecutor's Office could also appeal, provided that the defendant "remains inert and an unspeakable injustice is configured in his conviction in the face of the discovery, after the appeal judgment, of evidence of his innocence."

[144] Grotrian (2009), p. 162.

[145] Grotrian (2009), p. 238.

[146] Badaró (2024), p. 690. The protective provision of the American Convention is as follows: "the accused acquitted by a final judgment cannot be subjected to a new trial for the same facts." There is a recent work that deals with possible situations criminal-procedural resulting from res judicata of convictions in light of the principle of *favour rei*: Queiroz (2012), pp. 46–47.

[147] Zanoide de Moraes (2010), p. 369.

5.7.2 *The Broad Concept of the Presumption of Innocence*

Once separated, the *favor rei* and the *in dubio pro reo*, reaching a broader concept of presumption of innocence as a fundamental right norm, is a less arduous task. It follows, in the broad conceptualization, the classification according to which the presumption of innocence is both a *treatment norm* and an *evidentiary norm*, and, still, a *judgment norm*.

By the first denomination, the presumption of innocence observes, "as much as possible, that the accused is not given any guilty treatment before the final judgement of any conviction decision."[148] In the second, it is imposed that "to have a legitimate conviction decision or to request any type of restriction to the rights of the accused during the prosecution, it is necessary that the accuser presents incriminating and lawful evidence." Finally, in the third sense, it is demanded from the judge that "he demonstrates that that incriminating material is sufficient to give him the factual certainty to decide against the accused."[149]

If the presumption of innocence, as seen here, encompasses the meanings of *favor rei* and *in dubio pro reo* (and not the opposite),[150] one can return to the distinction between it and the equality of arms in criminal proceedings.

5.7.3 *The Distinction Between Equality of Arms and the Presumption of Innocence*

The presumption of innocence does not confuse with the equality of arms, even though the premise attached to the *favor rei* of mitigation of the imbalance between accusation and defense in criminal proceedings (according to the approaches of Gilberto Lozzi and Alexandra Vilela) brings the two notions a bit closer.

The *favor rei*, in the aspect of *favor defensionis*, disparages accusation and defense in criminal proceedings. And it does so with a view to unbalancing the clear situation of advantage that the body of criminal prosecution has in comparison with the defense. Moreover, for reasons that go beyond the present research, the *favor rei* is much more linked to the justifications for privileged treatment of the accused than

---

[148] Zanoide de Moraes (2010), p. 405.

[149] The wide range of exemplary situations and the related doctrinal repertoire can be seen, in Brazilian doctrine, in the work of Zanoide de Moraes (2010), pp. 405 and foll. By the way, for the author, only in the third sense that the *in dubio pro reo* has application in criminal procedural law, since it would be a pure judgment norm.

[150] A different stance from the one adopted, for example, by Vilela (2005), pp. 73–81, which follows a very broad criterion of *favor rei* and, as for the *in dubio pro reo*, adopts the understanding that it would be a norm linked to the "issue of evidence production and the distribution of the burden of proof" (p. 77).

to the operability of the criminal proceedings itself, a topic dear to the equality of arms.[151]

Thus, the problem of the justification of equal treatment may even manifest itself in a similar way in the equality of arms and in the presumption of innocence, but the latter, in the facet of *favor rei*, has a clear contour of defensive privilege, for which it is justified, to achieve other extraprocedural values, the procedural inequality.

Moreover, it is understood that the equality of arms is more linked to the possibility of the parties bringing the arguments under equal conditions to the judge so that the demands are impartially appreciated. Such a perspective is largely linked, as already anticipated, to the conception of adversarial or party criminal proceedings. On its part, the existence of the *favor rei* is deduced from the conception of the Rule of Law that the criminal proceedings—by the consequence it can have on the individual right at stake—translates.

Maurício Zanoide de Moraes explains that the *favor rei*, as a facet of the presumption of innocence,

> should guide the infraconstitutional criminal procedural legislative formation so as not to elaborate laws abstractly non-conforming to that constitutional provision, both in the judicial scope, to guide the choice of the interpretation most favourable to the accused.[152]

Besides the distinction on the theoretical level, the presumption of innocence (and the *favor rei* as one of its meanings) draws its foundation, within the scope of the ECHR, from Article 6, 2.[153] The equality of arms, as already seen, is based on Article 6, 1, of the ECHR.

In the Brazilian constitutional plane, continuing the distinction, while the presumption of innocence and its meanings (*favor rei* and *in dubio pro reo*) derive from Article 5, LVII, of the Federal Constitution, it is argued here that the foundation of the equality of arms is another: Article 5, *caput*, of the same document. Thus, although it is possible, at least in the facet of the *favor rei*, to gather a certain approximation between equality of arms and presumption of innocence, it is certain that, even by the fact that the *favor rei* (as a decision-making vector guided by an axiological criterion incident on the judge and on the legislator) is one of the aspects of the presumption of innocence, the equality of arms does not confuse with it.

The equality of arms may eventually have a foundation similar to the *favor rei*, but will not necessarily have with other unfolding of the presumption of innocence in a broader sense. Therefore, again, it does not confuse with the *favor rei*: while this is a content of the principle of the presumption of innocence, the equality of

---

[151] This cut makes it easier to separate both. This is because it is known that, outside of a certain process—in which such situations of advantage or disadvantage from side to side may appear—the *favour rei* has ideological justifications. Such justifications can be seen both in the *in dubio pro reo*, which is related to the management of doubt risks, like in the criminal review *pro reo*. As said in Chap. 1, the ideological justifications of the equality of arms—equalising the equals or unequalizing the unequals—are tested in the process.

[152] Zanoide de Moraes (2010), p. 369.

[153] "Any person accused of an offence is presumed innocent until their guilt has been legally proven" (Lozzi, 1968, p. 11). See also: Bacigalupo (1992), p. 78.

arms is not contained in another criminal procedural principle. It has autonomy and, given any similarity with the *favor rei*, one could even risk saying that its normative scope, at this point, confuses with that of the presumption of innocence.

Both the presumption of innocence and the equality of arms, therefore, have the *favor rei* as a possible applicative meaning. Thus, as said at the beginning of this chapter, we continue to define what the equality of arms *is not* so that, then, its concept can be purified.

5.8 The *Legal Aid* and Substantial Equality

There is no application of the equality of arms in the criminal process if the material notion of equality is not applied. In this regard, the precedents and the interpretation given, especially within the scope of the IACHR and even in the distribution of procedural costs—mainly in the cases of the ICTY discussed—are relevant.

The defense of the introjection of material equality in the process implies care in the automatic assimilation of the notions of adversariality and equality of arms, and for this reason, once again, a certain separation is justified. As already said, the adversarial process is certainly conducive to the principle, not being indispensable to its development.

The caution is taken to separate, conceptually, the adversarial criminal process from the equality of arms because, either by what the most attentive European doctrine has already said,[154] either by the Inter-American scenario (legal system inserted in a socio-economic context different from the model in which the system of *common law* was gestated and developed), there are sufficient reasons to distinguish them.

Thus, and in this regard, if it is common the lesson according to which the innate differences between accuser (with the exclusivity of moving the power of legitimate coercion) and accused make impossible the equal distribution of possibilities in the criminal process, the equality of arms has to take care of another serious issue: the introjection, in the criminal process, of social inequalities or, if not that, as seen in the scenario of the ICTY, of the very costs for the defense of citizens accused of complex conducts that often cause revulsion and, not infrequently, have high financial significance.

The backdrop of what is known, from the American and English examples of *legal aid*,[155] consists exactly in preventing socio-economic inequalities from being *forgotten* when moving to the strict scenario of the criminal process. The raison d'être of aid to the poorest in the criminal process, as Taruffo says, is precisely a charitable background action without which the (extraprocedural) difference between rich and poor, brought to the process, would be greatly disregarded. To this

[154] See topics 4.5 and 5.2.1 of this work.

[155] On this subject, see: Taruffo (2008), pp. 56 and foll.

is added, as seen in the analyses of the ICTY cases, that regardless of the fortune of the accused, often the defense needs funds to be able to effectively produce the evidence it deems pertinent.

If the need for *legal aid* is disregarded, the application of the equality of arms does not occur. The conclusion attends not only to the ideology of the *welfare state*, but also to that of the *fair trial*, applicable to cases of crimes against humanity—even the most abominable—with which, for example, the ICTY was confronted.

Without considering mechanisms for rebalancing forces (from outside to inside) in the criminal process, there is no talk of equality of arms and, then, *Fiat justitia, pereat mundus.*[156]

5.9 The Usefulness of the Theory of Principles in the Conceptualization of Equality of Arms

As it stems from equality, the principle of equality of arms cannot be conceptualized without rescuing, albeit in a very summarized way, the main features already pointed out here. To get to this part of the work, it was indicated that equality of arms is a principle.

With a justification identical to that of this text, Masha Fedorova, in a work here already so often cited, also structures the legal reasoning according to which equality of arms, in the theory of fundamental rights, is a principle, and not a rule.

From the perspective of the author, with support from Sarah J. Summers, also referred to in this text, "the idea of balancing is a vital part of understanding the purpose of the principle. The understanding of the nature of equality of arms as a principle usually sets the starting point of its examination in a criminal prosecution."[157]

By the conception followed here, the criterion of distinction between the rule and the principle is that according to which what varies from norm to norm (that is, from rule to principle) is the form of incidence in the concrete case. Thus, it is not because it is more or less fundamental or sectoral, but rather if the incidence is *all-or-nothing* or, on the contrary, through considerations (optimization command).

Equality, as is known, is part of the norms of this latter category, as taught by Robert Alexy himself,[158] or, among Brazilians, Virgílio Afonso da Silva.[159] And, justifiably, stemming, in our conception, equality of arms from equality itself and not from the contradictory—which allows for wider incidence, as already justified in the work—it has the characteristic of a principle, and not a rule.

In the investigation of what equality of arms is in the criminal process, and from its treatment as a principle, it is important to repeat that a broad concept of factual

---

156 Gomes and Mazzuoli (2009), p. 99.

157 Summers (2007), p. 10.

158 Alexy (1997), Chap. 8.

159 Silva (2009), p. 71.

support for the fundamental right norm is followed. With this, it is meant that, a priori, there is no field in which the precept of equality of arms cannot be applied.

By admitting the broad factual support of the fundamental right norm, if on the one hand space is opened for the incidence of the principle, on the other, its non-incidence in certain situations means that such non-application resulted either from a violation (not admitted), or from a restriction (admitted). In no case is it a matter of a priori prohibition in incidence.

This is because the doctrine is adopted according to which the protection derived from principled fundamental norms confers protection prima facie to the extent legally admissible. The particular theory of restricted factual support is not followed, since there would be an a priori prohibition on the incidence of the norm in certain situations from a prior filtering of the incidence of the protective norm. If such a theory were followed, there would be an incidence with a definitive character.[160]

The adoption of a broad factual support and the separation of the contradictory make it possible for the principle of equality of arms to apply in procedural phases where the contradictory would not apply. Examples of this are the penal execution and the pre-judicial phase of criminal prosecution. Hence, in rescuing the lesson of Virgílio Afonso da Silva,

> every action, state or legal position that has some characteristic that, considered in isolation, is part of the 'thematic scope' of a certain fundamental right must be considered as covered by its scope of protection, *regardless of the consideration of other variables*. The definition is purposely open, since it is precisely this openness that characterises the breadth of protection. Also the individualised response to the same question – what is protected *prima facie*? – follows the same open character.[161]

And so, given that the factual support of the fundamental right norm is composed of "what is protected" (its scope of protection) and by that "against which it is protected" (state intervention),[162] one can imagine, in the delimitation of the incidence of the norm, the following questions to be answered: (a) Being a fundamental right norm, what level of state intervention is required for effective protection? (Only from the Legislature? The Judiciary? The Executive? All of them? Some of them?); (b) What are, properly, the so-called *goods of life* protected?; (c) What is the subjective and objective extent in the criminal process, that is, on *whom* does the norm apply and in *which situations*?[163]

The treatment of the equality of arms from the adoption of a broad factual support makes problematic the situations of limitation and restriction of the fundamental right. In a word: such an approach places at the central point the very delimitation of the broad factual support.

---

[160] That is: *definitely* there would be one or another area not covered by the principle, such as situations arising in preliminary investigation or criminal execution.

[161] Silva (2009), pp. 109–110.

[162] Silva (2009), p. 71.

[163] These are, with some terminological variations, the questions asked by Zanoide de Moraes (2010), p. 362, pertaining to the delimitation of the scope of protection of the norm studied there.

This is because, regarding the limitations and restrictions of fundamental rights, the external theory is followed. And according to it, as already mentioned before, the limit of the fundamental right is not something *internal*, of the right itself (because, if it were, something that in theory is taken as a principle would more resemble a rule), but rather deduced from considerations with others that oppose it.[164]

In this particular, as could already be perceived from some judgments of the ECHR and the ICTY, the rule[165] of proportionality[166] may indicate the best way of applying the principle of equality of arms to provide greater protection in the concrete case. Being a fundamental right principle-norm, the equality of arms has broad factual support, and it is only after the weighing and justifications that accompany any intrusions in each concrete case that its concept is discovered.

If there is justification for not following the egalitarian notion of treatment between accused and accuser in the criminal process, it is not an illegitimate state intervention, but a restriction on the exercise of the fundamental right. This is what is seen, for example, in the abstract provision of the possibility of the official accuser making use of some of the expedited means in the search for information to clarify possible crimes, such as the measure of telephone interception.

On the other hand, if the disparate treatment results from a norm or act without adequate constitutional justification,[167] there will be a violation of the principle of equality of arms. Examples of this, to be deepened in the next chapter, can be seen in the so-called scenic conception of courtrooms that disrespects the parity performance of the defense and prosecution representatives; in the participation of the Public Prosecutor's representative in courts as *custos legis*; and in the opening of views to the Public Prosecutor's Office to express itself orally or in writing after the defense, as was the case with its response to the accusation.

Thus, as the external theory is followed regarding the restriction of fundamental rights, with the equality of arms, the concept to be achieved depends on the concrete justification for, in weighing, considering its application or not in a given situation.

As it is a principled norm, and as the broad criterion is followed in setting the factual support, it should always be inquired about the existence of constitutional justification for the restriction of its exercise, with which the situations of restriction (legitimate) and violation (illegitimate) of the principle of equality of arms in the criminal process are distinguished.

---

[164] Recapping: "The definition of the definitive content of the right is, therefore, defined *from the outside*, from the existing factual and legal conditions" (Silva, 2009, p. 140).

[165] Proportionality, for Virgílio Afonso da Silva, "has the structure of a rule, because it imposes a definitive duty: if it is the case to apply it, this application is not subject to factual and legal conditions of the concrete case. Its application is, therefore, made in whole" (2009, p. 168). The author, on this subject, attentive to the terminological variation on what would be proportionality, does not definitively close the doors to multiple nomenclatures. However, he emphasizes that the form of incidence is that of a rule.

[166] On this subject, see: Marzaduri (2007), pp. 378–381.

[167] The mention made is to the scope of protection of the norm proposed in the so-called *alternative model*. This model was dealt with in topic 1.2 of this work.

5.10 The Concept of Equality of Arms in the Criminal Process

5.10.1 The Relativity of the Concept

In 1937, Giuseppe Guarneri said that "the parties, while asking for justice, must be placed in the process in absolute parity of conditions." If it is impossible to fully agree with such teaching, which starts from the equality of arms in civil process, to say that, in the criminal process, the equality of arms is "a dream"[168]—a good part of it can be rescued in the search for an operative concept of equality of arms in the criminal process.

By the theoretical development of the theme since the first half of the last century, the idea that there should exist an *absolute* parity of conditions between accuser and accused is not sustained. This is because—and here is a reason not to fully agree with Guarneri—the theory of principles leads to the taking of the fundamental right norm (as is the equality of arms) as applicable prima facie and not in an a priori and absolute way. And, just like the very concept of equality, relative in its essence, the equalities between the parties are not absolute.

5.10.2 Decomposition of the ECHR's Conceptual Synthesis

The equality of arms, as seen from the repeated position of the ECHR, is equivalent to the reasonable opportunity given to each party to present their case—including their evidence—under conditions that do not put them at a substantial disadvantage vis-à-vis their opponent. Such a broad concept, repeated in the context of international criminal procedural law, can be decoded in order to reach some early conclusions in the work.

5.10.2.1 The *Weapon* as an *Opportunity*

When we discuss *opportunity*, we examine the *weapons* available to each party. This is because there is no mention of the competence of the defender as opposed to that of the accuser, or to the weapons in the sense of written or spoken reasons to the judge, as arguments for this or that thesis. At this point, when conceptualizing equality of arms as an *opportunity*, the exposition made by Mauro Fonseca Andrade of three positions that could exist regarding what would be such a weapon, whose distribution would be egalitarian, is relevant.

---

[168] Guarneri (1947), p. 119. The understanding that equality of arms in the criminal process is a dream is on p. 136 of the aforementioned article.

The Brazilian author reviewed Carnelutti's understanding that the *weapon* could correspond to the "reasons or the foundations of the positions assumed that the parties can expose to the judge," that is, it would equate to "word and persuasion." Then, he highlighted Goessel's position, according to whom the *weapon* would be simply and purely the competence of the professional (defender or accuser).[169]

Between the two theoretical currents, there is that one, followed by Gimeno Sendra, that the *weapon* in the criminal process should be understood as "situation, means, opportunity or possibility," indicating that "accusation and defence with the same tasks, means, situations, opportunities to present and propose evidence, to allege, request, refuse and appeal."[170]

This third lesson, recurring in judgments presented in this chapter, is the one accepted here. The breadth of the scope of the principle, given its broad factual support, should include the word *weapon* in the sense of "means, situations, opportunities, or possibilities, so that the parties can, on equal terms, demonstrate the validity and correctness of the arguments - or reasons, as Carnelutti prefers - that will be presented to the judge or court."[171]

From this, we resort to the theory of fundamental rights to answer the first of the three questions listed about the scope of protection of the norm (What state interventions are necessary for the implementation of the principle?): both the Judiciary (norm of treatment) and the Legislature (issuing laws that attend to the egalitarian situation in the process) are demanded. This means that the *disrespect* to equality of arms can equally come from judicial decisions that do not respect the egalitarian distribution of forces in the process between accusation and defense, and from normative acts that disregard the procedural equality that should permeate each legal situation.

5.10.2.2 What Is *Reasonable* in the Concept of Equality of Arms

Then, how *reasonable* the opportunity should be referred to the principled aspect of the fundamental right norm; that is, the application of equality of arms will always depend on factual situations, indicating that, in the concrete case, any imbalance in the presentation of the arguments of each party has been justified, or not.

---

[169] Andrade (2008), p. 165. The criticisms of the Brazilian author of the two theoretical currents are found, in the referred work, on pp. 167–168. Against the first current, it would be useless the equality of words, that is, of exposition of theses, if before that equality in the aptitude of the use of the word or the thesis was not instituted. Against the second, the excellence of the lawyer would be useless if the law did not distribute the procedural opportunity so that it can manifest itself. This second hypothesis, according to the author, was metaphorically considered a large-calibre weapon, but without ammunition.

[170] Andrade (2008), p. 166. The lesson of the Spanish professor says that the principle is fulfilled when, "in the procedural performance, both the accuser and the accused enjoy the same means of attack and defence and identical possibilities of allegation, proof and challenge" (Sendra, 2007, p. 91).

[171] Andrade (2008), p. 168.

According to the theory of fundamental rights, here we must discern between what is a restriction (lawful) to the exercise of the fundamental right and what is, on the contrary, an illicit state intervention, constituting a violation.

Hence, the concept includes the procedural introjections of economic differences that have occurred outside the process, but which can be clarified within it, such as the availability of financial resources for defense and prosecution to investigate sources of evidence. Hence, also, the reminder, here, of constitutional justifications for, for example, the accuser's access before the defense to specific means of producing evidence, such as wiretapping.

Once again, the adoption of the theory of principles implies affirming that, in the broad factual support, there is no a priori situation in the criminal process that motivates the exclusion of the incidence of equality of arms. Its non-incidence in certain justified situations does not mean an affront to the principle, but, being an adequate restriction, conforms to it.

In other words, by the external theory of restrictions to principles, it is only after the balancing test that we will diagnose whether the presentation of parity arguments in a situation of equality or inequality has been *reasonable* or not. This is because, as we have seen, the contour of the principle is outlined not from its internal characteristics, but after the balancing.

5.10.2.3 What Is a *Party* in the Concept of Equality of Arms

The word *party*, right after the reasonable opportunity that is given to it, should be understood in a broad sense, so much so that the very concept consecrated by international criminal procedural law also ends with the word *opponent*.

And this for the following reason: there is *an opponent* in the criminal process, that is, *a party* in a broad sense, whenever someone imputes an accusation to a third party or, in some way, addresses them with an act of state coercion—arrest, search measure, seizure, asset seizure, etc.

This restores the notion that the principle is independent of the procedural phase. It is enough that there is a conflicting interest between the freedom (or, to some extent, the right to it linked in the scope of the criminal process) of someone and the request of another.

Thus, the third question regarding the scope of protection of the principle (subjective and objective extensions) is answered: the people affected by the norm are the *opponents*, in a broad sense, that is, not necessarily the *parties* (in the formal sense), as there is a duality of interests even before the judicialization of criminal prosecution.

On the objective side, it is affirmed that parity applies throughout the arc of criminal prosecution, that is, from the moment there is any indicative measure that a subject is criminally investigated, until their interests do not oppose those of some representative of the state (or not) who sustains an antagonistic interest (that is, even in criminal execution).

Apparently, the principle really approaches equality and not contradiction, so the understanding of the incidence of the principle of equality of arms even before the judicial phase of criminal prosecution[172] and after the final judgement of any conviction is already in criminal review. The entire criminal process must, therefore, be *equitable*.

As argued from the theory of fundamental principles embraced in this text, such a perspective also privileges the broad support of the incidence of the norm of equality of arms.

5.10.2.4 The *Presentation of the Case* in the Concept of Equality of Arms

The connection of the concept to the *presentation of the case* goes beyond the notion of contradiction because it implies the analysis of the principle not only from the dynamic point of view (action and reaction), but as a norm of treatment of those involved, regardless of the acts of each party.

In other words, *presenting* a case involves both the criminal complaint to the court, and the indication of any imputation to someone—even if prodromic, that is, prior to the judicial phase of the criminal process—as well as any defensive request, including appeal, and in the phase of criminal execution.

Precisely because of this breadth, the evidentiary issue is one aspect, but not the only one, to be taken into account in the formulation of the concept. The examples seen in the judgments, by the way, about the issue of access to confidential documents or those that have been analyzed by the opposing party, are significant to support what is exposed here.

5.10.2.5 The *Evidence* for the Concept of Equality of Arms

Before considering the *evidence* in the criminal process—which would bring a connection with the contradiction—it is necessary to instrumentalize the *access to information*, that is, the *access to sources of evidence*. This means a rule of equal treatment before entering the rules of presentation, admission, and argumentation of evidence in the criminal process. After all, without equality of arms in terms of access to future evidence, the contradiction is not instrumentalized, afterwards, *about* that evidence.

[172] In the sense of the text, in Brazil, for example: Badaró (2024), p. 95; Fernandes (2005), p. 327; Malan (2012), p. 297. In comparative criminal procedural law, exemplarily: Fedorova (2012), pp. 19, 115 and foll; Ambos (2011), pp. 105/80; Kohlbacher (1978), pp. 14/5.

5.10.2.6 The *Substantial Disadvantage*

Finally, and as a decomposition that could even be read as a final set, the *substantial disadvantage* means the complement of weighing (*substantial* is something that depends on a judgement of ponderation, just like the term *reasonable*, already dealt with in the first part of the concept), accompanied by the concern with equality of treatment of those involved in the process (the *advantage* or the *disadvantage* necessarily imply a relationship of equality or inequality, but not of contradiction or reciprocity).

5.10.2.7 The *Opponent* Component of the Concept

The relationship with the *opponent* indicates that the focus of equality of arms is not the relationship of the parties with the judge—impartial representative of the state—but the relationship between them themselves.

Hence, again, the conceptual separation between equality of arms and adversarial proceedings, and also between it and a cooperative structure in criminal proceedings, in which the parties would have a role of collaboration with the search for the possible truth in the most prominent criminal proceedings than the intuitive objective of enforcing their opposing interests in the sustenance of their theses.

To answer the second indicative question of the scope of protection of the norm (the goods protected by it), one must take equality of arms not only as a norm of treatment (from the judge to the opponents in criminal proceedings), but also as a norm of judgement (assessment in each judicial decision on observance, as enabling to reach a fair decision).

5.11 Our Concept of Equality of Arms for Criminal Proceedings

Equality of arms in criminal proceedings is the equal distribution, during the criminal proceedings—from its pre-judicial phase to the executive—to those involved who defend opposing interests, of opportunities to presentation of oral or written arguments and evidence with a view to prevailing their respective theses before a judicial authority.

Whenever there is a clash of interests in criminal proceedings, to the extent justifiable from equality, it is necessary to establish, in the broadest possible sense, equality of aptitude for the prosecution and defense to explore all possible arguments for the convincing of their reasons before an impartial body.

Because its constitutional root is equality, its application does not depend on situations pre-established by law, but on each of the justifications, in concrete cases, that may be able to explain the balancing in a way to motivate its total incidence, its restriction, or, eventually, its non-application.

Because of all this, if it is impossible to think of examples capable of indicate a closed catalogue of cases in which equality of arms can be configured in criminal proceedings (hence why to move away from an attempt, because fruitless, of a list of situations in which the principle would apply), on the other hand, it is also impossible to a priori establish cases in which it should not apply. Thus, it can be said that it is no longer a matter of saying whether the principle of equality of arms *exists* or not in criminal proceedings. This is assumed as uncontroversial.

The issue to be addressed, and on which we will discuss later regarding the Brazilian case, is the measure of incidence; that is, the cases in which the principle does not justifiably apply, and the consequences that arise when there is no justification for the removal.

References

Alexy, R. (1997). *Teoria de los derechos fundamentales*. Centro de Estudios Constitucionales.

Almeida, J. C. M. d. (1973). *Princípios fundamentais do processo penal*. Revista dos Tribunais.

Ambos, K. (2006). El Tribunal Europeo de Derechos Humanos y los derechos procesales: igualdad de armas, procedimiento preliminar participativo y el art. 6 CEDH. In *Temas de derecho penal internacional y europeo*. Marcial Pons.

Ambos, K. (2009). *Confidential investigations (article 54(3)(E) ICC Statute) vs. disclosure obligations*: The Lubanga case and national law. *New Criminal Law Review, 12*(4).

Ambos, K. (2011). *Temas fundamentales del derecho procesal penal*. (Tomo I). Instituto Ecuatoriano de Derecho Penal e Investigaciones Criminológicas.

Andrade, M. F. (2008). *Sistemas processuais penais e seus princípios reitores*. Juruá.

Bacigalupo, E. (1992). Presunción de inocência, "in dubio pro reo" y recurso de casación. In E. V. Martinez (Ed.), *Derechos fundamenatles y justicia penal: Liber Amiculorum*. Editorial Juricentro. San Jose da Costa Rica.

Badaró, Gustavo Henrique Righi Ivahy (2012) O empate no julgamento da ação penal de competência originária do STF: absolver por quê? Available at: http://www.conjur.com.br/2012-out-22/gustavo-badaroem-empate-presuncao-inocencia-assegurada

Badaró, G. H. R. I. (2024). *Processo penal* (12th ed.). Thomson Reuters.

Barreto, I. C. (2005). *A Convenção Européia dos Direitos do Homem anotada*. Coimbra Editora.

Bettiol, G. (1966). *Istituzioni di diritto e procedura penale*. Cedam.

Burgorgue-larsen, L., & Úbeda de Torres, A. (2011). *The Inter-American Court of Human Rights: Case law and commentary*. Oxford University Press.

Cassese, A. (2008). *International criminal law*. Oxford University Press.

Centro de Estudos da Procuradoria Geral do Estado de São Paulo. (1997). *Instrumentos internacionais de proteção dos direitos humanos*. Centro de Estudos.

Chiavario, M. (1991). *Presunzione d'innocenza e diritto di difesa nel pensiero di Francesco Carrara*. Rivista Italiana di Diritto e Procedura Penale.

Cole, R. J. V. (2010). *Equality of arms and aspects of the right to a fair criminal trial in Botswana*. Stellenbosch University.

Costa, T. F. d. (2012). *A (des)igualdade de armas nas providências cautelares sem audiência do requerido*. Almedina.

Cruz, R. S. M. d. (2002). *Garantias processuais nos recursos criminais*. Atlas.

Damaška, M. (1986). *The faces of justice and State authority: a comparative approach to the legal process*. Yale University Press.
Elisa T. (2012). The principle of equality of arms: Part of the right to a fair trial. *Law Review Judicial doctrine and case-law online quarterly publication*, v. II, issue 4.
Fanego, C. A. (2009). *Exigencias en relación com la prueba testifical contenidas en el articulo 6.3.d. del CEDH*. Centro de Estudios Constitucionales.
Faranda, C. (1968). *The "par condicio" in criminal proceedings*. Giuffrè.
Fawcett, J. E. S. (1987). *The application of the European Convention on Human Rights*. Clarendon Press.
Fazzalari, E. (1966). Process. In A. Azara & E. Eula (Eds.), *Novissimo Digesto Italiano* (Vol. XIII). UTET.
Fedorova, M. (2012). *The principle of equality of arms in international criminal proceedings*. Intersentia; School of Human Rights Research.
Fernandes, A. S. (1999). *Processo penal constitucional*. Revista dos Tribunais.
Fernandes A. S. (2005). *O equilíbrio na investigação criminal*. DPJ.
Ferrua P. (2007). *Il 'giusto processo'*. 2. ed. Zanichelli.
Gamble, R., & Dias, N. (2009). Equality of arms is a blessed phrase: Its meaning under international law. *Sri Lanka Journal of International Law, 21*, 187.
Giostra, G. (2020). *Primeira Lição sobre a Justiça Penal*. Tirant lo Blanch.
Gomes, L. F., & Mazzuoli, V. d. O. (2009). *Comentários à Convenção Americana Sobre Direitos Humanos: Pacto de San José da Costa Rica*. Revista dos Tribunais.
González, A. D. (2010). *El principio de igualdad de armas en el sistema procesal penal colombiano*. Grupo Editorial Ibañez.
Grevi, V. (2000). *Alla ricerca di un processo penale "giusto": itinerarie e prospettive*. Giuffrè.
Grinover, A. P. (1990). *Defesa, contraditório, igualdade e par condicio na ótica do processo de estrutura cooperatória*. Forense universitária.
Grinover, A. P., Gomes Filho, A. M., & Fernandes, A. S. (2009). *Recursos no processo penal* (6th ed.). Revista dos Tribunais.
Grotrian, A. (1994). *Article 6 of the European Convention on Human Rights. The right to a fair trial*. Council of Europe Press.
Guarneri, G. (1947). *Sul problema dell'uguaglianza di armi nel processo penale*. Rivista di Criminologia e Diritto Criminale.
Harris et al. (1995). *Law of the European Convention on Human Rights*. Butterworths.
Hartmann, A., & Schmidt, R. (2012). *Strafprozessrecht: Grundzüge des Strafverfahrens*. Verlag.
Hies, J. (2009). *Das fair-trial-Prinzip und seine Bindungswirking für den Rechtsanwalt als Strafverteidiger*. Disserttion de Verlag im Internet GmBH.
Karam, M. L. (2009). *Juizados especiais criminais: a concretização antecipada do poder de punir*. Revista dos Tribunais.
Knoops, G.-J. A. (2004-2005). The dichotomy between judicial economy and equality of arms within international and internationalised criminal trials: A defence perspective. *Fordham International Law Journal, 28*, 1566.
Kohlbacher U. (1978). Verteidigung und Verteidigungsrechte unter dem Aspekt der "Waffengleicheit" Miteiner kritischen Analyse der geltenden Regelungen, insbesondere im Bund und im Kanton Zürich. Dissertation der Rechts-und staatswissenschaftlichen Fakultät der Universität Zürich zur Erlangung der Würde eines Doktors der Rechtswissenschaft.
Kohmann, G. (1974). *Waffengleicheit im Strafprozess?* J.C.B. Mohr (Paul Siebeck).
Lozzi, G. (1968). *Favor rei e processo penale*. Giuffrè.
Malan, D. (2012). *Investigação criminal defensiva no processo penal*. Revista Brasileira de Ciências Criminais, São Paulo, n. 96.
Marczak, E. (2000). *Das Fairness im Prozess*. Höhen Rechtwissenchaftlichen Fakultät der Universität zu Köln.
Marzaduri, E. A. (2007). *La parità delle armi nel processo penale*. Quaderni Constituzionale.
Moreno, F. C. (2002). *Las garantias constitucionales del proceso penal* (2nd ed.). Editorial Aranzadi.

Mustafa, A. A. H. (2007). *Equality of arms as a fair trial guarantee: A comparative study of India and European Court of Human Rights*. Central European University, Budapest.
Negri, S. (2005). The principle of "equality of arms" and the evolving law of international criminal procedure. *International Criminal Law Review, 5*. Netherlands.
Nicolitt, A. (2012). *Manual de processo penal*. Elsevier.
Paz, M. C. C. (2001). *La igualdad de armas: de la teoria a la realidad*. Cuadernos de Doctrina Y Jurisprudencia Penal.
Prado, G. (2024). *Curso de Processo Penal* (Vol. I). Marcial Pons, Madri.
Queiroz, P. (2012). *A coisa julgada no processo penal brasileiro como instrumento de garantia*. Coimbra.
Rainey, B., Wicks, E., & Ovey, C. (2014). *The European Convention on Human Rights*. Oxford University Press.
Rangel, P. (2012). *Direito processual penal*. Atlas.
Roberto, W. (2011). *Paridade de armas no processo penal*. Fórum.
Rodrigues, J. N. d. C. (1991). *Sobre o princípio da igualdade de armas*. Revista Portuguesa de Ciência Criminal.
Roxin, C. (2000). *Derecho procesal penal*. Editores del Puerto.
Sandermann, A. (1975). *"Waffengleichheit" im Strafprozess*. Zu den rechlichen Grundlagen dieses Rechtsinstituts. Inaugural. Dissertation zur Erlangung der Doktorwürde einer Hohen Rechtswissenchaftlichen Fakultät der Universität zu Köln.
Schroeder, F.-C., & Verrel, T. (2011). *Strafprozessrecht*. Verlag C.H. Beck.
Sendra, V. G. (2007). *Derecho procesal penal* (2nd ed.). Editorial Colex.
Silva, V. A. d. (2009). *Princípios e regras: mitos e equívocos acerca de uma distinção*. Revista Latino-Americana de Estudos Constitucionais.
Summers, S. J. (2007). *Fair trials: The European criminal procedural tradition and the European court of human rights*. Hart Publishing.
Summers, S. J., & Jackson, J. (2012). *The internationalisation of criminal evidence. Beyond the common law and civil law traditions*. Cambridge University Press.
Taruffo, M. (2008). *El proceso civil adversarial en la experiencia americana: el modelo americano del proceso de conotación dispositiva*. Temis.
Trechsel, S. (With the assistance of Sarah J. Summers) (2005) *Human rights in criminal proceedings*. Oxford University Press.
Ubertis, G. (2006). *Argomenti di procedura penale* (Vol. II). Giuffrè.
United Nations. (2008). *Selected decisions of the Human Rights Committee under the Optional Protocol* (p. 9). United Nations.
Valente, M. M. G. (2009). *Processo penal* (Vol. I). Edições Almedina S.A.
Vieira, R. S. (2013). *Paridade de armas no processo penal*. Revista dos Tribunais.
Vilela, A. (2005). *Considerações acerca da presunção de inocência em direito processual penal*. Coimbra Editora.
Vivanco, J. M., & Bhansali, L. L. (2004). *Procedural shortcomings in the defense of human rights: An inequality of arms*. Oxford University Press.
Volk, K., & Engländer, A. (2013). *Gundkurs StPo* (8th ed.). Verlag C.H. Beck.
Wąsek-Wiaderek, M. (2000). *The principle of "equality of arms" in criminal procedure under Article 6 of the European Convention on Human Rights and its functions in criminal justice of selected European Coutries: A comparative view*. Leuven University Press.
Wilson, R. (2008). *"Emaciated" defence or a trend to independence and equality of arms in internationalised criminal tribunals?* Washington College of Law Research Paper.
Zanoide de Moraes, M. (2010). *Presunção de inocência no processo penal brasileiro: análise de sua estrutura normativa para a elaboração legislativa e para a decisão judicial*. Lumen Juris.
Zapater, E. B. (2004). *La noción de un proceso penal con todas las garantías*. Manuales de Formación Continuada.
Zappalà, S. (2004). The prosecutor's duty to disclose exculpatory materials and the recent amendment to Rule 68 ICTY RPE. *Journal of International Criminal Justice, 2*, 620.

Chapter 6
Equality of Arms in the Brazilian Criminal Process

6.1 Delimitation of the Chapter's Object

Having arrived at an operative concept of equality of arms in the criminal process, it is time to test its application in Brazilian criminal procedural law.

In this chapter, therefore, an attempt is made to make a diagnosis from chosen procedural situations in which sometimes the principle applies, sometimes it does not. An attempt is also made to justify its incidence and its removal in the specific cases selected for analysis.[1]

Thus, whether because it has been assumed that the principle of equality of arms has a broad factual support (there is not a priori denial of incidence in certain situations), or because the so-called external theory has been followed (its conformation and, with it, the distinction between restrictions and limitations depend on concrete situations of weighing), at the time when its incidence in each legal situation will be discussed, the denial of incidence will be addressed now as a limitation (lawful), now as a restriction (unlawful) to the fundamental right.

In specific situations, a parallel will be drawn between the current criminal procedural law and that projected in Brazil, with the vicissitudes already verified in the legislative process of the Bill in the Chamber of Deputies.[2]

[1] Consideration of specific procedural consequences of the application or not of the principle of equality of arms in each chosen situation is not part of this chapter and was not the scope of the research from the beginning. To deal, in addition to the concept and diagnosis, also with the possible extension of the legal consequences of the (non)application of the principle would lead the dissertation to a different direction than imagined and proposed. This is a possible work to be done in the future.

[2] Bill No. 8.045/2010, which is currently being processed in the Chamber of Deputies, results from the final wording given, in the Federal Senate, to PLS No. 156/2009, as the Senate's version of the draft Criminal Procedure Code embodied in Report No. 1.636/2010.

R. S. Vieira, *Equality of Arms in Criminal Procedure*,
https://doi.org/10.1007/978-3-032-03663-6_6

The guiding threads of the approach to the incidence of the principle of equality of arms in the Brazilian criminal process do not arise exclusively from the subjects to whom such principle is directed (since the opposition of interests is clear between the antagonists, so that the principle does not depend exclusively on the notion of party in criminal process).

Considering the phases of the process, they also arise from the approach from four temporal arcs: preliminary criminal prosecution, criminal action of a condemnatory nature, appeals and challenging actions, and finally, criminal execution.

In the four procedural stages, there is jurisdictionalization of the opposing interests (to a greater or lesser extent in some and others, and it is striking the lesser jurisdictionalization of cases in the first and last phase, precisely the birth and death of the potentialities of defense and attack on fundamental rights). In them, the logic of case presentation should prevail in a situation of relative balance between the antagonists, with justifiable distinctions being observed.

In each of the phases, the treatment given to the recipients of the norm (on the passive pole: if investigated, if accused, if appellant or patient, if convicted; and on the active pole: Public Prosecutor's Office or victim acting in the investigative phase, in the evidentiary phase of the criminal process of knowledge, in the appeal phase or in manifestation in challenging actions or in criminal execution) varies, but what makes the approach useful is the application of equality of arms in the chosen temporal arc.

Due to the broad factual support, the principle of equality of arms is not dependent on evidentiary issues (e.g., opportunities for parity presentation of evidence elements of those involved in the criminal process; access to documents and information), nor is it tied to deadlines (equality of distribution for prosecution and defense, initial and final terms of counting), nor is its incidence circumscribed to the dynamic issues of hearing (design of hearing rooms, orders of questions from party to party) or criminal procedural march (logic of responses to the accusation and who speaks last in the criminal process).

By privileging the broad notion of factual support, equality of arms is present in various situations.

This way of thinking implies two difficulties: the first consists in justifying the incidence of the principle in the widest possible range of situations, and also in justifying cases of removal; the second refers to the approximation that the principle of equality of arms can have with some other themes dear to the criminal process, such as *favour rei*, the presumption of innocence and the adversarial principle. After all, there are occurrences where it would be possible to say that the principle of equality of arms applies when, in truth, the reason for being of this or that institute is another (e.g., criminal review, infringement appeals).

If the previous chapter dealt with the second difficulty, now it is time to deal with the first.

6.2 Equality of Arms in Preliminary Investigation: Active and Passive Knowledge

Before the criminal action is instituted, there are no parties in the criminal process. Even so, it is possible to notice the opposition of interests at stake, which is perceived from the dual function of the preliminary investigation and also from the substantial notion of accusation that is already formulated in it.

Regarding the first aspect, on the one hand it is affirmed that the criminal investigation has the role of investigating facts with a view to instructing a future criminal action—that is, it can be seen as a precautionary procedure for searching for information elements so that the accusation formulates the so-called *opinio delicti*—and, on the other hand, it is assumed that it is a "procedure to protect the accused," according to the words of Canuto Mendes de Almeida.[3]

In the first conception, as Nereu José Giacomolli emphasizes, if the preliminary investigation aims to provide an "accusatory basis," it also serves as an "accusatory filter." Therefore, according to the author, such an investigation has the function of "enabling and, at the same time, preventing the exercise of criminal action."[4]

In the second function, the notion does not tie itself to the technical concept of accusation brought to court nor to the way it is carried out in preliminary investigation, whose act that indicates it is the indictment, as a "draft of a possible accusation."[5]

[3] Specifically, to the criminal process, and without any communication to the theory of principles itself and its application in this legal field, Canuto Mendes de Almeida said that the so-called *preliminary instruction* "gives the defence the faculty to dissipate suspicions, to combat indications, to explain facts and to destroy prevention at birth; it provides means to promptly unveil the lie and to avoid the scandalous publicity of the trial. All research, investigations, testimonies, and diligences are subjected to serious examination to, in advance, reject everything that does not generate serious presumptions" (1973), p. 11. In a different view, and although attentive to the new theory of fundamental rights followed here, with a view specifically also directed to the criminal procedural field, Aury Lopes Júnior (2012), p. 272, assumes that "*the function of avoiding unfounded accusations is the main foundation of the investigation preliminary*, as, in reality, avoiding unfounded accusations means clarifying the hidden fact (provisional and probability judgment) and thus also ensuring society that there will be no abuses by the state's persecutory power. If impunity causes serious social unrest, more serious is the harm caused by irresponsibly prosecuting an innocent person." Such a lesson was reinforced in a later edition (2024), p. 110. Gustavo Badaró lists as objectives of the police inquiry not only the collection of elements for the initiation of criminal action, but also so that the holder of the criminal action can request precautionary measures (2024), p. 132. In the strict sense of the collection of "set of state acts aimed at determining the authorship and materiality of a criminal offence," see: Nicolitt (2011), p. 69.

[4] (2011), pp. 50–51.

[5] Pitombo (1987), p. 38. The text was also reproduced in *Work in Criminal Process.* Organization and notes Maria Eugênia Gil (2018), pp. 141/207. The indictment has "endo and extraprocedural effects" (Giacomolli (2011), p. 112), in the extent that it formalizes the value judgment of the delegate about a certain author and crime (internal influence) and inserts information about the person in databases of public security agencies (external influence). With the promulgation of Law No. 12.683/2012, which amended the provisions of Law No. 9.613/98, the indictment even became a cause for dismissal, without prejudice to remuneration and other rights provided by law, until the

As already mentioned, the content of the drafted accusation matters more than the form in which the act of accusation is presented. Hence, the incidence of the principle of equality of arms does not depend on the formal act of indictment, but on decisions during the preliminary investigation that attribute to a certain person the quality of suspect of the investigated fact.

Taking care to see in the preliminary investigation the citizen's guarantee against future accusations brought to court without the minimum substrate of information that makes the criminal demand useful (and therefore less defamatory to the accused), it is considered, in the forthcoming Code of Criminal Procedure, to delimit the "identification of sources of evidence" as the objective of criminal investigation.[6]

It is particularly due to the formulation of the judgment (even if preliminary) of imputation to someone for the commission of a certain action or omission that is criminally relevant that the accusation in the criminal process and in the investigation prior to the criminal action depends on what Marta Saad calls a "judgement of probability" of someone having committed a crime.

In the author's words, the "accusation is revealed either by formal act (indictment, complaint), or by the way the person is treated, in fact,"[7] which expands the defensive possibility in the investigative phase.

The conception accepted here takes as an accusation not only the act determined by the police authority—indictment and other specific acts of the same authority (representations for preventive detention, *ex vi* of Art. 13, IV, c.c. 311, CPP; representation for search and seizure measures, *ex vi* of Arts. 241 and ss., CPP;[8] representation for a precautionary measure of seizure in the criminal process, *ex vi* of Arts. 127, CPP and 4° of Law n° 9.613, in the wording conferred by Law n°

return of the public servant indicted to his functions (Art. 17-D). Badaró and Bottini (2012), pp. 359–361, have already expressed the unconstitutionality of such provision.

[6]Article 8° of PL n° 8.045/2010, in progress in the Chamber of Deputies. Paulo Rangel's lesson indicates that this concept (identification of sources of evidence) could already be used currently in the conceptualization of the police inquiry and its object, which is the preliminary investigation. For the author, the concept is already in the Code of Criminal Procedure of Portugal ("Set of diligences aimed at investigating the existence of a crime, determining its agents and their responsibility and discovering and collecting evidence, in order to decision on the accusation" Article 262, item 1. Still according to Rangel (2012), p. 71, "the investigation has the clear character of avoiding the initiation of an unfounded criminal prosecution by the Public Prosecutor's Office in view of the foundation of the criminal process, which is instrumentality and criminal guarantee." We do not agree with the author when he argues that "there being no accusation in the police inquiry, but, yes, mere investigation of facts, the indicted does not need to defend himself" (p. 75).

[7]Saad (2004), pp. 263–264.

[8]In our opinion, the provision of Article 241 of the Code of Criminal Procedure is unconstitutional, either because it means a circumvention of the inviolability of the domicile linked to the situation of flagrante or exhibition of a warrant (Art. 5°, X, CF), or because, if the search is carried out directly by the judge, he is stripped of the judicial function and disguises himself as an investigator. In this sense, see: Badaró (2024), p. 346. Particularly about the impossibility of a search carried out—except in cases of flagrante—by the police authority without a warrant, see: Pitombo (1999), p. 126. From this author, still: (2008), pp. 65–66.

12.683/2012; representation for temporary arrest, under the terms of Art. 2°, Law n° 7.960/89)—but also requests formulated by the Prosecutor's Office body with a view to the future offering of complaint.

From the imputation in a broad sense, therefore, a range of defensive actions in the criminal process opens up,[9] as there is even a constitutional guarantee (Art. 5°, LV) that provides for the defense of the accused in general.

In this regard, the text under consideration in the Chamber of Deputies (PL n° 8.045/2010), in its Article 9, provides:

> For all legal purposes, the legal status of 'investigated' is characterised from the moment the first act or investigative procedure is carried out in relation to the person on whom there are indications of authorship or participation in the practice of a criminal offence, regardless of the formal qualification attributed by the authority responsible for the investigation.

Even so, the exercise of the right of defense, inherent even to the investigative phase, does not necessarily allow to see the concretization of the principle of equality of arms, neither at all times, nor in all possible situations.[10]

This is justified, including by the care that must be taken in taking the notion of equality of arms as a principle and, from there, as seen in a previous chapter of the work, separating its possible justifiable limitations from its restrictions, to arrive at its practical application.

As a backdrop to the incidence of the principle of equality of arms in preliminary investigation, one can point out what is here taken as knowledge of the investigation.

The expression *knowledge of the investigation*, for this work, and in didactic terms, has two sides: a passive and an active.

The passive side consists of receiving the information from the investigation that concerns you, that is, *coming to know* the ongoing investigation. The active side, on the other hand, as opposed to *coming to know* the investigation, consists in presenting relevant information to it in favor of the investigated, in the same measure as it happens with the collection of evidence for the formation of the *opinio delicti* of the future accuser.[11] Thus, the passive and active sides of the expression *knowledge of the investigation* are, for this work, to come to know and to make known; or, still, such notion is equivalent to making something come to you (the knowledge of the investigation) and, on the other hand, to take the information you have somewhere (to the investigation).

---

[9] Saad (2004), p. 233.

[10] Even if the *moment* and the *situation* in which the principle of equality of arms coincides with the manifestation of the right of defense in the preliminary investigation, it is not lost sight of that the separation between equality of arms and right of defense is in the observation previously exposed that equality draws the foundation of constitutional equality, and not from the exercise of the right of defense. And equality of arms, in terms of knowledge of the investigation, instrumentalizes the right of defense.

[11] Emblematically, Giacomolli speaks of *parity of forces* in the preliminary investigation (2011), p. 57.

The manifestations of its incidence are distinct and, therefore, so will be the approaches to its manifestation and its delimitation.

6.2.1 *Passive Knowledge: Instructional Acts and Investigation Acts*

The one who suffers an accusatory charge already in preliminary investigation has the inalienable constitutional right to know, in the greatest possible amplitude, everything that is in the investigative procedure.[12]

Such access to the investigation documents is the main indicator of the equality of arms at this stage of the criminal prosecution, and one could only consider limitation (read: with justifiable constitutional reasoning) to the incidence of the principle if justifying factual situations led to such a conclusion; otherwise, there would be a violation of the principle.

Being a principle and not a rule, it is impossible to establish a priori the measure of the incidence of the principle of equality of arms in preliminary investigation, just as it is impossible to anticipate the measure of what is given to the investigated to know.[13]

In other words, there is no way to avoid or guarantee, in principle, the situation of balance vis-à-vis your opponent,[14] as it is not possible to say *what* the investigated can or cannot access, nor *what* he can present to the preliminary investigation.

Being a situation of application of a constitutional principle, and not a rule, evidently, the mandate of optimization of application in the greatest possible efficacy prevails. Besides, one does not start from the premise of application *tout court*, but, rather, of an application prima facie, to be tested in a concrete situation.

Even though it has been noticed, in the previous chapter, that access to the content of the investigation (that is, to the documents of the case) is a capital form of manifestation of the equality of arms, in Brazil, with the enforcement of Binding Precedent No. 14 of the Federal Supreme Court,[15] a supposed solution to the

---

[12] "The right to be aware of the charge is a necessary prerequisite for the right to react. There is no way to react without knowing" Fernandes (2002), p. 113.

[13] Hence, there is also a clear separation between *equality of arms* and *right of defense*: to some extent, in the preliminary investigation, without the incidence of the first principle, one does not reach the second.

[14] As there is no *party* in the preliminary investigation, neither is there a thought of an *opponent*. Even so, the principle applies, insofar as the *presentation of the case* is already at stake and there is, even if prodromically, the antagonism between the accuser and the accused.

[15] Binding Precedent 14 was a point of arrival, and not a starting point, for the solution of known problems in preliminary investigation. Its mention as an example is given not to try to bring it as a justification for the theory of fundamental rights followed, but rather—even if its own binding content, to some extent, may confuse the interpretation of what is a principle and what is a rule—to explain how central this problem is in the investigative phase of the Brazilian criminal process.

problem was quickly reached without discussing, from the application of the constitutional principle, the possible criteria for solving the difficulty. Anyway, with the issuance of the Precedent and the current discussion in the plane of Brazilian positive law, the first point of the question imposes that we deal with the so-called *ongoing diligences*.

From such ongoing diligences, one can speak of the situation of *advantage* of one of the poles of the prodromic relationship already existing between defense and accusation, as such *diligences*, if represented by the police authority or requested by the Public Prosecutor's Office, have the state apparatus in their favor, especially because they are taken ordinarily with the primary purpose of instructing the drafted accusation.[16]

With this, and to limit the principiological norm of fundamental right, the non-access to the diligences is justified. As Marta Saad indicates from lessons drawn from João de Deus Cardoso de Mello, Sérgio Marcos de Moraes Pitombo and Canuto Mendes de Almeida, it is inherent to the preliminary investigation the conceptual separation between *instructional* acts and acts *of investigation*.[17]

In summary, while the *instructional* acts would be those intended to inform, instruct, present data and, finally, document to the judge and the prosecutor the result of the investigations (since what was instructed in the preliminary investigation may or may not be repeated in contradictory instruction in court), the

---

Here is its content: "It is the right of the defender, in the interest of the represented, to have broad access to the elements of proof that, already documented in an investigative procedure carried out by an agency with judicial police competence, relate to the exercise of the right of defence" (published on 9th February 2009, p. 1). In the same sense is the provision of Article 11, of PL No. 8.045/2010, under consideration in the Chamber of Deputies: "It is guaranteed to the investigated and to his defender access to all material already produced in the criminal investigation, except in what concerns, strictly, the ongoing diligences. Single paragraph. The access referred to in the *caput* of this article includes broad consultation, notes and reproduction by photocopy or other technical means compatible with the nature of the material." The same scope is present in Article 27, which provides for the necessary understanding of those summoned for the purpose for which they are summoned. It is without reason to be, however, in light of equality of arms, the provision of Article 66 of the text now under consideration in the Chamber of Deputies, when it provides that at the time of interrogation in the preliminary investigation phase the investigated does not have the right to know of the "already identified sources of proof" (Art. 66, I, c.c. single paragraph).

[16] Take as an example the wiretapping, which aims to produce evidence in criminal procedural instruction, but not defensive evidence, a priori. It is no wonder that the accused does not have even active legitimacy to request the measure (Art. 3°, Law No. 9.296/96). In a critical view of the device and exactly for this reason, see: Streck (2001), pp. 78–81. And, with clear mention of the principle of *parity of treatment*, Gomes and Maciel (2012), p. 146, conceive, exceptionally, the hypothesis of telephone interception *pro reo*. They use, for this purpose, the breadth of the word *criminal instruction* (it is not directed at the defense or the accusation) and the example of the public servant who needs this means of evidence research to argue that what may seem to be passive corruption is nothing more than active corruption.

[17] Saad (2004), pp. 165 and ss. The lessons of the authors referred to are found on pp. 171–175.

investigative, in the synthesis of Sérgio Marcos de Moraes Pitombo, would be those of tracking the fact and its authorship.[18]

The relationship between the two, according to the lesson of Joaquim Canuto Mendes de Almeida, would be the following:

> 'Investigation' consists in the search for what is hidden: the collection of evidence often depends on investigation. The 'investigation' produces pre-procedural results: the police chief or deputy, after feeling these results in themselves, is the one who, by undertaking the written record of them, creates, so to speak, the informative elements of conviction.[19]

The investigated person, in summary, should be afforded the right to know of the instructive acts, but not of the investigative ones[20] that may still be in progress.[21] Denying access to the former means violating not only the right to defense, but also

---

[18] "The *investigation* consists in inquiring, in a methodical and continued way, about a certain reported occurrence. Whoever investigates only traces the fact—which seemed to him illicit and typical—its circumstances, as well as possible authorship. The *investigation* or inquiry can lead to a simple *proposition*, it is up to the *instruction* to conclude whether the mere *statement* is true or false. As a rule, and therefore, the *investigation* precedes the *preliminary instruction*. Already, in both phases of criminal prosecution, the *instruction* shows itself as an activity—which the *proposition*, simple or qualified, provoked—directed and tending to collect or produce evidence, about the existence of a fact, which is depicted as illicit and typical; and, also, to indicate the agent, or agents. In the preliminary phase, or preparatory to the criminal action, of a condemnatory nature, the judicial police carry out acts of *investigation* and others of *criminal instruction*, likely to be repeated, in court, or not" Pitombo (2001), p. 344. The position of Aury Lopes Júnior (2025), pp. 117/2, is also known, who, attached to the Spanish doctrine, separates the *acts of proof* from the so-called *acts of investigation*. It happens that the author concludes "that the IP only *generates acts of investigation*, and, as such, of limited probative value. It would be a contradiction to grant greater value to an activity carried out by an administrative body, often without any contradiction or possibility of defence and still under the cloak of secrecy." As it seems to us that the police inquiry does not produce only such acts of investigation, but also acts of proof, the rigorism of that separation is not followed here. author. Nereu José Giacomolli points out: "in certain situations, in forensic praxis, the elements collected in the pre-procedural phase have determining entity of the decision superior to those collected in the phase procedural, in court, such as telephone interceptions and technical-scientific evidence" (2011), p. 99. In the sense of this text, with the policing of instruction, see: Andrade (2009), pp. 529 and foll.

[19] Almeida (1973), pp. 211–212.

[20] The Brazilian Institute of Procedural Law proposed the Amendment No. 3 to the text of the current PL No. 8.045/2010 (at the time, the document analyzed by the IBDP was the original PLS No. 156/2009). Where in the future Code of Criminal Procedure it may be provided for "ongoing diligences" of which the investigated person has no reason to know, the Institute proposed that the expression be "ongoing precautionary measures, in course, whose knowledge to the investigated or defender can harm the effectiveness of the act." Indeed, the wording would be more precise and also the connection of non-communication in the records of situations that, if revealed, could compromise the investigation. From a perspective more faithful to this research, indeed, it could be affirmed that the wording suggested by the IBDP would allow the visualization of the principle from its broad factual support, and, likewise, that its restriction would only occur in certain concrete situations, to be proven factually. Thus, in addition to the broad factual support in the delimitation of the application of the principle, it is a matter of interpretation that would also privilege its external limit of incidence, all in accordance with what has already been developed in this work specifically about the theory of fundamental rights.

[21] Also in this sense: Zanoide de Moraes (2008), p. 47.

the equality of arms between the opponents. After all, in this way, there will be unjustified disadvantageous treatment to the investigated person, preventing them from presenting their arguments to the Judiciary in a position equal to that which the accuser will enjoy.

The assumption of this criterion for the conformation of the principle of equality of arms in this situation seems to fit the exposition of the theory of principles followed in this work, either because concrete situations of incidence are not excluded *a priori*, or because it works with the factual justification capable of restricting (with constitutional basis) its scope in one or another situation.

6.2.1.1 Passive Knowledge: Two Examples of Limit to the Internal Secrecy of the Preliminary Investigation

In this text, we do not agree to honor the interpretation given to Article 20 of the current Code of Criminal Procedure[22] to construct from there the rule of limitation of knowledge to the elements of information to the investigated person, being the hypotheses of procedural arrest—in which such knowledge is made possible—mere exceptions.[23]

As for the procedural situation of the investigated person (arrested, free or target of some other measure of procedural constraint), there is no distinction as to the scope of the secrecy of the inquiry (Art. 20, CPP), even because the constitutional extract of secrecy in any procedural situation depends on *intimacy* and *social interest* (Art. 5°, LX), which overrides the old rule of the current Code of Criminal Procedure.[24]

The justifications for secrecy are independent of the accused being in this or that situation, that is, free or arrested. And, thus, access to the elements of information from the preliminary investigation should also not depend on whether the investigated person is free or arrested.

An infraconstitutional rule that follows the path of this interpretation offends the principle of equality of arms in the bias of the necessary access to the elements of information available in the records, in the same way as they were made available to the representatives of the state (whether they are police authorities, or

[22] "The authority will ensure in the inquiry the secrecy necessary for the elucidation of the fact or required by the interest of society." The model from the point of view here criticized is the understanding of Marcellus Polastri Lima (Ambos, 2008, pp. 54 and foll.). Nereu José Giacomolli (2011), p. 92, is right when he emphasizes that the incidence of Article 20 of the Code of Criminal Procedure is for *outside* the procedure, that is, *external secrecy*; in the author's words, "as far as third parties are concerned." So also Maurício Zanoide de Moraes: "The belief that this persecutory phase is usually secret, with publicity being the exception, can no longer prevail" (2008), p. 44.

[23] Marcellus Polastri Lima argues, in this regard, that "secrecy does not prevail as in the case of the inquiry of a free suspect, and this happens precisely in view of the arrest of the suspect, in view of the restriction of individual freedom that requires greater transparency from the act" Ambos (2008), p. 56.

[24] On this subject, see: Malan (2009), pp. 171–172.

representatives of the Prosecutor's Office). There is no reason to, in the current preliminary investigation system, deny the investigated person (repeat: taken in a broad sense, from the incidence of substantial accusation addressed to him) access to all the elements of information that it is possible to give.

By the way, and to deal with the issue in a way close to equality of arms, Maurício Zanoide de Moraes teaches:

> The limitation of internal publicity, in turn, even if for a period, has the immediate effect of creating an inequality in the prosecution, since it only occurs for one part of the prosecution, namely the subject investigated/accused, remaining unrestricted internal publicity for the other acting subjects (Judicial Police and Prosecutor's Office).[25]

Hence, from the constitutional premise of the hypotheses of secrecy and publicity (at least internal, that is, covering at least the investigated), the factual criterion delimiting the justification for imposing secrecy on certain information to the target of the preliminary criminal prosecution is factual.

From adherence to factual limitation, the constitutionality of positive law provisions is analyzed. And in each factual situation, interests in criminal procedure are weighed—or not. Such weighing, moreover, must always observe the prevalence of the involved fundamental right (equality of arms), potentially violated, and not the result of an interpretation that allows its violation.

Even if the equality of arms, as a principle, is opposed to another procedural principle, care must be taken not to annihilate its fundamental core. That is: from the very weighing can come its minimum application contour, but not its total reduction of effectiveness, making it null. Or (what is even worse in the theory of fundamental rights): taking a conflict between principles as if it were rules and, thus, with the argument that one would be weighing a principle in conflict with another, simply revoking it.

Even so, there will be situations where the incidence will be mitigated; it is worth noting that the state, especially in the criminal process, should be the protector of the fundamental rights involved, and not the protagonist of their violation. This means that, just like the principle of equality of arms, publicity should also be guaranteed to the greatest extent possible, since it is also a fundamental guarantee inherent to the criminal process.

Moreover, to the target of criminal prosecution, the exercise of other fundamental rights (such as the right to be heard, the right to a full defense, the possible defensive reaction to the charge) is only instrumentalized when the first and fundamental step is guaranteed: to know, just as the prosecution knows, the elements of information contained in the preliminary investigation of the facts that concern him.[26]

---

[25] (2008), p. 43.

[26] Giacomolli (2011), p. 92. Only in this way is the provision in Article 8, 2, b, of the Inter-American Convention on Human Rights ratified in Brazil in 1992 by Decree No. 678. Rogério Lauria Tucci (2004), p. 212, footnote no. 5, says that "the publicity of procedural acts constitutes, as seen, guarantee of the right of defence, situation in which the exceptions to the rule are very limited."

Therefore, the cases in which the investigated person will not be informed—without offending the equality of arms—must be diagnosed from empirical findings that test the limit of the fundamental right in question. And only from this is it possible to diagnose the limitation to the principle of equality of arms (adequate constitutional reasoning) or its violation.[27]

Two examples can clarify this point, each in its own way: on one side, the suspension of the confidentiality of telephone communications (Law No. 9.296/96) presents case-by-case situations in which the removal of publicity, temporarily, can be justified; on the other hand, the procedural collaboration[28] (Law No. 8.072/90,[29] Law No. 9.034/95,[30] Law No. 9.080/95,[31] Law No. 9.613/98,[32] Law No. 9.807/99,[33]

---

[27] "Therefore, any law is not legitimate, even though approved by the National Congress, according to constitutional legislative process, that prohibits the publicity of the acts of criminal prosecution to, for example, make it more agile or so that those involved do not exercise full defence (full defence and technical defence). Such laws, although formally correct, would be disproportionate in substance and, therefore, illegitimate" Zanoide de Moraes (2008), p. 42.

[28] In a strict sense, it is the "agreement between the accused and prosecution, in which information is provided about the criminal offenses investigated and their authorship in exchange for procedural benefits such as immunity, the *non-prosecution agreements*, and the *plea bargain*, enshrined in the North American legal system" Lauand (2008), pp. 64–65.

[29] Article 8, single paragraph: "The participant and the associate who denounces the gang or mob to the authority, enabling its dismantling, will have their sentence reduced by one to two thirds." The same law provided a cause for reducing the sentence to the agent who, in the crime of extortion through kidnapping committed by a gang or mob, "denounces it to the authority, facilitating the release of the kidnapped, will have their sentence reduced by one to two thirds" (Art. 159, § 4, CP).

[30] In crimes committed in a criminal organization, the sentence will be reduced by one to two-thirds when the spontaneous collaboration of the agent leads to the clarification of criminal offenses and their authorship.

[31] It included the single paragraph of Article 16 of Law No. 8.137/90: "In the crimes provided for in this Law, committed in gang or co-authorship, the co-author or participant who through spontaneous confession reveals to the police or judicial authority the entire criminal plot will have their sentence reduced by one to two thirds." The same Law No. 9.080 inserted § 2 to Article 25 of Law No. 7.492/86, dealing with an identical cause for reducing the sentence.

[32] In the wording conferred by Law No. 12.683, of 2012, § 5 º: "The sentence may be reduced by one to two thirds and be served in open or semi-open regime, allowing the judge to refrain from applying it or to replace it, at any time, by a sentence restrictive of rights, if the author, co-author or participant collaborates spontaneously with the authorities, providing clarifications that lead to the investigation of criminal offences, to the identification of the authors, co-authors and participants, or to the location of the goods, rights or values object of the crime."

[33] Article 13: "The judge may, ex officio or at the request of the parties, grant judicial pardon and the consequent extinction of punishability to the accused who, being a first offender, has collaborated effectively and voluntarily with the investigation and the criminal process, provided that this collaboration has resulted in: I – the identification of the other co-authors or participants in the criminal action; II – the location of the victim with their physical integrity preserved; III – the total or partial recovery of the product of the crime. Single paragraph. The granting of the pardon judicial will take into account the personality of the beneficiary and the nature, circumstances, severity and social repercussion of the criminal fact." Article 14: "The indicted or accused who voluntarily collaborates with the police investigation and the criminal process in identifying the other co-authors or participants in the crime, in locating the victim alive and in the total or partial recovery

Law No. 11.343/2006,[34] Law No. 12.529/2001[35]) exposes cases of risk of the first phase of criminal prosecution bordering on secrecy, without justification.

In regulating the cases of lifting the secrecy provided for in Article 5, XII, of the Federal Constitution, Law No. 9.296/96 provides that the accused does not have prior access to the request for telephone interception (Art. 3). It also provides that, during the interceptions, the person who is aware of the elements produced and in the process of being produced is the representative of the Public Prosecutor's Office (Art. 6). The participation of the investigated person only occurs (Art. 9) in the proposal of the incident of non-utilization of the means of evidence search. In such a situation, it is empirically noted that the prior contact of the investigated person with the ongoing diligence would remove its effectiveness.

In this case, in addition to the already discussed distinction between *acts of investigation* and *acts of instruction*, and once the investigation acts are documented in the instruction that can be debated, there is a need for full access by the investigated person not only to the material that documents the wiretaps (transcription reports), but also to the media themselves.[36]

The possibility of declaring the preliminary investigation secret is not justified, therefore, in light of Article 20 of the Code of Criminal Procedure. The case-by-case analysis of investigative effectiveness is what should weigh the immediate knowledge of the investigated person to all information data or determine that immediately after the documentation of everything that was collected (acts of instruction), the same information, with the same depth and ease, is provided to the investigated person, addressed to the representative of the Public Prosecutor's Office.

That is, one should not wait for the instigation of a future judicial phase of criminal prosecution to give the investigated person full knowledge of these information elements. If it is about presenting the case in a non-disadvantageous situation, it is useless to deal with the principle and defend its observance if it is allowed to wait for the so-called *deferred contradiction* for the phase of criminal action to only then give the investigated person the possibility of using in his favor information already

of the product of the crime, in case of conviction, will have their sentence reduced by one to two thirds."

[34] Article 41: "The indicted or accused who voluntarily collaborates with the police investigation and the criminal process in the identification of the other co-authors or participants in the crime and in the total or partial recovery of the product of the crime, in case of conviction, will have their sentence reduced by one third to two thirds."

[35] The so-called *leniency agreement* has legal provisions in Articles 86 and 87, applicable to those accused of committing offenses against economic order, crimes provided for in Law Nos. 8.137/90 and 8.666/93, as well as those committed in a gang or mob (Art. 288, CP).

[36] Access to information is not purely and simply a matter of *deferred contradiction*, even though there is still no contradiction (in mere access), given the absence of action and reaction. Although this separation between contradiction and equality of arms has already been discussed previously, here the case is indeed one of equality of arms, because access to the relevant documentation allows the investigated (i) to present their case in a less disadvantageous situation than that of the one(s)—deputy and prosecutor—who already know(s) the content investigated; (ii) and only from this to structure your future and hypothetical reaction to the formal accusation.

documented in the records on which the Public Prosecutor's Office was able to comment.

On the other hand, the risk of cases of procedural collaboration becoming true secret procedures, made between accusers (in a broad sense, since there is not yet a party in the criminal prosecution) and accused, affronts the equality of arms. This is because it prevents the *accused*, already in the phase where the accuser has knowledge of the information elements extracted from the collaboration of a co-investigator, from knowing in the same depth the act already carried out, and can, therefore, present his case in a condition that does not make it disadvantageous vis-à-vis the accuser's.

In the words of Mariana de Souza Lima Lauand:

> The collaborator's statement cannot be a secret document. Full access must be guaranteed to the co-defendant and his defender so that they can develop the best defensive strategy, and the act must be redone, in the judicial phase, so that they can exercise the contradiction.[37]

The distinction between equality of arms, contradiction, and right of defense is, once again, important. The first step to be able to *react* to an *action* taken in criminal prosecution—which, if contrasted, can influence the defense—is the knowledge of the same elements to which the representatives of the prosecution body have access. In the case of procedural collaboration—or, as commonly known in Brazil, *plea bargain*[38]—this is particularly important. After all, such plea agreements, although they reduce or extinguish the penalty of the one who *informs*, have probative effectiveness against the accused.

Once again rescuing the premise of the distinction between *acts of instruction* and *acts of investigation*, if the procedural collaboration is carried out in the preliminary phase of criminal prosecution, there is an act of instruction, that is, an act whose probative effectiveness is addressed to the court. Therefore, Mariana Lauand is right again when she states that,

> once the collaborator has made an accusation against a third party, the co-defendant must become aware of the content of the statements, and he must be allowed, accompanied by his defender, to refute the allegations and propose diligences that he deems necessary to prove his innocence.[39]

Thus, when we talk about *deferred contradiction* on the information elements resulting from procedural collaboration, it is necessary to distinguish the

---

[37] Lauand (2008), p. 76.

[38] Lauand (2008), p. 61, footnote no. 164.

[39] Lauand (2008), cit., p. 76. In 2003, Sérgio Marcos de Moraes Pitombo also (Jun./Aug. 2003), p. 3, warned: "The involved should never be treated as a stranger, in preparatory or preliminary procedure. To distance him, to obstruct the exercise of the right of defence, which is not confused with the contradictory, breaks the Constitution of the Republic. To hide from him the intercourses, during the administrative procedure, prevents the discovery of the achievable criminal truth, to the detriment of society and ethics administrative."

contradiction (its essential notion) and *how deferred* it is (that is, for how long can we wait to exercise the contradiction) from the notion of equality of arms defended here.

The *contradiction* presupposes the knowledge of the content of the cooperative agreement between accuser and accused, particularly the narration made by the informer who attributes responsibility to the accused. Such knowledge is linked to the equality of arms because to establish a reaction (the contradiction to the content) to the accusation strengthened with the content of the information collected in a plea bargain, it is necessary, as a premise, that it is known.

The *deferral* of access to information, as seen in situations of wiretapping, should not wait for the initiation of the procedural phase of criminal prosecution.[40]

The accusatory charge will have existed before (and, as such, it will have prevented the accused, in knowing the elements thrown against him, can bring to light facts or defensive versions that assist in criminal prosecution or contradict untruths resulting from the agreement, or that he produces information elements in his favor), and there will already be a substantial accusation addressed to him—the accused.[41] The conditions that he will have to present his case to the court are disadvantageous, without there being a sufficient argument based on the effectiveness of criminal prosecution.

In the example of a plea bargain, therefore, it seems that the observance of the principle of equality of arms in the pre-procedural phase of criminal prosecution follows the dissenting vote of Min. Marco Aurélio, when, in the 1st Chamber, the Supreme Federal Court judged the *HC* no. 90.688, in the year 2008.

In that judgement, the Minister established—in our view, rightly, even though there the idea of the right of defense was conveyed, and not of equality of arms—that the defense has a legitimate interest in "knowing not only those who signed the aforementioned plea bargain agreement but also its content, aiming even at the opposition to what was asserted in the indictment." Also, as we have argued here, the Minister affirmed that, in light of the equality of arms, it is fundamental that the understanding is honored according to which the agreement "cannot serve for criminal prosecution and remain unknown to the defence."[42]

---

[40] There is disagreement with the position of Gustavo dos Reis Gazzola (2009), p. 179.

[41] From the confusion between equality of arms and contradictions, the argument of the non-existence of contradictions in preliminary investigation also does not convince. First, because what is taken care of is equality of arms, and not contradictory; and second because the very plea bargain is already an exercise of the contradictory, insofar as whoever behaves as a whistleblower aims to improve his situation in the course of criminal prosecution, and there is a defensive strategy of reaction to accusation, that is, a defensive contrariness to the accusation. Therefore, whoever denounces, to his measure, exercises the contradictory, and there is no reason for the denounced not to rebut the narratives collected at this stage.

[42] STF, *HC* no. 90.688, 1st T., Rel. Min. Ricardo Lewandowski. j. 12.02.2008, *DJe* 25.04.2008. The highlighted passages are part of the vote of Minister Marco Aurélio. This was not the decision made by the Brazilian Legislative Power. Indeed, with the advent of Law 13.964 of 2019, specific novelties were added on the topic of procedural collaboration in Brazil. And, with regard to the detail now in question, it was provided, in a new wording given to Article 7, §3, of Law 12.850/2013,

6.2.2 Active Knowledge: The Defensive Investigation

The manifestation of the equality of arms in the first phase of the criminal prosecution does not end with the *knowledge* on the part of the investigated. It also has its active side, that is, *what is brought to knowledge*, no longer from him, but on his part, to the criminal prosecution. In other words, it is not only important what *reaches* the investigated, but also what *comes from him* to the investigation.

If there were not the side that is here called *active* in relation to the content of the investigation, one could not speak of an egalitarian notion—presentation of the case with a view to avoiding disadvantage vis-à-vis the opponent—applicable in this phase. It is about this that Gustavo Badaró argues that denying the right to defensive investigation means "defending an inadmissible iniquity, violating the equality of arms."[43]

Particularly, it was preferred to deal with the passive and active sides of knowledge of the investigation because, with this methodological choice, it does not take the defensive investigation as synonymous with a possible *right to evidence* in the preliminary investigation.[44]

And this is because, when imagining the defensive investigation in criminal prosecution, more important than the *right to evidence* is the right to bring the information already collected to the investigation files.

Even if this can admit the approximation of one of the facets of the right to evidence (the admissibility of bringing to public investigation what was collected in private investigation), these are passive and active sides of the knowledge of the investigation. Thus, in addition to separating the approach to the right of evidence production (which is not the focus of this work), the parity between accuser and accused, from the point of view of presentation of the criminal case (even before the granting of production of information elements or even means of evidence search), becomes clearer.

Precisely because of this, Articles 14[45] and 184[46] of the Code of Criminal Procedure, linked to the notion of requests for diligence or, in the case of the latter, expert evidence, are not sufficient to deal with the equality of arms under the prism of bringing to the files the informative elements that can be important in presenting the case for the defense.

that: "The plea bargain agreement and the testimonies of the collaborator will be kept confidential until the receipt of the indictment or the criminal complaint, it being forbidden for the magistrate to decide on its publicity in any circumstance." Regarding the theme of procedural collaboration, it is suggested to read the work of Vinícius Gomes de Vasconcellos (2023).

[43] (2024), p. 95.

[44] Says Badaró: "The right to evidence presupposes a right to investigation" (2024), p. 166.

[45] "The offended, or his legal representative, and the indicted may request any diligence, which will be carried out, or not, at the discretion of the authority."

[46] "Except in the case of a body of crime examination, the judge or the police authority will deny the expertise requested by the parties, when it is not necessary for the clarification of the truth."

The methodological choice avoids dealing with the term *evidence* at this procedural stage and focuses on the active side of the investigated, clearly the function of presenting relevant information to his defensive theses in the same measure (or in a comparable measure) as the collection of information for the formation of the *opinio delicti* of the future accuser is done.

And dealing with the approach on the active side of the knowledge that the investigated has before the content of the criminal prosecution allows to rescue the idea of a filter of the preliminary phase of the prosecution. If this phase, while serving to inform the sources of evidence to the future accuser, also aims to avoid reckless and unfounded accusations, there are greater chances of the investigated bringing his information elements to the files and avoiding the initiation of a criminal action against him. After all, "the investigation is a relevant phase in the criminal process both for the prosecution and for the defence."[47]

The very idea of defensive investigation can have its roots supported by two very distinct findings is important for the work. Some see its foundation in the parallelism that has been noticed in the Public Prosecutor's Office increasingly acting actively in the investigative phase (in fact, an investigative directorship[48]): the Public Prosecutor's Office investigates; therefore, the defense can also investigate.[49] Another aspect does not depend on the defensive investigation of the investigative role of the Public Prosecutor's Office, since it is recognized that the police primarily collect accusatory elements, not defensive ones.[50]

The structure of the preliminary investigation, whether in the inquisitorial nature, in the limitation of defensive requests or in the common outcome that consists in the formation of the *opinio delicti* of those who have the monopoly of accusation (or, in exceptional cases, the individual to whom the state granted extraordinary legitimacy for this), it is created to formulate an accusatory judgment.[51]

So much so that this is only the *first phase* of criminal prosecution, which, by the way, to have the *second phase* inaugurated, is satisfied with indications of authorship and proof of the materiality of the investigated criminal offense (Article 395, CPP). And such hypotheses are much more permissive than the barriers to rejection of the initial (Art. 395, CPP) or of summary acquittal (Art. 397, CPP, in which one always notices one or another word indicative of intensity: *manifest* and *evidently*).

---

[47] Fernandes (2005), p. 319.

[48] The issue of the Prosecutor's Office being able to fully assume the investigative function is not the focus of this work. However, the so-called direct criminal investigation of the Prosecutor's Office was the subject of Extraordinary Appeal No. 593.727 and ended up being recognized as decided by the plenary of the STF. On another opportunity, we were able to express our opinion against such a possibility: Vieira (1999), pp. 11–12.

[49] André Augusto Mendes Machado (2010), pp. 46–47, cites the warnings of Antonio Scarance Fernandes, José Barcelos de Souza, and Marcos Alexandre Coelho Zilli. From the latter, in fact, it is gathered that "the strengthening of the powers of one of the parties in the procedural relationship cannot be designed without a corresponding strengthening in favour of the opposing party."

[50] Machado (2010), p. 46.

[51] In this sense, see: Rascovski (2012), pp. 122–123. See also: Badaró (2024), p. 166.

It is difficult not to verify that the idea of ending the criminal prosecution in the first phase is exceptional. This is proven, in practice, with the volume of *habeas corpus* denied on the argument that, with terminological variations, only the *premature* ending of criminal prosecution in this phase is admitted in cases of *extreme doubts* on the atypicality or something worth it.[52]

Hence, as André Augusto Mendes Machado rightly says, "as a way to ensure effective equality between the parties in the criminal prosecution and the right of defense of the accused, the defensive investigation must be admitted in both systems that adopt the ministerial investigation as well as the police."[53] At this point, a significant moment in Brazilian criminal procedural law is noted.

6.2.2.1 Active Knowledge: Defensive Investigation in PL n° 8.045/2010

The bill that is being processed in the Chamber of Deputies with a view to establishing a new Brazilian Code of Criminal Procedure is halfway to the consecration—in the aspect of active knowledge of criminal investigation—of the equality of arms between prosecution and defense. This is because, if today there is no provision for defensive investigation, in the scenario of projected Brazilian criminal procedural law, Article 13[54] brings a greater possibility of defensive action with a view to

[52] There is in Brazilian criminal procedural law an almost automatic jurisprudential understanding that, with the end of the first phase of criminal prosecution, the second should begin. It is always repeated, even if not always with due attention to the concrete case, the exceptionality that would be the *premature* closure of criminal prosecution, when, in fact, it seems to us, there should not be any bias *pro societate*. Representative of the opposite direction and therefore worthy of being observed is the ruling of the 5th Chamber of the STJ, which is correct, according to which, "The Federal Constitution enshrines, as a consequence of the presumption of innocence (art. 5°, LVII) the in dubio pro reo. It must be recognised that the in dubio pro societate cannot be used to fill evidentiary gaps" (*Habeas Corpus* no. 851907, under the rapporteurship of Justice Daniela Teixeira, published on 18th March 2024).

[53] Machado (2010), p. 46. About the Prosecutor's Office collecting, naturally, elements of information that endorse the hypothesis (future) accusatory, see: Fernandes (2005), p. 327.

[54] Article 13: "It is allowed to the investigated, through his lawyer, public defender or other agents with express powers, to take the initiative to identify sources of evidence in favour of his defence, he can even interview people. § 1° The interviews conducted in the form of the *caput* of this article should be preceded by clarifications about their objectives and the formal consent of the people heard. § 2° The victim cannot be questioned for the purposes of defensive investigation, unless there is authorisation from the judge of guarantees, always safeguarding his consent. § 3° In the hypothesis of § 2° of this article, the judge of guarantees may, if necessary, set conditions for the conduct of the interview. § 4° The requests for interview should be made with the necessary discretion and reserve, in working days and during business hours. § 5° The material produced may be attached to the inquiry files, at the discretion of the police authority. § 6° The people mentioned in the *caput* of this article will be civilly, criminally and disciplinarily liable for the excesses committed."

introducing into the investigation the sources of evidence diagnosed in favor of the defense.[55]

Even so, if the text being processed in the Chamber of Deputies prevails, defensive investigation will not have been as broad as possible, notably when the Italian criminal procedural law and its provisions of *indagine difensive* are taken as a reference point.[56]

In the Italian context, taken as a reference for comparative law for Brazilian defensive investigation,[57] Law No. 397/2000 brought equality of arms in the sense of production of sources of evidence between the Public Prosecutor's Office and the accused insofar as, for example, it provided "the possibility for the defender to carry out investigative acts similar to those of the Public Prosecutor's Office and the Judicial Police and attributing the same probative value to the result of the defensive investigation and that of the public investigation."[58] And this should be so that "the defense is endowed with the same capacities and the same powers of the accusation"[59] to the limit of what is factually possible.

In Brazil, however, the discipline under discussion in the Chamber of Deputies does not provide for the regulation of the limits of defensive action in the collection of sources of evidence, so that the legislator, in a somewhat timid way, limited itself to establishing the possibility of identifying "sources of evidence in favor of his defense, even being able to interview people" (Art. 13, *caput*). Anachronistically, it was still left to the discretion of the police authority to join the material produced by the defense (Art. 13, § 5°).[60]

Hence, the pertinent warning from Gustavo Badaró that, "without a specific regime that ensures the accused's lawyer powers to carry out, by himself or through private investigators, investigative activities, its effectiveness will be diminished."[61]

If there is still no equality of arms in the preliminary investigation in its active aspect, for it to be effective (hence it is said of *case presentation* in a non-disadvantageous situation), the minimum that one should imagine for the principle to be obeyed seems to be the following.

---

[55] On another occasion, we stated that, in defensive investigation, the defense can also become the "protagonist of the sources of evidence" Vieira (2011a), p. 376.

[56] In Brazilian doctrine, see: Machado (2010), pp. 127 and foll. See also: Malan (2010). Also: Azevedo et al. (2004), p. 7. Gustavo Badaró notes that, in addition to peninsular law, defensive investigation can be seen, in American law, as a consequence of the Sixth Amendment, which ensures the *right to counsel* (2024, p. 96).

[57] Machado (2010), p. 127.

[58] Machado (2010), p. 147.

[59] Rascovski (2012), p. 123.

[60] Vieira (2011a), pp. 376–377.

[61] (2024), p. 95. In this regard, and still focusing on equality of arms, Diogo Malan (2009), p. 175, states: "It is worth mentioning, even, that the lack of regulation of defensive investigation and of infrastructure to carry it out is one of the main factors fostering structural inequality between the parties in criminal proceedings in our country."

As a first step, the provision to be included in the Code of Criminal Procedure should avoid the anachronism of leaving to the discretion of the police authority the attachment of the informative elements brought by the defense (even because the final recipient of the information collected in the investigation is not the delegate, but the public or private accuser, who formulates the *opinio delicti*, and the judge, who accepts or rejects the initial). After this, and it is repeated, as a minimum criteria for the conformation of the principle within the scope of positive law, three situations can be imagined.

The first is the prerogative to carry out inspections and investigative diligences, which is already foreseen for the Prosecutor's Office of the Union (Art. 8°, V, Complementary Law n° 75/93) and of the States (Art. 26, I, "c," Federal Law n° 8.625/93), but not to the constituted lawyers and neither to defenders of the union or, for example, those of the Public Defender's Office of São Paulo.

The second is the power to issue notifications and summons, in general, for the collection of testimonies, provided for the members of the Prosecutor's Office of the Union (Art. 8°, VII, Complementary Law n° 75/93) and of the States (Art. 26, I, "a," Federal Law n° 8.625/93), but not to lawyers and public defenders.

And the third, more complex, is the one pertaining to the power of requisition[62] of diligences, to public and private bodies, provided for the Prosecutor's Office of the Union (Arts. 8°, II, IV and IX, Complementary Law n° 75/93) and of the States (Art. 26, I, "b," II, III and IV, Federal Law n° 8.625/93) and, in a different measure, provided for the Public Defender's Office of the Union (only for the guarantee of the safety of its members—Art. 8°, XIX, Complementary Law n° 132/2009) and for the Public Defender's Office of the State of São Paulo (only when in play the relationship with public bodies—Art. 162, IV, State Complementary Law n° 988/2006), but non-existent for lawyers.

It is said to be a situation of complex application because the requisition is an administrative act resulting from a vertical power relationship. It is possible to

[62] The power of requisition, even when used within the scope of criminal procedure, is not detached from administrative law. Requisition is an example of an "order," as an administrative act, "unilateral, discretionary, of authoritarian will manifestation, by which it is imposed on a Public Administration body, or a private individual, action or omission, to which they are obliged" Bandeira de Mello (2007), p. 566. The requisition, beyond the strict concept of administrative law—"administrative act of compulsory taking, for use in the collective interest, of a private individual's property, with subsequent return, compensating the prefixed or actual losses suffered as a result of this temporary loss of its own use" (p. 569)—is an act in which a vertical power relationship underlies. Unlike the request or the requirement, the requisition is not a request, but an order, a determination. As we are dealing here with the "power of requisition" within the scope of an already initiated investigative procedure, it does not seem reasonable for such a vertical power relationship to assist the side that will produce information elements with an accusatory bias, and not to establish the same prerogative for the one who may need to produce information elements for defense. Moreover, and because it is a power of requisition in an investigation already underway, as the entity that has the requisition power (Public Prosecutor's Office) will act, in the criminal case, as a party (interested, therefore), there is no reason to leave this observation aside, in favor of the state form with which the body (accuser) presents itself in the first phase of criminal prosecution.

imagine the granting of the power of requisition, on a larger scale, to the bodies of the Public Defender's Office (of the union and the states), but it would be difficult to foresee, in criminal procedure, the granting of power inherent to a coercive administrative act, as is the requisition to the constituted lawyer.

In any case, and even in the face of this apparent limitation imposed by administrative law, whenever the power of requisition is established on one side (normally, the holder of the exercise of the power of requisition will be a public entity), it seems reasonable that the same prerogative of command is also provided to the other side, under penalty of privileging, in criminal procedure, not only the inequality of forces (to bring to the records the element that may only matter to the accusation or defense), but also the administrative canon to the detriment of equality (bringing, for the preliminary investigation, the subject-subordinate relationship, which is irrelevant).

Moreover, the tone that moves the opposing interests of the accused and accuser is not of administrative law, just as it is not the one that moves the search for information (even if by an official entity) in criminal procedure in order to try to prove the accusatory hypothesis.

In criminal procedure, there is no, in the research of informative elements (accusatory or defensive), administrative law relationship between the requesters and the recipients of the order. This is because the position of the investigated before the state that accuses him, even in a preliminary phase, is not that of a subject, but that of a subject of rights. Similarly, the position of the representative of the state, in this same phase, is not assimilable to that of sovereign power, but rather to that of the state representative who has the constitutional function of both developing the investigation of the facts, as to hold the criminal action.

Hence, in the name of maintaining the so-called power of requisition to the body of future public accusation, the same coerciveness must be extended to public defenders (this exists in a small measure, as already seen) and to constituted and appointed lawyers (so that they do not find themselves in a disadvantageous situation in relation to public defenders).[63] In other words, if the impediment to this is indeed the issue involving the administrative law side, let the same powers of request be granted to those involved—all: accusers and accused—and no longer, as is done today, the power of requisition with a bias to the accusation body.

The three situations seem to be imperative in achieving the equality of arms in the active bias of criminal prosecution, that is, in the possibility of the investigated *bringing to the investigation* his theses. If these measures are not configured, one cannot say that there is equality of arms in the active aspect of the knowledge of the criminal investigation. It is not a mere limitation—or contour—of the right. It is the minimum that can be expected, justifiably, to make the principle of equality of arms apply at this moment and in this activity of criminal prosecution.

This is because the act of researching the sources of evidence is not a one-way street—even in the investigation. After all, the public interest in seeking to prove the

[63] Therefore, the understanding of João Pedro Chaves Valladares Pádua (2009), p. 13.

materiality and authorship of a certain fact is no less legitimate than that other interest—equally public, as it stems from the right to defend oneself from the pre-procedural accusatory burden—which the investigated must use the means available to try to avoid having a criminal action instituted against him.

The right to defense, as specifically stated in criminal procedural doctrine, even if prodromically (as is the case), is "analogous to the right of action,"[64] that is, it is the reverse of the coin according to which the ownership of the future exercise of the right of action must be opposed to the ownership of the exercise of the right of defense.

Such a perspective provokes a new way of thinking, including, about the investigated being able to use, for example, the so-called means of evidence research abstractly made available to the body that accuses him even in the pre-procedural phase. In justification, one can point out the possibility—not uncommon—that, to deny the probable authorship of a certain criminal offense, it may be necessary for the investigated to request the breach of fiscal secrecy of a person then alien to the investigation, and on whom initial suspicions may fall from previous defensive investigation work.

The possibilities of breaking secrecy, observed the specific legal reasoning pertinent to the adequacy of the measure, should be opened even if the author is the investigated, as both have an interest in bringing to the records the widest range of possible information to justify their future manifestations (of accusation or defense).

Another example is in a situation in which, to deny having been the author of a certain telephone conversation, and once having indications—from previous private and lawful investigative diligences—of who it may be, the investigated himself presents the request for suspension of the telephone secrecy of a certain person.

If, specifically in civil procedural doctrine, it is understood that "*defence* is the *negative counterpart* of the power of action, that is, it is the set of powers and faculties that allow the defendant to oppose the plaintiff's claim, pleading for its rejection,"[65] there is no reason to discard the concept for criminal proceedings.

Even in a pre-procedural dimension, there is activity (even if prodromic) of a party in the process. Hence, to observe the equality of arms from the accusatory burden dumped on someone, one must open the range of opportunities equal to those available to the accuser.

[64] Malan (2009), p. 153.

[65] Dinamarco (2024), pp. 401–402.

6.3 Equality of Arms in the Procedural Phase: Criminal Action, Until Judgment

If in the preliminary phase of criminal prosecution there is no specific provision for moments to have procedural chances so that the case is presented in non-prejudicial situations when compared to the presentation of the opposing party, and if there is no predefined moment in which a substantial accusatory burden is directed at someone, with the second phase of criminal prosecution, the opposite happens.

While in the preliminary procedure there is no fixation of the moment in which the accusation and the defense take place, nor in what form they appear, in the judicial phase of criminal prosecution the moment in which someone is considered a defendant in a criminal action is defined; deadlines are set for the defense and the prosecution to manifest themselves; and evidence to be produced is defined, observed the contradiction.

Therefore, if up to here the equality of arms has been addressed from the point of view of the knowledge of the investigation (passive and active sides), in a criminal action until the first-degree decision, it is possible to deal with moments and pre-established situations to diagnose the incidence of the principle of equality of arms.

This is not to say that, in the first phase, the principle of equality of arms does not apply, or that it is more *dynamic* (since there is no rigidity in the procedure, as seen in a condemnatory criminal action). What happens is that, by the way the preliminary investigation is conducted, the safest position for the diagnosis of the principle, in light of the concept reached in the previous chapter, is to focus directly on the knowledge on the part of those who already have to defend themselves.

More than that, the prediction of clear moments in which the equality of arms is presented in the second phase of criminal prosecution does not make this principle more *static* than its possible presentation in the first phase. It just happens that, because there are formal parties in the criminal process in the second phase and also because there is greater rigor with the sequence of acts to be developed until the final decision, the perception of equality of arms in this phase is clearer.

The indicative moments of manifestation of the principle of equality of arms in the Brazilian criminal process, in the judicial phase of criminal prosecution until the judgment on the merits, are the following, each with peculiar treatments: response to the accusation, production of evidence, presentation to the court, and observance of deadlines.

Before dealing with them, however, the topic requires an approach, albeit brief, on the incidence of equality of arms in two capital examples of consensual criminal procedural law: the penal transaction and the immediate application of penalty, in the summary procedure provided for in the project of a new Code of Criminal Procedure.

6.3.1 Equality of Arms in Penal Transaction and Immediate Application of Penalty (Art. 283, PL n° 8.045/2010)

The idea of consensus between accuser and accused is what animates both the well-known institute of penal transaction (Arts. 72 and ss., Law n° 9.099/95), as well as the institute of immediate application of penalty dealt with in the so-called *summary procedure* of the new Code of Criminal Procedure project underway in the Chamber of Deputies (Art. 283, of the Bill No. 8.045/2010).[66]

From the essence of the idea of agreement between those involved in both situations—which are distinguished in the hypotheses of admissibility and in the formalization in which both occur in the procedural scene—the idea of agreement between the parties emerges.

And hence the consideration about the equality of arms, along with the assumed autonomy of will and freedom to *transact* (in the case of the penal transaction) or to request immediate application of penalty (in the case of what is doctrinally already called in Brazil as bargain).

After all, in any legal business, one of the requirements for validity is the autonomy of the will of those involved. For criminal procedure, it is important to consider the equal treatment between the Public Prosecutor's Office and the accused, particularly the balanced situation between both. Without this, it cannot be said that the consequence of the transaction or the immediate application of a penalty in the *summary procedure* respects the equality of arms.

And that is exactly where the problem lies. Not necessarily in the abbreviated application of penalty, but in what it consists of, from the point of view of the treatment of the parties in the criminal process, its foundation. In other words, concerning the equality of arms, it is not about consensual criminal justice, but one of its core elements for the system of positive law in Brazil. What does not exist, at this point, is consensus itself.[67]

It is argued here that, considering the principle of equality of arms, the cognitive aspect of the facts debated in the process (brought to the judge) is not as important

---

[66] In the plane of current law, also the conditional suspension of the process (Arts. 89 and ss., Federal Law No. 9.099/95) can yield the same discussions that follow. But here it is not about the conditional suspension of the process because, in this case, there is typically no imposition of penalty, but subjection to procedural burdens. That is, although the situation of disadvantage in the negotiation aspect may remain the same, the immediate consequence in the case of the penal transaction and in the bargain is much more dramatic than that seen in the conditional suspension of the process. Because of this distinction, it is noted that the position of the parties deserves the same discussion carried on in sequence when we talk about the transaction and the bargain; it is not about the conditional suspension of the process.

[67] "Consensus does not mean imposition of the will of one subject over the other, for example, the interest of the prosecution in getting rid of the investigative procedure or the judge in ending the criminal process soon, but a horizontal discussion, not hierarchized of the solution of the criminal problem, that is, with more communication between the procedural subjects" Giacomolli (2009), p. 60. Also: "The announced negotiation is far from being inspired, as would be the essence of any contractual model, in autonomy and equality between the parties." Karam (2004), p. 39.

as *how* the procedural situation was configured from the situations of *advantage* or *disadvantage* of one party over the other.[68] And, about this, it is very difficult not to perceive the advantageous situation of the public accusation (either in the penal transaction or in the immediate application of penalty) when compared to that of the accused.[69]

It is not about a true agreement based on equality of treatment to the antagonistic sides, but, as Geraldo Prado pointed out some time ago considering the transaction (in a lesson also suitable to the new figure of the bargain), about something that seems to dress itself in the technique of "adhesion contracts" and that, thus, ends up generating a "forced conviction" directed to the accused. Even more, it transforms "the courtroom into a business counter."[70]

The inequality in the treatment of the subjects is inherent to the two negotiating figures and, as it is assumed in this work, it has no reasonable measure.

This is because, even if a rigid parallelism between the accuser and the accused is unthinkable, mainly because the loss of freedom is a contingent notion to only one of the sides, the situations in transaction or in bargaining are a one-way street. Only one party has something to gain from the agreement, and that party is the prosecution. And so, it is by the realization that, whether the agreement (of transaction or bargain) is made or not, this party—the prosecution—loses nothing.

Thus, in the transaction, the request of the representative of the Public Prosecutor's Office is the immediate application of a non-custodial penalty (Art. 72, Law No. 9.099/95), when precisely the abstract typical figure allows, if the due criminal process with a conviction has elapsed, the imposition of the same non-custodial penalty.

That is: to the accusing body, the *risk* of proposing the immediate application of penalty is only that of getting rid of the contradictory discussion that could result in an acquittal or conviction decision, to, in time (and process) economy, see the penalty already imposed. To the accused, however, accepting the proposal is equivalent to not running the *risk* of an acquittal or, at most, a conviction that would result from criminal instruction, necessarily not imposing a custodial penalty. Who has something to lose with such an agreement, from the start,[71] therefore, is only one of the consenting parties: the accused.

---

[68] That is: the instructional deficit would already be an important issue to deal with, because what is achieved with the penal transaction and with the bargain is an imposition of criminal penalty without in-depth discussion of the criminal issue. On this point, see: Reale Júnior (1997), pp. 25–31.

[69] As already mentioned here, and it is recognized to be the conformation of the Brazilian Criminal Process: the accusing body has, abstractly, broader powers of research and evidence production. In the issue of consensual justice, this point—the confirmation known of the Criminal Process—does not arise, because, in that case, exactly the possibility of *agreement*, of a *legal transaction* to be celebrated between the representative of the accusation and the accused person.

[70] Prado (2003), pp. 193 and 196.

[71] An interesting hypothesis is the one in which the information in the records are frankly unfavorable to the accused, that is: when, in theory, it is advantageous to celebrate the agreement compared to the prognosis of conviction and loss of primariness. Such a situation, however, results from concrete circumstances, and the weighing of the choice, given the prognosis of conviction, should

In the application of penalty upon request, dealt with in Bill No. 8.045/2010, the imposition of penalty in the terms in which the paragraphs of Article 283 regulate means an authentic conviction decision, albeit resulting from mere ratification. Thus, with the waiver of evidence production by those involved and with the confession of the accused, it can be considered the immediate imposition of a criminal penalty, whether custodial or alternative.

To the prosecuting body, the advantage lies, once again, in the anticipated conviction, with the dispensation of evidence production and, therefore, with the dispensation of the risk of not proving the hypotheses presented initially. To the accused, on the other hand, waiving effective contradiction, but imposing on him the burden of confession to be entitled to the *summary procedure*, this agreement is also detrimental, as it removes the possibility of reaching a final acquittal decision.

Whether in the transaction or in the bargain, the situation of advantage of the accuser is so patent that one can even remember the lesson taken from the Italian doctrine by Maria Lúcia Karam that, in these negotiations, one side (the prosecution) has "the knife and the cheese in hand," while the other (the accused) may suffer blackmail.[72]

Returning to the point that unites the two figures, and from the perspective of the situation of advantage of one of the parties compared to the other, one must ask, with Geraldo Prado: "is it possible, in fact, to consider the absence of coercion and equality of opportunities in activity directed at punishment for the practice of criminal offenses?"[73]

The answer that is assumed in this work is negative, that is, one cannot imagine that the two parties are treated in the same way, or, at least, given the natural distinctions, from a reasonable discrimination, in the situation of a criminal transaction and bargaining. The clearly prejudiced party is the accused, and exactly there lies the violation of the equality of arms.

About this, Diogo Malan (in analysis of the bargain, but espousing a point of view that applies, also, to the criminal transaction) argues that the principle of equality of arms has its "essential core" "mortally violated," since the new institute ends up "hypertrophying the powers of the accuser: the latter, in practice, replaces judge and jurors, concentrating the powers to formulate the accusation, judge the cause and fix the penalty."[74]

---

not prevail over the presumption of innocence and, thus, over the possibility of discussing the contours of the cause in contradiction. The general rule of disadvantage for the accused, therefore, remains.

[72] (2004), p. 39. The colloquial terms are from the referred work. This work will not explore in detail the existence or not of *blackmail* as a critical point of systems that adopt in varying measures the institute of *plea bargain*. The focus here is the advantage of one side in the imposition (a *contradictio in terminis*) of these agreements, whether they are coated or not with blackmail, that is, *overcharge*.

[73] (2003), p. 184.

[74] (2010), pp. 2–3.

Here, then, is the intermediate point between criminal investigation and the instructional process in which the principle of equality of arms would have everything to strongly apply—given the theoretical premise of the agreement of wills, which presupposes equality in the treatment of the parties—but it is really not consecrated.

6.3.2 *Response to the Accusation*

The first moment in which the accused can rebut arguments from those who accuse him so that his situation is not seen at a disadvantage before the Judiciary is the so-called *response to the accusation.*

The opportunity provided for in Article 396 of the Code of Criminal Procedure indicates that the response to the accusation is a mandatory piece for the valid development of the process, either for summary acquittal, or for judicial reanalysis[75] of the aptitude of the complaint, conditions of action, procedural assumptions, and just cause.[76]

The response to the accusation is a fundamental piece of the Brazilian criminal process and indispensable to the configuration of the equality of arms.

[75] "There can be, therefore, no binding of the judge with the previous decision that received the complaint, under the terms of art. 396, *caput*, of the CPP, since there is no preclusion or any other mechanism that makes the act immutable or not subject to reform. Legal impossibility of the request, illegitimacy of parties, ineptitude of the complaint, are topics that can be reviewed, even after the receipt of the complaint. If such situations are verified, even if the complaint has already been received, the judge must extinguish the process, without judgment on the merits" Badaró (2024), p. 421.

[76] The Code, with the wording given to Article 396 by Law No. 11.719/2008, began to provide two procedural moments that have generated intense doctrinal debate: that of the receipt of the initial before the defensive response (Art. 395, CPP), and the one following such response, of Article 399, CPP. In doctrine, there is a division between those who understand that from 2008 there are two moments, successive, for the receipt of the complaint (Grinover et al., 2009b, chap. XIII, item 2; Fernandes & Lopes, 2008; Fernandes (2002), pp. 61 and foll.), those for whom the moment of receipt of the accusation is indeed that of Article 396, of the Code of Criminal Procedure (Lopes Júnior, 2025, p. 902. The author is categorical: "one thing is what the law says, another is what we would (very much) like it to say, but it does not"), and those who understand that the moment of receipt of the accusation is that of Article 399, CPP (Badaró, 2009, pp. 123–180; Rangel, Paulo (2012), p. 528—the author, in fact, believes that "the legislator committed a serious fault within the area of the wording of the receipt of the complaint and deserves a red card" Prado (Sept. 2003), pp. 4–5; Nicolitt (2012), p. 267. In the STJ and STF, the prevailing understanding currently seems to be that the moment of receipt of the complaint is the one provided for in Article 396 of the Code of Criminal Procedure (within the scope of the STF: Ag. Reg. in Criminal Action no. 630, plenary, under the rapporteurship of Justice Ricardo Lewandowski, published on 22nd March 2012. In the STJ: *Habeas Corpus* no. 138.089, 5th T., under the rapporteurship of Justice Felix Fischer, published on 22nd March (2010). On this point, the only unanimity reigning in the doctrine is in the harsh criticism made to the legislator, particularly because even when the legislative process is underway, the expression *will receive it*, which appears in the current Article 396 of the CPP, was not originally included.

After all, from it, and as there is no preclusion regarding the appreciation of the conditions of action, procedural assumptions and just cause, it can result both a sentence that ends—already at this moment—the criminal process with the confrontation of the issues of criminal procedural law that underlie the accusation (active illegitimacy of part), as well as a sentence that analyses the contours of culpability, illegality and typicality of the fact. Furthermore, with the response, the extinction of punishability as a cause of acquittal in the criminal process (Art. 397, CPP) began to be dealt with.

Therefore, problems arise that, more than affecting the interpretation of the moment of receipt of the initial, concern the possibility of the defensive arguments being taken into consideration with the same weight that is given to the accusatory ones.[77]

---

[77] An interesting problem is the possible coincidence between the subject to be brought in response to the accusation and in exception (Arts. 95 and ss., CPP). This can happen with the condition of the action of legitimacy *ad causam* (subject ventilated both in response to the accusation, given there is no preclusion in the matters provided for in Article 395 of the Code of Criminal Procedure, as well as in a specific exception, under the terms of Article 95, IV, CPP). Another example is the discussion of the jurisdiction of the court (in the same way, ventilated in the response to the accusation, by virtue of Article 395, II, CPP, and the finding that it is a matter that cannot be precluded, as well as in its own exception provided for in Article 95, II, CPP). In addition to the duplication for the argumentation of the matters, there are still two points to draw attention to: the first is that, in the case of the declinatory, the hearing of the representative of the Public Prosecutor's Office is provided for (Art. 108, CPP); the second is that, precisely because the Public Prosecutor's Office is taken as the *custos legis*, it was the body included as liable to suffer the exception of suspicion (Art. 104, CPP). It is argued here that the duplication of the treatment of different matters is a consequence of the 2008 procedural reform, particularly by virtue of Law No. 11.719/2008, which changed the procedural matter of the criminal process in the first instance. Before such a change, there was no provision for the matters to be faced by the magistrate for the preliminary analysis of the complaint, but only the provisions of exception. As the new discipline of the procedural moment of receipt of the initial brought to the accused a wider range of defensive action, and to the magistrate a more objective range of analyses of the initials, it is understood that the vehicle in which the defensive reaction is formulated matters less than its content. It is not because the reaction is made in exception that, just for that, the Public Prosecutor's Office is given a view, the same not happening when the reaction is made in response to the accusation. In the same sense, but from another perspective, the 2008 procedural reform missed a good opportunity to—as it seems to be due and has been said in this text—remove from the representative of the prosecution body the duty of impartiality analogous to that required of the magistrate and of the court officials. Therefore, it is assumed that Article 104 of the Criminal Procedure Code is unconstitutional, since it offends the constitutional principle of equality of arms (since the Public Prosecutor's Office is part of the criminal process and, logically, the party does not have a duty of impartiality analogous to that of the magistrate); and that the matters dealt with by the defense, even if in their own exceptions, if covered by the limits of the matters to be brought in response to the accusation, do not justify, by the vehicle in which they are ventilated, referral to the Public Prosecutor's Office to comment on them. A different situation occurs if the exception is deduced after the response to the accusation, in situations where the reason is subsequent. In these cases, if the Public Prosecutor's Office, as a party, has not had knowledge to be able to comment on the existence or not of the subsequent reason that originated the exception, there is a plausible reason for it to comment. Regarding the moment when the impeding fact can arise, specifically regarding the hypotheses of suspicion or impediment of a magistrate, see: Dotti (Apr./Jun. 1993).

6.3.2.1 The Effective Response: Access to the Records, Contact Between Lawyer and Accused, Reasonable Time

The first of the problems arises from the effectiveness of the response and corresponds to the point of contact between the equality of arms and the right of defense. This is because, for the response to the accusation to be apt to reflect the matters that can be listed at this stage, the accused and the defender must be able to delve into the contours of the elements from which the accusation is built.

Hence, it is fundamental, as already said, that the accused is given the opportunity to the fullest extent to access the entire content of the investigation, as it is based on the details contained in the documents on which the accusation is based that he will be able to structure his reaction. Thus, as the first step towards observing the equality of arms in the procedural phase, one must pay attention to the total availability to the accused, whether free or imprisoned,[78] of all the information elements that are in the records.

If the *standard* cognitive of the accuser is more qualified than what is available to the defendant, the equality of arms in the criminal process is violated. After all, the minimum that should be offered to the one who defends against the accusation is that he knows the same elements of valuation that were brought to the knowledge of the accuser. More than that—and here the equality of arms approaches the right of defense—the response to the accusation depends on the exhaustion of the guarantee of free, prior, and reserved contact between lawyer and client.[79]

Unlike the accusation, the presentation of the defensive piece results from the exercise of two wills that come together: that of the accused, who has the factual elements to transmit to the lawyer and always exercises his self-defense, and that of

[78] Particularly in the case of an accused person in custody, the example of wiretapping and what is made available to him can indicate respect or violation of the equality of arms: as we know, the audios captured from documents that are attached to the process as transcriptions of the intercepted conversations. Commonly, copies of the process are made available to the accused and defenders, in which such transcriptions are documented along with the media of the captured conversations. The accused person in custody, evidently, has the right to listen to the intercepted conversations, in addition to just reading the transcribed ones, as it is his voice that appears (or not) in the audios, and no one better than the accused himself (the recipient of the initial and then, of the sentence) has the mnemonic capacity to work the contexts in which such conversations happened. This is, moreover, an exercise of self-defense. To consider, because the accused is in custody, that he cannot listen to the *wiretaps* included in the investigation simply because he is in custody (as this is what reduces the state denial that barely hides behind arguments such as logistical lack of availability of rooms and equipment to listen to the audios within the penitentiary establishments) violates the broad defense (in the bias of self-defense) and, particularly in distinction between those who are in custody and those who are free, establishes an odious—because without legal reason—limitation of the exercise of the right of the accused person in custody when compared to the one who will respond free to the accusation. The argument of the technological difficulty of guaranteeing the prisoner to listen to the dialogues does not convince, especially these days, when technological devices are used to produce so many means of proof and research of proof in the criminal process.

[79] Article 7°, III, Law No. 8.906/94 (from the perspective of the *munus* of the lawyer, be it public or private); Art. 8°, 2, "d," of the CADH (from the perspective of any citizen who is being prosecuted). From the perspective of the right to defense, see: Kehdi (Nov. 2005), pp. 12–13.

the professional who technically explores and translates for the procedural and criminal purposes the matters discussed with the assisted.

Because structurally the defensive manifestation depends on the observance of the two manifestations of will (accused and lawyer) in conjunction, the limitation in the free exercise of one of them (if the accused does not have access, personally and directly, to all the elements on which the accusation is based) or in the intertwining of both (if the contact between accused and lawyer is not free and reserved) removes from the defensive piece its possible effectiveness. Thus, it puts the defense, at this procedural moment, at a disadvantageous situation when compared to that of the accusation, which developed the accusatory line without any undue state limitation. The clash, at the procedural moment, between the written pieces—accusation and its initial counterposition—becomes unequal.

For this reason, the equality of arms, in this particular, integrates with the necessary knowledge of the information elements contained in the records, with the right of defense (regarding the contact and the unimpeded communication that must exist between lawyer and client). Even more than that, however, reasonableness must be observed in the time granted to the defense for its manifestation at this procedural stage.

This is because the CADH, in Article 8, 2, "c," provides, in addition to the *means*, the *time* suitable for the preparation of his defense. And when one imagines the incidence of the principle of equality of arms in the Brazilian criminal process, one must necessarily take it as "adequate time for the preparation of the defence" alongside the "adequate time for the preparation of the accusation." Especially because the guarantee of a reasonable duration of the process (Art. 5, LXXVIII, CF) is given to the individual himself.

Thus, and as the response to the accusation is a mandatory piece in which all matters of interest to the accused can be brought to consideration, there is no rigor in the peremptory fixing of the period provided by law: ten days, from the citation of the accused (Art. 396, CPP). About this, some criteria can be reached so that the division of opportunities between accusation and defense at this stage of the criminal process does not favor the argument of one side or the other.

The first and most common criterion would be the distribution of deadlines in the exact terms of Article 46 of the Code of Criminal Procedure. If the prosecution discharges, in situations without great complexity and in cases of defendants at large, to deduce accusation within fifteen days from the receipt of the records (or five days in case of defendants in custody), one could expect the defense to discharge, in the decade provided by law (Art. 396, CPP), to rebut the accusation.[80] Such a criterion, however, is insufficient for more than one reason.

---

[80] The situation of responding to the accusation in a circumstance resulting from a criminal action of private initiative of the offended is not dealt with here, because the exercise of the right to complaint is a consequence of the right to action and is not linked to the rigid prediction of initial action-reaction in criminal proceedings. The logic of the distribution of specific deadlines, therefore, at the procedural moment, does not arise in the context of the criminal action private of the offended. The discussion is not on the same plane, that in Brazil it is possible, as has been stressed,

The first is that if the accusation is granted a period of fifteen days to send to the court a mere accusatory hypothesis (or, in terms of Min. Cezar Peluso, a "proposal for a model of sentencing" – *HC* no. 83.301, 1st T., *DJ* 06.08.2004) that may come to be confirmed after due criminal process, providing a shorter period for this hypothesis to be rebutted results in inequality of opportunities in the presentation of theses.

After all, the accusation narrates the fact happened under the perspective that justifies the instigation of the criminal action, while the defensive effort goes beyond the mere narrative of what happened, since it can address the treatment of hypotheses of lack of criminal action, lack of just cause, ineptitude of accusation and, still, descend to the minutiae of substantive law (typicality, illegality, culpability).

The minimum that should be obeyed, therefore, is the equality of deadlines between the accusation and the defense, even in less complex cases. For this reason, the provision of the decade of Article 396 of the Code of Criminal Procedure seems to be unconstitutional.

On the other hand, neither ten nor fifteen days may be sufficient for the defensive manifestation, in more complex situations in which, moreover, neither does the accusation discharge the presentation of the initial within the period provided by law.

Regarding such complex situations, it is worth mentioning the proposition of Rafael Braude Canterji and Roberta Coelho Verlang. For the authors, from the observation of the equality of arms in the criminal process, the criteria for flexibilization of the decade provided in Article 396 of the CPP can be the following: "in cases (a) in which a longer period was granted to the Prosecutor's Office for the offering of a complaint than that provided for by law; (b) with a high number of defendants; (c) of considerable complexity; and (d) with a large amount of documents to be analysed."[81]

Thus, the deadline for the submission of the response to the accusation, besides not being reasonable to pre-establish in ten days (less than that provided for the accuser), is not peremptory and nor can it be comparatively less than the expected (or granted, since improper) for the accuser.

Even though *a priori* it is not said *what* the reasonable time is to respond to a certain accusation—but admitting that the limit of ten days is unconstitutional because, at its root, it creates inequality of time between accusation and defense to *formulate* and *rebut* the accusation[82]—it can be affirmed that, in situations in which

---

even the filing of a criminal complaint in a subsidiary way to the offering of the indictment, in the event of an excessive deadline for the offering of the indictment (Art. 5°, LIX, CF; Art. 29, CPP).

[81] Canterji and Verlang (Mar. 2012), p. 6.

[82] The understanding remains the same even if the initial piece was crafted in less time than provided by law. The preparation of the indictment in less time than provided in the legal parameter does not mean that the defense is also required, symmetrically, to prepare the response in less time than provided by law. And, in case of a defendant in custody, even if the deadline for the preparation of the indictment is reduced, this does not mean that the defendant's deadline should also be reduced. The accused is in custody due to state coercion, and the greater speed in offering the indictment is a measure that benefits him (Art. 5°, LXXVIII, CF). The procedural speed, however, and here it is reiterated that it is a measure for the benefit of the accused himself (which cannot be

the conditions treated by Rafael Canterji and Roberta Verlang do not exist, the minimum is that the defense enjoys the same time that the accusation had to formulate its arguments.

In complex situations, and because it is a principle-based rule, the granting of a more extended deadline may be necessary for the presentation of an effective response and, thus, to respect the equality of arms at this stage and to comply with Article 8, 2, "c," of the CADH.[83]

6.3.2.2 The Issue of Opening Views to the Accusation After the Defensive Response

It has been observed frequent return of the records to the accuser so that he can express himself at a time after the defensive response and before a judicial decision about it. Given this, the treatment of the equality of arms in the criminal process requires specific attention.

The issue now is not the *response* itself, but the *reply in the criminal process*, opening a new view to the accuser either to face the defensive theses, or to inform him of the documents joined.

Allowing double judgment of the accuser (as he will have expressed himself first when subscribing to the initial, and then when becoming aware of what will have been argued by the defense), for only then to have judicial appreciation together on the accusation and the defense, may offend the equality of arms in the criminal process.

In this sense, the possibility of offense to the principle of equality of arms is assumed here because, in truth, not every and any second intervention of the accuser will be inappropriate. A technical cut must be made for better exposure of the matter.

---

interpreted, therefore, against him), does not override the guarantee of a reasonable time for the defense to respond to the accusation in the most effective way possible.

[83] An interesting question, raised by some, lies in the concern with the deadline for offering the response to the accusation in case of passive joinder. Although the topic is not close to the equality of arms (relationship between accused and accuser), it may mean a break in equality among the accused themselves, given that it is possible that whoever is cited *last* also responds *last* to the accusation and, thus, will have had more time to produce the defensive piece. To avoid not a "disparity of arms among the accused," but a risk of having a more effective possibility that some would have, to the detriment of others (even though in parallel they all address the same accusation), Luis Guilherme Vieira (2010), pp. 607 and foll., proposes the analogous application of Article 241, III, CPC, which provides for the start of the civil contestation period after the joining to the records of the last receipt notice or executed citation mandate. In the same sense, André Nicolitt (2012), p. 272, points out: "whatever the procedure, if there is multiplicity of defendants, the deadline for the presentation of the written defence will start counting from the joining of the last executed mandate and not from the actual execution of each mandate."

6.3.2.2.1 Specific Situations: The Scope of Article 409 of the Code of Criminal Procedure and the Separation Between Response to the Accusation and Procedural Exceptions

If, in response to the accusation, it conveys a matter that should be dealt with in its own exception, the Code of Criminal Procedure provides, in paragraph 1 of its Article 396-A, that the exception be filed and processed separately, according to Articles 95 to 112.

Thus, the question may arise of, in response to the accusation, a defense being supported by a lack of procedural presupposition or condition for the exercise of the criminal action (Art. 395, II, CPP).

Such matters may coincide with the hypotheses provided for in exceptions, as is the case with the incompetence of the court (Art. 95, II, CPP), illegitimacy of party (Art. 95, IV, CPP), lis pendens (Art. 95, III, CPP), and res judicata (Art. 95, V, CPP). They result in the recognition of the lack of a valid presupposition for procedural development (in case of court incompetence), lack of action condition for the criminal action (in case of an illegitimate party), or lack of just cause for the criminal prosecution (in case of lis pendens and res judicata).

To treat the response to the accusation separately from the exceptions when the matters conveyed by the defense fit in both the manifestations (response and exception), the procedural technique requires that the matter be also seen separately from the expositions of the procedural piece presented by the defense. In other words, if there is direct exposition in the defensive piece of a thesis that should be exposed in exception, the relevant part of the piece presented as a response to the accusation should be processed as such; otherwise, not.

Thus, in a situation in which the question arguable in exception does not come, in the response, as a thesis to be directly faced by the magistrate, but results from the granting of the request presented in the response to the accusation (that is, when the matter of the exception arises as a consequence of judicial agreement with defensive request exposed in the response), in which it is debated, for example, the typicality of the criminal question or another aspect of relevance for the response to the accusation, the matter should continue to be treated in the amplitude of the response to the accusation.

An example that explains this point of view deals with the apparent competition of criminal norms and their possible consequences at this procedural stage. The question involves an indictment for conduct typified as misdirection and a situation in which, in response to the accusation, it is postulated that the framing of the same conduct in a crime against brand (Art. 190, I, Law n° 9.279/96).[84]

---

[84] Just like this, others could be imagined: a request for reclassification of conduct formulated in response to the accusation in proceedings for crimes against life. In this case, if the request is accepted by the magistrate, for recognizing the excess of the charge in the indictment, any reclassification of *attempted homicide* to *serious bodily harm* will result in a change of jurisdiction. The defense's request, however, will not have been brought in any exception, but in a pure and simple response to the accusation.

The proposed separation means that, if the *cause* of the defensive manifestation is the incompetence of the magistrate or the active illegitimacy *ad causam*, the exception procedure should be followed, in the relevant defensive chapter[85] (which, in this case, will be double: one piece with two arguments, dealing with incompetence, and the other with active illegitimacy—all according to Art. 110, § 1°, CPP).

If this does not happen, that is, if the incompetence or the illegitimacy of part is a *consequence* of the acceptance of another request made in response to the accusation (as is the case of discussion of the framing of the conduct in the situation of apparent competition of criminal norms), the right remains that of the response to the accusation. In this case, from the granting of the relevant request of the response will arise, or not, the recognition of incompetence or illegitimacy *ad causam*.

However, if the defensive manifestation is mainly about competence (and illegitimacy *ad causam*), the rite to be followed will be that of the exceptions. There, by virtue of Article 108 of the Code of Criminal Procedure, a manifestation is opened to the opposing party to speak (the Prosecutor's Office[86]). But if this does not happen, if the possible consequence of the granting of the request directly elaborated in the response is the eventual displacement of competence, there is no sense in determining the opening of views to the opposing party to manifest itself in opposition to the response to the accusation.

What is evident from such separation is that the exceptionality of the new manifestation of the Prosecutor's Office, in this case, will not result from the response to the accusation, but specifically from the rite provided for the exceptions. That is, if the situation is characterized as an exception, and not as response—from which will depend the judicial determination to, once brought the matter in response to the accusation, determine the registration in separate from the piece within the limits of the matter that should be deducted as exception—the new manifestation does not occur *because of the* and *in* response, but *because of the* and *in* exception.[87]

From another perspective, in the coincidence between the matters dealt with in the response to the accusation and those pertaining to conditions of action and procedural assumption, attention should also be paid to the equality of arms.

This is because, if it is certain that the rite of these exceptions resembles that of the exception of incompetence (Art. 110, CPP), more than the distinction between

[85] The technical solution can bring difficulties in the day-to-day forensic, where the most common is that the defensive pieces do not separate each *defensive chapter*, making it difficult and possibly exhausting to separate part of the defensive piece that should be filed separately for processing as an exception.

[86] The Code does not expressly deal with the manifestation of the Public Prosecutor's Office in the exception of illegitimacy. It merely deals with similarities between various exceptions with the procedure provided for the exception of incompetence (Art. 110, CPP). In our view, these examples in which the opening of views to the Public Prosecutor's Office can be discussed prove that its treatment in the process must be that of a *party*, and not that of *custos legis*.

[87] Explaining: the response to the accusation parades several theses. Two of them are specifically about the illegitimacy of the party and incompetence. The magistrate may, in the analysis of the defensive response, know the two parts cited as *exceptions* and determine the separate filing of the same piece, observing the limit that the exception will only deal with those two points.

the defensive thesis coinciding with that of exception being the main thesis or not in the response, here one should consider the moment in which situations that could fit separately in exceptions (ex.: incompetence and illegitimacy of part) arise.

Thus, one can have greater security in the interpretation of the matter in the specific case and understand the reasons why views are opened, or not, to the opposing party to the defense after the presentation of its response to the accusation.

On the other hand, in situations of res judicata or lis pendens, the fact impeding the new process (for the criminal process: the fact obstructing the existence of the just cause of the new process, once the pendency of the lawsuit or the authority of res judicata is established) may have occurred after the offering of the indictment. Such a fact may also, eventually, have occurred before the offering of the indictment, but, justifiably, the subscriber of the initial did not know of its occurrence.

In one or another hypothesis, the situation is analogous, for the accusation, to the *discovery of new evidence* in the case of admissibility of criminal review (Art. 621, III, CPP). Only by this reasoning is it understood that a new opening of views to the accusatory body does not offend the equality of arms.

Conversely, if the fact obstructing new criminal prosecution was already (or should be, in the situation of having a certificate proving the events or exposure of the matter,[88] in the records, before the offering of the indictment) known to the subscriber of the indictment, there is no reason to collect a new manifestation of the accusatory body. From such a perspective, the manifestation of the accusation does not occur to equalize the forces between accusation and defense, but by an imperative of procedural loyalty: the actors of the criminal process are offered the same possibilities of knowledge of the facts to be judged.

And at this point, the new manifestation of the Prosecutor's Office should not be given about the defense as a whole, but only about the matters dealt with in the documents to which until then there was no access, or to the defensive arguments referring to lis pendens or res judicata that were not known to the representative of the accusation.[89]

Therefore, from this second perspective, if the exceptional and justified hypothesis does not occur, and if the limit of the manifestation is not observed, the new opening of views to the Prosecutor's Office to speak about the defensive considerations will be offensive to the equality of arms and will put the defense at a disadvantage before the accusation.

[88] The hypotheses are distinct: if the proof of the thing judged is enough for the certificate, to deal with lis pendens, as the two criminal proceedings follow their courses, it is not uncommon for such an obstructive cause of just cause of the second act to have to argue about the objective and subjective coincidences of one and another criminal cause.

[89] For if the thesis of the response to the accusation had already been exposed in the records and, even so, a complaint was filed, this means that, even implicitly, the accusatory body already disagreed. Hence, it will not be reasonable to open a view for it to be spoken about with the response to the accusation. After all, it has already manifested itself once before offering the complaint, disagreeing with the defense.

Finally, a situation can be foreseen in which the defense manifests itself with the presentation of new documents. In this case, even due to the procedural loyalty that, as seen, must guide the paritary manifestations in the criminal process, it is advisable to determine the opening of views to the opposing party so that it can manifest itself within five days. The limit of the new accusatory manifestation must also be observed, that is, on the documents presented and the consequences arising from the defensive request attached to them.[90]

Apart from these hypotheses, there is no room for a new accusatory manifestation about the defensive response, under penalty of offending the equality of arms.

6.3.2.2.2 The Undue Reply in the Criminal Process: Offense to the Equality of Arms

Except in the exceptional situations indicated, the practice of determining a new opening of views for the Prosecutor's Office to manifest itself after the response to the accusation can lead to unequal and unjustifiable treatment of the parties in the process. Allowing two manifestations of the accusation against one of the defense and, concretely, admitting that the thesis of the initial has more efficacy than the response implies an advantage of the accusation before the defense.

Thus, except for exceptional cases, the practice of giving views of the process with the defensive manifestation to the accuser before deciding on the complaint and its response inverts the logic of the criminal process. This is because it ends up transforming the defensive piece (a reaction to the accusation) into an object of a new accusatory refutation. That is, the accusation is the one that, after offering the initial, refutes the defensive theses.

The Superior Court of Justice has already expressed its opinion on the disrespect that this practice brings to due process on more than one occasion.[91] This point of view is also known from the doctrinal point of view here adopted.[92] However, as

---

[90] It is collected, by analogy, the provision of Article 409 of the Criminal Procedure Code, which, in the wake of the legislative change brought with Law No. 11.689/2008, brought to the Jury Court's rite, in this same initial phase, an authentic "reply, from the Public Prosecutor's Office or the complainant, to respond to the preliminary allegations made by the accused or by the complained" Badaró (2008), p. 63. The analogy is justified because, as it seems, this would have been the *mens legis* to also encompass Law No. 11.690/2008, notably because both laws result from the same studies, from the same commission of jurists (chaired by Professor Ada Pellegrini Grinover). In the legislative process, as it seems, the projects took different directions, but the idea that unified them—at this point, the idea of reply in criminal procedure—seems to be the same.

[91] *Habeas Corpus* no. 172.345, 6th T. Rel. Des. Convoked Celso Limongi, *DJ* 19.08.2010. *Habeas Corpus* no. 128.591, 5th T., Rel. Min. Arnaldo Esteves, *DJ* 01.03.2010. It should be noted that, in recent years, a current trend has emerged in the Superior Court of Justice, which understands that there is no offense to due process in the presentation of a reply by the Public Prosecutor's Office, when the accused alleges "issues that, if accepted, may prevent the continuation of the criminal action." In this sense: AgRg in REsp 1893579 SP, 6th T. Rel. Min. Rogerio Schietti Cruz, *DJ* 21.06.2022.

[92] Decaro (Dec. 2011), pp. 13–14.

there is a precedent from the Supreme Court pertaining to the matter, it is important to deal with it, albeit briefly, to highlight the position taken in this work.

When judging the *Habeas Corpus* no. 105.739, the 1st Chamber of the Supreme Federal Court, in a case reported by Min. Marco Aurélio, understood that the opening of views to the Prosecutor's Office for a new manifestation, in light of the defensive response, would not imply illegal constraint because:

> It is inappropriate, in this case, to transport to this phase the imperative order alluding to the final allegations, when, here yes, considering even a precedent of my own, cited in the initial - Habeas Corpus no. 76.953/MT -, it is impossible to reverse the order provided for by law, hearing, after the presentation of the final allegations by the defence, the Prosecutor's Office.

In the aforementioned case, according to the fractional body of the Supreme Court, "the hearing of this [Prosecutor's Office] took place at a peculiar moment, strange to the space destined for the final allegations, even before the designation of a hearing. What happened, in this case, was the observation of a medullary principle of the criminal process - the contradictory."

The decision highlighted here deserves repairs from the perspective of the equality of arms, assuming the conceptual premise of the prohibition that one of the parties presents its case before the Judiciary in a concretely more advantageous situation than the other. And, even from the perspective of the contradictory, the argument developed in the judgment is dangerous, as it leaves room for the possibility of eternalizing the discussion prior to the decision on the initial.

After all, once a view is opened for the Prosecutor's Office in the exercise of the contradictory, not without reason, the defense (already invoking a facet of the *favor defensionis*) will claim for itself the prerogative of speaking last, with which, to provide the contradictory, there should be a view opened, then, to the defense.

More than that, it is understood that, at least in this procedural phase (of analysis of response to the accusation), the contradiction does not occur, so that the Prosecutor's Office knows the defensive arguments and can manifest itself on them.

It is imagined, in fact, the opposite situation: the contradictory, in this case, has the function of exactly allowing the defense to position itself in opposition to the accusatory arguments—as it is the one who must react to such arguments—and not that the accusation, based on refutations already exposed by the defense, tries to endorse its hypotheses.

It is undeniable that, with a view to the equality of arms, when granting two possibilities to the accuser to convince the magistrate about the correctness of his accusatory hypothesis, against only one possibility of the defense trying to refute the accusation, it opens up to the one who accuses a greater aptitude to see his arguments considered by the judge.

And even from the perspective of the contradictory, such a point of view does not seem to be the most correct, as the accused will not be able to rebut the new accusatory arguments, whether in case they endorse the aptitude of the complaint, the presence of just cause or the conditions of the criminal action, or, still, the fulfilment of procedural assumptions (Art. 395, CPP); be, with redoubled reason, in case the accusation deals again with issues related to the absence of causes that allow for summary acquittal (Art. 396, CPP).

6.3.3 *Equality of Arms in the Collection of Evidence and Its Exploitation in Court*

After the judicial analysis of the possible situations in the phase of Articles 396 to 399 of the Code of Criminal Procedure,[93] with the provision of the criminal instruction, a new treatment of the equality of arms in the criminal process begins.

In the instructive phase of the criminal action, one can deal with the incidence of the principle of equality of arms under two approaches: one of them has to do with the judicial treatment given to requests (in a broad sense), whether they come from the prosecution or the defense; the other refers to the spatial distribution of the hearing rooms.

In both perspectives, it is imperative to retain that, in a public criminal action, although the Public Prosecutor's Office is a representative of the state, its action in the criminal process is eminently interested, or that is, it is an activity of *part*.

In this regard, it is fundamental to remember something that has already been said here: the activity of those who plead in court for the success of the initial request is an activity of part, and not of law enforcement. Only by considering the representative of the accusing body as a party in the criminal process is it possible to move forward, then postulating the application of the principle of equality of arms in the criminal process.[94]

Having said that, as has already been seen in the approach to the breadth that is to be given to defensive investigation, and after having dealt with the equivalence of the possibilities of investigation to those who accuse and those who defend, with the issue under debate in the criminal action there is no need to dispute: the right to evidence belongs to both parties; neither more to one, nor more to the other.

The analysis of requests for production of evidence in a broad sense, therefore, must be rigorously critical regardless of the party that formulates them, whether it is the defense or the prosecution. After all, both are—logically, even—interested parties; and there is no legal reason to privilege the request coming from one party to the detriment of that coming from the opponent. Both defense and prosecution complete each other in the exercise of the same right, although in opposing poles: the right of action.

[93] Which means to say, in the wake of understanding espoused by the STF: a *positive* (aptitude of the complaint) and a *negative* requirement (non-incurrence of the initial in any of the items of Article 395 of the CPP) (*HC* no. 104.420, 2nd. C., under the rapporteurship of Justice Ayres Britto, published on 2nd May 2012).

[94] In the sense of this text and with criticisms of the conception of the criminal process that exalts formalism in the performance of the judge and the official accuser as representatives of a public body and discredits the defensive action due to *private* interests, see: Pádua (2009), p. 156.

6.3.3.1 The Procedural Instruction and the Treatment Given to the Requests of the Parties

The balance in the treatment of procedural subjects and—to stick to one of the details of the principle of equality of arms—the prohibition of disadvantageous treatment of one party in favor of the other implies that one analyzes with maximum neutrality the requests made, whether they come from the prosecution or the defense.

Thus, it is easy to see that, in this specific approach, the equality of arms is intertwined with the very contradiction, given that once a request is made, the opportunity for argumentative rebuttal must be given before deciding on it, under penalty of, without necessity supported by some reason, criminal procedural caution, deciding *inaudita altera parte*. Dealing with this detail invites two reflections.

The first, already advanced, lies in the observation that, even with criminal action in progress, there are requests that by their very nature prevent the immediate contradiction from being opened. One can cite, for example, the case of possible precautionary measure requested by the representative of the accusation that, if given the opportunity to the defense to disobey it, will take away the desired effectiveness of the provision sought (Art. 282, § 3°, CPP), or even the request for possible telephone interception that is justified, still within the scope of criminal action, in the terms of the aforementioned Law No. 9.296/96. These are exceptional situations that justify the removal *hic et nunc* of equality of arms, particularly in its aspect of approximation with the contradiction.

The second reflection that should be made in this regard is of a critical nature: defensive requests, as a rule, are treated opposite to what is given to those accusatory, for the simple (and widespread) reason—which does not even have legal provision—according to which one should open views to the prosecuting body to first opine on the defensive request and only afterwards collect a judicial decision. This way of thinking starts from the mistaken premise that the Public Prosecutor's Office in criminal prosecution is not a party, but rather a law enforcement officer, an assistant to the judge.

With this, it is assumed that the representative of the accusing body, if he does not have the same impartiality as the judge, could equate himself to the judicial authority in the sense that from him would come a better understanding of the application of the law to the concrete case. This thinking does not have approval within the scope of the present work.[95]

Defensive requests, like those of the prosecution body, come from a party that acts in favor of its interests. And interests are exercised, in the criminal process,

[95] Very appropriately, João Pedro Chaves Valladares Pádua (2009), p. 13: "If this argument prevails, then, as now seems obvious, all the evidentiary - and procedural in general - activity of the defence deserves a kind of presumption of discredit, since it, unlike the other actors in the process, has to protect private interest. And this, for what particularly interests here, translates into the fact that, unlike the judge or the Public Prosecutor's Office, the defence has no *power* to assist it in its task of gathering elements to support and even constitute its evidentiary activity - after all, it is a 'private', 'interested' party."

either by the accusing state, by the private accuser, or by the accused himself. There is no way to think differently, since the judge does not have as his assistant the one whose constitutional task is to develop the prosecution.

The examples of this criticism of the second reflection are the most common and can range from opening views to the Prosecutor's Office in requests for revocation of preventive detention during the criminal action (the Article 316 of the Code of Criminal Procedure does not provide for the need for the judge hear the prosecution before deciding the defensive request), to requests for indication of witness evidence made by the defense at the time it responded to the accusation (similarly, Article 396-A of the Code of Criminal Procedure does not provide for a new hearing of the representative of the prosecution on the convenience of hearing the defense witnesses; and from there it also does not extract the defensive duty to indicate in advance the relevance of hearing the listed witnesses).

Given the need to ensure the greatest possible equality in the judicial phase of criminal prosecution, there is no way to treat one side of the dispute with greater rigor than the other, or as if it deserved greater credit for representing public *interest* or *private*.

The *party*, in any process, because it behaves as interested in defending the interests it represents, must always have the same respect and the same credit attributed to the opposing party. Whether it is a defense of public, social, individual, or collective interest, the interest defended is the interest of a procedural party. Nothing more than that, whether in civil or criminal proceedings.

There is no exemption for either the defense or the prosecution in the criminal process, as both defend their interests, even if the defensive interest is, concretely, individual and the accusatory, abstractly, public. No predisposition to either side in the criminal instruction is admitted, under penalty of, including, the judicial authority losing its impartiality, which is the first attribute of the judge.

There is no, in the criminal process, *better* or *worse*; nor who defends a more or less worthy interest of the magistrate's attention. There are opposing interests that deserve the same attention and, for that very reason, always dispense the same consideration from the judge. In not observing this, there will be a disadvantageous situation to one of the sides, thus injuring the equality of arms.

Having presented such considerations, which should be observed in all requests made in court, whether they are from the prosecution or the defense,[96] we analyze

[96] To privilege the contradiction inherent to the process, it should, whenever possible, safeguard the defensive manifestation about the requests coming from the accusation before deciding on them, because the contradiction is a *two-way street* and not a *one-way street*. Regarding such a *two-way street*, a good example of the care that the parties' requests deserve is the discipline of the change of venue, under the terms of Article 427 of the Code of Criminal Procedure, with wording attributed by Law No. 11.698/2008. Before the legislative change, the then current Article 424 of the Code of Criminal Procedure provided—whether the request came from any of the parties—the opinion of the Attorney General of Justice (about which, by the way, the Summary No. 712 of the STF was valid, about a case of change of venue requested by the prosecution, when the defense was required to be heard). Now, given the non-repetition of the requirement, the situation that exists is the following: to the request formulated by the prosecution, in general, the defense is not

key moments in which the principle must be observed, namely: that of precautionary measures in the criminal process and the production of evidence in court.

6.3.3.2 Equality of Arms in Requests for Personal Precautionary Measures

In matters of personal precautionary measures, with the advent of Federal Law No. 12.403/2011, the principle of equality of arms began to be applied. That law gave a new wording to Article 282 of the Code of Criminal Procedure to include the following: "Except in cases of urgency or danger of ineffectiveness of the measure, the judge, upon receiving the request for a precautionary measure, will order the notification of the opposing party, accompanied by a copy of the request and the necessary documents, the case remaining in court" (§ 3).

Here we see the placement of the matter of imposition of precautionary measures—from the least invasive to, *ultima ratio*, preventive detention (Arts. 319 and 320, CPP)—dependent on the manifestations of the two parties in the criminal process. The legislative novelty is particularly important because, in the absence of a counterclaim in the criminal process guided by public initiative criminal action (there is no counterclaim), the new provision, more than implementing the adversarial principle, determines that the defense now has the possibility of convincing the judge that its reasons are better than those presented by whoever formulated the request for imposition of any precautionary measure.[97]

To observe the principle of equality of arms in matters of the imposition of precautionary measures, however, two warnings must be heeded.

The first refers to the judicial analysis of "urgency and danger of ineffectiveness of the measure," as, since it is a precautionary measure, there may arise the interpretation that just because it is *precautionary,* the request for the measure, the

heard, and vice versa; finally, if the measure is decreed *ex officio*, no other party is heard. This first understanding that can be extracted from the new provision does not favor, however, the isonomic treatment of the parties, mainly because the lack of dialogue about the requests for change of venue may weaken either the prosecution or the defense. Therefore—and hence the *two-way street*—the understanding of Gustavo Henrique Righi Ivahy Badaró (2008), p. 116, seems to be correct: "It will be better to continue to respect the contradiction, with the possibility that each party can manifest itself about the other's request, or that both are heard, when the measure results from the judge's representation."

[97] Methodologically, it was preferred to deal with precautionary measures in this sub-item of the work (in the part about the procedural instruction, and not about the investigation) because the system followed by the Code links the measures, as a rule, to requests from the parties, and a *party* exists when the criminal action has started, even if it prodromically manifests itself in a preliminary investigation. The reason, therefore, was twofold: to avoid duplication of the approach (now in the investigation, now in the instruction) and to prefer convenience in the exposition (the Code, here, predominantly speaks of *parties*, and this was followed, in the sequence of the criminal process, by the approach at this moment).

non-opening of manifestation to the party interested in contradicting the arguments there exposed, would be justified.[98]

Such a way of thinking contradicts the new system of precautionary measures in the measure in which, precisely because there is a range of measures that go from the *least* to the *most* invasive in terms of restriction to freedom, it disregards that their fungibility is only achieved if the party on whom each one will fall expresses itself on the suitability and necessity of each one of them.[99]

For example, a request for night-time home confinement (Art. 319, V, CPP) can be easily replaced by a measure of prohibition of absence from the District (Art. 319, IV, CPP), depending on the proof, on the part of the recipient of the measure, that it fits better in the case of convenience to the instruction due, for example, to night shift work. About this first warning, it can be said: it is not because the measure is *precautionary* that it should be decided without hearing the arguments of the opposing party.[100]

And this leads to the second warning, namely, that it is not because the criminal action is mostly moved by an official body that the formulated request (now precautionary) should be weighed with advantage in relation to that which in some way contradicts it.

It has already been said, and here it is insisted: in the matter of precautionary measures, the equality of arms is not achieved from the provenance of the request, but from the arguments that are read in it. And the request for imposition of a precautionary measure is nothing more than a part of the main request, coming from those who have legitimacy and interest to do so. Thus, the logic of interest makes it

[98] Guilherme de Souza Nucci (2011), p. 31, seems to be of this opinion when he states that "the tendency, in the scope of precautionary measures, will be the prevalence of cases of urgency or danger in delay (*periculum in mora*), justifying the decree *without prior hearing* of the accused or defendant. After all, many of the measures replace imprisonment, which is why they carry the same character of indispensability."

[99] And yet, from another perspective, it minimizes the application of basic norms of due process. In this regard, Antonio Magalhães Gomes Filho (2011), p. 45, has an important warning, made not on the level of the cautionary situation, but on the technique of cognition: "The summary or superficiality of the cognition carried out so that the judge issues the cautionary provision, does not remove the inescapable observance of the guarantees of the *due process*, which the Constitution ensures to those who are facing the possibility of suffering a restriction of rights, especially when it comes to personal freedom (art. 5°, LIV, of CF/1988). [...] In a democratic state, a judicial decision cannot be conceived in which the reasons of those interested in the provision are not taken into account." André Nicolitt (2011), p. 33, warns that, although in the matter of preventive detention the contradictory will become deferred, the range of so many other precautionary measures, different from prison, justifies the prior contradictory to the decree of personal precautionary measures.

[100] In this regard, Aury Lopes Júnior (2011), p. 15, emphasizes: "Even though it is a distinguished unknown of the Brazilian cautionary system, the contradictory is very important and perfectly compatible with some situations of cautionary protection." The author understands that the most suitable field for the prior contradictory to the decree of the measures is that of substitution, of accumulation, or of revocation of cautionary measures. For his part, the cases of preventive detention in which there is a danger of escape would be the suitable field for the contradictory, not prior, but subsequent to the decree of the measure (pp. 15–16). Of similar opinion is Luiz Flávio Gomes (2011), pp. 71–72.

not presuppose greater suitability to a request (precautionary or main) by the fact that it comes from this or that party in the criminal process.

Both parties are equally interested. And the request for imposition of a precautionary measure is simply and simply a part, a slice (precautionary) of the main request.

Thus, even if there was care in the assessment of requests in light of the criteria of urgency and danger of ineffectiveness of measures (as seen above) the judicial authority took the request coming from the Prosecutor's Office (in investigation or in criminal action – Art. 282, § 2°, CPP) as endowed with a priori plausibility without attributing the necessary counterweight to the defensive arguments, there would be no obedience to the system in force in Brazil with the advent of the aforementioned legislative change.

Obedience to the equality of arms, in matters of precautionary measures, depends on the equal consideration given to the defensive argument when compared with the attention addressed to the request for imposition of a precautionary measure. And this is justified not only to eventually decide not to decree the requested measure, but to decide, if necessary, for the imposition of other(s) more attentive to the canons of positive law of *necessity*, *adequacy,* and *personal conditions* of the recipient (Art. 282, I and II, CPP).

6.3.3.3 The Distribution of Spaces in the Courtrooms

In addition to the equality of consideration that the parties deserve at the time of assessing their requests, in criminal hearings, the observance of the principle of equality of arms is even more visible.[101]

The acts performed in criminal hearings are, even for the public outside the procedural ritual, the way in which criminal justice happens. For this reason, specifically regarding the architecture of the courtrooms, it is important to remember that, as stated in 1991 in a judgment of the European Court of Human Rights, "*justice must not only be done; it must be seen to be done.*"[102] Thus, even if the spatial distribution of the courtrooms is not the main or the only aspect of the equality of arms in the criminal process, it should reflect the role played by the parties.

As in Brazil, the issue is still little debated; here, first the lesson of comparative criminal procedural law is remembered, and then situations already faced are taken care of. With this, we reach the crucial point of the question, which is the treatment given to the accuser and the accused in the courtroom.

In the scenario of comparative law, in its Norm of Performance, Coordination and Transition (Legislative Decree No. 271, of July 28, 1989), which followed the new Code of Criminal Procedure of 1988, Italy gives an example of a provision pertinent to the matter. There, in Article 146, it was expressly provided that:

[101] We have already expressed our opinion on this: Vieira (Dec. 2011b).

[102] *Borgers v. Austria, Application* No. 12.005/86, judged on 30 October 1991.

> In the courtrooms, the benches reserved for the Prosecutor's Office and for the defenders are placed on the same level and facing the judging body. The private parties sit next to their own defenders, unless there is a need for caution. The chair for the witnesses is placed in such a way that these people are visible to the judge and the parties.[103]

In Portugal, Eduardo Maia Costa, Judge of the Supreme Court of Justice, pondered that the principle of "equality of arms" has a central role. For the author, there must be a "new courtroom." The magistrate said:

> The parties, in addition to being equidistant from the judge, must be on the same plane. Hence, unquestionably, the Prosecutor's Office cannot maintain the prominent plane that has always been that of a justice body, which always imposes on it a duty of impartiality and objectivity identical to that of the judge, it is there above all one of the parties in dispute, the one that formulated the accusation, which, it is true, is not obliged to defend in the final allegation, but which has the functional duty to explore in all its potentialities in order to its success. In summary, the principles of the accusatory and equality of the parties impose a strict equality of rights at the hearing between prosecution and defence, and consequently an equal positioning in the judicial scene.[104]

If, as already seen, the concept of equality of arms in criminal proceedings requires that equal opportunities be distributed to the parties to present their arguments in such a way that neither side is at a disadvantage before the judge, it is necessary to spatially readjust the format of the hearing rooms in Brazilian criminal procedural law.

Here, however, there are few examples of change; it being certain that, if at the level of positive law there is no requirement in this sense, it is opportune to first outline the current scenario of the problem, to then, and from an old precedent of the Supreme Federal Court, reach its core.

It is currently known that the Lia Pires Institute, based in Porto Alegre, produced a study on the spatial distribution of places to the prosecution and the defense, especially in judgments to be delivered by the jury court. According to that study,[105] "there is no legal, political or institutional reason to avoid that the Defence is in the same position as the Prosecutor's Office before the jurors and the community. On the contrary, the democratic criminal process guarantees equality between the parties."

In the same sense, there is a decision rendered by the 1st Criminal Court and the Special Criminal Court of the Restinga Regional Forum (Porto Alegre) in an administrative procedure moved by the Public Defender's Office which, incidentally, took as unconstitutional the legal provisions that grant to the representatives of the Prosecutor's Office the prerogative to sit to the right and on the same plane as the

---

[103] Article 146 on the norms of action of the new Italian Code of Criminal Procedure. In this regard, Lattanzi and Lupo (1990), p. 147, in attention to this norm, remember the procedure that was followed during the legislative process that resulted in this wording of the norm of action.

[104] Costa (2010), p. 359.

[105] In the research developed by the said Institute, a judgment was reported in the Court of Justice of Rio de Janeiro (Writ of Mandamus no. 35/2004, 7th Criminal Chamber, under the rapporteurship of Justice Eduardo Mayr, 3rd November 2004).

magistrates, distinguishing, with this, from the position of seats of the public defenders.[106]

In São Paulo, a federal judge working in a Criminal Court of that Judicial Section filed a Complaint in the STF under the argument that a decision granting a Writ of Mandamus by the Federal Regional Court of the 3rd Region dealt with a matter that concerns the entire National Judiciary, specifically regarding the distribution of spaces in hearing rooms.[107]

The issue there has to do with the provisions of Ordinance No. 41, of 1st December 2010, which determined "the adaptation of the hearing room" so that the "platform under the table and seat reserved for the federal judge, so that everyone present is on the same plane." That Ordinance also determined that it should be provided

> place in the hearing room for the worthy representative of the Federal Prosecutor's Office, immediately to the right of the judge, in the first seat, followed on the same side by the seats of the worthy Federal Public Defenders, appointed lawyers, ad litem and 'ad hoc'.[108]

Among the *consideranda* of the Ordinance are extracted "the constitutional procedural principle of isonomy or equality of arms between the parties, as well as the necessary equidistance and material and formal impartiality of the judge."[109]

Later, on 13 April 2012, the National Council of Justice also faced the matter. There, although important theoretical considerations were made for the resolution of the theme, the procedure was extinguished without appreciation of its merit due to a pending decision of the Supreme Federal Court, which, in the understanding of the reporting Councillor, would prevent a definitive manifestation of the Council.[110]

Within the legislative process of the Bill that is being processed in the Chamber of Deputies (Bill No. 8.045/2010), the Brazilian Institute of Procedural Law (IBDP) suggested a modifying amendment, in the specific chapter of the Jury Court procedure, so that, in the popular judgment, the Prosecutor's Office has "a seat in a

[106] Administrative procedure no. 02/2011, decided by Judge Mauro Caum Gonçalves on 19th June 2011. In the reasoning of that decision, an understanding was gathered, which is supported in this work, that the Prosecutor's Office, in a criminal action, is a party and not a law enforcer.

[107] Complaint no. 12.011, under the rapporteurship of Justice. Carmen Lúcia. In such constitutional action, the Federal Council of the Brazilian Bar Association, the National Association of Public Defenders, the National Association of Federal Public Defenders, and the Public Defender's Office of the Union were admitted as *amici curiae*. In ADIn 3.962, the National Association of Labour Magistrates (ANAMATRA) also questions the spatial distribution in the hearing rooms. As Minister Carmen Lúcia understood that that entity would not have active legitimacy to propose the objective demand, she monocratically denied the request. The case is in the appeal phase.

[108] Ordinance No. 41/2010, items I and II.

[109] Especially in the discussed concrete situation, see: Dotti (2012), pp. 1071–7.

[110] Consultation 0000422-19.2011.2.00.0000, under the rapporteurship of Councillor Marcelo Nobre, decision of 13.04.2012. The question in the STF that prevented the CNJ from commenting on the topic is that of Complaint no. 12.011.

position of equality and equidistance with the defender, in relation to the presiding judge," and that the accused has it "next to his defender."[111]

The plenary of the Supreme Federal Court dealt with this theme when judging the Direct Action of Unconstitutionality No. 4.768, proposed by the Federal Council of the Order of Lawyers of Brazil[112] and the Direct Action of Unconstitutionality No. 4.896, proposed by the same entity, the latter under the rapporteurship of Min. Luiz Fux.[113]

All these scattered manifestations have as their central point the distribution of physical spaces to the parties in hearing rooms. All of them challenge, with various grounds, Article 18, I, "a," of the Complementary Law No. 75/93—which provides for members of the Prosecutor's Office of the Union the prerogative to sit "on the

[111] As justification for the Modifying Amendment No. 102, the IBDP understood that: "If the project is concerned with the scenic aspect of the Jury Court, which is relevant, it is really important that the accused does not sit in an inferior position, sitting in the dock, below his defender, which also hinders the interaction between technical defence and self-defence. But it is not enough, it is necessary to ensure that the defence and the prosecution are positioned in a relationship of equality and equidistance in relation to the presiding judge. With this, it avoids the influence that the Prosecutor's Office would be on the side of the judge." There is a Bill (PLP No. 179/2012) that gives a new wording to Article 18, I, "a," of the Complementary Law No. 75/93. By the aforementioned bill, whenever representatives of the Prosecutor's Office of the Union present themselves "as parties in the process," they will not have the prerogative of sitting to the right and on the same plane as the judicial authorities. As justification for the aforementioned project, one can read that there are "numerous manifestations and criticisms regarding the disparity currently practiced by first instance judges in terms of equal and impartial treatment between prosecution and defence, especially when it comes to the place where the parties should sit, seeming that there is a certain supremacy of the member of the '*parquet*' over the other party." In the State of São Paulo, Bill No. 730/2013 is being processed, which "determines the placement of all tables intended for parties, lawyers, members of the Prosecutor's Office and judge on the same physical plane, in all hearing rooms of all courts in the State."

[112] The ADIn followed an internal study, within the Federal Council of the Brazilian Bar Association, which can be seen from Protocol No. 02038/2011. In the ADIn, under the rapporteurship of Justice Carmen Lúcia, the National Association of Members of the Prosecutor's Office (CONAMP) was admitted as *amicus curiae*, and the Brazilian Institute of Criminal Sciences (IBCCRIM) applied for admission as *amicus*. The application for admission and, separately, the arguments used by IBCCRIM as memorials are available at: <www.ibccrim.org.br>. In the aforementioned judgment, the majority of the members of the Supreme Court understood that the prerogative of representatives of the Prosecutor's Office to sit to the right of the judges does not offend the equality of arms in what is linked to the scenic conception of the courtrooms. The Ministers Gilmar Mendes and Ricardo Lewandowski were defeated, and particularly with a focus on the aspect of violation of the equality of arms, and to a different extent, Minister Rosa Weber, who circumscribed the need for equalization of position between the representative of the Prosecutor's Office and technical defense exclusively in trials by the Jury Court (j. 24.11.2022).

[113] As in ADIn 4.768, the Brazilian Institute of Criminal Sciences (IBCCRIM) applied for admission to the case as *amicus curiae*. The memorial of the *amicus*, as well as the application for admission, can be consulted directly on the website of the Brazilian Institute of Criminal Sciences (www.ibccrim.org.br). The aforementioned case was extinguished without merit judgment not only because, in the view of the eminent Rapporteur, the petition did not cover all the legal matters in question, but also because it resembled the one referred to here (ADI 4768), which had already dealt with the subject (J. 18.10.2023)

same plane and immediately to the right of the single judges or presidents of the judicial bodies before which they officiate"[114]—and Article 41, section XI, of Federal Law No. 8.625/93.[115] Such provisions do not hide the proximity (including symbolic) between the judge and the party.

On this matter, in a judgment of 17 May 1994, the 2nd Chamber of the Supreme Federal Court was able to decide, when confronted with the issue from the wording of Article 18, I, "a," of Complementary Law No. 75/93 in the face of Article 400 of the Military Penal Procedure Code,[116] that the Prosecutor's Office officiating before the Military Justice is a party and, for this very reason, it could not be granted a seat on the platform, on the same bench as the military board.

In that precedent, it was argued, among other premises, that one according to which equal treatment of the parties is inherent to due legal process. Hence, it is "undeniable that the Prosecutor's Office of the Union with the Military Justice acts as such, given the ownership of the criminal action."

There, the Ministers of the Supreme Federal Court also said that Article 18, I, "a," of Complementary Law No. 75/93 "cannot be potentiated to the point of blending judges and parties," it is not possible to neglect, therefore, that "members of the Prosecutor's Office and lawyers are in a situation of equality."[117]

That aforementioned appeal in a writ of mandamus was equipped, including an opinion from Professor Ada Pellegrini Grinover. The author, although she remained faithful to the understanding that they would be synonymous, the *equality of arms* and the *par condicio*, resumed theoretical considerations about the role of the parties in the criminal process and about the very importance of complying with the equality of arms at the criminal hearing.

From the first perspective, she asserted it is necessary that "the parties represent opposing interests in relation to the definition and qualification of the fact to be declared. The partiality of the parties is essential to the judicial function at the time

[114] Provides for the organization, duties, and statute of the Federal Prosecutor's Office.

[115] Organic Law of the Prosecutor's Office, Article 41: "The prerogatives of the members of the Prosecutor's Office, in the exercise of their function, in addition to others provided for in the Organic Law: [...] XI - to take a seat to the right of the Judges of first instance or of the President of the Court, Chamber or Panel."The prerogative of sitting to the right of the judge in courtrooms does not hide a valuation in the choice of place. In countries with a Catholic majority, as is the case in Brazil, the prayer of the *Creed* is known, according to which Jesus Christ "is seated at the right hand of God the Father Almighty."

[116] Decree-Law No. 1.002/69, Article 400: "Having to his right the auditor, to his left the officer of higher rank or older and, in the other places, alternately, the other judges, according to their ranks or seniority, with the clerk at a table near the auditor and the prosecutor at a table reserved for him - the president, at the first meeting of the Justice Council, will make in loud voice, standing, uncovered, the following commitment: 'I promise to appreciate with impartial attention the facts that are submitted to me and to judge them according to the law and the evidence of the case'. This commitment will also be made by the other judges, under the formula: 'So I promise'."

[117] RMS 21.884, 2nd T., under the rapporteurship of Justice Marco Aurélio, published on 25th November 1994.

of analysis, as well as at the time of synthesis the impartiality of the judge is necessary." [118]

Still from this perspective, Ada Pellegrini Grinover said:

> action and defence do not exhaust, evidently, in the power of impulse and in the use of exceptions, but unfold in that set of guarantees that, in the arc of the whole procedure, ensure to the parties the possibility bilateral, effective and concrete, to produce their evidence, to put forward their reasons, to appeal from decisions, to act, finally, using all the wide range of powers and faculties by which one can dialectically prepare the spirit of the judge. The parallelism between action and defence is what ensures to the two subjects of the instituted contradictory before the judge the concrete possibility of, on equal terms, perform the procedural acts capable of asserting their rights in court in interests. On equal terms, as it was said.[119]

On the second perspective, that of equality of arms, the author understood

> by *par condicio* or equality of arms, the principle of balance of situations, not equal but reciprocal, as they are, in criminal process, those of the offices of accusation and defence. And, as I wrote, the balance of situations is what guarantees the true dialectical opposition of the parties. Here is the contradictory identify itself with the *par condicio,* and not with the formal equality, leaving, it also, the static plane to insert itself in the dynamic. [120]

The opinion, besides disapproving the "corporate posture that wants to claim for the legal operators of a certain category a position of privilege in relation to the other," and criticizing the then perceived "corporate vanities,"[121] Ada Grinover predicted something that is now on the agenda.

It is that the author, still in 1993, imagined the following situation: "And tomorrow the Complementary Law of the Public Defender's Office may prescribe the same prerogative, in benefit of the members of the career." [122] Said and done.

Complementary Law No. 80/94, with the amendment of Complementary Law No. 132/2009, which organizes the Federal Public Defender's Office, provides, in its Article 4, § 7, that the "members of the Public Defender's Office is guaranteed to sit on the same level as the Public Prosecutor's Office."[123]

The discussion about the architectural configuration of the courtrooms[124] only reflects the essence of the issue, that is, it is the appearance of the root of the

---

[118] (1998), p. 313.

[119] (1998), p. 314.

[120] (1998), p. 315.

[121] (1998), pp. 317–318.

[122] (1998), p. 317.

[123] The old Statute of the Brazilian Bar Association (Law No. 4.215/63) had as a provision of one of the rights of the lawyer to "take a seat to the right of the Judges of first instance, speak sitting or standing, in courts and Tribunals, and request by order of Seniority" (Art. 89, XIII).

[124] That is, the well-known analysis of the architectural distribution in three models: (a) the current model, in which the Prosecutor's Office is located next to the magistrate, on a higher level than the other chairs in the courtroom; (b) The "T" model, in which the magistrate occupies the top of the "T," along with the secretary/clerk of the courtroom, at the same level as the other chairs in the room, while the Prosecutor's Office and the defense sit face to face; (c) the "U" model, in which the magistrate occupies the central part of the "U," along with the secretary/clerk of the courtroom,

problem. The crux of the matter is the congruence between the spatial arrangement and the equal treatment that should be given to the parties. Hence, it is understood to be convenient the spatial division of the courtrooms in a way that respects—even symbolically—the equality of treatment that the accuser and the accused, along with their defender, deserve.

In cases where proximity between the Public Prosecutor's Office and the judge is foreseen (either on the same platform, or at a different height, but with the prerogative of *sitting to the right* of the judge), the spatial division still prevalent in Brazil today offends the equality of arms.

Such division means the potential for the accuser to be seen, by the defendant and his defender, as closer to the judge than they are, and for, externally, the holder of the criminal action to be confused with the judge or with some of his assistants, even an assistant of the impartial body.

None of these situations should be favored, because, under any perspective, the physical proximity between accuser and judge is indicative that the accusatory arguments may be better received than those of the lawyer and the accused.

Furthermore, the spatial distribution in courtrooms currently predominant in the Brazilian criminal process violates the equality of arms because it enhances the disadvantage of the accused before the accuser in circumstances in which the orality of the arguments requires that both be given exactly the same treatment.

6.4 Equality of Arms in Appeal Situations and Challenge Actions

In appeal situations and in autonomous challenge actions, the incidence of the principle of equality of arms presents itself as a topic of debates as important as they are underdeveloped in academia and in courts.

Regarding the first group (appeals), it is worth noting the logical consequence that should be respected in the treatment given to the accusing body. After all, an appeal is a "mere prolongation of the already existing procedural relationship," that is, it does not constitute a "new procedural relationship." [125]

---

the defendant or witness sits facing the magistrate, on the inside of the "U," while the Prosecutor's Office and defense line up face to face on the two external faces, in opposition and equality (as discriminated by Councillor Marcelo Nobre, of the CNJ, in Consultation 0000422 – 19.2011.2.00.0000). In the criminal justice courtrooms of the state capital of São Paulo, for example, the partition of the rooms in the "T" model prevails, which seems to be reasonable.

[125] Grinover et al. (2009a), p. 27; Badaró (2024), p. 594; Nicolitt (2012), p. 548. Although the authors deal with *procedural relationships*, the lesson of the continuity of the legal situation (and not procedural relationships) is taken advantage of. About this, Aury Lopes Júnior deals with an *appellate procedural situation* (2025), pp. 1177–1179.

As for autonomous challenge actions, which in turn give life "to a different procedural legal relationship,"[126] the contours of the incidence of equality of arms, although not systematically resulting from the already established procedural situation, are no less important.

Before dealing with examples that antagonize the interests of the accused and the accuser in the criminal process in appeal situations and in challenge actions, it is necessary to address an aspect that permeates the systematics of appeals: the inequality of arms on the static plane. This is perceived by reflecting on the so-called appeal *ex officio* (Arts. 574 and 746, CPP). [127]

If from the perspective of appeal theory one can argue about the origin of the necessary appeal[128] and even about its reception in the Brazilian criminal procedural scenario post 1988, as it is an extension of the right of action,[129] the fact is that, being it still existing in Brazilian criminal procedural law, the prevailing understanding is that it would be a mere *condition of effectiveness of the decision.*

In any case, within the narrow limits of this work, it is established the understanding that the provision of such necessary appeals—or, if preferred, *conditions of effectiveness of decisions*—offends the equality of arms. This is because, without

[126] Grinover et al. (2009a), p. 27; Badaró (2024), p. 594; Nicolitt (2012), p. 548. In the words of Ada Pellegrini Grinover et al. (2009b), p. 344, the complaint is "a simple procedure of a disciplinary and corrective nature, whose objective is to safeguard the competence or the authority of the decisions of the courts." It is neither an action (it does not inaugurate a new procedural situation), nor an appeal (it is not a continuity of the pre-existing one), but an exercise of the right to petition. Even so, the bifrontism criticized here is noted, because from the provision of Articles 13 and 16 of Law No. 8.038/90 (which regulates the institute of the complaint in the STF and in the STJ), it is foreseen that the Prosecutor's Office acts, alternatively, now as a possible legitimated, now—if it has not subscribed to the complaint—as *custos legis*. This text does not agree with the duplicity of action of the same body. Particularly with regard to the complaint, it also does not agree with the assignment of *custos legis* to the Prosecutor's Office, because, not having the nature of action or appeal, but rather of mere "special guarantee" (p. 337) to enforce a judicial decision already given, it does not even apply, in the procedure instituted by it, contradictory (pp. 337 and 344). The intervention of the Prosecutor's Office in this regard, not resulting from manifestation as a party, is not even necessary.

[127] In the first case, there is a necessary appeal or appeal *ex officio* "I - of the sentence that grants habeas corpus; II - of the one that immediately acquits the defendant on the basis of the existence of circumstance that excludes the crime or exempts the defendant from punishment, under the terms of art. 411"; in the second, "of the decision that grants rehabilitation."

[128] Ada Pellegrini Grinover et al. (2009a), p. 303, see the justification for the necessary appeal of Article 574, I, CPP, in the exposition of reasons for the Code (item XV). According to the authors, such a condition of effectiveness would exist at the time to prevent any grants of *habeas corpus* from remaining without subsequent control. However, they recognize that, "given the necessary notification of the sentence to the MP, the provision lost its meaning." Tourinho Filho (2012), pp. 424–425, reports different reasoning for the necessary appeals in the Brazilian criminal process. According to him, "the idea came with the Portuguese law."

[129] For André Nicolitt (2012), p. 551, the thesis of the condition of effectiveness of the decision is a "fallacious way of saying the same thing in another way, however, without being able to hide the fact that the second degree body ends up providing jurisdiction without having been provoked by the parties." The thesis, according to him, is even a *sophism*, and such an ex officio appeal is unconstitutional.

there being concretely the opposition between accused and accuser (hence the plane of analysis being here eminently static), a clear position of disadvantage of the accused before the accuser is established.

After all, every and any situation of appeals *ex officio* in the Brazilian criminal process results from a judicial decision that has favored the accused; that is, such a condition of effectiveness of the decision is only imagined from a confirmation by a higher body. Such an obstacle to the effectiveness of the decision favorable to the accused, evidently, makes your situation in any and all cases (even if the accuser does not take any action) disadvantageous to whoever accused you.

From the point of view of the focus on equality of arms, therefore, there is no way to disguise that the provision of ex officio resources in the Brazilian criminal procedural scenario sponsors inequality between the parties without constitutional justification.

Continuing, here we consider the aspect of obedience to the equality of arms in oral and written manifestations of the defense and the prosecution. For both cases, it is worth the *presentation of the case*, as already discussed previously before the Court.

The situations of incidence of the equality of arms here in question are as follows: opinions and oral arguments, with particular approaches about the *habeas corpus* and the criminal review.[130]

6.4.1 *Public Prosecutor's Opinion*

As there is no legal or regimental provision for a written opinion by the accused in the criminal process (even because, when the accused manifests, he does so in defense of his own interests), when starting the treatment of the incidence of the principle of equality of arms in the appeal scope, the starting point (and also the arrival, given the majority incidence of public criminal actions) is to take care of the performance of the Public Prosecutor's Office.

Not only for what has already been said (non-existence of the accused's opinion), but also because of the essentiality of the institution that is the Public Prosecutor's Office (Art. 127, CF), whenever its intervention in appeals or in actions of challenge as an opinion, it is assumed that the manifestation results from acting as the *law's overseer*.

[130] In this text, references to the writ of mandamus (governed by Federal Law No. 12.016/2009) as an action of challenge will be made strictly necessary and at points where it deserves consideration separate from those made for the *habeas corpus*.

6.4.1.1 Opinion in Appeals Resulting from Public Criminal Action

In appeal situations, where there is an extension of the legal situation debated at a lower level, the performance of the Public Prosecutor's Office must strictly obey the opposition between the accused and accuser, as set in the motivating demand of the appeal. Thus, if the criminal action motivating the appeal is of private initiative of the offended, the ministerial manifestation should be, indeed, as *custos legis*, because in this same situation, the representative of the body acted at the lower jurisdictional level.

This, however, does not happen if the criminal action that gave rise to the appeal situation is public, whether it was exercised by its holder (Public Prosecutor's Office), or by its eventual successor (the offended), because the performance of the individual does not denature the legitimacy of the official accusatory body to, even, resume the criminal cause.

In the case of public criminal action, the performance of the Public Prosecutor's Office results from the activity of the party. Hence, it is unsustainable the argument that the performance of the representative of the body—which is one and indivisible—is that of a party until the appealed sentence, and then, due to the new procedural stage, it becomes impartial, that is, supported exclusively in the performance of the role of *custos legis*.

In addition to what has already been said in a previous chapter, now the argument is reinforced: there is no sense in favoring the understanding of this change of behavior of the body depending on the procedural phase, taking it in the appeal phase as an *impartial party*. In this sense, Aury Lopes Júnior's lesson is collected according to which "impartial party is a two-headed monster."[131]

For the very reason of the existence of the monopoly of the accusation constitutionally imposed (Art. 129, I, CF), the understanding that the Public Prosecutor's Office can vary its way of acting in the process due to its phases, notably if it has exercised the ownership of the exercise of the criminal action.[132] As Aury Lopes Júnior says,

> in the criminal process, the MP is not and has never been an impartial party, even because if it is a party, it would never be impartial. Impartiality is an attribute of the judge, because he is not a party.[133]

It is also not possible, in the words of the same author, to agree with what was named a "hybrid and malformed position of 'opinion giver' in appeal situation."

Admitting a change of procedural costume depending on the phases (at one moment it is a party; at another it is *custos legis*) is equivalent metaphorically to seeing in the representative of the Public Prosecutor's Office a procedural chameleon whose shades would change according to the procedural stage.

---

[131] (2025), p. 238.

[132] An opposite understanding is that of Sérgio Demoro Hamilton (2011), pp. 553 and foll.

[133] (2025), p. 238.

According to the understanding endorsed even by a member of the Public Prosecutor's Office of the Union, with which we agree here:

> We really have to see that the Public Prosecutor's Office, in public criminal actions, is always the author (holder) of the action, regardless of the instance in which its bodies act, and this condition (plaintiff) remains absolutely unchanged by the circumstance of intervening in the second instance another member of the institution (Regional Prosecutor, Justice Prosecutor etc.). Moreover, the constitutional function of both representatives is rigorously the same: defence of the legal order, of the democratic regime and of the social and individual interests that are indisputable (CF, art. 127), regardless of the title under which they intervene. After all, the Attorney General of the Republic, the Deputy Attorneys General of the Republic, the Regional Prosecutors and Prosecutors of the Republic are the very Prosecutor's Office, and not distinct institutions.
>
> It goes without saying that, regardless of the distinction between author and guardian, the Prosecutor's Office body will always be able to plead for conviction or acquittal, review its own or others' positions, appeal etc., since those who represent it are not organs of accusation, but organs legitimized to accuse; after all, the figure of the relentless Prosecutor/Promoter who pursues convictions at any cost and who counts acquittals as defeats and convictions as victories has long been overcome.
>
> The most important thing, however, lies in the following: the distinction between author and guardian of the law, despite being traditional and recurrent, is unfounded, because it presupposes duality where there is or should be unity. Indeed, being a permanent institution, essential to the jurisdictional function of the State (CF, art. 127), its constitutional mission, in all processes in which it intervenes, is always the same, regardless of who represents it (Promoter, Prosecutor etc.) and the entity or degree of jurisdiction (court, tribunal, councils etc.) in which it operates. Moreover, being a one/indivisible institution, it does not seem reasonable that it can be represented, autonomously, by more than one member in a single and same process, often to reiterate the same arguments. Indeed, for this very reason, no one proposes that, in the first instance or in original criminal actions, two Promoters/Prosecutors should act, one as the author of the criminal action, the other as guardian of the law. [134]

The disregard for the role of the Prosecutor's Office as a party in recourse situations arising from public criminal actions (whether or not the holder has discharged his exercise) has serious consequences for the equality of arms in the Brazilian criminal process.[135] This is because, in recourse situations in which dialectics must be observed,[136] the representative of the same body will have presented the case for

[134] Queiroz (Jul. 2012), pp. 16–17 (also available at: <http:// pauloqueiroz.net/sobre-a-intervencao-do-ministerio-publico-em-segundo-grau/print/>. Accessed on: 5 Oct. 2012).

[135] It was not without purpose that Aury Lopes Júnior (2012), p. 1201, understood to be a "dangerous imbalance in the procedural appeal situation" the understanding that sees in the role of opinion maker an exemption that does not comply with the role of part. In the same sense and explicitly, although in most of his text he referred to the order of oral arguments in the courts, see: Toron (2003), pp. 91 and foll. On p. 94, the author deals with practical situations: "after and with much frequency, exterminating the equality of arms and the contradictory, comes the ministerial opinion of the second instance, with renewed and substantial arguments in favour of the accusatory thesis, advocating for the provision of the colleague's appeal from the first degree."

[136] Ada Pellegrini Grinover et al. (2009b), p. 36, point out that the dialectic of appeal must impregnate "the entire *iter* procedural," because "it has own aspects when it comes to appeals: the appellant must decline the reasons why he requests the review of the decision, because only in this way the opposing party can present its counter-reasons, forming the indispensable contradictory in

the first time to the adjudicating body *a quo*. Then, a new representative (the person changes, but not the institution), under the title of *opinion*, will offer an understanding still coming from the entity that embodies the non-delegable ownership of the exercise of public criminal action.

There are regimental norms that reflect this violation of the equality of arms. For example, within the Internal Rules of the Supreme Federal Court, the Attorney General's Office has open views, in cases of habeas corpus appeals, for a period of two days (Art. 52, VIII, c.c. 311). In addition, in any case of criminal appeals, it also has open views to act as *custos legis* (Art. 52, XIII) and the deadline for manifestation is fifteen days (Art. 5°, § 1°).[137]

In the Internal Rules of the Superior Court of Justice, the situation is similar, as it provides for the manifestation as *custos legis* of representatives of the Attorney General's Office both in habeas corpus appeals (Art. 64, III), as well as in criminal appeals (Art. 64, X). Thus, a period of twenty days is granted for the collection of opinion in special appeal (Art. 256), of five days in ordinary appeal in writ of mandamus (Art. 248), and of two days in habeas corpus appeal (Art. 245).

In the Federal Regional Court of the 3rd Region, Article 60, IX, grants views to the representative of the Federal Prosecutor's Office in "criminal appeals, recourses and other criminal procedures." And Articles 241 and 242, in the situation of appeal for crimes whose predicted penalty is detention or imprisonment, respectively impose periods of five and ten days for the issuance of an opinion.

All the examples taken from court regulations, in addition to innovating in terms of the possibility of double manifestation of bodies responsible for criminal

---

appeal matter." The authors defend the theoretical point of view, although they pay attention to the wording of Article 601 of the CPP, which allows the appeal to rise and its judgment without reasons. They cite, in this regard, judgments of the STF that proclaim there is no nullity in case of a judgment without defensive reasons or counter-arguments to the accusatory appeal. A more current position of the STJ signals agreement with the authors' point of view: "The argument that the reasons for the appeal constitute a procedural piece that is dispensable is contrary to the understanding of this Court, which considers it essential to present the reasons for the appeal. According to the judgments that I am about to collate, if the reasons are not presented by the lawyer appointed by the defendant, he should be notified to appoint a new patron and, if he indicates or remains inert, a Dative Defender or the Public Defender should be appointed, for the attachment of the reasons for the appeal" (STJ, REsp n° 1.931.154, under the rapporteurship of Felix Fischer, published on 06th May 2021).

[137] It is, moreover, particularly striking the provision of Article 48 of that Regiment, which provides that the "Attorney General of the Republic takes a seat at the table to the right of the President." If about the scenic aspect of the courtroom has already been spoken previously in this work, opportunity in which even the almost mythical aspect that means "sitting on the right" of someone was not neglected, the provision in question is complicated even because it allows the privileged spatial division regardless of the representative of the Attorney General's Office ostentatiously such a position due to the role of part or supposed law enforcement. In a word: already problematic the two-headed consideration of the Prosecutor's Office (part and law enforcement), allowing it to sit on the right, pure and simple, makes the problem even more clear, because one cannot imagine legal validity in a provision that says: "sit on the right and that's it," just because he is Attorney General of the Republic and nothing more.

prosecution—as the Code of Criminal Procedure does not provide for them—unbalance procedural equality in terms of accusatory and defensive manifestations.

Because of this imbalance, they prevent the guarantee, in the best possible measure, of equal efficacy, on both sides, that each argument to be analyzed by the adjudicating body should have. Thus, they establish a disadvantage vis-à-vis the written presentation of the case to the Court, even if part of the accusatory argument comes formally labelled as *opinion.*[138]

In addition to what has been exposed here, Rogério Schietti Machado Cruz warns that "the Prosecutor's Office is given the opportunity to express itself again, through an opinion, and the same chance is not given to the defence, which engenders a manifest inequality of treatment between the parties, contradicting the axiom that '*the author should not be allowed what is not allowed to the defendant*'."[139]

According to this author:

> Regardless of the nature of the *Parquet's* performance in the appellate instance - party or mere law enforcer - the fact is that a very important procedural piece was attached to the case by the same body that promoted the criminal action, this body being governed by the principles of unity and indivisibility, from which it is irrelevant to claim that the indictment was signed by a prosecutor and the opinion by a justice prosecutor. Both, in reality, speak on behalf of the same institution.[140]

As, in the words of Rogério Schietti Machado Cruz, the Prosecutor's Office will have "produced, in addition to the reasons or counter-reasons, an opinion, its position is of clear superiority - at least numerically - in relation to the defence, since it only presented the piece that initiates the appellate procedure," there is an offense to the notion of equality of arms. This is because it prevents the system from giving the parties the same opportunity to present their cases in situations that do not configure as disadvantageous.

The solution that is considered in such a scenario, either to safeguard the performance of the Prosecutor's Office in a public criminal action as the accusing party that it is, or to obey the equality of arms that should manifest itself in the appellate instance, particularly in the documentary aspect of the matter (that is, in parity written manifestations), is to suppress the regimental provision of the representative of the Prosecutor's Office's opinion in every and any appellate situation, except for the special situations of criminal action exclusive to the offended party.

---

[138] Example of this imbalance can be seen, hypothetically, in a second-degree judgement in which the representative of the Prosecutor's Office (state or federal), in a single piece, presents the counter-arguments to the appeal of several co-defendants and the opinion on the appeals filed by the defenses and by the Federal Prosecutor's Office itself. The apex of the imbalance (although ironically there one can even see the body really behaving as it is imagined to be correct: part in the procedural situation, even though along with the counter-arguments there is formally the presentation of another piece) can be seen in manifestations that, thus, present in a single piece the counter-arguments of defensive resources and opinion of the Prosecutor's Office.

[139] Cruz (2002), p. 121.

[140] Cruz (2002), pp. 121–122.

Such a suggestion is not new, as José Frederico Marques already had the understanding that such performance of the Prosecutor's Office's body as law enforcer in appellate situations "seems somewhat bizarre." In the words of the author:

> The Prosecutor's Office is constituted, primarily, as an organ of criminal action and the punitive claim of the State. So much so that the prosecutor can make oral arguments before the appellate panel and there debate the case, *ex vi* of art. 610, single paragraph, of the Code of Criminal Procedure. And it is clear that he can intervene or take part in the oral debate, as an organ of the accusation. Moreover, it does not fit well with the contradictory structure of the national criminal process, and with the guarantees of the defendant's defence, that an organ invested with clearly persecutory functions speaks last.[141]

Paulo Queiroz advocates for the same modification of positive law:

> it seems unsustainable the intervention of the Prosecutor's Office in the second degree in criminal actions only as 'custos legis', a position that often offends the contradictory and the breadth of the defence. In the future the performance of the MP as an opinion maker should be abolished, if it was indeed received by the Constitution.[142]

As already indicated in Chap. 3, the only hypothesis in which, at least in light of the equality of arms, it would make sense to honor the opening of views for the Prosecutor's Office's body to manifest itself as *custos legis* would be, exclusively, that of a criminal action of private initiative of the offended party. In no other intervention can one sustain the change of role, which would depend solely and exclusively on the procedural phase of the criminal matter, confusing the role of party in public criminal action with that of law enforcer.

6.4.1.2 Opinion in Challenge Actions

In challenge actions, of which the most frequent examples in criminal procedure are the criminal review and the *habeas corpus*,[143] even though the reasoning is similar to what has been seen so far, some nuances need to be clarified.

The first one is that, unlike what happens with appeals, autonomous challenge actions are not equivalent to mere extensions of the procedural situation already in progress in the lower court. There is no adherence to the maintenance of the party situation in the lower jurisdictional degree.

But this does not mean that the Prosecutor's Office's opinion should be unconditionally honored. In this respect, a separation between the criminal review and the *habeas corpus* is necessary, notably because these are two very singular actions. In each of them, the configuration of the Prosecutor's Office's manifestation requires particular care.

---

[141] Marques (2000), pp. 254–255.

[142] (2012), p. 2.

[143] There are very few nuances in the security mandate, which is why, as already warned in this text, most of the warnings made about the *habeas corpus* will also be directed to that constitutional remedy.

6.4.1.2.1 Opinion of the Public Prosecutor in Criminal Review

In the case of a criminal review resulting from a public action, the Public Prosecutor's Office was involved throughout the entire procedural arc until the judgment was finalized.

And if the revision request exists, it logically results from the success of the criminal action brought at a lower level by the representative of the Public Prosecutor's Office, who, at the end of the process, requested the conviction of the accused.[144]

The peculiarity of the incidence of the principle of equality of arms in criminal review, especially in the manifestation of the Public Prosecutor's Office, is, once again, to justify its intervention in this specific action. Will it be as a *party*? Will it be as a *custos legis*?

As can be seen, the functional delimitation of the performance of the subjects in the criminal process surrounds the various manifestations that each of them can display in the criminal prosecution, specifically the manifestation of the accusatory body.

Here, it is possible to separate two perspectives: one in which the manifestation of the Public Prosecutor's Office may offend the equality of arms, as well as being useless; and another in which the manifestation of the Public Prosecutor's Office in criminal review will serve other purposes, typical of contestation in the action.

In the first perspective, the Public Prosecutor's Office would act as a guardian of the law; in the second, as a party.

Thus, from the first of the two perspectives, there is no sense in imagining that the superior representative of the same body should give an opinion in the revision action. If it is considered that the body does not act as a party in the revision action (and hence the revision action is taken as a single-party process[145]), in the situation

---

[144] The exception to this logic is dictated by Article 385 of the Criminal Procedure Code, already treated in this work. According to that device, it would be possible for a final judgment to be passed even if the Prosecutor's Office had, at the end of the process, postulated acquittal. Returning to the general rule with which we are working here, this is the argument of Aury Lopes Júnior (2025), p. 1341, to deny the Prosecutor's Office the possibility of appearing as the proponent of the revisional action. In the wake of the coherence that should guide the positions of the Prosecutor's Office, we adhere to the following words of the author: "We do not see how an artificially created part to be the natural contradictor of the passive subject (always remember the absurdity of speaking of *impartial-part* in criminal proceedings) have legitimacy for the action of criminal review, in favour of the defendant, to deconstruct a sentence criminal conviction that only occurred because there was an accusation (carried out by the same Prosecutor's Office, one and indivisible)." Anyway, there is considerable doctrinal opinion in the sense that the Prosecutor's Office does, indeed, have active legitimacy *ad causam* in criminal review. In this regard, see: Tourinho Filho (2012), pp. 716–718; Greco Filho (2009), p. 430.

[145] It was precisely the theoretical strangeness of a single-party criminal action that made Sérgio de Oliveira Médici (2000), p. 263, not take the criminal review as an action, but as a constitutional guarantee "whose foundation consists in the defence of the convicted in the face of a sentence characterized by judicial error." For the author, there would be the following perplexities in the case of taking the review as action: "even if the convicted is considered the *author*, who will be the

of the revision action aiming to rescind a sentence resulting from a public criminal action, a decision favorable to the revisionist necessarily disqualifies the exercise of the public accusation that has become final.

From this perspective, the performance of the representative of the Public Prosecutor's Office in criminal review tends to oppose the defensive request. There is no way to see the performance of the body, therefore, as a guardian of the law.

Due to this reason, the ministerial performance through an opinion in criminal review diminishes the effectiveness of the defensive argument to be taken to the judging tribunal and operates, in truth, as a counterpoint to the argument of the revisionist.

Such performance can be seen as analogous to that which occurs in criminal instruction with a view to the issuance of a sentence. Thus, even if eventually the ministerial manifestation comes to, at the end (and in criminal review this happens in a single moment, *ex vi* of Art. 625, of the Code of Criminal Procedure), agree with the terms of the request of the revisionist, not even for this reason its activity (just like in ordinary criminal instruction) ceased to be interested.

Still, regarding the point of view that does not consider the performance of the Public Prosecutor's Office as that of a party opposed to the revisionist, it is noted that there is an imbalance in the procedural situation. Given the finding that the request challenges the terms of the criminal action that ruled in favor of the condemnatory request of the Public Prosecutor's Office,[146] the performance of this same body does not appear to be impartial.

More directly, even than the ministerial performance in opinion offending the equality of arms, such a manifestation is a piece without utility, since the Judiciary does not need an auxiliary body to appreciate the facts exposed in the criminal review. The Public Prosecutor's Office, even for those who understand that in criminal review it is not a party, can also not be legally considered *amicus curiae*, even because such a procedural figure, only recently widespread in Brazil, does not

---

opposite party (the *required* or the *defendant* of the *revisional action*)? It will be said that it is the state. In this case, who represents it? The State Attorney General and the Union Attorney General are not cited for the defense of the public entity. The Prosecutor's Office, called to opine in the criminal review, does not represent the state or the union. It manifests freely, for or against the request, not intervening in the review as *opposite party* to the convicted" (p. 248). In his criticism of the conception of criminal review as action, Médici remembers an article by Sérgio Pitombo, according to whom, in the criminal review, "it is enough to remember that in the criminal review there is no passive party. It is not seen the *actio trium personarum*" (pp. 251–252). The article by Sérgio Pitombo is *Constituição da República e processo penal* (1996), pp. 133–139.

[146] There is no possibility in the Brazilian criminal procedural system for the victim to also appear on the passive side of the criminal review. As Maria Elizabeth Queijo (1998), p. 186, points out: "There is no provision for the victim's intervention in the criminal review. The assistant to the prosecution, in our system, is only allowed to qualify until the judgment becomes final." Therefore, in a private criminal action initiated by the victim, it cannot be affirmed, once again, that the performance of the Prosecutor's Office is that typical of the party in a criminal process. In this case—and only here—is where the Prosecutor's Office will officiate as *custos legis*. In this exceptional situation, it is necessary to recognize that the process of the criminal review, because of this, resembles the so-called process *of a single party*.

resemble either the parity performance in the process, or the constitutional conformation of the Public Prosecutor's Office.[147]

Such digressions do not directly result from behaviors of the Public Prosecutor's Office in practice, but are confined to the abstract observation of the current Brazilian criminal process. That is, they are not because the body of the Public Prosecutor's Office can privilege the accusatory thesis, but occur because the opinion is unnecessary for the judgment by the judging body.

Hence why it is tainted—if it is to honor the point of view that denies the performance of the Public Prosecutor's Office in criminal review as a party, that is, if it is to give interpretation to such an article as if it did not encompass an authentic contestation—as unconstitutional the provision of Article 625, § 5°, of the current Code of Criminal Procedure, which determines the necessary opening of views to the prosecutor for the collection of an opinion within ten days.

The Public Prosecutor's Office, in a revision action, besides not *needing* (that is, participation is not even necessary) to give an opinion for the better judgment to be given by the Judiciary, does not *have to* (that is, participation has no constitutional justification) manifest with the aura of impartiality.[148] If it does so, it will offend the equality of arms.

If it was previously stated to be absurd to talk about an *impartial party*, here it can be said that the impartiality of the body does not coincide with the opinion that goes against the position taken by a member of the same accusatory body.

And, to escape from the inconsistency noted in the general rule, the representative of the body, even if merely as an advisor, tends to weaken the presentation of the case by the revising party. Thus, the equality of arms is offended.

Let it be reiterated that the practical situation is known, occurring in a few cases, of total or partial agreement by the Public Prosecutor's Office with the revision request.

It will be said that, in this case, there is no counterpoint to the defensive claim, nor reinforcing the ministerial thesis sustained since the beginning of the prosecution. It happens that even this manifestation is of interest, as is always the case when the representative of the body alone, but at a different level of jurisdiction, deals with the criminal action that has become final after the prosecution's request has been granted.

From a second perspective, the Public Prosecutor's Office's action in criminal review can be considered as that of an authentic contradictor to the request made by the revising party. In this case, there is no violation of the equality of arms because

[147] The teaching of Sérgio de Oliveira Médici (2000), p. 249, is respectable, according to whom the prosecutor "does not advocate, does not represent the party, does not seek triumph. He speaks for the enforcement of the law, when opining in criminal review." The question is, in our opinion, the usefulness of this opinion itself, if it is taken as an opinion, and not an interested manifestation.

[148] Except in the exceptional situation of a criminal review triggered in the face of a criminal process that has become final moved by the victim, in a private criminal action initiated by the individual. Only in this case will the Prosecutor's Office not have an interested performance in the cause, and then, its performance can be valid as that of a law inspector.

the natural reaction to the defensive request, although labelled as *opinion* (Art. 625, CPP), allows the court to perceive the two facets of the right in question, presented by the revising party.

The equality of arms operates there, as well as the contradictory, given the opposition of interests at stake in the criminal review. And this, then, is taken as an impugnatory action.

Still from this perspective, the Public Prosecutor's Office is the arm that represents the "Administration-State,"[149] protecting its interests on the passive side of criminal reviews.[150]

The criminal review is projected, therefore, to defend the interests of the state that existed in the criminal instruction of criminal actions (if then the better analysis of the facts was first protected to, once proven, satisfy the executive protection, now the interests of the state are protected both in relation to the maintenance of the final conviction decision, as well as in relation to the patrimonial effects inherent to any success in the revision request).[151]

For the Public Prosecutor's Office's manifestation in criminal review to be admitted without offending the equality of arms, it is necessary—even if this means a different interpretation of the wording of the Code of Criminal Procedure (there it states that the Public Prosecutor's Office gives *opinion*)—to consider it as a party and not as a guardian of the law. The only way out of this understanding is, once again, the clear situation of the criminal action brought exclusively by the plaintiff that has resulted in a final conviction.

Only in this way, including the consideration of the criminal review as an action, has reason to be in the light of the dialectical opposition of the revising party's request. And only in this way can the usefulness of the Public Prosecutor's Office's manifestation be seen.

6.4.1.2.2 Opinion of the Public Prosecutor's Office in *Habeas Corpus*

Except in the exceptional situation of a criminal review triggered in the face of a criminal process that has become final moved by the victim, in a private criminal action initiated by the individual. Only in this case will the Prosecutor's Office not have an interested performance in the cause, and then, its performance can be valid as that of a law inspector.

In the case of *habeas corpus*, the hypothesis becomes more interesting—as it is common for the procedural situation motivating the action to be ongoing—and also

[149] Grinover et al. (2009a), pp. 243 and 257. In the same sense, see: Rangel (2012), p. 1065.

[150] Queijo (1998), p. 186.

[151] Badaró (2024), p. 695. The author explains that, in the criminal review, the opinion "has the nature of a true contestation" and that, in the case of cumulation of requests (proceedings of the revision and compensation for judicial error), the Prosecutor's Office acts as a procedural substitute for the Public Treasury. André Nicolitt reminds that the so-called opinion of the criminal review "has a true nature of response to the request for review" (2012), p. 587.

more difficult—as the position taken that the *writ* is an autonomous action and not a resource has other consequences.

In addition to the two technical peculiarities (ongoing cause and systematic placement of the role of the Public Prosecutor's Office in *habeas corpus*), a third one of a formal nature arises, with Decree No. 552/69. The question is, then, more complex than that verified in criminal review.

From the first aspect to be dealt with (the finding that the *habeas corpus* deals with challenging some point noted in ongoing criminal prosecution), once again, with a focus on public initiative criminal action, the ministerial action as an opinion offends the equality of arms between prosecution and defense.

With this, it is affirmed, as already done on other occasions, that the action of the Public Prosecutor's Office as *custos legis* will have its reason to be, without offending the equality of arms, in the specific case of criminal action of private initiative of the offended. Examples of this: if the patient impugns the criminal action for lack of just cause (Art. 648, I, CPP), it is because he understands that the accusatory initial should not have been received;[152] if he impugns the authority as incompetent (Art. 648, II, CPP), it is because the motivating question will have been addressed to the magistrate by the Public Prosecutor's Office; if he argues for the cessation of the originating reason for coercion (Art. 648, III, CPP), it is because the Public Prosecutor's Office will have requested the measure.[153]

If the situation is of inadmissibility of bail when the law authorizes (Art. 648, V, CPP) and in being the situation of bail as counter-caution, the Public Prosecutor's Office becomes aware of the terms of the arrest within 24 hours to give an opinion on it (Art. 306, CPP); and, in the case of alternative autonomous precautionary measure, bail does not even depend on its consent (Art. 333, CPP).

The situation of procedural nullity (Art. 648, VI) touches directly on the Public Prosecutor's Office, given that it is responsible for the exercise of criminal action that is presented before the court; and when the punishment is extinguished (Art. 648, VI),[154] if the judge has not recognized it ex officio, he will necessarily have heard the Public Prosecutor's Office at the lower level (Art. 61, single paragraph, CPP).

Thus, in *habeas corpus*, the Public Prosecutor's Office, as a rule, has already expressed an opinion on the issues that, if not resolved at the lower level, require

[152] Except for the possibility of the request for *habeas corpus* being for the recognition of the lack of just cause for the investigation itself. In this situation, it is possible that the Prosecutor's Office has not even opined yet.

[153] In the case of precautionary arrest, for example, if the judge can decree a preventive arrest ex officio during the criminal action, during the investigation phase, this depends on an express request, among others, from the Prosecutor's Office (Art. 311, CPP). Hence, either the Prosecutor's Office will have *agreed* with the coercion, or will have requested it, or, in the last case, will have already risen against it, with which its role as an opinion maker in a higher degree will be even more unnecessary, since the patient will have already used the arguments of the prosecutor who officiated in the lower degree to instruct his request and present his arguments.

[154] Obviously, this is the general rule in which the criminal prosecution moves for public initiative criminal actions.

analysis at a higher level. More than that, these are situations that often taint the procedures adopted even by the various representatives of the Public Prosecutor's Office, which is why it is difficult to sustain the argument that, at a higher level—and only for this reason—the performance of the same body is disinterested, that is, impartial.

And if in a criminal review the action has already become final, in *habeas corpus*, even if it is not said to exist, the prolongation of the criminal action, there is an approximation with the appeal situations. After all, it is not uncommon for the issues brought in the constitutional remedy to aim to modify, in favor of the patient, situations still *sub judice* that can be the subject of preliminary appeals.[155]

Hence, even if the hypothesis is not of an appeal per se, the performance of the Public Prosecutor's Office in the opinion in *habeas corpus* resembles that of a typical appeal, as there is an interest of the body in upholding the criminal action and its terms.

This means, in the courts, allowing the prosecution to enjoy greater opportunities to argue in favor of its theses than the defense, which, even having initiated a new demand (the *habeas corpus* is an autonomous action), takes the initiative as a result of the course of criminal prosecution, which believes that its terms should be rediscussed by another judicial body.

From this perspective, just as in criminal review, also in *habeas corpus,* the distinction between impugnatory action and appeal is not sufficient to assess compliance or non-compliance with the principle of equality of arms. This is because in autonomous impugnatory actions, there is a tendency for the Public Prosecutor's Office to act as a party or, at least, as an antagonist to defensive interests, which indicates an offense to the principle of equality of arms.

Such finding makes the situation of autonomous actions even more offensive to the equality of arms insofar as, precisely because such manifestations are not formally partial—that is, they do not have formal adherence to the position that the Public Prosecutor's Office followed at a lower level in the criminal action motivating the action—having an aura of impartiality, the accusatory arguments gain efficacy in the courts to the detriment of the defensive ones.

In response to this warning, Rubens Casara believes it is "inadmissible that the Public Prosecutor's Office, at the second level of jurisdiction, expresses itself, before the collegiate judgment, in cases in which the prosecutor or Federal Prosecutor in exercise at the first level of jurisdiction has already expressed himself."[156]

---

[155] Gustavo Badaró (2009), p. 233, sees the "enormous similarity" of the *habeas corpus* with appeals in situations where the *writ* is used not for the immediate protection of freedom, but in a preventive function, "to avert an imminent threat to freedom of movement."

[156] (2011), p. 754. Even more: "As they believe in an 'impartial party', the magistrates begin to identify with the Prosecutor's Office (the State counts the crime and the criminal) and reserve for the accused (the other/the other party) a natural distancing" (pp. 745–746).

The problem, then, is similar to what has already been seen in criminal review: one imagines the specific action in which the Public Prosecutor's Office is not a natural opponent of the petitioner.

It is emphasized in this text that, even if under a formal guise, the Public Prosecutor's Office does not appear as a *party* in *habeas corpus*, its manifestation tends to serve as a counterpoint to the interests represented by the petitioner. It will not be so in the case of acting as a guardian of the law in cases of *habeas corpus* that arise from an issue arising in a criminal action of private initiative of the offended.

Dealing with the assumption of the role of the *party* in *habeas corpus* leads to the second question, which unfolds with the following question: after all, in *habeas corpus*, who is the legitimate passive *ad causam*? If it is not admitted that the criminal process of the action of *habeas corpus* is the so-called *single-party criminal process*, then who is the antagonist of the petitioner? At this point, Chiovenda's premise, discussed in Chap. 3 of this work, is repeated.

The *party* is the one who asks for legal protection or against whom some protection is requested. And, bringing the then deepened lesson to the scope of *habeas corpus*, in the current wording of the Code (Art. 654, § 1°, "a," CPP), the passive legitimation *ad causam* will fall on the representative (assuming that the illegal coercion was practiced by a public agent) of the body that determined the segregation of freedom of someone.

In the words of Ada Pellegrini Grinover, Antonio Scarance Fernandes, and Antonio Magalhães Gomes Filho, "the passive party in the action of *habeas corpus* is the *coercer*, that is, the person responsible for the act of restriction or threat to the right of freedom of movement, whose illegality is pointed out by the petitioner."[157]

Far from ending controversies, the doctrinal lesson raises at least two new controversies. The first of them begins in the complementation of the own authors, according to whom "since the coercer is an organ or public authority, it is undeniable that there will be a joint lawsuit between this and the state, represented in the action of *habeas corpus* by the Public Prosecutor's Office."[158]

It is not defended here the idea that the Public Prosecutor's Office can act as a joint defendant of the so-called passive party in *habeas corpus*.[159] Systematically, it

[157] (2009), p. 280. In the same sense, in the most recent Brazilian doctrine, see: Nicolitt (2012), p. 590; Badaró (2024), p. 681; Greco Filho (2009), p. 423. Besides the authors cited, no great doctrinal attention was paid to the theme of the *passive* legitimacy of the action of *habeas corpus*. Except for José Frederico Marques (2000), p. 479, the other authors did not even position themselves in relation to this theme. This is the case, for example, of Pontes de Miranda (1962), pp. 500–501, who, when dealing with passive legitimacy in *habeas corpus*, did not specify *what* makes the authority a passive part of the *writ*; of J. M. Othon Sidou (1989), who did not deepen the passive side of the *legitimatio ad causam*. Inocêncio Borges da Rosa (1942) also did not deal with passive legitimation in *habeas corpus*, and the same omission was noted in the work of Eduardo Espínola Filho (1965).

[158] Grinover et al. (2009a), p. 280.

[159] Although all the most recent authors cite the well-known work of Grinover, Scarance, and Magalhães, none of them followed them in their texts to say that the Prosecutor's Office, in *habeas corpus*, can behave as a passive litisconsort. It is not understood what would be the justification to

does not justify the joint lawsuit if the Public Prosecutor's Office officiates at a hierarchical level higher than that in which the coercing authority officiates. In addition, the Public Prosecutor's Office does not suffer the effects of the decision to be rendered in *habeas corpus*.[160]

As a rule, the coercive acts come from members of the Judiciary, there is no reason to place the representative of the Public Prosecutor's Office in the passive pole of the action of *habeas corpus* when the passive party of that constitutional action (the responsible for the coercive act) is responsible, in a situation of impartiality, for the conduct of the case in which the constraint arose.

Admitting the proposed joint lawsuit situation would offend the separation procedural between who is impartial (the judge, considered as coercing authority) and who is partial (the Public Prosecutor's Office, party in the criminal action and, now, joint defendant in the situation of *habeas corpus*).

Thus, structurally or functionally, it is difficult to reach the conclusion of the authors in the sense that the Public Prosecutor's Office, in *habeas corpus*, could function as a joint defendant of the pointed coercer. Furthermore, in light of Article 46 of the Code of Civil Procedure, the connection that would animate the interests of the joint defendants (Art. 46, IV, CPC) would be insufficient to justify the

define the Prosecutor's Office (officiating at a hierarchical level higher than that in which the coercive act was pronounced) as a litisconsort of the coercive authority. The Prosecutor's Office does not suffer the effects of the decision to be pronounced in *habeas corpus* and, as in general the coercive acts come from members of the Judiciary, there would be no reason for members of the Prosecutor's Office to be situated in the passive pole of the demand when precisely the main party (from which the coercive act emanates) is responsible, in a situation of impartiality, for the conduct of the proceedings in which the alleged constraint arose. Structurally or functionally, it is difficult to reach the conclusion of the authors that the Prosecutor's Office, in *habeas corpus*, could function as a litisconsort of the pointed coercive entity. In addition, in light of Article 46 of the Civil Procedure Code, the connection that would animate the interests of the litisconsorts—Article 46, IV, CPC—would be insufficient to justify the duplication in the passive pole. This, without dealing with the non-existence, in the criminal process of *habeas corpus*, of "communion of rights or obligations" (Art. 46, I, CPC). Fundamentally there is another disagreement with the authors: the definition of the Public Prosecutor's Office as a litigant of a procedural subject annihilates the logic of the separations of the functions of each procedural subject, as it does not agree to place, on the same plane of passive legitimation, an impartial entity (the judge) and another partial one (the Public Prosecutor's Office).

[160] If the representative of the Public Prosecutor's Office is pointed out as the coercive authority, the judge will not be his litigant. The pointed-out representative of the Public Prosecutor's Office will behave as the passive part of the *habeas corpus*. In this hypothesis, any opinion from the same body at a different jurisdictional level puts the issue on other levels. Once the coercion pointed out as illegal comes from the Public Prosecutor's Office itself, again, its action as an opinion would not be impartial. From the perspective of a procedural party, formally acting as an opinion of the one and indivisible body could indicate as possible the manifestation. Even so, there is no joint litigation (among the representatives of the Public Prosecutor's Office), given that the manifestation is from a single body only with a variation of jurisdictional degree. In this case, the offense to the equality of arms would remain: both the coercive authority and the opinion writer would act guided by the same interest, in a situation of advantage over the patient. In other words, if the coercer is the representative of the Public Prosecutor's Office, acting as a law enforcer is even more unfitting. In this same situation, if the action is taken as a party, it offends the equality of arms.

duplication in the passive pole. And this without mentioning that in the criminal process of *habeas corpus,* there is no "communion of rights or obligations" (Art. 46, I, CPC).

The second controversy lies in the very manifestation of the coercing authority, which occurs as part of the optional *information* that are demanded from it by the body that will come to know of the petition (Arts. 662 and 664, CPP).

This is the phase in which, taking the coercing authority as legitimized *ad causam* passive in the action of *habeas corpus*, there may be some opposition to the interests of the petitioner. The problem of this tenuous judicial manifestation lies in itself (in light of the very knowledge that has been given to the higher degree of the matter *sub examinem*), insofar as the *information* does not mean an exercise of contradiction exercised before the court that will come to judge the *habeas corpus*.

And they could not be, because, as Aury Lopes Júnior reminds,

> the request for information, as the expression evidences, is an objective report and detailed of the state of the process. Obviously, there is no 'contradiction with the judge' (which would be a complete procedural absurdity), nor should the coercing authority make a 'defence' of its act. Judge is not a party, there is no 'contradiction' or possibility of manifestation that exceeds the narrow limits of the objective provision of the requested information.[161]

The action of *habeas corpus*, therefore, is special also because it is structured to privilege the rapid understanding of the facts under consideration. And that is why the procedure is accelerated, demanding from the authority responsible for the tainted act only the information (often, in a short time). To start treating this authority as a genuine contradictor in the *writ*, besides denaturing the desired speed in the process, would mean dangerously placing the editor of the coercive act in an antagonist position to the petitioner.

And thus opens the risk of a procedural situation in which the judge, pointed out as the coercive authority, and the petitioner, who represents the interests, in the *habeas corpus*, of the person to be judged, still, at a lower level, by that same judge.

In this circumstance, even because of the specificity of the *habeas corpus*, the analysis of the equality of arms between the antagonists is delicate.

This is because it cannot be said that there is—in situations where the coercive authority is a representative of the Judiciary—between the coercive authority and the person who suffers the coercion, a typical relationship of antagonism, in the way that each of the parties defends their own interests and opposes, and, therefore, acts with their own weapons.

From this perspective, in fact, it is argued that, in the wake of the specificity of the action of *habeas corpus*, the passive legitimation entitles the coercive authority to only inform the judging body of the situation that occurred, as a justification for the decision taken.

In most cases (where the coercion comes from a public body and, including, members of the Judiciary), it cannot be said that there is *opposition* of interests

---

[161] (2025), p. 1374.

between the coercive entity and the patient, such as is noted in ordinary criminal actions, that is, in situations where there really are two opposing interests—and clearly partial, one accusatory and the other defensive—that demand impartial jurisdictional appreciation.

Hence, the justification for caution with the provision of information, if the pointed out coercive authority is a member of the Judiciary.

The justification for the decision taken—whether to receive the initial, whether to issue arrest warrants, for example—cannot go beyond the strict limit of the *habeas corpus*, under penalty of the coercive authority, to inform the constitutional remedy's judging body of the reasons for the decision taken (which logically believes to have been correct), influence the very conduct of the case, originally.

And this point—namely, the overflow of the technical and necessarily impartial justification about a decision taken in the course of the process to enter into the value consideration about the case itself, still *sub judice*—would be a technical absurdity and an attack on the impartiality of the judge or the body of the court pointed out as coercive authority in the process that still runs under its responsibility.[162]

As a visible restraint in the contradiction of the coercive authority to the terms of the petition is justified, and yet it is not understood that the Prosecutor's Office could behave as a passive litisconsort[163] in the *habeas corpus*, the concern about the basis of its manifestation in the *writ* returns.

After all, if the representative of the Prosecutor's Office is not a party in the *habeas corpus*, his performance will be that of *custos legis*.[164]

Thus, the warning mentioned earlier is recalled: the Public Prosecutor's Office, although not formally a party in *habeas corpus*, manifests itself in a tendential way and, in this measure, its intervention affects the equality of arms, by unbalancing in detriment of the petitioner the game of forces inherent to the process of *habeas corpus*.[165]

---

[162] A different situation, in view of what is being argued here, is the one in which the pointed out coercive body is the Public Prosecutor's Office. Partiality is not expected in the criminal prosecution of those who have the accusatory function defined even constitutionally. That is, in a case in which the coercive authority is the Public Prosecutor's Office, a parallelism between the antagonism of the initial legal situation and the one created with the filing is tolerated.

[163] It has already been said, in topic 3.6 of this work, that the only hypothesis of passive joint litigation would be the one in which the public accuser resumes the ownership of the criminal action then initiated subsidiarily by the private party. Regarding this, see: Gomes Filho (1997), p. 151.

[164] The presumption of the constitutionality of normative acts is not transplanted to criminal procedure, as a justification to—just like the Attorney General of the Union acts in abstract control actions of constitutionality—defend the constitutionality of the contested act (Art. 103, § 3°, CF). Besides the problem not being posed even by analogy (since the illegal constraint does not enjoy a *presumption of non-occurrence*, unlike what happens with the *presumption of constitutionality* of normative acts whose unconstitutionality is argued), the *habeas corpus*, par excellence, has nothing of an objective process, contrary to what is taught to be one of the characteristics of the abstract process of constitutionality control.

[165] In cases where the action tending against the interests of the patient is not verified, and in which the body of the Public Prosecutor's Office even agrees with the terms of the filing, it only endorses

On one side, the conformation of the *writ* involves the petitioner (who speaks on behalf of the patient); on the other, the coercive authority, who informs the reasons for having edited the challenged act.

The Prosecutor's Office is not a party—not even as a litisconsort—in the structural design of the *habeas corpus* in Brazilian law. Therefore, obeying the structure of the specific action, the manifestation that occurs is necessarily as *custos legis* and, thus, structurally unnecessary for the judgment of the *writ*.

Furthermore, as the performance of the Prosecutor's Office in *habeas corpus* will have succeeded another from the same body that has officiated at a lower level[166] (except in the case of a situation in a private criminal action of the offended party that has given rise to the *habeas corpus*), the opinion tends to function as a counterpoint to the defense theses.

And there lies the offense to the equality of arms in the criminal process of *habeas corpus*, given its institutional design of informality and speed with a view to guaranteeing as effectively as possible the right to freedom: the relationship that exists is between the petitioner and the coercive authority, and not between either of them and the Public Prosecutor's Office officiating in *habeas corpus*.

Finally, a word about the Public Prosecutor's opinion in *habeas corpus*: there is no provision for such a possibility in the current Code of Criminal Procedure and Decree-Law No. 552, of 25 April 1969, is its legal basis.[167]

It happens that this Decree-Law is based on Article 2, § 1, of Institutional Act No. 5, of 13 December 1968, and the very provision on which it is based established the exceptional legislative power of the President of the Republic because he could then, "declare the recess of the National Congress, the Legislative Assemblies and the City Councils, by Complementary Act, in a state of siege or outside it, only returning to function when summoned by the President of the Republic." Thus, "once the parliamentary recess is declared, the corresponding Executive Power is

---

the terms of the initial and, with this, has a dispensable participation in the process of *habeas corpus*. That is, as it has been stated here: either the Public Prosecutor's Office opposes the defensive request and, by doing so, violates the equality of arms, or, otherwise and in minority hypotheses where this does not happen, its participation does not assist in the resolution of the issue.

[166] Except for the hypotheses of filing a *habeas corpus* against a coercive act attributable to police officers without the Public Prosecutor's Office having yet been aware of it in the original criminal prosecution, and the hypotheses of *habeas corpus* filed against illegal coercion exercised by private individuals.

[167] Article 1°: "The Public Prosecutor's Office will always be granted, in Federal or State Courts, a view of the records related to processes of 'habeas corpus' originating or on appeal by a period of 2 (two) days. § 1° At the end of this period, the records, with or without opinion will be concluded to the rapporteur for judgement, regardless of agenda. § 2° The view to the Prosecutor's Office will be granted after the provision of information by the coercive authority unless the rapporteur understands it unnecessary to request them, or if requested, they have not been provided. § 3° In the judgement of the cases referred to in this article the oral intervention of the representative of the Public Prosecutor's Office will be ensured." Article 2°: "This Decree-law will come into force on the date of its publication, repealing article 611 of the Code of Criminal Procedure and other provisions to the contrary." The manifestation of the Public Prosecutor's Office in writ of mandamus is optional (Art. 12, single paragraph, Law No. 12.016/2009).

authorised to legislate on all matters and exercise the powers provided for in the Constitutions or in the Organic Law of the Municipalities."

This Decree-Law No. 552/69 repealed Article 611 of the Code of Criminal Procedure, which provided that, "when the appeal is for *habeas corpus*, the attorney general will not have access to the case files."

The connection of Decree-Law No. 552/69 with the Brazilian dictatorship still deserves an addendum: the 1967 Constitutional Charter provided that the body of the Public Prosecutor's Office of the Union would represent that entity in court (Art. 138, § 2, Federal Constitution of 1967).

Such findings prove the connection that existed between the Ministry Public of yesteryear and the Central Power. As far as the guarantee of *habeas corpus* is concerned, one can well understand the purpose of the ministerial intervention—including to the point of a Decree-Law repealing an express provision of the Code of Criminal Procedure—to the detriment of the equality in the effectiveness of the defense arguments.

It is necessary, at the specific point of the decree, to pay attention to the material unconstitutionality and the possibility of discussing, even, its non-reception.[168]

The dual perspective of work is assumed insofar as the provision of the decree-law that establishes inequality of arms in the criminal process offends the principle of equality, enshrined in Brazilian constitutional law (Art. 5, II, CF).

From the perspective of concentrated control of the constitutionality of norms, since the advent of the Allegation of Non-Compliance with Fundamental Precept (ADPF), it has become possible to exercise such control even in the face of acts issued under the aegis of previous constitutions (Art. 1, sole paragraph, I, Federal Law n ° 9.882/99).

[168] In Brazil, the doctrine of supervening formal unconstitutionality is not prestigious. Moreover, from this point of view, there would be another underlying discussion. The very Code of Criminal Procedure was issued by decree-law, during the Constitution of 1937. Formally, therefore, one could question the repeal of the article of the Code of Criminal Procedure by Decree-Law No. 552/69, insofar as the two acts would be of the same normative species: decree-law. This discussion, besides being fruitless by account of the already reported impossibility of arguing the supervening formal unconstitutionality, yields before the finding of the material defect of unconstitutionality, to which this text alerts. And although under the prism of material unconstitutionality the question is posed under the parameter of the current Constitution, it is possible new argument to argue that, at the time of the issuance of Decree-Law No. 552/69, it could not be considered valid. This is because the normative field of action via decree-law of the then current Constitution, defined in Article 58, I and II, was delimited to *national security* and *public finances*. In his analysis of the word *national security*, Geraldo Ataliba (1967), pp. 51–63, listed all the constitutional provisions that could fit into the concept and taught that such matters should be related "with the existential and functional conditions of the State, as provided by the constituent legislator." In the lesson of that publicist, "the concept of national security - resuming the theme that was being developed - for the special effect of specifying the matter that can be the object of normative action by the President of the Republic, through *decree-law*, is stricter than the general constitutional concept of security." And the matter dealt with in Decree-Law No. 552/69 does not deal with national security, but with a procedural and specific aspect of the *habeas corpus*, which is the granting of possibilities—previously forbidden by the Code of Criminal Procedure—of written and oral manifestation to the representative of the Public Prosecutor's Office.

Already from the perspective of the issue of the reception of the norm by the new order constitutional—especially because, with the understanding settled in the Supreme Federal Court with Adin 2 according to which reception would be a matter of intertemporal law and is not subject to constitutional control—it would be possible the concrete exercise of the judgment of reception of the norm by the members of the Judiciary.

By the first criterion, with the handling of the Allegation of Non-Compliance with Fundamental Precept, the validity of the impugned legal norm could be assessed. Already by the second, observing the breadth of active legitimacy, the problem raised with Decree-Law n ° 552/69 would be treated from the perspective of the norm's validity.

In both situations, therefore, the provisions of the said decree-law could be questioned in the light of the offense to the equality of arms.

The treatment of the Public Prosecutor's Office's actions in written submissions in *habeas corpus*, as seen, is complex, and the possible solutions to ensure the equality of arms are not simple. There may not even be a situation close to the ideal.

This is because the body's actions can hardly be seen as disinterested and detached from the previous manifestation of representatives of the Public Prosecutor's Office in the criminal prosecution that has given rise to the *habeas corpus*. It is not by acting in a different phase of the criminal prosecution that, just because of that, the body ceases to be interested and assumes an aura of impartiality.

Even so, the Public Prosecutor's Office is not a party in the action of *habeas corpus*, and cannot act as a litigant of the party that holds the passive legitimation *ad causam*, which is the coercive authority. He does not have the duty to inform the court about the acts that occurred and are tainted with illegal constraint, nor the function of contradicting the terms of the petition.

The Public Prosecutor's Office is not part of either the active side (unless it acts as a petitioner), nor the passive side of the *habeas corpus* action (unless it is its own representative pointed out as the coercive authority). Therefore, it cannot manifest itself as if it were a party, even if as a litigant.[169]

Given this, as the manifestation occurs as a *custos legis*, the opinion exemption calls attention again: it is not conceivable, in this work, merely because of the procedural phase of the criminal prosecution, the Public Prosecutor's Office acting sometimes as a *party*, sometimes as a law enforcer. Hence, from this perspective (of a law enforcer), the Public Prosecutor's Office's action in *habeas corpus* unbalances

---

[169] Again, the example helps in the exposition of the matter. In the *Habeas Corpus* no. 121.216, judged by the C. 5th. Chamber of the STJ and reported by Min. Jorge Mussi (j. 19.05.2009), the Public Prosecutor's Office figured as the petitioner. In the interesting question debated—new systematics of questions in criminal hearing, according to Article 212, CPP—in the STJ, an opinion was collected from the Subprosecutor-General of the Republic. The example elucidates the impossibility of taking the opinion-giver as a party in the procedural situation that involved the petitioner and the respondent, as the authority pointed out as coercive was the Court of Justice of the Federal District. The same example reminds, still, of the impossibility of seeing in the opinion body a litisconsort of the authority pointed out as coercive (in the case, the Court of Justice of the Federal District).

the relationship of antagonistic interests between the petitioner and the coercive authority.

The participation to give an opinion, therefore, is a cause of breaking with the principle of equality of arms insofar as, structured the *habeas corpus* for the debate on the coercive act (therefore, the opposition to the act is from the petitioner and the initial legality judgment is from the coercive authority itself), the participation of this third party (the Public Prosecutor's Office) potentially contradicts the interests of the petitioner and reinforces those of the coercive authority.

Finally, the existence of Decree No. 552/69 proves that the structure originally provided for by the Code was indeed the most correct: the Public Prosecutor's Office should not (would not) manifest itself in actions of *habeas corpus*.[170]

The diagnosis of such a scenario indicates that it is knowingly a non-ideal situation: removing the possibility of the Public Prosecutor's Office to manifest in *habeas corpus* results in a possible situation of advantage to the petitioner, since the passive party in the action of *habeas corpus* is only the coercive authority. And, in *habeas corpus*, unlike what happens with appeals, there are no counter-arguments to the defensive request.

However, considering the Public Prosecutor's Office as a litigant, or as representative of the state administration to manifest in the *writ*, is equivalent to underestimating the performance of the body, which is not disinterested, even though it formally appears as a law enforcer in the procedure of *habeas corpus*.

If, on the one hand, the structure of the process does not allow the Public Prosecutor's Office to appear as a party in *habeas corpus*, on the other hand, the structure of the body prevents it from being considered, in its performance, of a typical exemption of auxiliary figures of magistrates, as would be, hypothetically, the *amicus curiae*.

And, to conjecture with the performance as auxiliaries of the magistrates, it would be conceived again the performance of the Public Prosecutor's Office linked to one of the two state powers (Executive or Judiciary), as seen in the Brazilian constitutional orders prior to 1988—assuming such a position would mean a setback in the very independent institution acquired in 1988 by the Public Prosecutor's Office.

Admitting, with due caution, the imperfection of the proposed solution, it is suggested, for the observance of the equality of arms in this particular, that the possibility of the Public Prosecutor's Office acting as an opinion in cases of *writs* resulting from public initiative criminal action is removed.[171]

---

[170] Here, a distinction is made between public initiative criminal actions and those of private initiative of the offended. In the event of the *writ* resulting from an event in the last situation, the Public Prosecutor's Office can, indeed, manifest itself.

[171] Any theoretical or practical consideration regarding the situation of advantage that will come to the petitioners, given a certain fungibility between the use of *habeas corpus* and that of proper resources in the Code of Criminal Procedure, cannot be attributed to the solution suggested here. It is impossible to dispute with the Public Prosecutor's Office in *habeas corpus* in the same way as with resources. The possibility of handling more *habeas corpus* and fewer resources, because of

6.4.2 *Oral Intervention of the Public Prosecutor's Office*

The considerations already made about the Public Prosecutor's Office's opinion in appeals and autonomous actions of challenge are useful for reflection about its oral intervention. This is because it was the same Decree-Law No. 552/69 that dealt not only with the written intervention of the Public Prosecutor's Office in *habeas corpus*, but also its oral intervention (Art. 1°, § 3°). And it did so in both appeal cases and challenge actions.

One of the motives for the approach that will follow is in the provision of Article 41, III, of Federal Law No. 8.625/93, which guarantees to members of the Public Prosecutor's Office in the states the prerogative of "having view of the records after distribution to the Panels or Chambers and intervene in the sessions of judgment, for oral argument or clarification of matter of fact." The logic that justifies the ministerial performance in opinion and in oral arguments is the same.

The opportunity that is envisaged for the Public Prosecutor's Office to speak orally in cases without offense to the equality of arms is that of cases of criminal action of private initiative of the offended. Already, its oral manifestation in appeals arising from public criminal action in criminal review is only admitted if made as a party. In *habeas corpus*, as seen, there will be no room for such manifestation, unless the equality of arms is violated.

In addition to this generic perception, there is an additional particularity that should be analyzed concerning the incidence of the equality of arms in oral manifestations, namely, the order of manifestations of oral arguments in courts, whether in appeals or in challenge actions.

6.4.2.1 Order of Oral Arguments in Courts in Appeal Situations

In appeal situations, the premise that the representative of the Public Prosecutor's Office acts as a procedural subject must be respected. About this, in the judgement of the *Habeas Corpus* no. 87.926, prepared by the full body of the Federal Supreme Court, an important premise was established according to which it is

> difficult, if not illogical, to split the performance of the Public Prosecutor's Office in the appeal field, in a criminal process: there is no way to think that, at first instance, its representative acts only as a formal party and, at the appeal level – which, let it be noted, is merely a phase of the same process –, it strips off this function to start acting as a simple guardian of the law. A single and indivisible body, in the wording of art. 127, § 1, of the Constitution of the Republic, there is no way to admit that the Public Prosecutor's Office operates only as *custos legis* in the course of a process where, at a different stage, it has

---

this (in one case, the Public Prosecutor's Office would not offer an opinion and, thus, could not manifest itself on the content of the initial piece of the *writ*; in the other, the *Parquet* could manifest itself on the content of the appeal), proves two things: first, that the opinion is not disinterested; second, that perhaps we should rethink what are, really, the *parties* in *habeas corpus*—but there still does not include the Public Prosecutor's Office itself.

> already functioned, through another body, as the one in charge of the accusation, under penalty of violating the very accusatory syntax of the criminal process. The content of the legal opinion, in essence, exposed in the opinion or in the oral argument, is of little relevance in this theme. That is, even if in the opinion or in the oral argument the Public Prosecutor's Office postulates the acquittal of the accused, it always remains the body responsible for the accusation and does not cease to act or to be able to act as the party that it is. A different conclusion would lead to the conception of a process of a single party, the accused, which seems absurd in the face of a guarantor, accusatory, agonistic (sic) system, marked by the guarantee of contradiction.[172]

In that *habeas corpus*, the single paragraph of Article 610 of the Code of Criminal Procedure was analyzed, which provides for the manifestation of the Public Prosecutor's Office always after the defensive oral argument.

There, it was established, the interpretation according to which, in the case of an appeal coming from the accusation, who should give the last oral argument is the defense, to rebut the arguments of the appealing accusatory body.[173] The important thing here is to establish that if the appeal is accusatory, the defense speaks last; if defensive, it is the accuser who has the last word.

The observance of the equality of arms in the criminal process does not mean a rigid dispute over *who speaks last* in the criminal process. It is not true, in fact, that *he who speaks last, speaks better*. What is called *speaking* in the process is linked with the contradictory, that is, with the knowledge of the arguments of the opposing party, and not with the equality in the effectiveness of presenting the case of one party to the court.

From the perspective of the equality of arms, if it is the defense that appeals, allowing it to speak after the accusatory body means even a subversion of the principle, as it is the one who will be at a comparative advantage compared to the procedural situation of the accusation at the appeal stage.

After all, in cases of defensive appeals, imposing on the accusatory body (which here acts as a party) its manifestation before knowing the oral reasons of the appellant means demanding from the respondent party to speak without being able to rebut the arguments of the appealing party.

To sponsor the understanding that, even in defensive appeals, the defense *would speak last*[174] unbalances the equality of arms, this time to the detriment of the

---

[172] STF, *HC* no. 87.926, Plenary, reported by Justice Peluso, published on 25th April 2008 (pp. 8–9 of the vote of Min. Cezar Peluso).

[173] Similarly, the Supreme Court said that the provision of Article 143, § 2nd, of the Internal Rules of the Regional Court of the 3rd Region deserves a *constitutional reinterpretation*, as it does not distinguish in cases of prosecution's appeal if the defense should speak last. There, it also analyzed Article 470, VI, of the Internal Rules of the Court of Justice of São Paulo, which correctly provides that, being the case of an accusatory appeal, who speaks first is the appellant, that is, the prosecution.

[174] In the cited judgment of the Federal Supreme Court (*HC* no. 87.926), there is a passage from an old precedent, from 1979, in which the STF would have faced the theme already once. In that reported case, RE 91.661, reported by Justice Xavier de Albuquerque and judged on November 27, 1979, what would have happened was that the defense spoke before the prosecution in a trial session. The judgment, regarding the matter, is not clear (whether the appeal was defensive or accusa-

accusation. In this sense, and for what has been defended here, the point of view espoused by Douglas Fischer seems to be correct:

> When the *appeal is exclusive to the defence*, without deviating in absolutely nothing from the principle of contradiction, the equality of arms (*par conditio*) imposes that, *in this case*, the Public Prosecutor's Office has the opportunity to *contradict* what the defence intends. The *attack* is no longer from the holder of the criminal action, but from the defendant (or rather, *in favour of the defendant*), who does not agree with the decision rendered against him. In other words, the defence (or whoever appeals in its favour) should, indeed, speak last, because what is in play, at this moment, is the exclusive claim of the defence, no longer of the prosecution, already attended (it is true that in a *provisional* way, but attended). The claim (to conviction, even if partial) is no longer prosecutorial, but defensive (nullity, acquittal or, if less, reduction of conviction). Wanting the Public Prosecutor to speak *always before* the defence in case of exclusive appeal of the defence will generate the need for the *parquet* to have to *guess* what the defence intends to develop in its oral defence. It will not be allowed to *contradict* anything, but *try to contradict* based on mere conjectures of what, effectively, may be said from the tribune or eventually placed in the appeal in favour of the defence (*let's not forget: the oral argument is just a reinforcement to the appeal already put in the records*). A logical inversion of things, *maxima venia*. It is to give different weapons to parties, breaking the parity of the (true) *due legal process* and to the detriment of the prosecution (art. 563, CPP).[175]

What seems reasonable and ensures equality in the presentation of theses orally paraded by the appellants is the following scenario: in an exclusive appeal of the prosecution, it first supports its appeal reasons and then the defense exposes the reasons why the appealed decision should not be reviewed. Conversely, in the case of a defensive appeal, the same procedure is followed inversely.

In the situation of opposing appeals, however, so that neither the defense nor the prosecution is weakened—comparatively to each other—in their arguments, the solution considered is the full presentation of the theses paraded in the prosecutorial and, afterwards, defensive appeals.

In such cases, if the trial has not been split (given the prejudiciality that may exist with the acceptance or refutation of the theses of one appeal on the requests indicated in the opposing appeal), it should, after the joint report, first exhaust the oral argument of the Public Prosecutor's appeal and then the defensive one.[176]

---

tory), but in any case, the thesis that the defense should always speak last in the criminal process was endorsed.

[175] Fischer (2009). The agreement with the author is partial because, according to him, in the article, the Public Prosecutor's Office speaks twice and the defense only once, even if the case is an accusatory appeal. According to the author's reasoning, the Public Prosecutor's Office would speak before the defense on the accusatory thesis; this would then be rebutted by the defense and, still after, the word would return to the Public Prosecutor's Office, "to manifest only about the defence's appeal." As the article implies that this sequence should occur even in an accusatory appeal, there would be a breach of the equality of arms with the prosecution first defending *its* appeal and then *contradicting* the defensive rebuttal. If the hypothesis treated in the article was of a *defensive* appeal, the manifestation of the Public Prosecutor's Office could only be given once (after the defense), and not twice, as indicated there.

[176] The reason why—in cases of opposing appeals, of defense and prosecution—the trial begins with the accusatory appeal lies in the prevalence that should be given to the *favour rei* insofar as

Still in this hypothesis of judgement of defensive and prosecutorial appeals, if by chance the accused's lawyer has not been summoned for the purpose of making an oral argument in his appeal and in the prosecution's, the representative of the Public Prosecutor's Office who officiates in the court will not be able to make an oral argument and the trial date should be rescheduled, observing the need for regular summons to the accused's lawyer to be able to exercise the right to oral argument.

6.4.2.2 Oral Argument of the Public Prosecutor in Autonomous Impugnation Actions

In cases of impugnation action, we are not facing an extension of the ongoing criminal prosecution. With this, as already argued, as it is not part of the criminal process arising from the action of *habeas corpus*, the performance of the prosecution body is not even due, since it is unnecessary for mere assistance to the judging body. Its performance as a law enforcer will only have meaning if the *habeas corpus* discusses issues arising in a criminal action of exclusively private initiative.

In the case of criminal review, the oral manifestation is only justified if it is considered as a result of the activity of a party, that is, of the opponent to the request of the revisionist, as is settled in the majority of national doctrine.

Anyway, in a plenary body trial that faced the question of oral argument in *habeas corpus*, the Supreme Federal Court was able to face the issue and, by majority of votes, made a decision that draws attention to the incidence of the principle of equality of arms in Brazilian criminal procedure.

The reasons for the decision of the case portrayed below call the problem of the incidence of equality of arms and the oral argument of the Public Prosecutor, both in relation to the *habeas corpus*, and, even, in relation to the criminal review. It is the trial of the order question of the trial of the *Habeas Corpus* no. 102.732.[177]

In that case, as argued by the petitioner from the tribune, due to the patient having had preventive detention from a request signed by the Attorney General of the Republic and the Deputy Attorney General of the Republic, and, also, the indictment also having been signed by the Attorney General of the Republic, the Supreme Court was provoked to decide on the order of the oral arguments. The defense understood that the representative of the Public Prosecutor's Office in the trial session was not in the capacity of law enforcer, but of a party.[178]

---

that, not having the condemnatory decision appealed by both parties, the right to freedom is better protected by allowing defense the opportunity to *speak last*, that is, react to the accusation. Thus, it keeps in tune even with the logic of the criminal process since the indictment: the defense has the burden of *reaction* to the accusation, which is transplanted to the Court.

[177] STF, *HC* no. 102.732, Plenary, reported by Justice Marco Aurélio, published on 07.05.2010.

[178] As stated in the judgment of the referred *habeas corpus* (available at: <http://www.youtube.com/watch?v=RbsE2dyZCR4>), the reason for the disagreement of the representative of the Public Prosecutor's Office of the Union regarding the defensive plea would be in the finding that, in that case, the *habeas corpus* would present itself with the conformations of an appeal, hence

In the words of the Reporting Minister, there is no "an antagonistic party properly said in the *habeas corpus*. The procedural relationship [...] is shown taking into account the figure of the petitioner, the patient and the body pointed out as coercive."

On the other hand, as stated by the Deputy Attorney General of the Republic who was present at that trial session, Deborah Duprat, she—and not the signatory of the request for preventive detention directed at the patient—was present at the session precisely because of the impediment of the latter for having signed, in addition to the request for preventive detention, also the complaint addressed to the patient.

That is: the representative of the Prosecutor's Office at the trial session understood that the institution could be divided. If represented by one person, the activity could be seen as that of a *party;* but if represented by another person, the performance as *custos legis* would be safeguarded. Thus, as can be seen from the aforementioned trial session, a separation would be necessary—within the performance of the Federal Prosecutors—between author and body *custos legis*.

According to the reasoning espoused and to escape from the inconsistency here so often pointed out, it would be possible for a representative of the Prosecutor's Office to appear as *custos legis,* and another person from the same institution represented the body as a party.

In addition, the disagreement of the representative of the Attorney General's Office against the defensive plea placed in question of order resulted from the understanding that, in that case, the *habeas corpus* was presented "with the conformation of an appeal." It was then followed by the understanding that it should be allowed—taking the Federal Prosecutor's Office as the respondent—that "accusation and defence debate on equal terms."[179]

On that occasion, the principle of equality of arms in criminal proceedings was disregarded. On the one hand, there was the understanding that the *habeas corpus* could be equated to an appeal (or have its conformations from it), hence why the representative of the Prosecutor's Office defended the reasons for the contested decision. It happens that the *habeas corpus* is not an appeal and, therefore, the body of the Prosecutor's Office should not behave as a party in the constitutional action.

Even if, as already seen, the constitutional action sometimes resembles an appeal,[180]this is due to its use, and not to its structural conformation. Thus, even if

---

why the respondent should have the possibility to, "on equal terms," debate with the appellant the issues at stake.

[179] In this regard, just watch the recording of the trial session, from 27'44" (available at: <http://www.youtube.com/watch?v=RbsE2dyZCR4>). From the vote of Minister Carlos Ayres Britto it is inferred, on the one hand, the attachment to the argument that the Prosecutor's Office, in *habeas corpus*, acts as *custos legis* (and for this reason it would have bowed to the argument that such action would be safeguarded with the presence at the trial session not of the signatory of the indictment, but of the Deputy Attorney General); and, even so and in the same vote, His Excellency agreed with the argument that the *habeas corpus* there placed would have the features of an appeal, hence why it is necessary for the body of the Prosecutor's Office to know the defensive oral argument to make its own afterwards. Minister Celso de Mello treated the Prosecutor's Office, in the scope of *habeas corpus*, as a "necessary procedural subject."

[180] Badaró (2003), pp. 233–234.

such understanding is privileged, functionally there would be no way to demand an *equality of conditions* between the petitioner and the Prosecutor's Office, since structurally the body is not a party in *habeas corpus*. Nor could one, much less, attribute such *equality of conditions* if there are no reasons or counter-reasons in *habeas corpus*.

And, if the assimilation proposed by the representative of the Attorney General's Office between *habeas corpus* and appeal, the problem analyzed here would continue to exist insofar as the manifestation of the coercive authority would not even be appropriate. After all, the antagonism would be established between the said *parties*.

On the other hand, as decided by the majority, it was understood that the manifestation of the body of the Prosecutor's Office, even if as guardian of the law, would allow the oral argument to be delivered after that of the petitioner. Even so, there is no way to honor the subsequent oral manifestation of the Prosecutor's Office.

This is not due only to the non-existence of the idea, in the Internal Rules of the Supreme Federal Court, that in *habeas corpus* the accusation necessarily (and even lastly) manifests itself as a guardian of the law, but it is justified because the only legal basis of this understanding consecrated in jurisprudential practice rests on the already treated Decree-Law No. 552/69, which suffers from unconstitutionality.

In autonomous actions of challenge, whatever they may be, the performance in oral argument of the body of the Prosecutor's Office, if as guardian of the law, should be limited to cases of criminal action of exclusively private initiative.

The performance in criminal review, by the way, will only be justified if it occurs as a party.

If not, one ends up privileging, under the guise of impartiality, a manifestation coming from the accusatory body that reinforces the thesis of the author of the public criminal action and makes the procedural situation of the accused disadvantageous.

6.5 Equality of Arms in Criminal Execution

In matters of criminal execution, the treatment of equality of arms depends on two considerations: its jurisdictional nature and the legal position of the Prosecutor's Office. Once the two premises are established, the reason it is argued, in this work, the understanding that the principle of equality of arms also applies in criminal execution can become clearer.

The first,[181] which is jurisdictional and not administrative, makes it derive from the application of all the constitutional and criminal procedural norms inherent to

[181] Although in this work we do not delve into the minutiae of considering the execution of the sentence as a genuine autonomous process (assumed position) or as a mere procedure of the criminal process (position that is of Vicente Greco Filho, 2009, p. 110), one cannot fail to notice the strangeness of the very establishment of the legal situation of the execution of the sentence, result-

the fundamental guarantees of those who are involved in the criminal process. [182]The second, more attached to the central theme discussed here, refers again to the assumption of the role of the Prosecutor's Office as a party, that is, with an entity that represents interests (even if collective, public, social) and therefore acts as a party also in the criminal execution process.

From the first perspective, with the Penal Execution Law in force since 1984, Article 194 provides for the judicial procedure as the one that should guide the application of the dictates of the course of criminal executions. Such a provision, according to René Ariel Dotti, would already be enough to bury the old understanding that took the right of criminal execution as a relationship of administrative law.[183]

Still under this premise, the equality of arms, as a consequence of procedural equality in the field of positive law, is present in criminal execution. And, as developed in this work, it must have its incidence guaranteed in all concrete cases where the situations of the convicted person are antagonistically placed—it is about shortening the time of sentence compliance or enjoying benefits inherent to the duration and progression of the sentence regime—and those of the state representative who tutors the interest in seeing the execution of the imposed sentence satisfied.

ing from an official act of the judge. In light of the separation of functions between judge (since, being jurisdictional, there is effective judgment in execution of sentence, and on the most diverse issues, even if repeated times, such as temporary exits, regime regressions, recognition of remissions of sentence, regime progressions, issuance of release warrants, recognition of sentence extinction etc., according to Article 66 of the Law of Execution of Sentence), convicted and Prosecutor's Office, it is really to be questioned whether the execution of the sentence should begin by an act of the one who is—still—impartial, or by provocation of a party. It seems better would be if the provision of Article 105 provided that the beginning of the execution would be given by an act of impulse of the party (in this case: Prosecutor's Office), and not by a judicial act, of determination of issuance of a Guide Letter. The interest that moved the state (accuser, not judge) to see a sentence imposed on someone is the same (that this sentence be served), and by logical imperative is held by the same state (no longer accuser, but interested in the satisfaction of the right recognized in a sentence that has become final, but still, and in no way, not a judge). For Aury Lopes Júnior (2007), p. 373, an author who makes the warning here accepted, there is still another serious criticism of the inquisitorial nature of the Law of Execution of Sentence, since in it "the written form of the acts predominates, the adversarial and the right to defence are quite limited (technical defence), and, finally, the very res judicata can be violated."

[182] "The principles that govern the process of execution are basically the same as those of the process of knowledge" Médici Apr./Jun. (1993), p. 103.

[183] Dotti (Apr./Jun. 1985), p. 47. The author also alluded to items 88 and 92 of the statement of reasons of the very Law of Execution of Sentence to dismiss the old understanding that the system should be governed by administrative law rules. The Brazilian doctrine that delved deeper into the subject does not diverge, since the law came into force, about the eminently jurisdictional nature of the process of execution of sentence. In this regard, see, among many: Castilho (1988), pp. 98–99; Beneti (1996), pp. 43 and foll., and 63 and foll.; Grinover (1998a, b); Médici (1993), pp. 101–103; Amaral (Nov./Dec. 2009), p. 162; Cintra Júnior (Jan./Mar. 1995), pp. 115–120; Fernandes (Jul./Sept. 1993), p. 89; Franco (1986), p. 103; Dinamarco (2020), pp. 516 and foll.

It was about this that Alberto Silva Franco dealt with legality in criminal execution and mentioned, alongside the guarantees of jurisdiction, of ample defense and of the contradictory, the *equality of arms*.[184]

The criminal execution process is, therefore, as Ada Pellegrini Grinover teaches, "the instrument through which jurisdiction operates, for the judicial protection of the subjective rights of the sentenced and for the effective realization of the concrete command emerging from the sentence."[185]

As for the second premise, the Prosecutor's Office acts as a party also in the phase of criminal execution. This is because, as much as in criminal instruction, or even before, in preliminary investigation, it defends interests in the scope of the criminal process. The unavailability of these interests does not denature the activity of the Prosecutor's Office as that of a party, even in criminal execution.

In this regard, it is worth remembering the lesson of Antonio Scarance Fernandes. According to the author, "both in the process of knowledge, when the penalty is applied, as in the execution, when it is effected, the Prosecutor's Office is always a party, in the defence of this unavailable interest to punish the author of the crime."[186]

The assumption of such a point of view deserves an additional clarification that can make the connection between the first and second premises of this chapter more evident. This is because both for those like Vicente Greco Filho, who take criminal execution not as an autonomous process, but as a mere procedural phase of the criminal process—bringing it closer to the so-called *improper execution* of civil procedural law— as for those who understand it as a proper and autonomous procedural phase within criminal procedural law, the paritary position of the Prosecutor's Office as a procedural subject remains intact. That is: even if the conceptualization of the criminal execution process itself is not so focused, the treatment of the Prosecutor's Office as a party remains.

In fact, according to Vicente Greco Filho's position, it would be even simpler to sustain the understanding that the Prosecutor's Office acts as a party in criminal execution. As it is a procedure and not an autonomous process, in criminal

---

[184] Fernandes (1987), p. 100. Geraldo Prado (2006), p. 223, in a study dedicated to penal execution, accepted the expression of Fazzalari repeated by Antonio Magalhães Gomes Filho, according to whom, also in this phase of the criminal process and just like in the instructive phase of the process of knowledge, there must be a "symmetry of subjective positions." Dinamarco (2020), p. 517, in this regard, understand that in penal execution, as here defended, all the guarantees of the *due process law* and of the *contradictory*, among which is the "procedural equality," apply.

[185] (1987), p. 7. In this regard, it is worth highlighting a section of Summary No. 44 of the Criminal Process Tables (activity linked to the Department of Procedural Law of the Faculty of Law of the University of São Paulo, in a session of 8 November 1983): "As in every process, understood as a triple procedural legal relationship, the penal execution process is a process of parties, which assures the sentenced the guarantees of the 'due process law', directly derived from the Constitution, even in the silence of the Codes" (1987, p. 9). And also from Summary No. 85: "are fully applicable guarantees to the process of penal execution, as a consequence of the constitutional principles of the 'due process law', even if the procedural law does not expressly assure them, equality, broad defence, the contradictory, the double degree of jurisdiction, publicity" (p. 12).

[186] Fernandes (1987), p. 28.

execution the paritary positions derived from the criminal process of knowledge should be maintained.

On the other hand, accepting the premise according to which there is in criminal execution a new process and not a mere procedural phase of the ongoing criminal process provokes a debate about the possible role of the Prosecutor's Office. Only then can we talk about situations of advantage and disadvantage, at each procedural moment, between the parties in the criminal execution process.

And here, once again, the interest of the Prosecutor's Office emerges: no longer that of deducing the accusation with a view to achieving a judgment on the merits, but already that of guaranteeing the satisfaction of the right recognized in the criminal process of knowledge. In this sense, we can borrow the lesson from Ela Wiecko de Castilho, who understands the Prosecutor's Office as "a mandatory party in the execution process,"[187] from the observation that, when *requesting* and *appealing*,[188] it represents the interests of the state (and therefore acts as a party).

If in the process of knowledge, the interest represented by the Prosecutor's Office was that of confirming the original imputation formulated and thus imposed a conviction, in execution is the compliance with this same imposed penalty—resulting from a process that the Public Prosecutor's Office itself promoted and generated a condemnatory decision transited in res judicata—that animates it. In addition, the problem of the bifrontal action of the Public Prosecutor's Office during the cognitive phase of the criminal prosecution, prior to the transit in res judicata of conviction, is repeated in criminal execution.

Hence the need to make explicit the premise that, in both cases, the Public Prosecutor's Office should not act, in the case, sometimes as *custos legis*, sometimes as a party. After all, in both one and the other, there is clear antagonism between its manifestations and those of the then accused, now convicted. And where there is antagonism, given the opposing interests aimed at by the action of one and the other party, there are *opponents* for the purposes of applying the principle of equality of arms.

Touching on this point, Sidnei Beneti first recognizes that the "Public Prosecutor's Office, in the execution process, acts bifrontally," and then deduces that "the Public Prosecutor's Office is not, in the Brazilian system, tasked with carrying out the execution of the sentence, but rather, acts as a party."[189]

Although Article 67 of the current Penal Execution Law deals with the Public Prosecutor's Office as acting to "supervise the execution of the sentence and the security measure," one cannot fail to perceive its role as a party in the executive process, a role that was also in its cognitive phase prior to the condemnatory decision transited in res judicata.

---

[187] (1988), p. 86.

[188] The author (1988), pp. 85–86, presents no less than nineteen examples, with support in the Penal Execution Law, of situations in which the Public Prosecutor's Office exercises the power of *request* in penal execution, in clear activity of part.

[189] (1996), p. 75.

To officiate as *custos legis* really implies the problem of the bifrontal action of the Public Prosecutor's Office, and it seems to be here the exact point that needs to be corrected: the action of the one who watches over the execution of the right recognized by an executive title is that of a party, and not that of a law enforcement officer. The interests represented by the Public Prosecutor's Office, both in the instruction phase of the knowledge process and in the execution process are the same, identically unavailable, and expensive in both phases of the criminal prosecution.

Regarding the symmetry existing between the procedural party that acted in the knowledge process and the procedural party that acts in the execution phase, the understanding of Antonio Scarance Fernandes is correct, for whom (with the emphasis on following the author's theory of the relationship procedural), also in execution:

> The three main subjects of the legal relationship are easily identifiable: the judge, the MP and the convicted. The MP and the convicted are parties, each watching over a certain interest. The former wants the command of the condemnatory sentence to be effective and that the resocialisation of the sentenced is done without prejudice to social guarantee. The sentenced wishes that: the execution does not exceed the limits of the criminal judgement and that all rights guaranteed by law are guaranteed to him, such as the progression of the sentence, temporary leave, attendance at schools etc.[190]

Still on the premise that the Public Prosecutor's Office acts as a party in criminal execution, it is opportune to remember that the jurisdictionalization of the phase executive of the criminal prosecution would make no sense, as it brings with it the incidence of the rules inherent to due process. This would not happen if, also in execution, the structure of the process were not dialectical.

In other words, it would make no sense to move from the merely administrative to the jurisdictional nature of criminal execution[191]—applying with this, in the final phase of the criminal prosecution, all the range of rights and guarantees of due process—if even so it could be imagined that in the execution phase the process was of *single party*, a situation that would be to take the Public Prosecutor's Office as a mere law enforcement officer, being a party only the convicted.[192]

---

[190] (1993) p. 89. In a footnote, the author exposes, moreover, the comparative law lesson, with mentions to Italian (Alfredo Gaito) and Portuguese (Anabela Rodrigues) doctrines.

[191] Which, moreover, signals an evolution also in the field of comparative law, as reported by Grinover et al. (1994), pp. 331–336, in a joint study made about the situations in the legal systems of Brazil, Costa Rica, Argentina and Uruguay, with comparison in the provisions of the Model Code of Criminal Procedure for Ibero-America. While in Costa Rica, there is still no jurisdictionalization of criminal execution, both in Uruguay and in Argentina, there is a move towards greater jurisdictionalization. When focusing on the Model Code, it is understood that there is a greater jurisdictionalization in the executive phase of the criminal process and, moreover, the Public Prosecutor's Office is maintained in its role as a party in the criminal process.

[192] Thus, even if one may disagree with the consideration of Ada Pellegrini Grinover (1987), pp. 17–18, in the sense that the Public Prosecutor's Office, in criminal execution, can act both as a "partial party" and as an "impartial party," one agrees with her on the following: in execution, "the parties will be the MP and the sentenced, by his defender."

As already mentioned here, the assumption that the same body can act sometimes as a law enforcement officer (Penal Execution Law, Arts. 67 and 68), sometimes as a party, has no reason to be and breaks with the definition of roles of the actors of the criminal process. Therefore, central to the problem of the legal position of the Public Prosecutor's Office in the Brazilian criminal process as a whole, to understand the application of the equality of arms in the executive phase, one must necessarily take its action as that of a party, because it is a party and always has been throughout the process.

6.5.1 *Equality of Arms in Criminal Execution: Examples of Incidence and a Critical Point*

In any case, it must be observed that in criminal execution, the guarantee that there is no situation of disadvantage on one of the sides, or that is, between the parties in criminal execution—the Public Prosecutor's Office and the convicted. It is precisely for this reason that the Penal Execution Law, exemplarily in situations of remission of sentence (Art. 126, § 8°), imposition of a differentiated disciplinary regime (Art. 52, § 2°), and revocation of conditional release (Art. 143), always provides for the prior hearing of the convicted before any judicial decision.

In these three hypotheses, in which the criminal execution follows a jurisdictional model (Art. 194), it must be rescued, not without the critical point of the law still providing for a judicial decision without provocation from the interested parties,[193] the opportunity for the Public Prosecutor and the convict to have their arguments weighed on an equal footing.

The examples that are gathered from the penal execution law, therefore, and that are manifest in different situations, arise from the so-called *execution incidents*. In penal execution, there is no typical instruction in the molds of the criminal process in its cognitive phase. Hence, situations such as response to accusatory manifestations and position in courtrooms do not arise.

In penal execution, the instruction that is noted to exist pertains to this or that incident, to occurrences that have taken place during the course of the execution of the sentence itself; therefore, the equality of arms applies, specifically and punctually, to the requests made by both the Public Prosecutor, as well as by the convict, and to the egalitarian weight that the magistrate attributes to them.

Particular attention deserves the situation in which a sanction is imposed due to the commission of a serious offense. This is because Article 59 of the Penal Execution Law only deals with the procedure as dependent on regulation, and nothing more. Fortunately, Article 60 of the same Law only provides for access to the jurisdiction of the executive process in case of imposition of the differentiated

[193] What causes strangeness in the light of the *ne procedat iudex ex officio*, even more so in the context of criminal execution, which by essence limits individual freedom.

disciplinary regime, being certain, still, that the placement of the convict in isolation for up to ten days does not depend, as seen, on judicial order.

The situation is indeed important because it openly confronts the general rule of Article 194 of the Penal Execution Law (the procedure is not jurisdictional) and because it consists of a serious and indisputable imposition on the already limited right of freedom of the convict, without detailing the judicial scrutiny of the restrictive measures that may occur.

So much was fought for the jurisdictionalization of the execution phase of the sentence, and, even today, the anachronistic procedure, without jurisdictionalization, for the investigation of serious offenses persists. The warnings of Gustavo Octaviano Diniz Junqueira must be recalled here, for both reasons (either by obedience to the general rule, or by the need for a judicial decision in any situation that threatens individual freedom), who, when specifically addressing this issue, stated:

> As it is a procedure that can result in a restriction of individual freedom, we believe that the same guiding principles of the criminal process as a whole should prevail, that is, the *in dubio pro reo* in evidentiary matters and respect for defence instruments, respecting the peculiarities of the situation.[194]

As long as there is also no jurisdictionalization of this fundamental execution incident, there is no access to penal execution justice, with which there is (intuitively) no impartiality for a decision that imposes any measure resulting from a sanction due to the fulfillment of a serious offense. Still in the same measure, there is also no possibility for the arguments of the convict to be exposed (on an equal footing with any that oppose them) for legitimate appreciation.

That is why, if there are the various examples already seen of the manifestation of the principle of equality of arms in penal execution (which result from the jurisdictionalization of the executive phase of the criminal process), there is still a nodal point to be resolved: the imposition of a sanction in the course of the execution of the sentence due to the pointed fulfilment of a serious offense. In this case, there is still no equality of arms.

References

Almeida, J. C. M. d. (1973). *Princípios fundamentais do processo penal*. Revista dos Tribunais.

Ambos, K. (2008). *Processo penal europeu*: preservação das garantias e direitos individuais. (princípios processuais e análise da Convenção Européia de Direitos Humanos). Tradução, notas e comentários sob a perspectiva brasileira de Marcellus Polastri Lima. Lumen Juris, Rio de Janeiro

Andrade, M. d. C. (2009). *Métodos ocultos de investigação (plädoyer para uma teoria geral)*. Juruá.

Ataliba, G. (1967). *O Decreto-Lei na Constituição de 1967*. Revista dos Tribunais.

Azevedo, A. B. et al. (2004). *A preservação do devido processo legal pela investigação defensiva (ou do direito de defender-se provando)*. Boletim do Instituto Brasileiro de Ciências Criminais, n. 137.

[194] Junqueira and Fuller (2010), p. 28.

Badaró, G. (2009) O ônus da prova no *habeas corpus*: *in dubio pro libertate*. In G. Prado, & D. Malan, (Coords.). *Processo penal e democracia*: estudos em homenagem aos 20 anos da Constituição da República de 1988. Lumen Juris, Rio de Janeiro.
Badaró, G. (2024). *Processo penal*. – 12. ed. Thomson Reuters Brasil.
Badaró, G., & Bottini, P. C. (2012). *Lavagem de dinheiro: aspectos penais e processuais penais*. Revista dos Tribunais.
Badaró, G. H. R. I. (2003). *Ônus da prova no processo penal*. Revista dos Tribunais.
Badaró, G. H. R. I. (2008). *Tribunal do Júri: Lei 11.689, de 09.06.2008*. In M. T. R. d. A. Moura (Coord.). Revista dos Tribunais.
Bandeira de Mello, O. A. (2007). *Princípios gerais de direito administrativo* (Vol. 1). Malheiros.
Beneti, S. A. (1996). *Execução penal*. Saraiva.
Borges da Rosa, I. (1942). *Processo penal brasileiro* (Vol. IV). Livraria do Globo.
Canterji, R. B., & Verlang, R. C. (2012). *Prazo razoável para responder à acusação*. Boletim do Instituto Brasileiro de Ciências Criminais.
Castilho, E. W. V. d.. (1988) *Controle da legalidade na execução penal*. Sergio Antonio Fabris Editor, Porto Alegre
Cintra Júnior, D. A. D. (1995). *A jurisdicionalização do processo de execução penal: o contraditório e a ampla defesa*. Revista Brasileira de Ciências Criminais.
Costa, E. M. (2010). Para a democratização da sala de audiências. In: J. C. Lima & R. R. R. Casara (Coords.). *Temas para uma perspectiva crítica do direito*: homenagem ao Professor Geraldo Prado. Lumen Juris, Rio de Janeiro.
Cruz, R. S. M. (2002). *Garantias processuais nos recursos criminais*. Atlas.
Decaro, L. G. R. (2011). *Pode o ministério público manifestar-se sobre a resposta à acusação antes de o juiz a apreciar?* Boletim do Instituto Brasileiro de Ciências Criminais.
Dinamarco, C. R. (2024). *Instituições de direito processual civil* (Vol. 1, 11th ed.). Editora JusPodivm.
Dinamarco, C. R. (2020). *Instituições de Direito Processual Civil*. (Vol.1, 10a ed.). Malheiros.
Dotti, R. A. (1985). *A crise da execução penal e o papel do Ministério Público*. Giuffrè.
Dotti, R. A. (1993). *Suspeição de magistrado*. Revista Brasileira de Ciências Criminais.
Dotti, RA (2012) O princípio do equilíbrio das armas no processo penal. In J. Zilio, & F. Bozza (Orgs.). *Estudos críticos sobre o sistema penal*. Homenagem ao Professor Doutor Juarez Cirino dos Santos por seu 70° aniversário. Ledze
Espínola Filho, E. (1965). *Código de Processo Penal brasileiro anotado* (Vol. III). Borsoi.
Fernandes, A. S. (1987). O Ministério Público na execução penal. In: A. P. Grinover, & D. Busana (Coords.). *Penal execution*: Law no. 7210, of 11 July 1984. Max Limonad.
Fernandes, A. S. (1993). *Reflexos relevantes de um processo de execução penal jurisdicionalizado*. Revista Brasileira de Ciências Criminais.
Fernandes, A. S. (2002). *Reação defensiva à imputação*. Revista dos Tribunais.
Fernandes, A. S. (2005). O equilíbrio na investigação criminal. In F. L. Yarshell, & M. Zanoide de Moraes (Orgs.). *Studies in honour of Professor Ada Pellegrini Grinover*. DPJ
Fernandes, A. S., & Lopes, M. (2008). *O recebimento da denúncia no novo procedimento*. Boletim do Instituto Brasileiro de Ciências Criminais.
Fischer, D. (2009). *A ordem de sustentação oral nos processos criminais perante os tribunais: uma leitura acerca do espectro do que decidido pelo STF no HC n. 87.926-Sp*. Boletim do Instituto Brasileiro de Ciências Criminais.
Franco, A. S. (1986). A jurisdicionalização da execução penal. In *Temas de direito penal*: breves anotações sobre a Lei n. 7.209/84. Forense.
Gazzola, G. d. R. (2009). Delação premiada. In R. S. Cunha, P. Taques, & L. F. Gomes (Coords.). *Limites constitucionais da investigação*. Revista dos Tribunais.

Giacomolll, N. J. (2009). *Juizados especiais criminais, Lei 9.099/95: abordagem crítica: acordo civil, transação penal e suspensão condicional do processo; rito sumaríssimo* (3rd ed.). Livraria do Advogado.

Giacomolli, N. J. (2011). *A fase preliminar do processo penal: crises, misérias e novas metodologias investigatórias*. Lumen Juris.

Gomes Filho, A. M. (1997). *Ministério Público e acusação penal no sistema brasileiro.* Pena y Estado: Revista Latinoamericana de Política Criminal, Buenos Aires.

Gomes Filho, A. M. (2011). Medidas cautelares e princípios constitucionais: comentários ao artigo 282 do CPP, na redação da Lei 12.403/2011. In: Fernandes, Og (Coord.). *Medidas cautelares no processo penal*: prisões e suas alternativas: comentários à Lei 12.403, de 04.05.2011. Revista dos Tribunais.

Gomes, L. F. (2011). *Prisão e medidas cautelares*: comentários à Lei 12.403, de 04 de maio de 2011. Revista dos Tribunais.

Gomes, L. F., & Maciel, S. (2012). *Interceptação telefônica: comentários à Lei 9.296, de 24.07.1996.* Revista dos Tribunais.

Greco Filho, V. (2009). *Manual de processo penal.* Saraiva.

Grinover, A. P. (1987). Natureza jurídica da execução penal. In: A. P. Grinover, & D. Busana (Coords.). *Execução penal*: Lei n. 7210, de 11 de julho de 1984. Max Limonad.

Grinover, A. P. (1998a). A exigência de jurisdicionalização da execução na América Latina. In: *O processo em evolução.* 2. ed. Forense Universitária, Rio de Janeiro.

Grinover, A. P. (1998b). Igualdade de partes e paridade de armas: a posição do MP no Superior Tribunal Militar 1998. In: *O processo em evolução.* 2. Ed. Forense Universitária.

Grinover, A. P., Fernandes, A. S., & Gomes Filho, A. M. (1994). A exigência de jurisdicionalização da execução. In: M. Massa, & S. Schipani (Org.). *Un "codice tipo" di procedura penale per l'America Latina.* Forense Universitária

Grinover, A. P., Gomes Filho, A. M., & Fernandes, A. S. (2009a). *As nulidades da ação penal.* Revista dos Tribunais.

Grinover, A. P., Gomes Filho, A. M., & Fernandes, A. S. (2009b). *Recursos no processo penal.* Revista dos Tribunais.

Hamilton, S. D. (2011). O parecer criminal do Ministério Público perante os tribunais: ato essencial do Processo. In: M. L. Bastos, & P. S. M. C. d. Amorim (Orgs.). *Tributo a Afrânio da Silva Jardim*: escritos e estudos. Revista Síntese de Direito Penal e Processual Penal. Porto Alegre.

Junqueira, G. O. D., & Fuller, P. H. A. (2010). *Legislação penal especial* (Vol. 1). Saraiva.

Karam, M. L. (2004). *Juizados especiais criminais: a concretização antecipada do poder de punir.* Revista dos Tribunais.

Kehdi, A. P. d. A. (2005). *Sobre o contato via interfone entre advogado e cliente preso.* Boletim do Instituto Brasileiro de Ciências Criminais.

Lattanzi, G., & Lupo, E. (1990). *Norme di attuazioni di coordinamento e transitorie del nuovo Codice di Procedura Penale: annotate con le relazioni e con i lavori preparatori.* Giuffrè.

Lauand, M. d. S. L. (2008). *O valor probatório da colaboração processual.* Dissertação (Mestrado) – Faculdade de Direito, Universidade de São Paulo.

Lopes Júnior, A. (2007). Revisitando o processo de execução penal a partir da instrumentalidade garantista. In: Carvalho, Salo de (Coord.). *Crítica à execução penal.* Lumen Juris.

Lopes Júnior, A. (2011). *O novo regime jurídico da prisão processual, liberdade provisória e medidas cautelares diversas* (Atualizado): Lei 12.403/2011. Lumen Juris.

Lopes Júnior, A. (2012). *Direito processual penal* (9th ed.). Saraiva.

Lopes Júnior, A. (2025). *Direito processual penal* (22nd ed.). Saraivajur.

Machado, A. A. M. (2010). *Investigação criminal defensiva.* Revista dos Tribunais.

Malan, D. (2009). Defesa técnica e seus consectários lógicos na Carta Política de 1988. In G. Prado, & D. Malan (Coords.). *Processo penal e democracia*: estudos em homenagem aos 20 anos da Constituição da República de 1988. Lumen Juris.

Malan, D. (2010). *Sobre a condenação sem julgamento prevista no PLS 156/09*. Boletim do Instituto Brasileiro de Ciências Criminais.

Marques, J. F. (2000). *Elementos de direito processual penal* (Vol. IV). Milleninium.

Médici, S. d. O. (2000). *Revisão criminal*. Revista dos Tribunais.

Médici, S. O. (1993). *Processo de execução penal*. Revista Brasileira de Ciências Criminais.

Nicolitt, A. (2011). *Lei n° 12.403/2011*: o novo processo penal cautelar: a prisão e as demais medidas cautelares. Elsevier.

Nicolitt, A. (2012). *Manual de processo penal*. Elsevier.

Nucci, G. d. S. (2011). *Prisão e liberdade*: as reformas processuais penais introduzidas pela Lei 12.403, de 4 de maio de 2011. Revista dos Tribunais.

Pádua, J. P. C. V. (2009). *Poder de requisição para a defesa no processo penal: em busca da real paridade de armas*. Boletim do Instituto Brasileiro de Ciências Criminais.

Pitombo, C. V. B. (1999). *Da busca e apreensão no processo penal*. Revista dos Tribunais.

Pitombo, C. V. B. (2008). Licitude da prova obtida por meio da busca e da apreensão. In: C. S. Vilardi Sanchez, F. R. B. Pereira, T. T. Dias Neto (Coords.). *Direito penal econômico*: crimes econômicos e processo penal. Saraiva.

Pitombo, S. M. d. M. (1987). O indiciamento como ato de polícia judiciária. In *Inquérito policial: novas tendências*. Edições Cejup.

Pitombo, S. M. d. M. (1996). *Constituição da República e processo penal*. Revista Especial do Tribunal Regional Federal.

Pitombo, S. M. d. M. (2001). Breves notas sobre o anteprojeto de lei, que objetiva modificar o Código de Processo Penal, no atinente à investigação criminal. In: S. S. Shecaira (Org.). *Estudos criminais em homenagem a Evandro Lins e Silva*: criminalista do século. Ed. Método.

Pitombo, S. M. d. M. (2003). *Procedimento administrativo criminal, realizado pelo Ministério Público*. Boletim do Instituto Manoel Pedro Pimentel.

Pitombo S. M. d. M. (2018) *Obra em processo penal*. Organização e notas Maria Eugênia Gil. Editora Singular.

Pontes de Miranda, F. C. (1962). *História e prática do habeas-corpus: direito constitucional e processual comparado*. Borsoi.

Prado, G. (2003). *Elementos para uma análise crítica da transação penal*. Lumen Juris.

Prado, G. (2006). *Sistema acusatório: a conformidade constitucional das leis processuais penais*. Lumen Juris.

Queijo, M. E. (1998). *Da revisão criminal: condições da ação*. Malheiros.

Queiroz P (Accessed on: 5 Oct. 2012) Sobre a intervenção do Ministério Público em segundo grau., n. 75, jul. 2007. (also available at: <http://pauloqueiroz.net/sobre-a-intervencao-do-ministerio-publico-em-segundo-grau/print/>.). Boletim dos Procuradores da República, Brasília

Rascovski, L. (2012). A investigação criminal defensiva e o papel da defensoria pública na ampla defesa do investigado. In: ______ (Coord.). *Temas relevantes de direito penal e processual penal*. Saraiva

Reale Júnior, M. (1997). Pena sem processo. In: Pitombo, Antônio Sérgio Altieri de Moraes (Org.). *Juizados especiais criminais*: interpretação crítica. Malheiros.

Saad, M. (2004). *O direito de defesa no inquérito policial*. Revista dos Tribunais.

Sidou, J. M. O. (1989). *"Habeas data," mandado de injunção, "habeas corpus," mandado de segurança, ação popular: as garantias ativas dos direitos coletivos segundo a nova Constituição*. Forense.

Streck, L. L. (2001). *As interceptações telefônicas e os direitos fundamentais: Constituição, cidadania, violência: a Lei 9.296/96 e seus reflexos penais e processuais*. Livraria do Advogado.

Toron, A. Z. (2003). *O contraditório nos tribunais e o Ministério Público*. Revista dos Tribunais.

Tourinho Filho, F. d. C. (2012). *Processo penal* (Vol. 4, 34th ed.). Saraiva.

Tucci, R. L. (2004). *Direitos e garantias individuais no processo penal brasileiro*. Revista dos Tribunais.

Vasconcellos, V. G. d. (2023). *Colaboração Premiada no Processo Penal* (5th ed). rev. e atualizada. Thomsom Reuters Revista dos Tribunais.

Vieira, L. G. (2010). Paridade de armas: uma leitura constitucional dos arts. 3° e 396-a do CPP e 241, III, do CPC e o termo inicial de contagem do prazo para apresentação da resposta escrita no Processo Penal. In: J. C. Lima, & R. R. R. Casara (Coords.). *Temas para uma perspectiva crítica do direito*: homenagem ao Professor Geraldo Prado. Lumen Juris.

Vieira, R. S. (1999). *Ainda, investigação criminal direta do Ministério Público: poder implícito ou limite implícito? Proposta de novo enfoque*. Boletim do Instituto Brasileiro de Ciências Criminais.

Vieira, R. S. (2011a). *Os lugares nas salas de audiência penal*. Valor Econômico.

Vieira, R. S. (2011b). Traços adversariais no projeto de Código de Processo Penal: uma proposta para o estudo da paridade de armas. In: D. Malan, & F. Mirza (Orgs.). *Setenta anos do Código de Processo Penal brasileiro*: balanço e perspectivas de reforma. Boletim do Instituto Brasileiro de Ciências Criminais.

Zanoide de Moraes, M. (2008). Publicidade e proporcionalidade na persecução penal brasileira. In: A. S. Fernandes, J. R. G. d. Almeida, M. Zanoide de Moraes (Orgs.)

Zanoide de Moraes, M.. (Orgs.). *Sigilo e processo penal*: eficiência e garantismo. Revista dos Tribunais, São Paulo.

Chapter 7
Conclusive Aspects

At the end of the work, it is possible to succinctly record the conclusions reached. Beforehand, it is worth noting that the study of the equality of arms starts from the constitutional scenario, where equality is its main legal foundation.

The present approach to the constitutional norm of equality was supported by the theory of fundamental rights, according to which equality is a principle and not a legal rule. Being a principle, it is a norm that does not apply in each specific case as an *all or nothing*, but rather through criteria of weighting. In addition, such a perspective admits collisions between equality and other principles that can be opposed to it, in relation to which its minimum concept (external theory) arises. Still, according to the theory of fundamental rights, the principle of equality is also not excluded, a priori, from any situation (broad factual support).

Based on the premise of constitutional equality, it is possible to reach the equality of arms in criminal proceedings. The idea of parity goes back to equality between the parties involved in the process, and, therefore, the constitutional extract of equality is inseparable from the treatment given to the equality of arms in criminal proceedings.

In the historical evolution of Brazilian Criminal Procedure Codes—whether in the Imperial Code, or at the beginning of the republican period, when there was the promulgation of several and distinct state Criminal Procedure Codes—there is no concern from the legislator in dealing with procedural equality. The topic of equality of arms, then, was not on the agenda.

From the Vicente Ráo Project, some attention began to be given to the treatment of the principle of procedural equality. This, with variations of lesser or greater degree, was perceived in the original wording of the Code of Criminal Procedure of 1941 and in the changes suffered by the document until 2011. In such variations of treatment to the principle of procedural equality, the Hélio Tornaghi and Frederico Marques Projects were important reference points.

R. S. Vieira, *Equality of Arms in Criminal Procedure*,
https://doi.org/10.1007/978-3-032-03663-6_7

In the projected criminal procedural law (Bill No. 8.045/2010), there is concern with the topic of procedural equality and, thus, with the equality of arms in criminal proceedings.

Given the assumption of the principle of equality as a premise for the application of the equality of arms in criminal proceedings, it is necessary to revisit the concept of *party* in this context. For this, it is indispensable, to some extent, to have the aid of the theoretical construction of civil procedural law.

In criminal proceedings, when dealing with the so-called *party*, a study that focuses on the equality of arms should analyze the accuser, the accused (in a broad and strict sense), and the assistance. The construction of such a concept is attached to the interest that animates the participation of the subjects in the process and to the existence of antagonism of requests. And with this, the idea of Chiovenda about active and passive legitimation *ad causam* is rescued, depending on the origin and direction of the request for judicial protection.

In Brazilian criminal proceedings, the Public Prosecutor's Office acts as a party and not as a law enforcer. The establishment of this premise proved to be important for the study of the equality of arms in criminal proceedings, particularly because it situates the antagonism that drives the actions of both the accuser and the one who reacts to the accusation. From this perspective, and to give conformity to the incidence of equality of arms, the performance of the Public Prosecutor's Office in Brazilian criminal proceedings as *custos legis* is exclusively that in which the manifestation occurs in a criminal action of private initiative of the offended.

The adversarial criminal process is the most fruitful for the study of the equality of arms. Such a procedural system, however, does not resemble either the inquisitorial nor the accusatory, both considered as traditional systems of criminal proceedings. This is because it separates from both in origin and in historical and geographical development, as well as in the attribution of the prevalence of the role of the parties in the process.

Also, based on the procedural theory that best applies to the equality of arms, the word *process* was taken here not as a legal relationship, but as a set of legal situations. This is because the adversariality that is shown in the equality of arms is a notion that develops in a structure in which there is no cooperation between the parties, neither reciprocal nor necessarily with the state-judge.

The concept of equality of arms is constructed by precedents of international human rights protection bodies. There is no, in the Brazilian criminal procedural system, express norm that deals with the equality of arms. Nor could it be verified, in compared national systems, the provision of an express norm that could conceptualize the equality of arms in criminal proceedings.

In this particular, the concept comes from judgments of the ECHR (from the interpretation of Article 6, I, of the ECHR), of the ICTY, of the ICTR, of the IACHR, and of the interpretation given by the HRC to Article 14 of the ICCPR.

The synthesis that is extracted from the position of the international courts and the HRC regarding the concept of equality of arms in criminal proceedings is as follows: it is the reasonable opportunity given to each party to present their case—including their evidence—under conditions that do not put them at a substantial disadvantage vis-à-vis their opponent.

In addition to the judgments of the international courts mentioned, the doctrine of international criminal procedural law also contributes to the concept of equality of arms in criminal proceedings. Furthermore, beyond both contributions, it is possible to arrive at the definition of equality of arms in criminal proceedings from the interpretation that can be given to each word of the concept already extracted. The construction of the concept, moreover, depends on separating its incidence from notions dear to criminal proceedings that are close to it, such as *par condicio*, the presumption of innocence, and the adversarial principle.

Equality of arms in criminal proceedings equates to an equal distribution, throughout the criminal process—from its pre-judicial phase to the executive stage—to those involved who defend opposing interests, of opportunities to present oral or written arguments and evidence with a view to prevailing before a judicial authority their respective theses.

Such a principle is enshrined in Brazilian criminal procedural law. It exists not in an ideal and rigorously identical measure between the parties, but is reflected from the constitutional justification of equality, observing the factual distinctions between the positions taken in the criminal process.

Even so, in Brazilian procedural law, there are points where equality of arms applies and points where it does not apply. In this second case, sometimes there is a constitutional justification that indicates there is no offense to the principle, sometimes not. And when there is no justification, a violation is configured.

In the preliminary investigation, the equality of arms must apply, since there are opponents, and also that there is an accusatory charge in criminal proceedings. The measure of the observance of the principle, in that procedural phase, is given by what is here called double knowledge on the part of the investigated: passive and active.

For the first, equality of arms means that the investigated must be given broad knowledge of the content of the criminal prosecution, under penalty of sponsoring an unjustifiable situation of disadvantage before those who, prior to the criminal action, are already drafting an accusation against him. For the second, the investigated should be given the opportunity to bring to the investigation the information elements of which he has and which are useful for the defense of his interests.

Already in the scope of the criminal action, the equality of arms is manifestly manifested at various moments. At first, it manifests itself mainly in the question of positive law in the criminal transaction (and in the projected law, of bargaining). The incidence in these cases is problematic, as the premise of equality between who proposes the immediate penalizing measure and who accepts it is put, doctrinally, in check.

Then, in the situation of response to the accusation, the principle of equality of arms manifests itself either in the distribution of a deadline for a response symmetrical to the one used by the one who formulated the accusation, or in the need to, implement an effective response, reserved and unimpeded contact between the accused and the defender. In each perspective, what justifies treating these examples as equality of arms is the idea of preventing one of the parties from being treated in a situation of advantage over the other.

Still in the phase of response to the accusation, the equality of arms is fundamental in the reflection of whether to determine, or not, a new view of the accuser after the defensive response. There are several ways to deal with this subject, but, to prevent an unjustifiable situation of advantage to the accuser in the face of the accused, it is considered to deny the opening of new views to the accuser, except in exceptional situations justified in the text.

Then, in criminal instruction, the necessary adherence to the principle of equality of arms requires that the magistrate be given the same attention given to the requests formulated by the parties. The observance of equality of arms a priori excludes the possibility that requests coming from the accusatory body—whether it is public or private—have, by themselves, greater weight or credit than those coming from the defense.

In this particular, it is necessary to rethink the existence of requisition powers in the criminal process, tendentially directed to one of the parties (mainly the public accuser, except for exceptions provided for the Public Defenders of the Union and the States). Full observance of the principle of equality of arms in criminal proceedings, about this, demands either that the defense be extended the requisition power in a symmetrical degree to the accusatory, or that such power be extirpated from the criminal process, since it is linked to the notion of overlapping state interest to the individual.

As for the distribution of courtrooms, it is a measure to be rethought so that equality of arms is also complied with in forensic ritualistics. It is not possible that, in symmetry of antagonistic positions, the accused and accuser are seen by the recipients of justice as distinctly close to the judge, that is, with one of them being closer than the other.

The scenic conception of the courtrooms, moreover, is the most visible aspect, although not the only and not the most important, in which the problem of equality in the attribution of the roles of the parties in the criminal process is manifested.

In appeal situations, equality of arms is respected if and to the extent that the accusatory body strictly safeguards its role as a party in the criminal process. Hence, it is impossible to favor—except in situations of private criminal action of the offended—manifestation, oral or written, as an opinion, that is, as a *custos legis*.

In turn, in situations of impugnation action, the role of the party in the criminal process must also be ensured in criminal review, under penalty that the manifestation of the Public Ministry, although labelled as *opinion*, offends the equality of arms. It is necessary, therefore, to favor the lesson according to which, in criminal review, the Public Ministry is an antagonist of the author of the action, and not a disinterested and impartial entity.

In *habeas corpus*, the equality of arms in the criminal process is problematic because the parties in the special action are the petitioner and the coercive authority. Hence, it is impossible for the Public Prosecutor to participate as a party. Still in this context, the participation of the Public Prosecutor as *custos legis* is not justified—except in cases of private criminal action by the offended party that motivated the *writ*—under penalty of offending the equality of arms. This is because the manifestation of the Public Prosecutor as *custos legis* formally appears as impartial, but either tends to be contrary to the interests of the patient in *habeas corpus* (in the case of *habeas corpus* not petitioned by the Public Prosecutor), or is an anomalous intervention (in the situation where the *habeas corpus* is petitioned by the Public Prosecutor itself).

Regarding Decree-Law No. 552/69, which repealed Article 611 of the Code of Criminal Procedure, it can be said that it is materially unconstitutional. Thus, in concentrated control of constitutionality (Fundamental Precept Noncompliance Claim), it is necessary to argue unconstitutionality. It can also be objected, in concrete situations, that its provisions were not received by the current constitutional text.

If the legal understanding that there is no formal unconstitutionality subsequent to the new constitutional order prevails, at least in relation to the material field, unconstitutionality can be argued.

This affirms, even in regard to *habeas corpus* (except for the situation of *writ* resulting from criminal prosecution in which the criminal action is of private initiative by the offended party), that there should not be intervention of the Public Prosecutor, either in terms of written manifestation, or in terms of oral manifestation.

It is finally asserted that the equality of arms also applies in criminal execution, since there is opposition of interests and typical antagonism of parties between the convicted and the Public Prosecutor.

MIX
Papier aus verantwortungsvollen Quellen
Paper from responsible sources
FSC® C105338

If you have any concerns about our products,
you can contact us on
ProductSafety@springernature.com

In case Publisher is established outside the EU,
the EU authorized representative is:
Springer Nature Customer Service Center GmbH
Europaplatz 3, 69115 Heidelberg, Germany

Printed by Libri Plureos GmbH
in Hamburg, Germany